## Praise for *Financing Failure*

"Paulson, Geithner, and Bernanke told the American public a pack of lies and misrepresentations during the subprime crisis. Where other authors merely parroted these untruths, Vern McKinley calls them on it in this very carefully researched book. *Financing Failure* shows us the appalling lack of logic in regulators' responses to financial crises and how, sadly, we can expect more of the same in the next crisis. McKinley has produced an excellent history of the flawed analysis of financial crisis policy of the last century."

—**Jean Helwege**, Professor of Business Administration, University of South Carolina; Former Senior Economist, Federal Reserve Bank of New York; Former Economist, Board of Governors of the Federal Reserve

"Reading Vern McKinley's *Financing Failure* will lead you to a logical conclusion: Failure should be allowed to happen just as success should be allowed to happen. Mr. McKinley demonstrates not only that we have gone to great extremes to keep failure from happening, but also to protect the turf of the regulators who have intervened to keep it from happening. We have done this by putting at risk great sums of public funds and by creating fear in the public mind on the consequences of financial failure. To get a balanced view of the experience we are still going through, this book is a must read."

—**William Wallace**, Professor of Economics, University of North Texas; Former Staff Director-Board of Governors of the Federal Reserve; Former Chief Operating Officer of the Federal Reserve Bank of Dallas

"Vern McKinley's analysis of the recent bailouts of the financial institutions includes the most comprehensive research of the actual underlying discussions that I have seen. The book raises important concerns about the basis of several of the government's decisions which effectively reallocated tremendous amounts of the nation's wealth. It is also startling to note how little transparency that the analysis behind these institutional and governmental bailout actions has received to date. This track record of government intervention does not inspire confidence that the Dodd-Frank legislation will lead to better outcomes in the future."

—**Michael W. Bell**, Retired Chief Financial Officer, CIGNA Corporation

"This is a phenomenal, detailed policy review of American bank bailouts from the 20th century onward, with a specific focus on the most recent crisis and its aftermath. . . . Underneath a wealth of interesting detail, McKinley identifies a 'corporatist' agenda supported by what might be called the coalition of the self-important: (1) Big banks (2) Regulators and (3) Politicians. . . . Throughout the crisis, McKinley was one of the few people who was trying to figure out what the policy-makers were actually doing, as opposed to imbibing thoughtlessly conventional narratives about what went wrong (embodied in the FCIC report and its dissents). On a moral level, when you consider, as McKinley does here, that the same regulatory agencies that precipitated the crisis gained power during the lawmaking period designed to remediate it, it is clear that we are far from addressing the financial and economic instability characteristic of our modern political order. Going forward, I suspect I will be returning to this book often. Well done."

> —**Matt Stoller**, Fellow at the Roosevelt Institute and former Senior Policy Advisor for Congressman Alan Grayson

"Our nation seems in the same sorry spot more than three years after the federal bailouts and government takeovers that 'rescued' our economy. Our credit has been downgraded, the stock market is on a roller coaster, our government continues its gangster ways in its attempts to run the private sector, the government-controlled housing market continues to be a mess, and our banks stand on a precipice. Unless our nation reckons with the truth behind the ongoing financial crisis, our economy (and our republic) will continue to flounder. A good place to begin this reckoning is with Vern McKinley's *Financing Failure*, which exposes the truth behind the bailouts—that government officials, some still in power today, cared little for the rules, the law, or even the facts."

> —**Tom Fitton**, President, Judicial Watch

"With this deeply researched and annotated account, Vern McKinley shows that in 2008—as in past financial crises—a panic among investors was matched by a panic among government officials and financial regulators. This book should be read by anyone willing to question the crisis narrative produced by the government to justify its actions and propagated by a credulous media."

> —**Peter J. Wallison**, Arthur F. Burns Fellow in Financial Policy Studies, American Enterprise Institute

# FINANCING FAILURE

THE INDEPENDENT INSTITUTE is a non-profit, non-partisan, scholarly research and educational organization that sponsors comprehensive studies in political economy. Our mission is to boldly advance peaceful, prosperous, and free societies, grounded in a commitment to human worth and dignity.

Politicized decision-making in society has confined public debate to a narrow reconsideration of existing policies. Given the prevailing influence of partisan interests, little social innovation has occurred. In order to understand both the nature of and possible solutions to major public issues, the Independent Institute adheres to the highest standards of independent inquiry, regardless of political or social biases and conventions. The resulting studies are widely distributed as books and other publications, and are debated in numerous conference and media programs. Through this uncommon depth and clarity, the Independent Institute is redefining public debate and fostering new and effective directions for government reform.

100 Swan Way, Oakland, California 94621-1428, U.S.A.
Telephone: 510-632-1366 • Facsimile: 510-568-6040 • Email: info@independent.org • www.independent.org

# FINANCING FAILURE

## A CENTURY OF BAILOUTS

VERN McKINLEY

The INDEPENDENT INSTITUTE

Oakland, California

The Independent Institute
100 Swan Way, Oakland, CA 94621-1428
Telephone: 510-632-1366
Fax: 510-568-6040
Email: info@independent.org
Website: www.independent.org

Cover Design: Christopher Buenventura
Cover Image: © Paul Taylor/Corbis
Interior Design and Composition by Leigh McLellan Design

*Library of Congress Cataloging-in-Publication Data*

McKinley, Vern.
  Financing failure : a century of bailouts / by Vern McKinley.
    p. cm.
  Includes index.
  ISBN 978-1-59813-049-2 (pbk.) -- ISBN 978-1-59813-053-9 (hbk.)

  1. Bank failures--United States--History. 2. Bank failures--Government policy--United States. 3. Banks and banking--State supervision. I. Title.
  HG2491.M365 2011
  332.10973--dc23

                                    2011027479

15  14  13  12  11                          5  4  3  2  1

What has will be again, what has been done will
be done again; there is nothing new under the sun[1]

"fly by the seat of your pants"
DEFINITION: to proceed or work by feel or instinct
without formal guidelines or experience[2]

Chicken Little: Help! Help! The sky is falling.
I have to go tell the king!
CHICKEN LITTLE is a story for teaching courage. Don't be
a chicken little. Don't be afraid. The sky is not falling.[3]

1. Ecclesiastes 1:9 (New International Version).
2. Definition number 2, *The Urban Dictionary*, http://www.urbandictionary.com/define
.php?term=fly%20by%20the%20seat%20of%20your%20pants.
3. E. L. Easton English online, "The Story of Chicken Little: A story for teaching courage,"
http://eleaston.com/chicken.html.

# Contents

Acknowledgments                                                    xi

Financial Scorecard                                               xiii

Introduction                                                        1

1   Bear Stearns—The Original Sin                                   9

2   Bailouts 101                                                   23

3   The Depression of the 1930s and the Interventions              39

4   After the Depression                                           61

5   The 1980s Financial Crisis and the Interventions               71

6   After the 1980s Financial Crisis                              103

7   The 2000s Crisis: The Fed and Treasury Intervene              119

8   The 2000s Crisis: The FDIC Intervenes                         233

9   The 2000s Crisis: TARP                                        257

10  Will the Dodd-Frank Changes Stop the Bailouts?                277

11  The Assessment of the History                                 299


APPENDIX  The Freedom of Information Act Lawsuits                 315

Selected Bibliography                                             355

Index                                                             363

About the Author                                                 381

# Acknowledgments

I APPRECIATE THE patience of Alex Tabarrok of The Independent Institute for waiting eighteen months before he received anything from me worth reading. Thanks also to those "anonymous commentators" that Alex relied upon to fill gaps and generally make the book a better read, and to Gail Saari of The Independent Institute for her work as production manager on a book with a topic that never seemed ready to close out.

Thanks also to Judicial Watch (Tom Fitton, Paul Orfanedes, Michael Bekesha) for representing me in my four Freedom of Information Act (FOIA) cases against the Board of Governors, Federal Deposit Insurance Corporation (FDIC), and Federal Housing Finance Agency (FHFA). Judicial Watch is a conservative, non-partisan educational foundation that promotes transparency, accountability, and integrity in government through litigation, investigations, and public outreach. Were it not for them, I would have had an unpleasant choice between either fully pursuing FOIA litigation on my own or writing this book. Both would not have been possible.

I would also like to thank Jean Helwege for her comments and work as an expert witness in helping me question just about everything the representatives of the Federal Reserve said or did during the most recent crisis; and Elizabeth Harrison for her research assistance, which included a number of on-point quotations that were inaccessible to me given my international travels.

I appreciated the detailed comments I received from Bill Osterberg, William Wallace, Michael Andrews, Robert Strahota, Marc Chu, Bob Abplanalp, Varoujan Avedikian, Joe Pomykala, George Gregorash, Phil Smith, and Matt Stoller. Useful comments were also provided by two anonymous FDIC staff members on historical and policy details. Also thanks to Adam Berkland of the

Congressional Oversight Panel (COP) for help in navigating details from the COP reports. Writing is a team sport. All errors and omissions are those of the author.

I also thank those who wrote the first wave of books on the financial crisis, including Andrew Ross Sorkin (*Too Big to Fail*), David Wessel (*In Fed We Trust*), Henry Paulson (*On the Brink*), William Cohan (*House of Cards*), and John Taylor (*Getting Off Track*), as well as Milton Friedman and Anna Schwartz for their classic work on monetary history including the Depression (*A Monetary History of the United States—1867–1960*).

And finally to my family: My brother Rich for commenting on a very early draft of this book that I was too embarrassed to show anyone else and for giving me a sense of direction on public policy issues thirty years ago. To Nona, Ruben, and Catherine for living with my early morning wake-up time to work on the book, even if it meant Daddy was sometimes not so active in the evenings during family time. To my mom and dad, who came of age during the Depression, an event at the core of the history outlined in this book; they instilled values of thrift and savings in my siblings and me, values that are sadly lacking in Washington today.

The views presented in this book are those of the author.

# Financial Scorecard

## 1910s

Senator Claude Swanson, shepherded the Federal Reserve Act through Congress for President Wilson

President Woodrow Wilson, signed the Federal Reserve Act into law

## 1930s

Joseph Broderick, superintendent of New York State Banking Department during failure of Bank of United States

President Herbert Hoover, signed legislation creating the Reconstruction Finance Corporation

Jesse Jones, chairman of the Reconstruction Finance Corporation

President Franklin Roosevelt, signed the Emergency Banking Relief Act into law

## 1980s

C. Todd Conover, comptroller of the currency during the bailout of Continental Illinois

William Isaac, chairman of the Federal Deposit Insurance Corporation (FDIC) during and in the aftermath of the bailout of Continental Illinois

Fernand J. St. Germain, congressman who scrutinized the bailout of Continental Illinois

L. William Seidman, chairman of the FDIC during much of the 1980s financial crisis immediately after William Isaac

Irvine Sprague, FDIC Board member throughout the 1980s

Paul Volcker, chairman of the Board of Governors of the Federal Reserve during the bailout of Continental Illinois

## 2000s

### *Board of Governors of the Federal Reserve*

Scott Alvarez, general counsel

Deborah P. Bailey, deputy director—Banking Supervision and Regulation Division

Ben S. Bernanke, chairman

Donald Kohn, vice chairman

Randall S. Kroszner, governor

Brian Madigan, director—Division of Monetary Affairs

Patrick Parkinson, deputy director—Division of Research and Statistics

Michelle Smith, director of the Office of Board Members

Coryann Stefansson, associate director—Banking Supervision and Regulation Division

Kevin Warsh, governor

### *Congress*

Senator Christopher Dodd, chairman of the Senate Committee on Banking, Housing, and Urban Affairs

Congressman Barney Frank, chairman of the House Committee on Financial Services

## Department of the Treasury

Henry M. "Hank" Paulson, Jr., secretary of the Treasury

Robert Hoyt, general counsel

Neel Kashkari, assistant secretary

Scott Polakoff, acting director—Office of Thrift Supervision

Robert Steel, under secretary of domestic finance; president and CEO of Wachovia

## Federal Deposit Insurance Corporation

Sheila C. Bair, chairman

John Reich, board member and director of the Office of Thrift Supervision

## Federal Housing Finance Agency

James Lockhart, director

## Federal Reserve Bank of New York

William Dudley, executive vice president—Markets

Timothy F. Geithner, president

Patricia Mosser, senior vice president—Markets

Brian Peters, senior vice president—Risk Management

## Securities and Exchange Commission

Christopher Cox, chairman

### White House

George W. Bush, president

Barack Obama, president and previously senator and presidential candidate

### Financial Industry Leadership

Jamie Dimon, chairman and CEO of JPMorgan Chase

Richard Fuld, chairman and CEO of Lehman Brothers

Harvey Miller, partner of Weil, Gotshal, and Manges

Alan Schwartz, CEO of Bear Stearns

Robert Willumstad, CEO of AIG

# Introduction

PROBABLY NO ISSUE during the most recent financial crisis aroused more passion than financial institution bailouts. Many polls during the height of the crisis in September 2008 showed overwhelming disfavor for the bailouts, but the results varied depending on the precise wording of the poll question.[1] Those that aligned themselves against the bailouts did so for a number of reasons: They were believers in the free market and dead set against the interventionist aspects of such bailouts; or they regularly support interventionist

---

1. See Associated Press, "Poll: Most Americans Against Bush's Bailout Plan," FoxNews .com, September 26, 2008 ("Just 30 percent of Americans say they support Bush's package . . . 45 percent say they oppose Bush's proposal while 25 percent said they are undecided."), http://www.foxnews.com/printer_friendly_story/0,3566,428921,00.html; "Public Blames Wall Street For Its Own Troubles, Opposes Taxpayer Bailouts," Los Angeles Times/Bloomberg.com, September 23, 2008, http://www.latimes.com/media/ acrobat/2008–09/42527811.pdf ("Americans are opposed to the use of taxpayer dollars to rescue ailing private financial firms by 55% to 31% with 14% not sure"), wording of the question as follows: "Do you think the government should use taxpayers' dollars to rescue ailing private financial firms whose collapse could have adverse effects on the economy and market, or is it not the government's responsibility to bail out private companies with taxpayers' dollars?"; but also see Pew Research Center for the People and the Press, "Most Approve of Wall Street Bailout and See Obama as Better Able to Address Crisis," http://pewresearch.org/pubs/963/wall-street-bailout-approval ("Reacting to initial reports of the federal bailout plan over the weekend, 57% said the government was doing the right thing, while 30% said it was doing the wrong thing"), but the wording of the question was as follows: "As you may know, the government is potentially investing billions to try and keep financial institutions and markets secure. Do you think this is the right thing for the government to be doing?"

economic policies, but decried these particular interventions as a "bailout of Wall Street."[2] Those supporting the bailouts were equally convinced of the righteousness of their position that the bailouts, combined with other interventions in the financial system throughout 2008 and 2009, "averted the imminent collapse of the global financial system."[3]

In the three years since the number of bailouts peaked in the latter part of 2008, the standard narrative in judging these most recent bailouts of financial institutions has been:

- The challenges faced by the Treasury Department, the Federal Reserve, and the Federal Deposit Insurance Corporation (FDIC), the primary agencies vested with the power to bail out financial institutions, were absolutely unprecedented in nature and the agencies needed expanded powers to respond to the crisis.
- Although the private sector was largely to blame for the crisis, all manner of terrible consequences impacting "Main Street" would have flowed from allowing the largest financial institutions to fail.
- The interventions by the government, although not perfect in execution such as when Lehman was allowed to fail, saved the economy from

---

2. For example, the so-called "tea parties" organized against government spending held in particularly low esteem those lawmakers who voted for the bailouts. "Nationwide Tea Party Protests Blast Spending," CNNPolitics.com, April 15, 2009, http://edition. cnn.com/2009/POLITICS/04/15/tea.parties/; David Stout, "The Wall Street Bailout Explained," *New York Times*, September 20, 2008, http://www.nytimes.com/2008/09/21/business/21qanda.html. One Republican senator, Robert Bennett, was ousted in a primary election in Utah, at least in large part because of his support for financial institution bailouts. See Shobhana Chandra and Jonathan D. Salant, "Utah Senator Bennett Loses Republican Party Renomination Bid," Bloomberg.com/*Businessweek*, May 9, 2010, http://www.businessweek.com/news/2010–05–09/utah-senator-bennett-loses-republican-party-renomination-bid.html. More recently, Lisa Murkowski lost a Republican primary, a loss that was also attributed in part to her TARP yes vote. Also see David Stout, "Q&A: The Wall Street Bailout Plan," *New York Times*, September 21, 2008, http://www.nytimes.com/2008/09/21/business/worldbusiness/21iht-21qanda.16325439.html?_r=1.
3. Chairman Ben S. Bernanke, "Reflections on a Year of Crisis," August 21, 2009, http://www.federalreserve.gov/newsevents/speech/bernanke20090821a.htm.

another Great Depression, avoiding a repeat of what the United States experienced in the 1930s.

It is expected that those involved in the bailouts would write glowing appraisals of interventions during the financial crisis.[4] The question is why there has not been a more detailed, critical analysis of the decisions made regarding the bailouts. A recent list of the top fifty business books published since early 2009 listed a great many books addressing the financial crisis, including some that focused on the bailouts.[5] Most of these latter books covered the private-sector side of the crisis, focusing on some of the individual firms that failed or nearly failed, such as Bear Stearns or Lehman Brothers; the surviving firms such as Goldman Sachs and JPMorgan Chase; or some of the unique characters involved in the crisis. This focus is natural given the allure of stories about quick ascensions and equally quick collapses, and it is consistent with the idea that the private sector was to blame for the financial crisis. The commercial success of movies like 1987's *Wall Street* during a prior turbulent time in recent U.S. financial history is just one example of this reliable formula. Interestingly enough, this blockbuster movie has been updated for the most recent crisis.[6]

A few of the books on the top fifty list did focus on policy issues. However, they take as a given that government intervention in the form of bailouts of financial institutions was absolutely necessary. Rather than questioning in a meaningful way whether these three previously noted narratives were true, these books perpetuate them as fact. The typical coverage of the crisis instead highlights the personalities involved on the government policy side (such as Chairman Bernanke, Secretary Paulson, or Federal Reserve Bank of New York

4. Henry M. Paulson, Jr., *On the Brink: Inside the Race to Stop the Collapse of the Global Financial System* (New York: Business Plus, 2010) [hereinafter *On the Brink*]. The subtitle alone evokes imagery of a Superman-like hero saving the global financial system from imminent collapse.

5. James Pressley, "Top 50 Business Books, 'Animal Spirits' to 'What the Dog Saw,'" Bloomberg.com, June 17, 2010. The list covered books published from January 1, 2009, to the date of the article.

6. *Wall Street: Money Never Sleeps* (20th Century Fox, 2010, Directed by Oliver Stone), http://www.wallstreetmoneyneversleeps.com/.

[FRBNY] President Geithner) or on the private-sector side (Richard S. Fuld, Jr., of Lehman Brothers; Jamie Dimon of JPMorgan Chase; and Robert B. Willumstad of American International Group [AIG]).[7]

There are a number of potential explanations for the lack of a critical analysis of the government's response. The most compelling reason is that these narratives have been perpetuated by a tripartite coalition of self-interested participants in both the financial collapse and the response to it. Simply stated, the members of this coalition, which is made up of (1) the largest financial institutions, (2) the financial regulatory agencies, and (3) the politicians who approved the bailouts, have a wildly overstated sense of self-importance. The largest financial institutions claim the financial system cannot survive unless their institutions individually survive. They practice what might be called "cafeteria capitalism." Cafeteria style, they pick and choose when they want to follow capitalist principles: they follow it when things are going well, but they beg for the intervention of the government when they are not. The bailout agencies that believed the horrific tales of the financial institutions, in turn, claim to have saved the economy from another depression without doing any long-term damage to the financial system. The politicians also claim that they saved the American economy with their bailout legislation. After all, they had to do "something." Senator Bob Bennett, who lost his U.S. Senate seat to a challenger from within his own party, said the passage

---

7. Two of the most prominent books addressing the most recent crisis that compile extensive detail on the individual bailouts but also largely accept the standard narrative are *In Fed We Trust* [hereinafter *In Fed We Trust*] by the *Wall Street Journal*'s David Wessel (New York: Crown Business, 2009) and *Too Big to Fail* [hereinafter *Too Big to Fail*] by the *New York Times*'s Andrew Ross Sorkin (New York: Viking, 2009). As Sorkin himself describes his book, it instead is a book about "people"; see Book TV, "Andrew Ross Sorkin, *Too Big To Fail*," Speech at Credit Suisse in New York City hosted by the Foreign Policy Association, http://www.youtube.com/watch?v=NDzlVpk_VKQ at the 4:00 mark ("I thought of this frankly less about institutions in a way that were too big to fail so much as I thought about it as people, who in their own way thought they were too big to fail and I wanted to tell that story from a human perspective."). See also TYTInterviews, "David Wessel—*In Fed We Trust*," August 6, 2009, run time = 12:33 http://www.youtube.com/watch?v=D_r-tzBNOfs; and ForaTV, "WSJ Editor Likens Economic Relief to Surgery," October 13, 2009, run time = 3:51, http://www.youtube.com/watch?v=RrkyESwcjJg.

of the core bailout legislation was "Congress's finest moment."[8] The members of this coalition have been collectively responsible for perpetuating a corporatist system in U.S. finance. Their support of that corporatism is intertwined and mutually reinforcing. They have done everything within their power not only to survive the crisis, but also to expand their influence under the bailout regime codified in the recently passed Dodd-Frank legislation.

This book will take a different approach to the crisis. Rather than focusing on people, this book will concentrate on the policymaking behind the decisions to bail out institutions, not just during the most recent crisis, but also earlier in history. The focus will be on how decisions were made, the data that informed those decisions, and the justifications for legislative changes in the wake of financial crises. What a review of the history reveals is a century of public officials making vastly exaggerated claims regarding the salutary effects of short-term government intervention and of long-term legislative changes, dating from the initial passage of the Federal Reserve Act in 1913 through the Dodd-Frank legislation in 2010. The history also reveals that the genesis of financial crisis was government policy, whether it was the mismanagement of monetary policy during the 1930s or the extraordinary push of consumers into homeownership leading up to the 2000s crisis.

In particular, this book will bring under scrutiny the policy decisions made during the most recent crisis by the Treasury Department, the Federal Reserve, and the FDIC. As the book will detail, a number of government oversight agencies such as the Government Accountability Office (GAO), the Congressional Oversight Panel (COP), and the Special Inspector General for the Troubled Asset Relief Program (SIGTARP), with their overlapping jurisdictions and perspectives on the bailouts, have looked at the individual interventions, but none has reviewed the policy basis for the entire range of bailouts. Openly questioning the policy basis cited by the Treasury, the Federal Reserve, and the FDIC leads to a completely different narrative:

---

8. This refers to the Troubled Asset Relief Program (TARP). Eleanor Clift, "The 'Former Member' Club," *Newsweek*, Dec. 17, 2010, http://www.newsweek.com/2010/12/17/congress-reflects-on-the-year-what-went-wrong.html.

- In looking at the history of such interventions during the last three major financial crises in the 1930s, 1980s, and the 2000s, one finds that rather than being unprecedented, the events and responses were actually a clear case of history repeating itself. The reality is that the parallels between many of these events, which were decades apart, are downright eerie.

- Notwithstanding the scary descriptions of impending doom by the various financial regulatory and supervisory agencies, there has never been any clear evidence presented that the failure of one of these large institutions would put the entire financial system at risk.

- With each passing crisis, the interventions got broader and more entrenched, the portion of the financial industry that was bailed out grew, and the number of agencies implementing bailouts multiplied.

- The most recent crisis was rife with regulatory breakdowns. The first stage of breakdowns occurred in the regulatory agencies in their role as an early warning system to raise a red flag at individual institutions. The second stage of breakdowns occurred in the interventions themselves, most of which were absolutely inconsistent with one another. These interventions did not instill confidence, but rather undermined it and gave the impression that the leadership of these agencies panicked and were simply "flying by the seat of their pants" in responding to the crisis.

- When these actions of the agencies were placed under scrutiny during the most recent crisis, rather than openly discussing the justifications for the interventions, the agencies did everything in their power to shield their actions from the scrutiny of outsiders under the vague mantle of avoiding further undermining of confidence. As a result, it has been necessary for anyone truly interested in researching the policy issues involved to bring suit against these agencies to extract details on the crisis. Some of the largest business and news organizations in the United States, including Bloomberg LP, Fox News Network, and the *New York Times*, as well as education foundations and private citizens (including the author), have brought suit since the beginning of the crisis seeking access to data on these transactions.[9]

---

9. The only exception to this limit on access has been for oversight entities with vested authority to gain access to such information, such as the new legislatively created COP

The final point of this series of conclusions is certainly salt in the wound for taxpayers. The idea that policymakers would use all the powers at their disposal to prevent outside analysts either from the media or the public generally from reviewing their decision-making, especially when vast sums of public funds were being placed at risk, is particularly galling. Though the extent and speed of the recent series of bailouts was extraordinary, as noted they were hardly unprecedented, as modern banking history is replete with examples of such publicly funded interventions. As a result, an historical analysis of bailouts is essential to understanding why we have become so reliant on such interventions.

---

and the SIGTARP, which were put into place to oversee the implementation of the TARP. Additionally, the GAO has also investigated many of the most recent bailouts, as well as many of the bailouts back in time. Probably the most prominent of the so-called Freedom of Information lawsuits against the government has been *Bloomberg L.P. v. Board of Governors of the Federal Reserve System*, which has been reviewed by the Supreme Court. The *Wall Street Journal* has also filed a number of Freedom of Information Act (FOIA) requests in this regard, as has the Fox News Network. See Review and Outlook, "Systemic Risk Stonewall," *Wall Street Journal*, September 1, 2010, http://online.wsj.com/article/SB10001424052748703467004575463781244452958.html?mod=WSJ_topics_obama; and *Fox News Network, LLC v. Board of Governors of the Federal Reserve System*, District Court Southern District of New York: 639 F.Supp.2d 384 (2009); U.S. Court of Appeals 2nd Circuit: 601 F.3d 158 (2010). Additionally, the author has brought multiple suits against the FDIC, the Board of Governors of the Federal Reserve, and the Federal Housing Finance Authority (FHFA), and his counsel on these cases, Judicial Watch, a conservative, non-partisan educational foundation, has also brought suit against these agencies (for a summary of such cases see the Appendix).

# 1

## Bear Stearns—
### The Original Sin[1] (March 2008)

DURING THE FIRST week of March 2008, the U.S. Securities and Exchange Commission (SEC) staff conducted an on-site inspection focused on Bear Stearns's liquidity pool. No significant issues were identified. Bear Stearns's liquidity pool stood at about $18 to $20 billion.[2]

At 1:29 p.m. on Monday, March 10, 2008,[3] Brian Peters of the Federal Reserve Bank of New York (FRBNY) informed staff at the Board of Governors in Washington and the other reserve banks that

> Bear's [credit default swap] spreads have blown out to 750 bp, and the stock is down substantially. There are considerable rumors on the Street of dealers and funds pulling away from Bear. We are in contact with the SEC. Please check with your firms to see if they have or are taking any

---

1. James Freeman, "Bear Stearns: The Fed's Original 'Systemic Risk' Sin," *Wall Street Journal*, March 16, 2009. Sudeep Reddy, "A Necessary Step or Slippery Slope?" *Wall Street Journal*, March 15, 2009.

2. SEC, "Timeline Regarding the Bear Stearns Companies, Inc.," 3 April 2008, 2 [hereinafter Bear Stearns timeline].

3. The format for the description of Bear Stearns that follows was drawn from "Plaintiff's Memorandum in Opposition to Defendant Board of Governors' Motion for Summary Judgment and in Support of Plaintiff's Cross-Motion for Summary Judgment," *McKinley v. Board of Governors*, Case 1:10-cv-00420, March 8, 2010, which was drafted by Paul Orfanedes and Michael Bekesha of Judicial Watch with comments from the author. http://www.scribd.com/doc/28064418/Opposition-to-Board-of-Governors-SJ-Motion -and-Statement-of-Facts.

actions (increasing haircuts, refusing assignments to them, or in any other way constraining credit) with respect to Bear.[4]

Meanwhile, that same day the SEC scheduled an on-site visit for Tuesday, March 18, to review Bear Stearns's first quarter financial results in more detail.[5] Bear Stearns started the week with a cash and liquid securities position of $18 billion.[6]

There were also concerns on that Monday afternoon about emerging public reports on Bear Stearns: "Apparently there was some misinformation in the press regarding Bear Stearns that caused the firm[']s [credit default swap] spreads to widen significantly and fueled rumors about potential liquidity problems."[7] Staff at the Office of the Comptroller of the Currency (OCC), which regulates national banks, also reportedly raised questions of their own. On Monday OCC staff became concerned about the potential exposure to Bear Stearns of banks that it regulates, and to that end staff of the agency began to call these banks. The calls were not about general exposures but were specifically about exposure to Bear Stearns. In a recounting of one of these conversations, a targeted banker was told, "Don't tell your traders and don't get out of any counterparty agreements that you have. But what's your exposure to Bear Stearns?" Of course the banker told his traders, bought puts, sold short, and

---

4. *McKinley v. Board of Governors*, Bates No. 09–0164–000001. All citations to Bates Numbers refer to the reference numbers in the Board of Governor's September 30, 2009 document production, Exhibit 4 available at http://www.scribd.com/doc/28064856 /Exhibit-A-Part-2-McKinley-Declaration-to-Support-Opposition. Email from Brian Peters, Federal Reserve Bank of New York (FRBNY) to various staff at FRBNY, other reserve banks and the Board of Governors of the Federal Reserve (hereinafter BOG) titled "Priority: Bear Stearns," March 10, 2008.

5. Bear Stearns timeline, 3.

6. Bear Stearns timeline, 3. Henry M. Paulson, Jr., *On the Brink: Inside the Race to Stop the Collapse of the Global Financial System* (New York: Business Plus, 2010) [hereinafter *On the Brink*], 100. David Wessel, *In Fed We Trust: Ben Bernanke's War on the Great Panic* (New York: Crown Business, 2009), 147–48, 153, [hereinafter *In Fed We Trust*]. William D. Cohan, *House of Cards* (Anchor Books: New York, 2009) [hereinafter *House of Cards*] 53.

7. *McKinley v. Board of Governors*, Bates No. 09–0164–000002, 000004. Email from Jon D. Greenlee to various BOG staff titled "Brian Sack info—Bear Stearns Priority Request" March 10, 2008.

got out of everything he could possibly get out of.[8] Despite these rumors and questions, an unnamed firm "adamantly stressed that it [was] continuing to provide liquidity to Bear Stearns."[9]

By Tuesday, March 11, at 2:36 p.m., a primary focus of FRBNY staff was on the reaction of large financial institutions (LFIs) to the troubles at Bear Stearns: "Several additional LFIs report gradual reduction in various lines to Bear, with most closely reviewing existing positions. LFIs generally seem satisfied with Bear's liquidity. Bear appears to be reducing [short-term] funding and staggering long-term debt, but don't seem interested in financing derivative/repo transactions with longer terms, unique structures, etc. LFIs' management appear [sic] cognizant of exacerbating problems via widespread/dramatic reduction in credit to Bear."[10]

By Wednesday, March 12, 2008, "an increased volume of [Bear Stearns's] customers expressed a desire to withdraw funds from, and certain counterparties expressed increased concern regarding maintaining their ordinary course exposure to, Bear Stearns."[11] This activity prompted Alan Schwartz, chief executive officer of Bear Stearns, to call FRBNY president Geithner that evening to discuss the precarious position of the firm, and the next day the SEC, the Treasury Department, and FRBNY staff discussed the status of Bear Stearns in more detail.[12]

---

8. *House of Cards*, 22–25.

9. *McKinley v. Board of Governors*, Bates No. 09–0164–000007 email from Peter Drake FRBNY to various FRBNY, Federal Reserve Bank, and BOG staff titled "Priority: Bear Stearns," March 10, 2008. The name of the firm providing liquidity was redacted under Freedom of Information Act exemptions 4 and 8.

10. *McKinley v. Board of Governors*, Bates No. 09–0164–000008 email from Bard Stermasi FRBNY to various FRBNY, Federal Reserve Bank, and BOG staff titled "Priority: Bear Stearns-Mar. 11," March 11, 2008.

11. The Bear Stearns Companies Inc. Proxy Statement Pursuant to Section 14a of the Securities Exchange Act of 1934 (hereinafter Bear Stearns Proxy Statement), April 28, 2008, 27 [hereinafter Bear Stearns Proxy Statement], http://www.scribd.com/doc/28064986/Exhibit-B-Bekesha-Declaration-to-Support-Opposition.

12. Alan Schwartz, interview by Financial Crisis Inquiry Commission (FCIC), email to Erik Sirri, Robert Colby, and Michael Macchiaroli, March 13, 2008. Bear Stearns timeline, 4.

At 2:33 p.m. on Thursday, March 13, 2008, Deborah P. Bailey, deputy director of the Board's Division of Banking Supervision and Regulation, notified members of the Board of Governors and senior staff that

> [FRBNY] and Board staffs are monitoring the situation. [FRBNY] staff is in ongoing contact with SEC staff and has asked them to keep the Federal Reserve [informed] as to the firm's liquidity profile including unencumbered cash positions, available secured and unsecured financing sources, and available Fed-eligible and non-eligible collateral. As of noon today, the SEC reported that the holding company has $12.5 billion in cash and has been able to roll "almost all" of its equity repos and all of its U.S. and European bank loans.[13]

Meanwhile, Bailey noted an SEC conclusion that "no notable losses have been sustained and that the capital position of [Bear Stearns] is 'fine.'"[14] That same Thursday "an unusual number of customers withdrew funds from Bear Stearns and a significant number of counterparties and lenders were unwilling to make secured funding available to Bear Stearns on customary terms."[15]

The staff of the Board of Governors and FRBNY was struggling under great time pressure and with questionable information to undertake the required analysis of Bear Stearns in order to understand the firm's operations, as well as the potential broader impact beyond Bear Stearns:

- "Coryann Stefansson just called and said that this is the info (still preliminary and probably not super accurate but kind of in the ball park at least) that she has about the exposure of major banks to Bear. . . .

---

13. *McKinley v. Board of Governors*, Bates No. 09–0164–0000010–11. Email from Deborah P. Bailey to Rita Proctor, Donald Kohn, Randall Kroszner, Kevin Warsh, Frederic Mishkin, Scott Alvarez, and Brian Madigan titled "Bear Stearns Update," March 13, 2008 [hereinafter Bailey email to Board members].
14. Bailey email to Board members. Reportedly, in a related quote, Chairman Cox of the SEC on March 11, 2008, had said in reference to a full range of investment firms (Goldman, Morgan Stanley, Merrill Lynch, Lehman Brothers, and Bear Stearns) that "We have a good deal of comfort about the capital cushions at these firms at the moment." *House of Cards*, 28.
15. Bear Stearns Proxy Statement, 27.

She also said that [REDACTED] should be on the list, but nobody could confirm it."[16]

- "Sorry if my details are sketchy but will try to provide more substance as we get information."[17]
- "I must say that I am not that comfortable with the accuracy, but we got the info from the teams."[18]
- "We have pulled together the exposure #s of the [large financial institutions] to [Bear Stearns] but the information is from the last monthly reports from the firm that are prepared by the exam teams. Board staff did not go out this week for a request on more current exposure information."[19]
- "Here is a report we received where [Bear Stearns] tried to identify the counterparties that they owed money to. The[y] claimed it was inexact (their systems are not set up to run that way), but ordinarily correct. Looks like it is only derivatives. Will provide more clarity as I can."[20]
- "While dated, attached is a spreadsheet folks here pulled together on what each firm had as of year-end 2007 w.r.t. their counterparty credit risk exposure to Bear."[21]

---

16. *McKinley v. Board of Governors*, Bates No. 09–0164–0000017. Email from Roberto Perli to Brian Madigan and William English previously forwarded by James Clouse, titled "Banks' exposure to Bear Stearns," March 13, 2008. The named firm was redacted under exemption 4 and 8 of the Freedom of Information Act.

17. *McKinley v. Board of Governors*, Bates No. 09–0164–0000033. Email from Deborah P. Bailey to Rita Proctor, Donald Kohn, Randall Kroszner, Kevin Warsh, Roger Cole, Scott Alvarez, and Frederic Mishkin, titled "BS Update," March 13, 2008.

18. *McKinley v. Board of Governors*, Bates No. 09–0164–0000033. Email from Deborah P. Bailey to Scott Alvarez and Roger Cole, titled "Re: BS Update," March 13, 2008.

19. *McKinley v. Board of Governors*, Bates No. 09–0164–0000034. Email from Deborah P. Bailey to Donald Kohn, Brian Madigan, Frederic Mishkin, Kevin Warsh, Randall Kroszner, Rita Proctor, Roger Cole, and Scott Alvarez, titled "Re: BS Update," March 13, 2008.

20. *McKinley v. Board of Governors*, Bates No. 09–0164–0000037. Email from Brian Peters to Deborah P. Bailey and Coryann Stefansson, titled "Fw: Largest Bank_Broker Group Exposure to BS Group.xls," March 14, 2008.

21. *McKinley v. Board of Governors*, Bates No. 09–0164–0000050. Email from Dianne Dobbeck to various staff at the FRBNY and BOG staff, titled "Bear Info From Team Rooms," March 14, 2008. It should be noted that this email was sent after the meeting started where the Board of Governors approved the Bear Stearns/JPMorgan transaction.

By 5:40 p.m. on Thursday, March 13, numbers were starting to come to-gether on firm level exposure to Bear Stearns for a broad range of institutions as circulated by James Sheerin at the Board of Governors: "Here are exposures to [Bear Stearns] that I have now."[22] These exposures have never been publicly released. By 7:00 p.m. that same evening, Bear Stearns calculated that its liquid-ity pool was down to $2.0 billion.[23] Although these were not bank depositors that were withdrawing their funds, the impact of the evaporation of funding sources from Bear Stearns had the same impact as a traditional bank run.

At 7:50 p.m. on Thursday, March 13, 2008, FRBNY staff learned of the pos-sibility that Bear Stearns would file for bankruptcy the following day. An email exchanged between FRBNY officials, including FRBNY President Geithner, noted: "SEC just received a call from [Bear Stearns Chief Risk Officer] Mike Alix indicating [that Bear Stearns is] uncertain about [its] ability to operate tomorrow. Likely to call us." Attached to a subsequent email were notes of a telephone conference between FRBNY staff and SEC officials regarding Bear Stearns, but details of the notes have not been publicly disclosed. A FRBNY official forwarded this same email to the Board of Governors' General Counsel, Scott Alvarez, at 8:15 p.m.[24] At 8:26 p.m. Board of Governors Deputy Director Bailey informed the members of the Board of Governors and other senior staff that Bear Stearns's "Chief Risk officer indicated that [Bear Stearns] will likely have 'trouble' opening tomorrow and will be under pressure. A great deal of uncertainty about ability to operate."[25]

---

22. *McKinley v. Board of Governors*, Bates No. 09–0164–0000029. Email from James Sheerin to Coryann Stefansson and Deborah P. Bailey titled "bear Stearns exposures," March 13, 2008.

23. Bear Stearns timeline, 4. *In Fed We Trust*, 154. *House of Cards*, 61. It is not clear whether the available cash balance dropped this quickly, whether different definitions of cash were used, if the $12.5 billion figure quoted in the email from the Federal Reserve was over-stated, or if the details from *In Fed We Trust* are inaccurate.

24. *McKinley v. Board of Governors*, Bates No. 09–0164–0000030–0000031. Email from Brian Peters to Thomas Baxter, William Dudley, Terrence Checki, Christine Cumming, Michael Silva, and Timothy Geithner titled "SEC just received a call from Mike Alix. . ." March 13, 2008.

25. *McKinley v. Board of Governors,* Bates No. 09–0164–0000033. Email from Deborah P. Bailey to Rita Proctor, Donald Kohn, Randall Kroszner, Kevin Warsh, Roger Cole, Scott Alvarez, and Frederic Mishkin titled "BS update," March 13, 2008.

That same evening Alan Schwartz, CEO of Bear Stearns called JPMorgan Chase Chief Executive Officer Jamie Dimon to determine if his firm could lend Bear Stearns as much as $30 billion or buy the company. Dimon informed Schwartz that a loan or outright purchase was impossible, but that JPMorgan Chase was willing to assist Bear Stearns in finding a solution to its liquidity problem.[26] During the evening of Thursday, March 13, representatives of JPMorgan Chase and officials from the U.S. Treasury Department, the FRBNY, and the Board of Governors engaged in discussions regarding how to resolve the liquidity deterioration at Bear Stearns. These discussions continued throughout the night. JPMorgan Chase made it clear during these discussions that it could not loan funds to Bear Stearns without some form of assistance provided by the government. JPMorgan Chase and another unnamed bidder were the only firms that expressed meaningful interest in Bear Stearns. Bear Stearns set up a data room for potential bidders to undertake due diligence, the process of reviewing assets of a firm for potential purchase.[27]

At 9:16 p.m. on Thursday, March 13, 2008, Board of Governors Vice Chairman Donald Kohn sent an email to the other board members and other senior staff stating:

> [Bear Stearns is] talking to [JPMorgan] but not clear what might happen. Right now it looks like without help holding company likely to file Chapt. 11 tomorrow—broker and other liquid entities should continue to operate, though obviously they wuillbe [sic] subject to runs. SEC has people in the firm and FRBNY likely to send someone over to look at positions.[28]

Elsewhere, between 10 p.m. and 11 p.m. on Thursday, Governor Randall Kroszner, in an online discussion with Vice Chairman Kohn, began to speculate about the

---

26. Jamie Dimon, interview by FCIC, October 20, 2010. Bryan Burrough, "Bringing Down Bear Stearns," *Vanity Fair*, August 2008, http://www.vanityfair.com/politics/features /2008/08/bear_stearns200808 [hereinafter "Bringing Down Bear Stearns"].

27. Jamie Dimon, interview by FCIC, October 20, 2010. Alan Schwartz, testimony before the FCIC, May 5, 2010. Bear Stearns Proxy Statement at 27–28.

28. *McKinley v. Board of Governors*, Bates No. 09–0164–0000034. Email from Donald Kohn to Deborah P. Bailey, Frederic Mishkin, Kevin Warsh, Randall Kroszner, Rita Proctor, Roger Cole, Scott Alvarez, and Brian Madigan titled "BS Update," March 13, 2008.

indirect impact of Bear Stearns's problems on the broader financial markets: "I think it is not just the direct exposure to [Bear Stearns] but the turmoil that this could cause in the entire [credit default swaps] market. These contracts haven't really been tested and the uncertaintu [sic] generated by a filing by a major player could have extreme consequences."[29] Kroszner did not offer any support for his speculation.[30] By 11:00 p.m. on Thursday, JPMorgan Chase had a team of specialists at Bear Stearns's headquarters reviewing its financial records to determine what action, if any, JPMorgan Chase could and would be willing to take.[31]

At 12:38 a.m. on the morning of Friday, March 14, 2008, Bear Stearns's chief risk officer emailed a FRBNY staffer a spreadsheet of banks and brokers having the largest exposure to Bear Stearns. By 1:03 a.m. this same Bear Stearns spreadsheet had been circulated to other FRBNY staffers and to officials at the Board of Governors.[32] By 2:00 a.m. investigators from the FRBNY joined JPMorgan and SEC staffers already at Bear Stearns's headquarters. One anonymous Federal Reserve staffer's wildly exaggerated take on the situation was as follows: "For the first time in history the entire world was looking at the failure of a major financial institution that could lead to a run on the entire world financial system. It was clear we couldn't let that happen."[33]

At 2:00 a.m. on Friday morning, March 14, 2008, FRBNY President Geithner called Vice Chairman Kohn and told him that he wasn't confident that the fallout from the bankruptcy of Bear Stearns could be contained, and at approximately 4:00 a.m. Geithner called Chairman Bernanke, who reportedly

---

29. *McKinley v. Board of Governors*, Bates No. 09–0164–0000035–0000036. Email from Randall Kroszner to Donald Kohn, Deborah P. Bailey, Roger Cole, Scott Alvarez, and Brian Madigan titled "BS Update," March 13, 2008. Calls by the author to Kroszner to discuss this "turmoil" were not returned.

30. The issue was raised by Deborah P. Bailey in an email earlier that night at 8:52 p.m., but again there was no clear basis for the speculative statement.

31. "Bringing Down Bear Stearns."

32. *McKinley v. Board of Governors*, Bates No. 09–0164–0000037–0000038. Email from Coryann Stefansson to Brian Peters, Deborah P. Bailey, and Sarah Dahlgren titled "Largest Bank_Broker Group Exposures to BS Group.xls," March 14, 2008.

33. "Bringing Down Bear Stearns."

"agreed that the Fed should intervene."[34] Around 5:00 a.m. on Friday, March 14, 2008, FRBNY President Geithner, Chairman Bernanke, Treasury Secretary Paulson, Governor Warsh, Vice Chairman Kohn, Tony Ryan, Bob Steel from Treasury, and Erik Sirri from the SEC participated in a conference call.[35] Jamie Dimon, CEO of JPMorgan, came on the line for a few minutes to provide input on his bank's role as clearing bank for Bear Stearns. He painted a dark picture, emphasizing that a Bear Stearns failure would be disastrous for the markets, and that the key was to get to the weekend.[36]

At 5:48 a.m. and 5:50 a.m., respectively, almost an hour after the conference call had commenced, the members of the Board of Governors and other board officials received, via emails forwarded from the FRBNY, spreadsheets titled "Bear Stearns exposure Mar 14 v1.xls" and "Bear Stearns Counterparty Credit Exposures March 14 Morning Call.xls."[37] These spreadsheets have not been released by the Board of Governors.

Approximately one hour later, around 7:00 a.m., "Geithner laid down the gauntlet. 'We've got to make a call here, because [repo] markets open at seven-thirty,' he said. 'What's it going to be?' The consensus was there. 'Let's do it,' Bernanke said."[38] The "it" was to have the FRBNY offer a short-term nonrecourse loan to JPMorgan, and JPMorgan in turn would extend credit to Bear Stearns.

---

34. John Cassidy, "Anatomy of a Meltdown," *The New Yorker*, December 1, 2008, http://www.newyorker.com/reporting/2008/12/01/081201fa_fact_cassidy.

35. *On the Brink*, 100. (Secretary Paulson notes that he was on the call "[s]till wearing the boxer shorts and T-shirt" he slept in.) Statement of Timothy F. Geithner, president and chief executive officer, FBRNY, before the U.S. Senate Committee on Banking, Housing, and Urban Affairs Regarding Actions by the Federal Reserve Bank of New York in Response to Liquidity Pressures in Financial Markets, U.S. Senate, April 3, 2008.

36. *On the Brink*, 100–101.

37. *McKinley v. Board of Governors*, Bates No. 09–0164–0000040 and 000042. Email from Deborah P. Bailey to Rita Proctor, Brian Madigan, Donald Kohn, Randall Kroszner, Kevin Warsh, Roger Cole, and Scott Alvarez titled "Bear Stearns cashflow," March 14, 2008, forwarding a 5 a.m. email from William Brodows of the FRBNY.

38. Kate Kelly, *Street Fighters: The Last 72 Hours of Bear Stearns, the Toughest Firm on Wall Street*, 69 (New York: Penguin Group, 2009).

Chairman Bernanke threw in a caveat to the deal: "I'm prepared to go ahead here only if Treasury is supportive and prepared to protect us from any losses."[39] Paulson admitted that he wasn't sure what legal authority, if any, that Treasury had to indemnify the Federal Reserve in this manner. He stated his position clearly notwithstanding any legal limitations: "I'm prepared to do anything. If there's any chance of avoiding this failure, we need to take it." After all, he later noted, the repo markets would open shortly—around 7:30 a.m.—and he wasn't about to drag in a lot of lawyers and debate any legal fine points. Shortly thereafter, Secretary Paulson called President Bush and informed him of the decision even though the Board of Governors of the Federal Reserve had not yet met to discuss or authorize the transaction.[40]

Despite the fact that the key decisions had been made, the data continued to flow. At 7:39 a.m., Coryann Stefansson, associate director of the Board's Division of Banking Supervision and Regulation, obtained and sent to Governor Kroszner a document setting forth data from the third quarter of 2007 regarding the value of credit default swaps held by the top twenty-five commercial banks. This was apparently a follow-up to the discussion on the fragility of this market.[41]

At 9:13 a.m., just as the meeting of the Board of Governors was about to convene, JPMorgan issued a press release announcing that "in conjunction with [the FRBNY], it has agreed to provide secured funding to Bear Stearns. . . . Through its Discount Window, [the FRBNY] will provide non-recourse, back-to-back financing to JPMorgan."[42] At 9:16 a.m., Governor Kevin Warsh sent an email to the heads of the twelve Federal Reserve Banks informing them of the following:

Bear Stearns is proving unable to find (sic) itself. This morning, the Board **will** vote under [Section] 13(3) to authorize the FRBNY to lend

39. *On the Brink*, 101.

40. *On the Brink*, 101.

41. *McKinley v. Board of Governors*, Bates No. 09–0164–0000044–0000045. Email from Coryann Stefansson to Randall Kroszner titled "Cds," March 14, 2008.

42. "JPMorgan Chase and Federal Reserve Bank of New York to Provide Financing to Bear Stearns," March 14, 2008, available at http://investor.shareholder.com/jpmorgan chase/releasedetail.cfm?releaseid=299381.

to JPMorgan Chase to on-lend to Bear Stearns. We will announce that action later this morning, following announcements by JPMC and BS. In addition, we will announce the following: 'The Federal Reserve is monitoring market developments closely and will provide liquidity as necessary to promote the orderly functioning of the financial system.'[43]

Around 9:21 a.m., approximately six minutes after the Board of Governors convened, Bear Stearns issued its own press release stating that it had "reached an agreement with JPMorgan . . . to provide a secured loan facility."[44] When the stock market opened at 9:30 a.m., the decision to "bail out" Bear Stearns was at least two hours old, and the public had been notified about the FRBNY's emergency financing of Bear Stearns.

At 9:39 a.m., apparently after the Board of Governors had formally authorized the transaction, Dianne Dobbeck of the FRBNY emailed FRBNY staff, board staff, and staff of other Federal Reserve Banks a spreadsheet of "counterparty credit risk exposure to Bear [Stearns]" for year-end 2007.[45] At 11:52 a.m., FRBNY Senior Vice President Jamie McAndrews emailed FRBNY President Geithner and other FRBNY employees a three-page draft memorandum: "I've drafted a set of arguments in favor of today's action for your review. I would appreciate any comments, as these are a first draft." However, the memo was not drafted for use at the board meeting at 9 a.m. In fact, this was two hours after the meeting was completed. Interestingly enough McAndrews, who drafted the memo, did not even attend the Board of Governors' meeting. FRBNY President Geithner forwarded the memorandum to Chairman Bernanke, Vice Chairman Kohn, and Governor Kevin Warsh by email, along with a notation

43. *McKinley v. Board of Governors*, Bates No. 09–0164–0000046. Email from Kevin Warsh to Timothy Geithner, Donald Kohn, Randall Kroszner, and various Federal Reserve Bank presidents titled "Note from Vice Chairman Kohn," March 14, 2008 (emphasis on "will" added by the author given the Board of Governors had not voted yet).
44. "Bear Stearns Agrees to Secured Loan Facility with JPMorgan Chase," *Businesswire*, March 14, 2008, http://www.businesswire.com/portal/site/homepermalink/?ndmViewId =news_view&newsId=20080314005441&newsLang=en.
45. *McKinley v. Board of Governors*, Bates No. 09–0164–0000050. Email from Dianne Dobbeck of FRBNY to BOG and Federal Reserve Bank staff titled "Bear Info from Team Rooms," March 14, 2008.

stating, "This is very good." Later that afternoon, at 1:54 p.m., Vice Chairman Kohn emailed a response to McAndrews and FRBNY President Geithner, stating, "Jamie, Nice job; you've made the case about as strongly as it could be made, and it's very helpful to have this spelled out." The email was 'cc-ed' to Chairman Bernanke and Governor Warsh. Four minutes later, McAndrews responded to Vice Chairman Kohn, stating, "Thanks very much Don, I'll work to incorporate your comments, and others I receive in the next day or two from people here." McAndrews "cc-ed" Chairman Bernanke, Governor Warsh, and FRBNY President Geithner.[46] It does not appear that the original or any subsequent version of the document have ever been produced publicly by the Board of Governors.[47]

A few days after the bailout of Bear Stearns was announced, the lawyers that Secretary Paulson did not want to talk to in the early morning hours of Friday, March 14, informed him that the Anti-Deficiency Act prevented Treasury from spending money without a specific congressional allocation. Treasury General Counsel Bob Hoyt stated it simply: "We can't do this." Treasury could not indemnify the Federal Reserve against losses as Secretary Paulson and Chairman Bernanke had wanted. Treasury Secretary Paulson was not pleased: "My God. I just told the president we have a deal."[48] All that Treasury could supply was a letter of support that recognized that Treasury had no power to cover losses of the Federal Reserve. It also acknowledged that if a loss was sustained on the Bear Stearns transaction, a reduced amount of funds would be given to Treasury by the Federal Reserve.[49]

On March 26, 2008, FRBNY attorneys sent attorneys at the Board of Governors a four-page memorandum "recount[ing] the legal advice that was provided by FRBNY legal staff to Board legal staff."[50] On April 2, 2008, attorneys at the Board of Governors prepared a sixteen-page memorandum that "recounts the

---

46. *McKinley v. Board of Governors*, Bates No. 09–0164–0000053–0000054. Email from Jamie McAndrews to Timothy Geithner, Meg McConnell, and William Dudley, titled "First draft of arguments in favor of today's action," March 13, 2008, with attachment "Arguments in favor of today's action.doc."

47. The Board has not identified whether *McKinley v. Board of Governors* Bates Nos. 09–0164–0000166–0000168 is a final version of this same memorandum.

48. *On the Brink*, 114.

49. *On the Brink*, 115.

legal advice that was provided to the Board on and around March 14, 2008 in support of staff's recommendation that the Board [of Governors] authorize under section 13(3) . . . FRBNY to extend credit to [Bear Stearns] indirectly through [JPMorgan]."[51] Neither of these memos has been released for public scrutiny.

On June 27, 2008, the Board of Governors released the minutes of its March 14, 2008, meeting. Nearly four months after the Board of Governors had acted, the minutes only disclose that "given the fragile condition of the financial markets at the time, the prominent position of Bear Stearns in those markets, and the expected contagion that would result from the immediate failure of Bear Stearns, the best alternative available was to provide temporary emergency funding to Bear Stearns through an arrangement with JPMorgan Chase. . . . Such a loan would facilitate efforts to effect a resolution of the Bear Stearns situation that would be consistent with preserving financial stability."

Among other necessary findings, the minutes summarily state only that the board had concluded that "unusual and exigent circumstances existed" and "Bear Stearns, and possibly other primary securities dealers, were unable to secure adequate credit accommodations elsewhere."[52] The Board of Governors did not identify the specific evidence it considered or how it analyzed that evidence.

---

50. *McKinley v. Board of Governors*, Bates No. 09–0164–0000185–0000188. *Vaughn Index*, attached to Thro Decl. as Exhibit F, at Item No. 36.
51. *McKinley v. Board of Governors*, Bates No. 09–0164–0000169–0000184. *Vaughn Index*, Item No. 35.
52. Board of Governors of the Federal Reserve System, "Minutes of the Board of Governors of the Federal Reserve System," March 14, 2008 [Bear Stearns Minutes].

# 2

## Bailouts 101

"Bank runs have a bad reputation."[1]

MANY TERMS HAVE been used as the most recent financial crisis unfolded to describe the events in real time: failure, run, and bailout. However, little effort has been dedicated to more clearly defining these terms; defining a central bank's role in addressing failures and runs; and defining the event when all of them reach their heights, a financial crisis. The following discussion addresses these concepts as they will be used in the ensuing chapters with focus on how their definitions changed in the wake of the Bear Stearns bailout.

### What Does It Mean When a Financial Institution Fails?

The problems at Bear Stearns started to become widely known with the deterioration of the value of its assets, most notably the troubles at two of its hedge funds.[2] Any time such losses occur they cause a reduction in the net value of a financial institution. Solvency is an indicator of net value measured by a calculation of the institution's assets in relation to its liabilities. At the same time as a drop in the net value, a financial institution usually also has difficulty

---

1. George G. Kaufman, "Bank Runs: Causes, Benefits, and Costs," *Cato Journal*, 7, no. 3 (Winter 1988), 559 [hereinafter "Bank Runs"].
2. Jody Shenn and Bradly Keoun, "Bear Stearns Rivals Reject Fund Bailout in LTCM Redux," Bloomberg.com, June 25, 2007, http://www.bloomberg.com/apps/news?pid= newsarchive&sid=a2mbR8rPyzto.

in accessing liquidity. Bear Stearns started having liquidity difficulties after the hedge fund losses came to light. As obligations came due some creditors may have been hesitant to place their funds at risk in an institution that seemed to be approaching insolvency.[3]

When a financial institution approaches insolvency or cannot meet the demands of creditors, it ultimately may lead to failure, a government-supervised closure of a financial institution.[4] Legal regimes governing financial-sector institutions vary, but most require revocation of an operating license or placement in bankruptcy or its equivalent either when all capital value is exhausted, when a large percentage of capital value is exhausted, or when a financial institution cannot meet the obligations of its creditors. Having a defined process under law for a financial institution to fail is a good thing, what is called an "exit strategy." This can be done either through a form of receivership or bankruptcy, the exit that Bear Stearns would have taken were it not for the intervention by the FRBNY. Absent such an intervention, the alternative to failure is to allow financial institutions to linger on, making investments and soliciting funds from creditors for an undefined period of time. Under those circumstances, the financial institution's owners have little at stake and thus a minimal incentive to control risk. This environment may ultimately undermine the competitive position of stronger, better-managed financial institutions.

In supporting such a financial-sector legal regime, one of the purposes of financial institution regulation, supervision, and oversight is to act as an advance warning system on failures in order to limit the losses sustained through the so-called "financial safety net." In the United States these programs, such as deposit insurance and central bank lending, were initiated during the early part of the twentieth century. Up until early 2008, the financial safety net had been almost exclusively reserved for insured depository institutions, such as

---

3. Bear Stearns timeline, 1–2. Adjustments made by Bear Stearns included increasing their reliance on secured funding and decreasing reliance on short-term unsecured funding.
4. It is conceivable that a well-run, solvent institution could be brought down through false rumors if funding is not made available, but such events have been very rare in the United States.

commercial banks.[5] The intervention to save Bear Stearns from bankruptcy was a dramatic change because the financial safety net was explicitly extended to cover a singular investment bank.

## What Does It Mean When a Financial Institution Has a Run?

Although Bear Stearns was not a commercial bank and did not have depositors that caused a traditional bank run, it did have short-term creditors that were able to withdraw their funding once the firm's difficulties became known. This is what led to its near collapse. A run occurs when a financial institution approaches insolvency, as concern grows about its ability to pay its obligations and there is an incentive for creditors to be first in line to withdraw funds.[6] Previously concern about runs was focused on commercial banks, a natural consequence of fractional-reserve banking, whereby an institution is required to maintain only a fraction of what has been placed in deposit available to repay depositors.[7] If depositors who are easily able to withdraw funds receive word that a financial institution is in a weakened financial state, they may ultimately "run" to the bank to withdraw their funds before other creditors if they are concerned that there may not be sufficient resources to pay all those who desire repayment. In the case of a financial institution that is insolvent or approaching insolvency, the run is the result of the insolvency, not the cause, if depositors are aware of the weak financial position.[8]

---

5. Federal Reserve Board—Remarks of Chairman Alan Greenspan, "The Financial Safety Net," Thirty-seventh Annual Conference on Bank Structure and Competition of the Federal Reserve Bank of Chicago, Chicago, Illinois, May 10, 2001. See also John R. Walter and John A. Weinberg, "How Large is the Federal Financial Safety Net?" *Cato Journal*, 21, no. 3 (Winter 2002).

6. Again, it is conceivable that a well-run, solvent institution could be brought down through false rumors if funding is not made available, but such an event is rare today.

7. An example of a run outside the context of fractional-reserve banking during the 2000s crisis was the Reserve Primary Fund. This fund still had a run because claims were filled at face value.

8. "Bank Runs," 563.

Bank runs have both good and bad effects. The good effect is the market discipline exerted on bank management. A run is a market signal that a bank is weak and is essentially a form of punishment for poor management of an institution. Since the inception of deposit insurance in the 1930s, insured depositors have had a limited incentive to monitor banks and cause a run as they are assured of payment up to their insured amount. However, deposit insurance has not eliminated runs, as uninsured depositors who are above the FDIC limit and other creditors still have an incentive to monitor a bank's condition and have an incentive to run on a bank.[9]

The bad effect of a run beyond the individual institution level is the potential for damage to the broader banking system and economy generally. Although a run is obviously devastating for an individual institution, for policymakers the implications of a contagion are of greater concern.[10] The term "contagion" refers to a state in the financial industry where a seemingly irrational negative cascading effect causes financial institution failures regardless of the institution's actual condition.[11] When the Board of Governors approved the Bear Stearns transaction, it specifically cited "the expected contagion that would result from the immediate failure of Bear Stearns" as one of the primary justifications for its action.

Contagion results from choices made by a broad range of creditors triggered by an individual institution run. Individual creditors who have withdrawn funds during a run have three choices as they contemplate what to do with their funds: (1) They can place their funds at another financial institution that is perceived as safer; (2) they can purchase a financial security or real asset that is perceived

---

9. Decades ago the process of a run was of the physical variety in that creditors showed up in the bank lobby, but as the methods for withdrawing funds have migrated to being more electronic than physical, the process of a run has transformed. Today, bank runs are a blend of the physical and electronic variety, with Bear Stearns almost entirely of the electronic variety. For a fictional depiction of a classic physical bank run see "The Bank Run," a clip from the Frank Capra movie *It's a Wonderful Life*, which was set in the 1930s. http://www.youtube.com/watch?v=qu2uJWSZkck. For a physical run during the recent financial crisis which also apparently included insured depositors, see the example of IndyMac in California: http://www.youtube.com/watch?v=2EnaU7D800M&feature =related.

10. "Bank Runs," 571.

11. Vern McKinley and Gary Gegenheimer, "Bright Lines and Bailouts," Cato Policy Analysis No. 637, April 21, 2009, 3 [hereinafter "Bright Lines and Bailouts"].

to be safer, such as a Treasury security or gold; or (3) they can hold funds in the form of currency outside the banking system. If option (1) is chosen, it will have little adverse impact on the overall financial system and contagion will be limited. However, if most of the withdrawing creditors fear the insolvency of all financial institutions or question the efficacy of fractional-reserve banking or other systems susceptible to runs and choose option (3), then there is a broader impact on the entire banking system. This is a classic case of contagion that could ultimately lead to a dramatic contraction in money and credit as severe as during the Great Depression of the 1930s.[12]

If a financial institution that has a run is soundly managed, solvent, and has sufficient collateral, it should be able to borrow in the marketplace and survive, ultimately avoiding a contagion effect. Under most circumstances, a run will not drive such a bank to failure. Alternatively, if in response to a run a weakened and barely solvent bank disposes of its assets at fire-sale or deeply discounted prices, it may push a solvent financial institution into insolvency. Although the SEC confidently deemed that Bear Stearns's capital position was "fine" just days before the FRBNY intervened, the fact that its funding dried up in March 2008 pointed to a different conclusion.

## What Is the Role of a Central Bank in Addressing Failures and Runs?

Bear Stearns was unable to borrow in the marketplace, and the Board of Governors approved a transaction under what is called lender-of-last-resort authority. The concept of a central bank as a lender of last resort has been a familiar part of financial crises throughout history, even before the Federal Reserve in the United States was constituted. The parameters of the role that a central bank should play in the midst of failures and runs were developed by two nineteenth-century monetary theorists: Henry Thornton and Walter Bagehot.[13] Although Bagehot

---

12. "Bank Runs," 563–65.

13. Bagehot is more often cited, but Thornton's earlier work preceded Bagehot's and made many of the same points. For a detailed analysis of the work of Thornton and Bagehot with regard to lender of last resort, see Thomas M. Humphrey, "Lender of Last Resort: What It Is, Whence It Came, and Why the Fed Isn't It," *Cato Journal*, 30, no. 2 (Spring/ Summer 2010), 333 [hereinafter "Lender of Last Resort"].

has been quoted often throughout the crisis, some of these have been summaries that are actually incomplete as to the scope of his writings.[14] A more complete summary categorizes the elements of central-bank lending during times of crisis as possessing the following traits:[15]

- **Announced pre-commitment**—The central bank gives advance notice that it will lend freely in the midst of a crisis.
- **High (penalty) rate**—For the offered relief in times of crisis, borrowers pay a stiff penalty in order to ration scarce liquidity resources and assure that institutions at least considered market options that were available.
- **Eligible borrowers and acceptable collateral**—The type of eligible borrower is broadly defined, in the sense that bankers and non-bankers are eligible, so long as the borrower has good collateral to offer.
- **Unsound institutions**—The quality of institutions eligible as borrowers is narrow and limited, excluding unsound institutions. So even a large institution should be allowed to fail if it is not sound. The role of the central bank is to limit the adverse impact of a failure on sound institutions.
- **Strengthening self-reliance**—There should not be an overreliance on the central bank, as the strain placed upon it should be limited.

To go back well before Bear Stearns to illustrate how a central bank should intervene as lender of last resort, there is a contemporary nineteenth-century example of Overend, Gurney, & Co. (hereinafter, Overend). Although it was an interconnected discount house that sparked a panic, it was allowed to fail in 1866.[16] Central bank intervention was focused on supporting the rest of the

---

14. An oft-quoted summary is from Paul Tucker (2009), "The Repertoire of Official Sector Interventions in the Financial System: Last Resort Lending, Market-Making, and Capital (90 KB PDF)," remarks at the Bank of Japan 2009 International Conference on the Financial System and Monetary Policy Implementation, Bank of Japan, Tokyo, Japan, May 27–28 ("Bagehot's famous dictum, in Lombard Street, was that, to avert panic, central banks should lend early and freely (i.e., without limit), to solvent firms, against good collateral, and at 'high rates.'")

15. "Lender of Last Resort," 347–53.

16. "Overend, Gurney & Co.," *New York Times*, January 31, 1869. "Lender of Last Resort," 353.

financial system after the institution's collapse. Bagehot was not concerned that an institution like Overend was allowed to fail, referring to it as "the model instance of all evil in business." He belittled Overend's business practices, noting "these losses were made in a manner so reckless and so foolish, that one would think a child who had lent money in the City of London would have lent it better."[17]

To justify the Bear Stearns and other interventions, some have invoked the name of Bagehot and then proceeded to rewrite his words in a manner that Bagehot himself would not recognize. Very much like the judge who inserts a personal interpretation of the Constitution based on modern conventions, these central bankers have replaced Bagehot's writings with their personal views. Brian Madigan, Director of the Division of Monetary Affairs at the Board of Governors during the crisis, demonstrates the invocation followed by the modernity justification: "Bagehot's dictum continues to provide a useful framework for designing central bank actions for combating a financial crisis. However, that framework needs to be interpreted in the context of the modern structure of financial markets and institutions and applied in a way that observes both legal constraints and a broad range of practical considerations." This explanation was accompanied by the rewritten standard for central-bank lending, which implies a much more expansive central-bank role than Bagehot imagined:

> In a financial crisis, markets may be dysfunctional and price quotes volatile or even unavailable, adding to the uncertainty in assessing firms' solvency. As a result, the decision as to whether to lend to a given firm can entail a significant measure of judgment—judgment both about the firm's solvency and about the possible market effects of the failure of the firm. Indeed, the ramifications of a possible default of a large financial firm in conditions of financial stress may be unclear—and, typically, time is short. Consequently, it is essential for a central bank to have the capability to assess the firm's condition and the quality of its collateral, on the basis of incomplete information, rapidly and effectively. It is also

17. Walter Bagehot, *Lombard Street: A Description of the Money Market* (London: Henry S. King and Co., 1873), 9, 107.

essential to be able to make quick and sound judgments as to the likely market effects of the possible failure of such a firm.[18]

There were clear market effects that flowed from the failure of Overend. However, this did not lead Bagehot to make the case for lending to such an obvious example of what he considered an unsound institution.

## What Is a Bailout of a Financial Institution?

Some argue that it is not sufficient to have a lender of last resort extend credit to sound institutions on good collateral. They reflexively conclude that large financial institutions like Bear Stearns just cannot be allowed to fail. The potential contagion aftereffects for large institutions are just too pronounced. This is especially the case during times of financial crisis, because the risk of runs and a contagion effect are supposedly too great. A bailout is often proposed as the solution to avoid large failures, just as in foreign policy the domino theory is used to justify military intervention.

However, there has never been a clear and robust articulation of the level of risk in the financial system that can cause a collapse. Presumably, there is some

---

18. Brian F. Madigan, "Bagehot's Dictum in Practice: Formulating and Implementing Policies to Combat the Financial Crisis," at the Federal Reserve Bank of Kansas City's Annual Economic Symposium, Jackson Hole, Wyoming, August 21, 2009. Lender of last resort authority is based on Federal Reserve Act Section 10B (12 USC 347b). The discount window through which the Federal Reserve Banks lend funds to eligible depository institutions on a short-term basis, secured by collateral, includes a primary credit program, available to depository institutions in generally sound financial condition; and a secondary credit program, available to depository institutions not eligible for primary credit. There is also a seasonal credit program for small depository institutions. See Declaration of Brian F. Madigan, *Bloomberg LP v. Board of Governors of the Federal Reserve System*, February 27, 2009, 3–4. Also see http://www.frbdiscountwindow.org. On the related issue of the perceived stigma that is applied to borrowing from the discount window, see Olivier Armantier, Eric Ghysels, Asani Sarkur, and Jeffrey Shrader, "Stigma in the Financial Markets: Evidence from Liquidity Auctions and Discount Window Borrowing During the Crisis," Unpublished Draft, March 15, 2010, http://www.unc.edu/~eghysels/papers/TAF_DW_stigma_AFA_Mar_15_10.pdf. For an international perspective of such lender of last resort functions see Dong He, "Emergency Liquidity Support Facilities," IMF Working Paper (WP/00/79), April 2000.

level of risk reached when there is a very high likelihood of contagion, what is referred to as systemic risk. This level of risk was certainly not clearly articulated as the harried bailout of Bear Stearns was unfolding. Advocates for bailouts have also never articulated the type of analysis that is necessary to support a bailout decision, as there are challenges with many common methods. For example, under a standard cost-benefit analysis it is very difficult to estimate the moral-hazard costs of a bailout. Alternatively, quantifying the benefits of a bailout is also speculative, as it involves estimating the fallout avoided from rescuing an institution, a difficult task indeed. Even though developing such an analysis is a challenge, it does not mean that the benefits derived from a bailout exceed the costs in all instances. In the case of Bear Stearns, it was simply assumed that the benefits of intervention exceeded the cost of the bailout.

Some policymakers would prefer to define bailouts narrowly. This is done in order to escape having their actions categorized as a "bailout," a word that is not looked upon in a positive light. For example, in a conversation with Treasury Secretary Paulson, then presidential candidate and Senator Barack Obama made a simple observation about intervening to take over the operations of Fannie Mae and Freddie Mac: "Bailouts like this are very unpopular." Paulson responded that the intervention regarding Fannie Mae and Freddie Mac wasn't a bailout in any real sense, noting that common and preferred shareholders alike were being wiped out, and that Treasury had replaced the CEOs. The implication is that despite the $200 billion of public funds that was committed to assure that debt holders in Fannie Mae and Freddie Mac did not lose their investment (most notably foreign governments, such as China and Russia), because shareholders were wiped out and management replaced, no one received a bailout.[19] Surely the benefit flowing to Fannie Mae and Freddie Mac debt holders constitutes a bailout. But for the extraordinary intervention by the government they would have very likely been at risk under a receivership scenario, as it is called in the context of Fannie Mae and Freddie Mac.

An alternative characterization has been offered by Robert Willumstad, the chief executive officer of AIG who simply decided to give bailout a new name: "I'm proposing a transaction, not a bailout. If we get the Fed's backing in exchange for collateral, I give you my word I'll sell every asset needed to pay you

---

19. *On the Brink*, 14, 18. *Too Big to Fail*, 222.

back."[20] Willumstad's comment does raise an interesting question. Even if an institution is a risky bet, as nearly everyone would agree AIG was in the fall of 2008, what if funds were extended to AIG and it simply paid back the government, with interest? That approach at first glance would seem to be a costless transaction that is simply a wash, from a government accounting perspective. But the transaction is not so easily characterized. It is not clear that interest costs are the only costs incurred in this type of transaction or that simple interest costs are the best measure to estimate the pricing for such a transaction. Additionally, such an intervention involves a subsidy that is not available to all businesses, a process of government choosing winners and losers.

Clearly a broader definition of bailout than the one offered by Secretary Paulson and one less euphemistic than offered by Willumstad of AIG is appropriate, which would include all manner of beneficiaries of public funds, including shareholders, creditors, or counterparties. With that in mind, a bailout is defined as an effort to avoid a contagion by means of:

- A government intervention through lending, equity injection, purchase of assets, assisted takeover, loan guarantee, or other tangible benefit or subsidy, or inaction through regulatory forbearance for a financial institution or group of financial institutions. In the case of a transaction, the repayment of funds extended must be at risk, either because the financial institution in question is unsound or repayment is not otherwise assured.
- The action taken is preemptive because the financial institution benefiting from intervention does not fail and go out of business through revocation of an operating charter and placement into receivership (commercial banks, Fannie Mae, Freddie Mac) or bankruptcy (noncommercial banks), but remains a going concern, thus benefiting creditors, shareholders, or counterparties of the financial institution who would otherwise be at risk of loss.[21] However, if a financial institution fails, but as part of a transaction uninsured depositors or creditors are paid off by the government on an ad hoc basis, it is still considered a bailout.

---

20. *Too Big to Fail*, 364.
21. This legal infrastructure was altered under the Dodd-Frank legislation.

- But for the bailout, the financial institution would "fail" and be forced to either go through receivership or bankruptcy in the prescribed legal form; or potentially have its role in financial intermediation disrupted.[22]

Under this definition, transactions that would not be considered bailouts would be the FDIC's purchase-and-assumption or payoff transactions, in which a troubled institution does not remain a going concern. Additionally, the exercise of the Federal Reserve's traditional lender of last resort powers to depository institutions in sound financial condition would not be considered a bailout if these loans are fully collateralized, and no preferential rate or subsidy is involved.

## What Is a Financial Crisis?

Treasury Secretary Paulson described the conventional logic behind the bailout of Bear Stearns: "All financial institutions depended on borrowed money—and on the confidence of their lenders. If lenders got nervous about a bank's ability to pay, they could refuse to lend or demand more collateral for their loans. If everyone did that at once, the financial system would shut down and there would be no credit available for companies or consumers. Economic activity would contract, even collapse."[23] But the problems at Bear Stearns certainly did not trigger the financial crisis. Most financial crises result from the deflating of asset bubbles.[24] In this case there was a bubble in mortgage-related assets and the deflating of that bubble led to reduced wealth and consumer spending and shifts from risky assets to safer assets.[25] The collapse of Bear Stearns merely

---

22. Definition, slightly modified, of a bailout drawn from "Bright Lines and Bailouts," 2–3.

23. *On the Brink*, 97–98.

24. Carmen Reinhart and Kenneth Rogoff, "This Time is Different: Eight Centuries of Financial Folly," see video of Carmen Reinhart at "May 3: 800 Years of Financial Crises," May 5, 2010, at http://video.ft.com/v/82349517001/May-3–800-years-of-financial-crises. She emphasizes the two human traits of arrogance and ignorance that permeates this 800-year history.

25. For a critique of the so-called amplification approach, see Nicole M. Boyson, Jean Helwege, and Jan Jindra, "Crises, Liquidity Shocks, and Fire Sales at Financial Institutions," July 23, 2010. Available at SSRN: http://ssrn.com/abstract=1633042.

signaled that the building imbalances in the economy were sufficient to place a large financial institution at risk of failure.

The turbulence during a financial crisis exceeds that of a period of mere financial fragility or financial instability, whereby vulnerabilities are evident or begin to impede the financial system. For an event to be considered a financial crisis, there needs to be a cessation of the normal functioning of the financial system. For purposes of this analysis, a financial crisis is a period of prolonged financial stress during which the corrective movement of imbalances in the financial system, often caused by government policy, lead to a combination of interrelated negative consequences, including:[26]

- Contraction in the flow of credit to households and businesses in response to the uncertainty of credit quality or the unwinding of a financial bubble;
- A significant decline in economic activity generally referred to as a recession as defined by the National Bureau of Economic Research (NBER). During financial crises, such recessions are usually more severe than a temporary decline and human costs in the form of high unemployment are sustained; and
- A significant number of financial institutions approaching failure, which may lead to concerns sufficient to cause runs and to which the policy response has often included bailouts, especially for large financial institutions.[27]

A contraction of credit is manifested in a reduced willingness of financial institutions or the marketplace to lend or to lend only at very high rates. Over time, one type of evidence of what is sometimes referred to as a "credit crunch" is the level of bank net loans and leases. Going back to the 1930s, the

---

26. See Mark Jickling, "Averting Financial Crisis," Congressional Research Service Report for Congress, Report RL 34412, March 21, 2008. This report notes that there is no precise definition of financial crisis, but then it proceeds to do a good job of detailing its elements.
27. These three events are shown in roughly their sequential order, although a number of factors will go into how the sequence of events will be presented and there is obviously some overlap in these events. For example, in the most recent crisis a credit contraction began to manifest itself in mid-2007, the recession as determined by NBER began in December 2007, and the level of bank failures really did not begin to rise dramatically until mid-2008 as bank failures are sometimes referred to as a lagging indicator.

**Table 2.1.** Years of Negative Year-to-Year Growth in Bank Net Loans and Leases

| Year | Growth |
|------|--------|
| 1938 | <4.3>% |
| 1942 | <11.1>% |
| 1943 | <0.3>% |
| 1991 | <2.8>% |
| 1992 | <1.0>% |
| 2009 | <6.0>% |

*Source*: Federal Deposit Insurance Corporation (FDIC), http://www2.fdic.gov/hsob/ hsobRpt.asp. Data for 2010 reveal an increase of 1.5 percent.

year-to-year change in net loans and leases has only turned negative three times: (1) during the 1930s and 1940s as the economy was mired in the Depression; (2) during the later part of the economic turbulence that happened in the 1980s and early 1990s; and (3) during the recent crisis (see Table 2.1).

Since the onset of the modern financial system during the Depression, there have been more than a dozen discrete recessions, the lengthiest of which are highlighted in the table on the next page (Table 2.2). Most of these more severe recessions, which reveal stress in the broader economy, were accompanied or caused by periods of financial crisis.

Financial-sector stress also manifests itself in the failure or near failure of banks and other financial institutions. This flows primarily from the write-down of assets as adjustments are made to address imbalances in the value of assets, most particularly in the aftermath of asset bubbles involving credit-funded assets. There have been three periods of significant financial institution failures in modern times during the 1930s, 1980s, and now 2000s, as detailed in Table 2.3.

Even though the number of failures during the most recent crisis pales in comparison to the earlier financial crises, the period from 2008 to 2011, from a financial institutions failure and assistance standpoint, was at least as severe or more severe than the prior noted periods. During the 1930s and 1980s, due to limitations on interstate and branch banking, many failing financial institutions were comparatively smaller and did not have a national or international presence like many of the failures during the 2008-to-2011 period. In contrast many very large financial institutions, including three of the largest commercial

**Table 2.2.** Business Cycle Contractions

| Peak in Activity | Trough in Activity | Length of Downturn (months)[1] |
|---|---|---|
| Aug 1929 (III) | Mar 1933 (I) | 43 |
| May 1937 (II) | June 1938 (II) | 13 |
| Feb 1945 (I) | Oct 1945 (IV) | 8 |
| Nov 1948 (IV) | Oct 1949 (IV) | 11 |
| July 1953 (III) | May 1954 (II) | 10 |
| Aug 1957 (III) | Apr 1958 (II) | 8 |
| Apr 1960 (II) | Feb 1961 (I) | 10 |
| Dec 1969 (IV) | Nov 1970 (IV) | 11 |
| Nov 1973 (IV) | Mar 1975 (I) | 16 |
| Jan 1980 (I) | Jul 1980 (III) | 6 |
| July 1981 (III) | Nov 1982 (IV) | 16 |
| July 1990 (III) | Mar 1991 (I) | 8 |
| Mar 2001 (I) | Nov 2001 (IV) | 8 |
| Dec 2007 (IV) | June 2009[2] | 18 |

*Source*: National Bureau of Economic Research (NBER), http://www.nber.org/cycles/cyclesmain.html.
1. Recessions lasting longer than one year are highlighted.
2. See National Bureau of Economic Research, Business Cycle Dating Committee, September 20, 2010 http://www.nber.org/cycles/sept2010.pdf.

**Table 2.3.** Clusters of Bank Failure and Financial Assistance Activity

| Period | Financial Institution Failures or Assistance |
|---|---|
| 1929 to 1940 | 10,110 |
| 1981 to 1993 | 2,920 |
| 2008 to 2011 | 380 |

*Source*: Federal Deposit Insurance Corporation. Report generated at http://www2.fdic.gov/hsob/SelectRpt.asp?EntryTyp=30. Data for the 2000s through mid-June 2011.

**Figure 2.1.** U.S. Bank Failures: Market Share 1934 to 2010

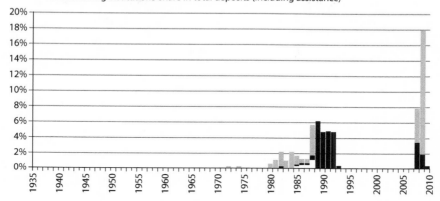

■ Failed banking institutions' share in total deposits (excluding assistance)
▨ Failed banking institutions' share in total deposits (including assistance)

*Source*: Luc Laeven and Fabian Valencia, "Resolution of Banking Crises: The Good, the Bad, and the Ugly," IMF Working Paper, WP/10/146, 19, Figure 7; cited source FDIC.

bank groups, Citigroup, Wachovia, and Bank of America, and a number of large investment banks, including Lehman Brothers and Bear Stearns, failed or otherwise required or applied for financial assistance. When judged by the percentage market share, the experience during the most recent crisis far exceeds that during the 1980s (see Figure 2.1).

Based on the business cycle data from NBER; the data on credit growth, and the financial institution failure and assistance data, we are left with three financial crises for analysis:

- The Great Depression beginning in 1929 and lasting into the 1940s (hereinafter referred to as the 1930s financial crisis);
- The post–stagflation period from the early 1980s to the early 1990s (hereinafter referred to as the 1980s financial crisis); and
- The most recent financial crisis beginning during 2007 (hereinafter referred to as the 2000s financial crisis).[28]

---

28. Although the shorthand 1930s, 1980s, and 2000s will be used, as these are the periods in which bailouts were concentrated, it is very clear that factors contributing to or fallout in the wake of these periods may have manifested themselves in prior or subsequent decades.

These periods are important, not only for the challenges presented as they were in motion, but also because during or in the aftermath of the crisis, legislative changes were made that shaped the response to the subsequent crisis. Most of the significant changes in financial legislation the past eighty years occurred during or in the aftermath of these three major financial crises.

**3**

# The Depression of the 1930s and the Interventions

"These reserve banks, practically under Government control and supervision, having a broad vision of financial matters, can be used to prevent dangerous inflation or ruinous depression. They will have a steadying influence on the finances of the country and produce that stability which is the most propitious for the growth and development of the Nation. This bill . . . makes impossible another panic in this country, with its distress and disaster, precipitated by Wall Street speculation with the reserves and deposits of interior banks."

> —Senator Claude Swanson of Virginia urging
> passage of the Federal Reserve Act in 1913[1]

---

**LEGAL SCORECARD:**

- Federal Reserve Act (1913)
- Trading with the Enemy Act (1917)
- War Finance Corporation (1918)
- Reconstruction Finance Corporation (1932)
- Emergency Relief and Construction Act (1932)
- Emergency Banking Relief Act (1933)
- Banking Act of 1933

---

1. 51 Cong Rec 430 (December 8, 1913).

THE FORCES BEHIND a financial crisis do not spontaneously erupt, but instead build up over many years or decades. In the decades prior to the 1930s, one of the more important events leading up to the Depression was the Panic of 1907, which led to the establishment of a central bank. Before the creation of the Federal Reserve in 1913, private clearinghouses were responsible for responding to individual banks that were in danger of failing. These clearinghouses were a central point of coordination for settling transactions among banks in a defined geographic area. The first clearinghouse in the United States was created in New York in 1853 modeled on versions in the United Kingdom.[2]

Before the creation of the Federal Reserve, when a bank experienced problems and word circulated of its weakness, other banks were then hesitant to lend to it. This eventually led to the bank running out of currency or failing to meet its end-of-day debt to the clearinghouse. The bank was forced to suspend operations and subject itself to examination by the authorities to determine whether it was illiquid, but solvent; or illiquid and insolvent (or at least below minimum required capital). A bank in the former group was allowed to reopen and loans from other member banks were coordinated by the clearinghouse. A bank in the latter group was required to either recapitalize or liquidate. In emergencies, banks would suspend converting deposits into currency, and the clearinghouse would issue to member banks certificates on the clearinghouse to assist in clearing. Once it was created, the Federal Reserve essentially took on the role of a national clearinghouse providing liquidity, especially during times of crisis. The clearinghouses remained and their operations were then limited to clearing and settlement of interbank claims.[3]

President Wilson relied heavily on Senator Swanson of Virginia to take leadership in gaining passage of the Federal Reserve Act.[4] In arguing for pas-

---

2. New York Clearing House—Historical Perspective, http://www.theclearinghouse.org /docs/000591.pdf.

3. "Bank Runs," 570. One example of a coordinated effort by the New York Clearing House was during the Panic of 1907 when five member banks of the clearinghouse and three nonmember banks were provided with assistance coordinated by the clearinghouse. Milton Friedman and Anna Jacobson Schwartz, *A Monetary History of the United States, 1867–1960* (Princeton, NJ: Princeton University Press / National Bureau of Economic Research, 1963), 159 [hereinafter *Monetary History*].

4. Henry H. Mitchell, "Claude A. Swanson of Pittsylvania," Pittsylvania Historical Society Packet, Spring 1992. http://www.victorianvilla.com/sims-mitchell/local/swanson/ca/ phsp1.htm.

sage, Swanson presented the example of the New York banks that he blamed
for recent financial panics:

> The banks in New York are dominated by the large financiers and specu-
> lators of this country, and these reserves have been used for their en-
> richment and not for the public good. By this great concentration of
> reserves here the few financiers who control these banks in New York
> have been able to precipitate panics and produce depression and finan-
> cial disturbance whenever their selfish interest dictated. The panic of
> 1907 has taught this Nation a lesson which it will never forget. It proved
> beyond dispute that the banks and financiers of New York felt no public
> responsibility for the bank reserves under their control. The panic of
> 1907 was precipitated by wild stock speculations in the city of New York,
> engineered by the financiers there who control the great banks.

He contrasted those actions with the expected actions of the proposed Federal Reserve Banks:

> The benefits which will accrue from these regional, or, as named in this
> bill, Federal reserve banks are great and many. The reserves of this Nation,
> which are needed in times of financial distress and stringency, will be held
> by those who have a public responsibility for their just and proper use,
> and not as now, by those who have such responsibility and no purpose of
> public benefit in their use. . . . I am satisfied that the Federal reserve board
> when constituted will wisely, faithfully, fearlessly, and patriotically dis-
> charge the duties conferred upon them to the benefit of the whole of the
> country and without favoritism to any. . . . I believe the present President
> of the United States, animated by only lofty and noble principles in all of
> his work, will select as members of this Federal reserve board men fully
> equipped, men with noble purposes and whose administration of their
> office will redound to the great betterment of this Nation.[5]

The Federal Reserve Act, in the first line of its text, codified this concept of
allocating reserves within the component parts of the financial system: "An Act
to provide for the establishment of Federal reserve banks, to furnish an elastic
currency, to afford means of rediscounting commercial paper, to establish a more

5. 51 Cong Rec 428, 430–32 (December 8, 1913).

effective supervision of banking in the United States, and for other purposes."[6] The concept of an "elastic currency" was intended to introduce more flexibility and discretion to the financial system, as the Federal Reserve was empowered to make substantial changes in the quantity of money over short periods of time.[7]

Well before the Great Depression, the Federal Reserve System received one of its first tests when there was a severe deflationary downturn in the United States that lasted for eighteen months, from January 1920 to July 1921.[8] The contraction was one of the most rapid declines on record, as wholesale prices and industrial production collapsed. Although the contraction was relatively brief, it ranks as one of the severest on record and was most likely attributable to adjustments in economic imbalances in the aftermath of the war, as well as maintenance of interest rates by the Federal Reserve at a very high level. Interest rates were reduced during the recovery to prerecession levels.[9] Even though the downturn led to an increase in bank failures (see Table 3.1), it did not lead to widespread bank runs or heavy withdrawals of currency that might have indicated a contagion.[10]

The time period that followed from 1921 to 1929 was characterized by fairly rapid economic growth without major contractions, regarded at the time as a "new era" of stability in the economy.[11] The 1920s were truly a wildcat era in banking during which the churn of competition led to a dramatic uptick in mergers and bank suspensions. From 1915 to 1920, approximately 500 banks suspended operations, or about 100 per year. In contrast, from 1921 to 1929, nearly 6,000 banks suspended operations, or at least one per day, with three per day during 1926 (see Table 3.1). The suspensions, which were concentrated in small institutions in small towns, were primarily caused by competitive pressures from large banks applied to small banks and by the agricultural difficulties of

---

6. Federal Reserve Act, Preamble (December 23, 1913).

7. *Monetary History*, 190.

8. See National Bureau of Economic Research, http://www.nber.org/cycles/cyclesmain. html.

9. *Monetary History*, 197 (Chart 16), 214, 231, 237.

10. *Monetary History*, 235. John R. Walter, "Depression Era Bank Failures: The Great Contagion or the Great Shakeout?," Federal Reserve Bank of Richmond, *Economic Quarterly*, Volume 91/1, Winter 2005, 46 [hereinafter, "Depression Era Bank Failures"]. *Monetary History*, 204 (Chart 18). This chart shows a relatively stable deposit-to-currency ratio in the range of 7 percent from early 1920 to mid-1921.

11. *Monetary History*, 240.

the 1920s.[12] This was a sustained period of bank failures, the length and extent of which had not been previously experienced in the United States.[13]

This increase in failures during relatively good economic times was transformed into what can only be described as a meltdown of the banking system. From 1929 to 1933, the United States experienced by far the most severe business-cycle contraction in recorded history, and it may have been the most severe in the whole of U.S. history. More than a fifth of the commercial banks in the United States holding one-tenth of the volume of deposits at the beginning of the contraction suspended operations because of financial difficulties (see Table 3.1), and when voluntary liquidations, mergers, and consolidations are added in the number of commercial banks fell by more than a third.[14]

Three discrete banking crises occurred, the first in late 1930 which included the most prominent bank failure of the period, that of Bank of United States (BOUS), the 28th-largest commercial bank in the country. It was the largest commercial bank failure, as measured by volume of deposits, up to that point

---

12. *Monetary History*, 249. Pre- and post-1921 suspensions are not entirely comparable as they are from different sources that apply a slightly different definition of suspension. There was also a wave of failures in Florida in the late 1920s due to land speculation, as there were nearly 100 failures there in 1928 and 1929. Friedman and Schwartz (269–70) are also critical of the Federal Reserve for a seeming lack of concern for the level of bank suspensions and the possible negative impact it might have on monetary policy and financial stability ("In retrospect, one notable omission from Federal Reserve literature is any policy discussion of bank suspensions, despite the much higher rate of suspensions than during any comparable earlier period. Each year the Board reported the melancholy figures of suspensions, properly classified as member and nonmember, national and state banks, and confined itself to noting that suspensions were in disproportionate number of nonmember rather than member banks, of banks in small communities rather than in large, and in banks in agricultural rather than industrial areas. It did not discuss methods of mitigating the effect on depositors of suspensions that did occur, or of reducing the rate of suspensions. And it did not recognize the possibility that a high rate of suspensions might undermine confidence in the banking system and lay the groundwork for subsequent runs.").

13. There was a spike in bank failures in the mid-1890s during a period of two severe recessions, but the level of failures peaked at about 500 failures in one year. "Depression Era Bank Failures," 44.

14. *Monetary History*, 299. The contraction from 1839 to 1843 is cited by Friedman and Schwartz as possibly comparable, although comparisons are difficult due to inconsistencies in historical data.

**Table 3.1.** Bank Failures 1919 to 1934

|      | Failures      | Contractions of note |
|------|---------------|----------------------|
| 1919 | 63            |                      |
| 1920 | 155           | Severe recession     |
| 1921 | 506           | Severe recession     |
| 1922 | 366           |                      |
| 1923 | 646           |                      |
| 1924 | 775           |                      |
| 1925 | 617           |                      |
| 1926 | 975           |                      |
| 1927 | 669           |                      |
| 1928 | 498           |                      |
| 1929 | 659           |                      |
| 1930 | 1,350         | Banking Crisis #1    |
| 1931 | 2,293         | Banking Crisis #2    |
| 1932 | 1,453         | Banking Crisis #3    |
| 1933 | 4,000 (est.)  | Banking Holiday      |
| 1934 | 61            |                      |
| 1935 | 31            |                      |

*Source*: *Monetary History*, p. 438.

in history. As early as 1927, bank examinations by the Federal Reserve Bank of New York (FRBNY) noted the riskiness of BOUS's heavy investment in real estate. The bank was also heavily invested in credits related to its own bank stock and insider loans. Ultimately these led to the bank's insolvency, which was accompanied by a depositor run.[15] Joseph Broderick, New York Banking Superintendent at the time, tried to arrange a merger for the bank in the months leading up to its December 1930 closure, insisting that BOUS was "solvent as a going concern." As a number of proposed mergers fell apart, Broderick then argued that BOUS's closure would lead to a domino effect on other banks: "I warned that its closing would result in the closing of at least 10 other banks in

---

15. Joseph L. Lucia, "The Failure of the Bank of United States: A Reappraisal," *Explorations in Economic History* 22 (October 1985), 405 [hereinafter Lucia Bank of United States].

the city and that it might even affect the savings banks. The influence of the closing might even extend outside the city, I told them."[16]

The FRBNY also spent some time assessing the collapse of BOUS, which was a Federal Reserve member bank and at the time of its closing had received $19 million in credit from the FRBNY, an unwise extension to such an unsound institution.[17] A merger was never completed, and BOUS was closed on December 11, 1930. However, the closure did not, as predicted by Broderick, lead to a rash of bank failures.[18]

The second crisis occurred in early 1931, a period during which deposits fell more dramatically than during the first crisis;[19] and the third crisis from the last quarter of 1932 to March 1933, which culminated in a nationwide banking holiday that extended from March 6 to March 13, in what was an unprecedented move that has not been repeated.[20]

---

16. *Monetary History*, 309–11. As Friedman and Schwartz note, the failure of BOUS was of particular significance, not only because of its noted size, but because its name had led many to regard it as an official bank, which was a blow to confidence. It should be noted that BOUS ultimately paid off 83.5 percent of its adjusted liabilities despite its having to liquidate so large a fraction of its assets during the difficult conditions it liquidated under. (Quote from statement of Joseph A. Broderick, New York State Superintendent of Banks: "I said it [the Bank of the United States] had thousands of borrowers, that it financed small merchants, especially Jewish merchants, and that its closing might and probably would result in widespread bankruptcy among those it served. I warned that its closing would result in the closing of at least 10 other banks in the city and that it might even affect the savings banks. The influence of the closing might even extend outside the city, I told them.")

17. *Monetary History*, 357–58. One New York banker apparently commented that the failure of BOUS "had shaken confidence in the Federal Reserve System more than any other occurrence in recent years." Friedman and Schwartz conclude that a limited understanding of the connection between bank failures, runs on banks, contraction of deposits, and weakness of the bond markets led to the limited response. Lucia Bank of United States, 409, 412, 414. It appears the FRBNY was even willing to accept ineligible paper in their transaction with BOUS.

18. Lucia Bank of United States, 414. Paul B. Trescott, "The Failure of the Bank of United States, 1930," *Journal of Money, Credit and Banking* 24, no. 3 (August 1992): 387, 392, 397.

19. *Monetary History*, 314.

20. *Monetary History*, 324–32. ("The banking holiday, while of the same species as earlier restrictions of payments in 1814, 1818, 1837, 1839, 1857, 1873, 1893 and 1907, was of a far more virulent genus. In these earlier restrictions, no substantial number of banks closed down entirely even for a day, let alone for a minimum of six business days.")

**Figure 3.1.** Ratio of Bank Deposits to Currency Held by Public

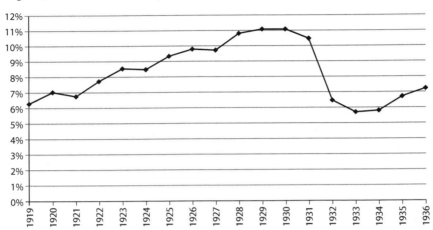

*Source: Monetary History*, pp. 801–4.

Bank failures were important to the overall spiraling contraction for two reasons:

- Failures involved capital losses to owners and depositors, transmitting the consequences of failure just as the failure of other business enterprises involved losses to owners and creditors; and
- Failures were the mechanism through which a drastic decline was produced in the stock of money. The failures greatly reduced the attractiveness of deposits as a form of holding wealth and so induced the public to hold less money relative to income than it otherwise would have held.

The second of these reasons, the decline in the money stock, was by far the more important of the two as the estimated losses were a mere $2.5 billion, but from 1929 to 1933 commercial bank deposits dropped by 42 percent, or $18 billion.[21] One good indicator of the extent of contraction in the stock of money caused by withdrawal of deposits is the ratio of deposits to currency. This ratio

---

21. *Monetary History*, 351–52.

plunged from roughly 11 percent in 1929 to less than 5 percent in 1933, returning to a percentage not seen since 1900 (see Figure 3.1).[22]

The first wave of failures in late 1930 may have resulted from poor loans and investments made during the 1920s.[23] As for the second and third crises, these were more self-reinforcing on the basis of runs followed by a cycle of banks facing pressure to liquidate assets, forcing a decline in market value of the assets. Impairment in the market value of assets held by banks, in particular in their bond portfolio, was an important source of impairment of capital, which led to bank suspensions, as opposed to the default of specific loans or of specific bond issues.[24] The weakened capital position of banks made them very vulnerable to even minor drains in liquidity.[25]

The Federal Reserve did not have the same incentives as the clearinghouses to maintain the liquidity of sound banks and failed to perform as well in dealing with the bank runs from 1929 to 1933 as the clearinghouses had in earlier panics.[26] The Federal Reserve's response was limited to a form of forbearance in allowing assets to be valued more liberally in bank examinations, thus deferring recognition of losses. In general, the Federal Reserve displayed little concern for suspended banks, most of which were not members of the Federal Reserve System.[27] Specific to monetary policy and the efforts to address the dramatic

---

21. *Monetary History*, 351–52.

22. *Monetary History*, 51–2, 175, 204, 273, 333 (Chart 31, panel 2), 799–808 (time series years 1867 to 1960).

23. *Monetary History*, 355. For example, BOUS had been troubled as far back as July 1929.

24. *Monetary History*, 319 (Open Market Policy Conference, January 1932: "Within a period of a few months United States Government bonds have declined 10 per cent; high grade corporation bonds have declined by 20 percent; and lower grade bonds have shown even larger price declines.") Other potential contributing factors cited included the increase in the federal deficit from $0.5 billion in 1931 to $2.5 billion in 1932 and to fear of "irresponsible" legislation.

25. *Monetary History*, 330. Recorded capital figures were widely recognized as overstating available capital, because assets were being carried on the books at a higher value than their market value.

26. "Bank Runs," 571. Gary Gorton, "Banking Panics and Business Cycles," *Oxford Economic Papers* 40 (1988).

27. *Monetary History*, 357–58.

conversion of deposits into currency, the response of the Federal Reserve has been described as inept and not in keeping with the Federal Reserve Act's concept of a flexible currency. Actions similar to those taken by the Federal Reserve itself in reversing the dramatic downturn in the early 1920s or those recommended by Bagehot could have prevented the collapse.[28]

The idea that this was a contagion that was not only catching up poorly managed institutions, but also strong banks, was probably best captured by Senator Carter Glass: "[W]hen weak banks begin to topple there takes place a disastrous psychology in the whole country that precipitates runs on strong banks that break them down."[29] There is some question as to whether the description of contagion taking down "strong banks" along with weak ones has validity, but this narrative was largely accepted at the time as the justification for government intervention.[30] This idea that contagion was at work in part led to the creation of the Reconstruction Finance Corporation and the Federal Home Loan Banks. Additionally, special powers were codified in the Federal Reserve Act.[31]

## The Reconstruction Finance Corporation—
## The Great Peacetime Precedent

The Reconstruction Finance Corporation (RFC) was the primary response by the Hoover Administration to the wave of bank failures in the early 1930s. In 1931, desperate to find some way to respond to the crisis, Hoover looked back to the war of a decade earlier. He used the War Finance Corporation (WFC) created during the Wilson Administration in 1918 as a model. This is an example of why some presidential scholars argue that actions during wartime in

---

28. *Monetary History*, 391–419.

29. Congressional Record 77 (May 19, 1933), S 3728.

30. For a case study of banks in Chicago during the Great Depression, see Charles W. Calomiris and Joseph R. Mason, "Contagion and Bank Failures During the Great Depression: The June 1932 Chicago Banking Panic," *The American Economic Review* 87, no. 5 (Dec. 1997), 863–83 [hereinafter "1932 Chicago Banking Panic"]. The authors conclude that failing institutions during the panic and failures during non-panic periods shared many of the same characteristics from a predictive standpoint.

31. *Monetary History*, 300.

the Wilson Administration laid the groundwork for heavy intervention in the economy more broadly during peacetime.[32] The justification of the WFC was narrowly targeted to wartime, as it was intended to enable banks to furnish essential credits for industries and enterprises necessary to the prosecution of the war. Liberty Bonds were issued to finance World War I, and before or after the issuance of Liberty Loans, which were tranches of the bonds, private banks were reportedly crowded out of the credit markets. In Europe many central banks had broader authority to lend to banks than the Federal Reserve and, so the argument goes, the WFC needed to be created to fill the role that central banks in Europe were undertaking. The act was intended to be "a war measure to give relief from this condition during war."[33] In fact, the WFC existed for a

---

32. For the text of the Act see United States Statutes at Large, 65th Congress, 1917–1919, Vol. 40, Part I, 506 [hereinafter Text of WFC Act]. The fact that many government programs under Presidents Hoover and Roosevelt were transformed versions of programs of Wilson has been highlighted by Ivan Eland: "Many conservatives blame Franklin D. Roosevelt for creating a permanent big government in the United States, and he certainly did contribute to it, but Wilson laid the groundwork by intervening in the economy during World War I on an unprecedented scale. . . . During the Great Depression, FDR merely brought back many of the wartime agencies and renamed then. He also used some of Wilson's people to manage them. . . . Thus, Wilson not FDR, is the father of the modern permanent big government. He did not create the massive peacetime welfare state, but he made it possible for Hoover and FDR to do so later." Ivan Eland, *Recarving Rushmore: Ranking the Presidents on Peace, Prosperity and Liberty* (Oakland: The Independent Institute, 2009), 223–5. For this and other reasons, in developing a rating system for presidents based on peace, prosperity, and liberty, Eland rated Wilson fortieth out of the forty presidents rated. For the relationship between the New Deal and World War I, see William E. Leuchtenburg, "The New Deal and the Analogue of War," in John Braeman et al., editors, *Change and Continuity in Twentieth-Century America* (Columbus: Ohio State University Press, 1964), 81–143.

33. War Finance Corporation Bill, House of Representatives, 65th Congress, 2nd Session, Report No. 369, March 9, 1918, 1–2. This report contains a letter from the Secretary of the Treasury William McAdoo: "The proposed act to incorporate a War Finance Corporation should be regarded primarily as a measure to enable the banks, both national banks and State banks and trust companies, to continue to furnish essential credits for industries and enterprises which are necessary or contributory to the prosecution of the war. . . . The government's borrowings . . . have tended to preempt the credit facilities of the banks and often to prevent them from giving needed and customary help to quasi-public and private enterprises. Many instances have been brought to the attention of the Secretary of the Treasury and of the Federal Reserve Board where industrial plants, public

mere seven months of wartime from April to November 1918, but it survived many years after the war. Its charter was extended in 1921 to undertake all manner of lending activity, primarily agriculture-related, and it ultimately closed its doors in 1931.[34]

Hoover considered the Depression the last phase of World War I and thought the economic collapse and the war were in many ways interlinked and the methods needed to address them similar.[35] In what can only be described as a seat-of-the-pants effort, much of the same language for the RFC was used from the WFC legislation, an early historical example of cut-and-paste legislation.[36] Hoover's annual message to Congress in December 1931 set out a plan to create the RFC, which was proposed to be a temporary agency to strengthen confidence in the economy:

---

*(footnote 33 continued)* utilities, power plants, railroads, and others have found it difficult, if not impossible to obtain the necessary advances to enable them to perform vital services in connection with the war because essential credits ordinarily available to them, are being absorbed by the Government itself. In Europe central banks are permitted to grant to banks and bankers loans upon stocks and bonds upon certain well-defined terms. . . ."

34. Randall Holcombe, "The Growth of the Federal Government in the 1920s," *Cato Journal* 16, no. 2 (1996).

35. James S. Olson, *Saving Capitalism: The Reconstruction Finance Corporation and the New Deal 1933–1940* (Princeton, NJ: Princeton University Press, 1988), 10 [hereinafter *Saving Capitalism*] ("I believe you will all agree with me that the destruction of life and property, the great tax burdens, and the social and political instability which resulted from the Great War have had large responsibility in its origins"). (Hoover remarked early in 1932 that the Depression was "like a great war, in that it is not a battle on a single front but upon many fronts.")

36. For example, in each act, Section 2 provides for precisely the same dollar amount of start-up capital for the agencies: $500 million. Section 6 of the RFC enabling act calls for replacing all references to "War Finance Corporation Act" in Section 5202 of the Revised Statutes of the United States with "Reconstruction Finance Corporation Act." See Text of WFC Act; and United States Statutes at Large, 72nd Congress, 1931–1933, Vol. 47, Part I, 5 [hereinafter RFC Act]. Former WFC employees were recruited to staff the RFC. Both were considered "temporary agencies" that were designed to "rejuvenate private money markets with injections of government funding." However, the RFC was "a startling departure in peacetime public policy." *Saving Capitalism*, 15.

In order that the public may be absolutely assured and that the Government may be in position to meet any public necessity, I recommend that an emergency Reconstruction Corporation of the nature of the former War Finance Corporation should be established. It may not be necessary to use such an instrumentality very extensively. The very existence of such a bulwark will strengthen confidence. The Treasury should be authorized to subscribe a reasonable capital to it, and it should be given authority to issue its own debentures. It should be placed in liquidation at the end of two years. Its purpose is that by strengthening the weak spots to thus liberate the full strength of the Nation's resources. It should be in position to facilitate exports by American agencies; make advances to agricultural credit agencies where necessary to protect and aid the agricultural industry; to make temporary advances upon proper securities to established industries, railways, and financial institutions which cannot otherwise secure credit, and where such credit advances will protect the credit structure and stimulate employment.[37]

The memory of the thousands of bank failures over the preceding years figured prominently in the development of the RFC by the Senate and the House of Representatives. However, almost no connection was made between the measures being taken under the guise of the RFC and the effort to stop the dramatic increase in bank failures other than to argue that the banks were truly solvent and that RFC loans would provide "accommodation."[38] A concluding paragraph of the House Report on the creation of the RFC reveals the faint hope that this previous wartime measure would slow down the dramatic rise in failures: "The restoration of credit and confidence is a necessary step if we are

---

37. President Herbert Hoover, "Annual Message to the Congress on the State of the Union," December 8, 1931. http://www.presidency.ucsb.edu/ws/index.php?pid=22933. See also letter from Secretary of the Treasury A.W. Mellon to Honorable Peter Norbeck, Chairman, Committee on Banking and Currency of the Senate regarding S.1, December 22, 1931.

38. This fact is mentioned in both the Senate and House reports. Senate Report No. 33, 72nd Congress, 1st Session, January 6, 1932, 2; House of Representatives Report No. 36, 72nd Congress, 1st Session, January 9, 1932, 2–3.

to find our way out of the present unhappy conditions. This is what it is hoped the legislation will accomplish."[39]

The RFC approach is considered a bailout because of the high risk of non-payment involved in advancing funds to such unsound financial institutions. The RFC provided assistance predominantly to weak institutions in an attempt to reduce the incidence of bank failures and limit deposit disintermediation.[40] Although the intended focus of RFC assistance was on banks with a chance of survival, analysis of the institutions provided with funding reveals that the probability of bank failure for those banks receiving RFC assistance was quite high.[41] Many of the endangered banks were not members of the Federal Reserve System and others, although members, lacked paper eligible for discount by the Federal Reserve.[42]

The intervention was an extraordinary step that goes against the historical narrative that President Hoover had a hands-off response to the Depression. He came under criticism from those who questioned his apparent abandonment of free-market principles to bail out financial institutions. Hoover described his initial meeting with Congressional leaders in October of 1931 as follows:

> I hoped those present would approve my program in order to restore confidence which was rapidly degenerating into panic. The group seemed

---

39. House of Representatives Report No. 36, 72nd Congress, 1st Session, January 9, 1932, 4.
40. RFC Circular #1, Washington, DC: U.S. Government Printing Office, 1932, as cited in Joseph R. Mason, "Do Lender of Last Resort Policies Matter? The Effects of Reconstruction Finance Corporation Assistance to Banks During the Great Depression," *Journal of Financial Services Research* 20, no. 1 (September 2001), 77, 78 [hereinafter "Lender of Last Resort Policies"]. Also see *Monetary History*, 427, which also details the small percentage of strong banks that received RFC Funding ("To avoid the suggestion that RFC investment signified a bank's weakness, some stronger banks which did not actually need new capital were asked to sell the corporation a modest amount of preferred stock or capital notes. According to [Jesse] Jones fewer than twenty of the more than six thousand banks into which the RFC put capital actually had no need of it.").
41. See Figure 8 in Charles W. Calomiris and Joseph R. Mason, "How to Restructure Failed Banking Systems: Lessons from the U.S. in the 1930s and Japan in the 1990s," National Bureau of Economic Research, Working Paper No. 9624, April 2003. This figure details that the predicted probability of bank failure based on exogenous characteristics for banks receiving RFC loan assistance was 50 percent.
42. RFC Senate Report, 3.

stunned. Only [Speaker of the House John Nance] Garner and [Senate Majority (Republican) Leader William] Borah reserved approval. The others seemed shocked at the revelation that our government for the first time in peacetime history might have to intervene to support private enterprise.[43]

The vehicle of the RFC provided the Congress with a unique approach in implementing an aggressive government-driven response:

It became apparent almost immediately, to many Congressmen and Senators, that here was a device which would enable them to provide for activities that they favored for which government funds would be required, but without any apparent increase in appropriations, and without passing any appropriations bill of any kind to accomplish its purposes. After they had done that, there need be no more appropriations and its activities could be enlarged indefinitely, as they were almost to fantastic proportions.[44]

The RFC began with seed capital of $500 million from the Treasury Department and initial authority to borrow up to $1.5 billion. The agency was empowered to make loans to financial institutions.[45] Despite nearly $2 billion of RFC loans in just over a year to thousands of financial institutions and other commercial enterprises, the financial system collapse continued unabated. The effectiveness of the initial round of loans in stemming the crisis was limited as the previously described wave of failures ensued in early 1933.

Those who were disappointed at the limited impact of the RFC as a response to the crisis argue that its initial implementation was simply ill-timed and poorly structured. So this argument goes, the forces leading to collapse may have been

---

43. Hoover, Herbert, *The Great Depression: 1929–1941* (New York: Macmillan Co., 1952) (vol. 3 of Hoover's memoirs), as quoted in Walker F. Todd, "History of and Rationales for the Reconstruction Finance Corporation," *Federal Reserve Bank of Cleveland Economic Review*, 1992 Quarter 4, vol. 28, no. 4, 24 [hereinafter "History and Rationales for RFC"].
44. *Saving Capitalism*, 43, citing Chester Morrill, Secretary of the Board of Governors of the Federal Reserve.
45. RFC Act, 5, 9.

too great to be counteracted by the funds made available by the RFC. Between October 1929 and March 1933, the nation's basic money supply fell from $28 billion to $19 billion, and gross national product fell from $103.1 billion to $55.6 billion. In the face of such a massive collapse, the billion dollars lent by the RFC to banks were of little consequence.[46] However, the minimal effectiveness of the RFC could also have been predicted given the absence of a clear connection between the legislative solution and the underlying bank failures.

Another "poor structure" argument regarding RFC loans was that the names of the recipients of the loans were publicized. Democrats in Congress properly intended this move as a transparency measure to safeguard against favoritism in the distribution of loans. Depositors correctly regarded information that a bank had received an RFC loan as a sign that the bank was financially weak, and disclosure of this information sometimes caused runs. The ensuing panic often put the bank in worse condition than before the loan was made. Indeed many banks refused to apply for loans, believing that the damage from publicity would outweigh the direct financial benefits of the loan.[47] However, the argument that such loans should not be publicized cannot be justified given that public funds were at risk. The individual institutions had to make a judgment whether they could limit the damage from any stigma associated with an announcement that they were taking RFC funding.

Another argument advanced by defenders of the RFC is that the agency was ineffective because it was required to take the strongest assets of a troubled

---

46. *Monetary History*, 325.

47. *Monetary History*, 325. A provision of the Emergency Relief and Construction Act passed in July 1932 was interpreted as requiring publication of the names of the banks to which the RFC had made loans in the preceding month, and such publication began in August. The inclusion of a bank's name on the list was correctly interpreted as a sign of weakness, and hence frequently led to runs on the bank. The effect was further increased in January 1933 when, pursuant to a House resolution, the RFC made public all loans extended before August 1932. See Section 201(b) of the Emergency Relief and Construction Act of 1932 ("The Reconstruction Finance Corporation shall submit monthly to the President and to the Senate and the House of Representatives, a report of its activities and expenditures under this section and under the Reconstruction Finance Corporation Act, together with a statement showing the names of the borrowers to whom loans and advances were made, and the amount and rate of interest involved in each case"). United States Statutes at Large, 72nd Congress 1931–33, Vol. 47, Part I, 712.

bank as security for the loan, which deprived the banks of assets needed to meet further demands for cash. One example cited in support of this proposition is Reno National Bank, which in April 1932 received a loan of $1.1 million on which the RFC took as collateral $3.0 million of the bank's best securities, leaving the bank in an illiquid state.[48] But clearly such a bank was not forced into taking the RFC funding and must have seen it as preferable to the alternative of not borrowing the $1.1 million from the RFC. Many of the banks helped by the RFC ultimately failed by March 1933 for lack of sufficient capital as the RFC was not authorized to provide such capital.[49]

It wasn't until March 1933 and the passage of the Emergency Banking Relief Act of 1933 that the RFC was able to provide capital to banks in the form of preferred stock.[50] The newly elected President Roosevelt also looked back to the First World War in his initial effort at addressing the banking crisis. He invoked the Trading with the Enemy Act, passed in 1917 to restrict trade with countries hostile to the United States, to justify the closing of the banks on March 9, 1933.[51]

---

48. See Lender of Last Resort Policies, 90.

49. *Monetary History*, 330–1 (Owen D. Young, deputy chairman of the board of directors of the New York Federal Reserve Bank, in comments before the directors, July 7, 1932: "Under present methods a loan from the Reconstruction Finance Corporation is largely used to pay off certain depositors before the bank ultimately closes, leaving the other depositors out on a limb because the Reconstruction Finance Corporation has gutted the bank of collateral in securing its loans. If this is all that is to be accomplished it might have been better to make no loans."). *Saving Capitalism*, 26.

50. United States Statutes at Large, 73rd Congress 1933–34, Vol. 48, Part I, March 9, 1933, 6 ("Sec. 304. If in the opinion of the Secretary of the Treasury any national banking association or any State bank or trust company is in need of funds for capital purposes either in connection with the organization or reorganization of such association, State bank or trust company or otherwise, he may, with the approval of the President, request the Reconstruction Finance Corporation to subscribe for preferred stock in such association, State bank or trust company, or to make loans secured by such stock as collateral, and the Reconstruction Finance Corporation may comply with such request. . . .").

51. National Emergency: Constitutional Questions Concerning Emergency Powers, April 11, 1973. ("However, research by the Special Committee soon disclosed that the United States has been in a state of declared emergency since March 9, 1933. At the request of President Roosevelt, Congress passed the Emergency Banking Act to meet the economic emergency of the Depression. This swift legislative stroke ratified the President's bank holiday declaration and allowed him to exercise what had originally been war powers in peacetime.")

Section 5(b) of the Trading with the Enemy Act gives the President the power to "investigate, regulate or prohibit . . . any transaction in foreign exchange, export or earmarking of gold or silver coins or bullion or currency, transfer of credit in any form . . . and transfer of evidence of indebtedness." The Emergency Banking Relief Act also allowed the RFC to purchase the preferred stock of banks. Many of Hoover's closest advisers stayed on during these first days of the Roosevelt Administration to provide assistance with implementation of the RFC equity program as they had written the legislation for the banking holiday and the preferred stock purchase program.[52] The description of the legislative approval process reveals the continuation of the seat-of-the-pants approach as the measure was introduced, passed, and signed in a single day:[53]

> The Speaker recited the text from the one available draft, which bore last-minute corrections scribbled in pencil. . . . With a unanimous shout, the House passed the bill, sight unseen, after only thirty-eight minutes of debate. . . . The Senate, over the objections of a small band of progressives [Senators Lafollette, Borah, Case, Dale, Nye, and Shipstead, together with Senator Costigan, the lone Democrat voting no], approved the bill unamended 73–7 at 7:30 that evening and at 8:36 that same night it received the President's [Roosevelt's] signature.[54]

The preferred stock option allowed the RFC to leverage its use of funds to a greater extent than the mere lending of its funds, but it also obviously did it with greater risk to the RFC than mere loans.[55] Initially, the RFC was seen by some as a government attempt to take over the banking system. They also imposed a

---

52. *Saving Capitalism*, 40.

53. Howard H. Preston, "The Banking Act of 1933," *The American Economic Review* 23, no. 4 (Dec. 1933): 585.

54. Leuchtenburg, *William E., Franklin D. Roosevelt and the New Deal: 1932–1940* (New York: Harper & Row, 1963), 43–44, as quoted in History of and Rationales for RFC, 7; *Federal Reserve Bulletin* 19 (1933): 115–18.

55. "Lender of Last Resort Policies," 77, details the progression of RFC activities from first making heavily collateralized loans, to relaxing collateral requirements on those loans, to recapitalizing banks directly through preferred stock purchases. Mason argues that RFC assistance to banks became more effective as default risk was assumed, as he measures effectiveness primarily by a reduced level of bank failures and notes that this required the government to bear substantial default risk, 77–78, 91.

difficult dividend and redemption burden on the banks. As in the case of earlier RFC loans, the banks thought the public might see the RFC capital investments as a sign of weakness.[56] President Roosevelt and his new RFC Chairman, Jesse Jones, began an offensive to get bankers to sell preferred stock to the RFC.[57] Jones asked the management of many of the country's largest and most prestigious financial institutions to sell preferred stock to the RFC to avoid a stigma from being placed on such transactions. Ultimately, a number of the country's largest banks, including National City Bank of New York, First National Bank of Chicago, and Continental Illinois Bank and Trust Company, agreed to sell preferred stock to the RFC.[58]

The biggest surge of preferred stock investment came with the Banking Act of 1933, which established the FDIC. Many of the 9,000 nonmember banks were not financially sound enough to qualify for deposit insurance, so the RFC invested in those banks and helped launch the FDIC. By the end of 1933, the RFC's investment of about $1 billion was a third of total bank capital.[59] Under the Banking Act of 1933, all Federal Reserve member banks became members of the FDIC Fund as of January 1, 1934. Banks that were not members of the Federal Reserve System were authorized to join the Fund upon certification

---

56. *Saving Capitalism*, 73.

57. Franklin Delano Roosevelt, Letter to Jesse Jones on a Plan to Admit Non-Member State Banks to the Deposit Insurance Fund, October 23, 1933, http://www.presidency.ucsb.edu/ws/index.php?pid=14541 ("Recently the Reconstruction Finance Corporation has urged banks needing additional capital in order that they might give credit to business men and farmers to secure that capital by the sale to the Reconstruction Finance Corporation of preferred stock. This is already being done in many cases. But we hope that all banks will take advantage of this opportunity to put themselves in an easy cash position to help in the work of recovery. . . . To accept the Government's offer to purchase preferred stock does not mean that a bank is weak but that it is eager to cooperate 'in the recovery effort to the fullest possible extent and thus undertake to put this additional capital to work. We are not thinking of idle capital. We are thinking of working capital—capital working for recovery.").

58. National City Bank of New York and Continental Illinois Bank and Trust Company sold $50 million of preferred stock to the RFC. *Saving Capitalism*, 78, 80, 125. "Banking Out of Hock," *Time*, November 27, 1939. First National Bank of Chicago sold $15 million. "Will Sell Stock to RFC; First National Bank of Chicago Limits It to $15,000,000," *New York Times*, November 11, 1933, 23.

59. *Saving Capitalism*, 82.

of their solvency by their state banking agency and examination by the FDIC. Approximately a thousand banks were found to be insolvent. Correction of their insolvency was accomplished through raising of funds locally, directors' guarantees, purchase by local interests of bad assets, or through investments by the RFC in capital obligations of those institutions.

After the preferred stock investment program, the RFC became heavily involved in the management of select institutions. The RFC's stake in Continental Illinois Bank and Trust Company gave it control of the bank, and it wielded that control to appoint Walter J. Cummings, formerly the first head of the FDIC, as chairman of the board. Jesse Jones, the chair of the RFC, also intervened regarding salaries paid to bank executives if he considered them "over-paid" to assure that the banks did not enrich themselves after receiving government largesse. Amendments to the RFC Act of 1933 required Jones to certify the appropriateness of the salaries paid by every corporation accepting loans and investment money. The intervention in Continental was necessary because it was a large correspondent bank in the Midwest that would have reportedly taken hundreds of smaller banks with it if it were closed. Additional cases where management changes were made included the Prudence Company of New York and the Maryland Casualty Company.[60]

In the aftermath of the capital injections and the genesis of deposit insurance the level of bank failures receded (see Table 3.1). The ratio of deposits to currency rose from its depths during the early 1933 bank holiday when it was just above 4 percent to more than 7 percent after 1934, but it never again reached the heights of the late 1920s (see Figure 3.1). It is difficult to distinguish any impact between the initiation of the FDIC and the RFC capital injections given they occurred simultaneously during 1933 and 1934. Although some credit has been directed to the RFC investments, clearly in the short run the guarantee of deposits through the FDIC was an overwhelming factor in reducing the level of bank failures.[61] And although the creation of the FDIC did not directly bolster the capital standing of banks as the RFC did, it reduced the likelihood of runs

---

60. *Saving Capitalism*, 125–26.

61. *Monetary History*, 427 ("The RFC played a major role in the restoration of the banking system as it had in the futile attempts to shore it up before the banking holiday"). *Monetary History*, 434 ("Federal insurance of bank deposits was the most important structural change in the banking system to result from the 1933 panic, and, indeed in our view, the

on banks. But that reduction of failures came at a price in squelching a market mechanism to punish poorly managed banks. Small depositors no longer had the incentive to monitor the condition of banks. Going forward, when owners of problem banks experienced a drop in capital, deposit insurance now gave them an incentive to fund risky investments with a ready source of funding in a gamble to turn around the fortunes of the bank, all under a guarantee backed by the federal government.

## Lending Under Unusual and Exigent Circumstances

It was also during the early 1930s that the Federal Reserve Act was amended to expand the authority of the Federal Reserve to lend beyond member banks. As part of the Emergency Relief and Construction Act of 1932, Section 13(3) was added to the Federal Reserve Act as part of a road construction measure designed to relieve unemployment. Subject to certain restrictions, Section 13(3) authorized Reserve Banks, "in unusual and exigent circumstances," to extend credit directly to "individuals, partnerships, and corporations."[62] A number of restrictions were placed on this lending and these restrictions made it unlikely that many non-banks could qualify for emergency advances from Reserve Banks. In fact, due to these restrictions and the availability of credit elsewhere the Reserve Banks made loans to only 123 business enterprises from 1932 until 1936, aggregating only about $1.5 million under Section 13(3). The largest single loan was for $300,000.[63] This power to lend would remain dormant for more than seventy years.

---

structural change most conducive to monetary stability since state bank note issues were taxed out of existence immediately after the civil war").

62. Section 210, United States Statutes at Large, 72nd Congress 1931–1933, Vol. 47, Part I, 715.

63. Walker F. Todd, "FDICIA's Emergency Liquidity Provisions," *Federal Reserve Bank of Cleveland Economic Review* 29, no. 3, 3rd quarter, 1993, 18–20. *Monetary History*, 321. Friedman and Schwartz barely mention this in their historical analysis (" The Emergency Relief and Construction Act of July 21, 1932, therefore permitted the Reserve Banks to discount for individuals, partnerships, and corporations, with no other sources of funds, notes, drafts, and bills of exchange eligible for member banks. Those powers were used to a very limited extent. Discounts for individuals, partnerships, and corporations reached a maximum of $1.4 million in March 1933. Authorization to make those discounts expired July 31, 1936.").

# 4

# After the Depression

"The provisions of the bill with respect to the circumstances under which such loans may be made, however, are not altogether clear, and the language might at some future time be interpreted to permit the [FDIC] to embark upon the general business of lending to banks."
> —Thomas B. McCabe, Chairman of the Board of Governors of the Federal Reserve System in an apparent invocation of a "turf war" with the FDIC, expressing concern that proposed new FDIC powers might conflict with existing Federal Reserve powers to lend to banks.[1]

---

**LEGAL SCORECARD:**
- Federal Deposit Insurance Corporation Act of 1950
- Reconstruction Finance Corporation Liquidation Act of 1953

---

AS THE DEPRESSION receded and the economy revived in the postwar period, the RFC and the other agencies and powers created during and in the aftermath of the downturn lingered. An era began where the Congress bestowed more permanent powers to intervene in the banking industry on the FDIC in the form of standing bailout powers.

---

1. Amendments to Federal Deposit Insurance Act, Hearings Before a Subcommittee of the Committee on Banking and Currency, United States, 81st Congress, 2nd Session, January 11, 23, and 30, 1950, 105 [hereinafter 1950 Senate Hearings on Open Bank Assistance].

## The Reconstruction Finance Corporation

The Reconstruction Finance Corporation (RFC), President Hoover's vehicle for saving the bank system, was originally supposed to be in existence for a mere two years, but it actually lasted for over two decades. It became involved in a wide variety of enterprises far afield from its original crisis lending and investment functions as it:

- Organized the Commodity Credit Corporation and used its loans to attempt to raise the price of agricultural products.
- Oversaw the Federal National Mortgage Association, the Electronic Home and Farm Authority, the Export-Import Bank, and the Disaster Loan Corporation, which were all subsidiaries of the RFC at one time.
- Purchased gold when the Roosevelt Administration attempted to drive up the price of the metal.
- Became heavily involved during World War II in war production and the purchase and stockpiling of strategic materials through the Defense Plant Corporation, the Defense Supplies Corporation, the United States Commercial Company, the Rubber Reserve Company, and the Metals Reserve Company.

After the war, the agency achieved independent status and as one commenter described it "became embroiled in a series of bribery and corruption scandals." According to a Senate investigation of 1951, securing an RFC loan through the Democratic National Committee had become a common practice.[2] In 1953, when Republicans controlled both the Presidency and the Senate for the first time in decades, the RFC Liquidation Act became law. The act called for the termination of its lending authority, liquidation of assets, and the winding up of affairs of the RFC as expeditiously as possible. It also transitioned many of its activities to other government agencies, including the Small Business Administration (SBA), which was created under the RFC Liquidation Act. The

---

2. Clark Nardinelli, "The Reconstruction Finance Corporation's Murky History," Heritage Foundation, December 21, 1983, 3, 11, 12.

SBA carried on the RFC's small business and disaster loan programs.[3] At the time of the act, the RFC still had dozens of regional agencies, numerous branch offices, and well over $1 billion in loans and investments. Efforts began immediately to consolidate offices, eliminate overhead expenses, and where possible place RFC loans and investments in the hands of private financial institutions.[4]

## FDIC Open Bank Assistance

As of 1950, the FDIC had a number of options under law regarding failing financial institutions. The institution was addressed on a closed-bank basis, whereby it was put through a specialized process analogous to bankruptcy but tailored to banks, and was not bailed out. This could be in the form of an insured deposit payout, where the institution was closed and placed into a receivership with the FDIC paying depositors the insured portion of their deposits. Additionally, there was also the purchase-and-assumption (P&A) transaction where the institution was closed and the FDIC arranged for an existing bank to purchase failed bank assets and assume its liabilities.[5]

About the same time as the winding up of the RFC, changes were proposed to these existing failing bank options of the FDIC using the RFC structure as a model.[6] The FDIC sought a new power beyond the power to undertake a

---

3. Reconstruction Finance Corporation Liquidation Act, Small Business Act of 1953, Public Law 83–163. United States Code Congressional and Administrative News, 83rd Congress, First Session, 1953, Vol. 1, 278.

4. For a summary of the state of the Agency and the process of winding down its operations see "Progress Report on RFC Liquidation," Hearing Before the Committee on Banking and Currency, United States Senate, 83rd Congress, 2nd Session, March 26, 1954, 2–4. In an interview, Milton Friedman noted the wind-up of the RFC as one of the few cases of a government agency being eliminated. (Milton Friedman: "Somebody mentioned the other day that the Reconstruction Finance Corporation, which was established in 1931 or '32, may have been allowed to die. I'm not sure about that one. But there are very few you can name."), http://www.achievement.org/autodoc/page/frioint-5.

5. Robert DeYoung and Jack Reidhill, "A Theory of Bank Resolution: Political Economics and Technological Change," January 31, 2008, 18 (Section on Direct Payouts and Assumptions 1935–1950).

6. Federal Deposit Insurance Corporation, "Open Bank Assistance," Chapter 5, in *Managing the Crisis: The FDIC and RTC Experience*, 151 [hereinafter *Managing the Crisis*].

closed bank transaction, referred to as open bank assistance (OBA). Like the RFC loan and investment programs, it involved advancing funds to open banks approaching failure as a preemptive measure to avoid their collapse. Creditors and shareholders at risk in a bank closure would be bailed out.[7] However, in contrast to the creation of the RFC which was during a depression and which was proposed as a temporary measure, the proposed FDIC OBA power was permanent. It could either be invoked during a severe financial crisis or during a time of relative financial-sector calm to address the case of a single troubled bank.

During hearings on the proposal, as the Congress assessed whether to grant the FDIC OBA authority, the question arose of a conflict between the new proposed FDIC powers and the lender of last resort powers of the Federal Reserve.[8] The concern was also expressed in a statement of then-Federal Reserve Board Chairman Thomas B. McCabe.[9] After all, both the Federal Reserve and FDIC would be expected to lend in cases where a bank found itself in financial difficulty. This potential conflict was considered resolved as lending by the Federal

---

7. Section 13(c), United States Statutes at Large, 81st Congress, 1950–51, Vol. 64, Part I, 888–89 ("In order to reopen a closed insured bank or, when the Corporation has determined that an insured bank is in danger of closing, in order to prevent such closing, the Corporation, in the discretion of its Board of Directors, is authorized to make loans to, or purchase the assets of or make deposits in, such insured bank, upon such terms and conditions as the Board of Directors may prescribe, when in the opinion of the Board of Directors the continued operation of such bank is essential to provide adequate banking service in the community. Such loans and deposits may be in subordination to the rights of depositors and other creditors.").

8. Amendments to Federal Deposit Insurance Act, Hearings Before a Subcommittee of the Committee on Banking and Currency, United States, 81st Congress, 2nd Session, January 11, 23, and 30, 1950, 68 [hereinafter 1950 Senate Hearings on Open Bank Assistance] ("Senator Robertson: Do you think that the language of section 13(b) which authorizes the FDIC to step in to prevent the closing of an insured bank, is so broad that there is the possibility of conflict there with the powers of the Federal Reserve Board . . .").

9. However, his suggested change was not adopted in whole, but clarifying changes were made. 1950 Senate Hearings on Open Bank Assistance, 105 ("The provisions of the bill with respect to the circumstances under which such loans may be made, however, are not altogether clear, and the language might at some future time be interpreted to permit the [FDIC] to embark upon the general business of lending to banks. It is understood that this power is intended to pertain only to distress cases which could not be handled by normal banking processes. In order to make clear that this is the case, we recommend that the provisions of section 13(b) be revised as follows. . . . ").

Reserve would be based on sound assets, while FDIC OBA lending would be based on distressed assets to commercial banks in danger of closing.[10] The OBA power was also restricted to cases where the institution's continued existence was "essential" to providing adequate banking services in the community.[11]

A primary justification for granting the power of OBA to the FDIC was that it would be the least costly method to resolve an institution and it would be very limited in scope. It would be a preemptive action and only address cases where a bank was in danger of closing. In so doing, it would be less costly to provide assistance that would avoid closure, rather than having the FDIC absorb the losses normally inherent in closing a financial institution.[12] Once it was

---

10. 1950 Senate Hearings on Open Bank Assistance, 69 (Mr. Woolen. "Answering the question, Senator, for the [American Bankers Association], we had not made objection to that section, and I think there is perhaps a distinction between the proposed powers for the FDIC and the powers resting in the Federal Reserve Board, in that in the latter case it is expected that loans are to be made on sound assets, and this provision aims at the treatment of distressed assets."). Also see 131–34 for a similar colloquy ("Mr. Wiggins. It will be noted that the authorization to make loans to or purchase the assets of an insured bank by the Insurance Corporation is for the purpose of preventing 'the closing of an insured bank or in order to reopen a closed insured bank.' In my opinion, this authority is highly desirable and in no way conflicts with the powers of the Federal Reserve System to make loans to or rediscount paper of member banks. This authority is for emergency use only and gives the Insurance Corporation a facility with which, at a time that it may find a bank in serious difficulty, it may act promptly with the objective of preventing, if possible, a bank's closing.").

11. *Managing the Crisis*, 153–54. "FDIC Assistance to An Insured Bank on the Ground That It is Essential in Its Community," Congressional Research Service, October 1, 1984, 3 [hereinafter "Essential in Its Community"].

12. 1950 Senate Hearings on Open Bank Assistance, 79 ("Mr. Oliver. If a situation develops, the [FDIC] should have power to take corrective steps to prevent trouble in a proper situation by giving temporary financial assistance rather than closing the bank or requiring it to merge with another insured bank with a resultant loss to the Corporation. It seems to us that this provision, to be exercised only in a proper situation, is a most constructive one. It is designed to prevent trouble rather than to pay off depositors or to require the merger of the bank with another one. We can see no possible objection to this provision. . . . Senator Maybank. I wondered about that provision. I didn't see how it could possibly be done except in the case of an emergency. Mr. Oliver. That was the intention. Rather than letting a bank get bankrupt and forcing the [FDIC] to lose, this is to prevent bankruptcy. It is to try to tide them over. It is a very feasible provision. I can't see any possible objection if it is limited, as suggested by the Senator.").

granted the OBA power in 1950, the FDIC did not use the power until 1971 for a tiny $11 million bank in Boston and it only used the power four times in total throughout the 1970s, all for relatively modest-sized banks.[13] But the precedent had now been firmly set in place. Rather than the previous standing process where a failing bank was reflexively shuttered and permanently resolved by the FDIC, the agency now had the power to apply discretion to the failing bank resolution process and allow a bank to avoid closure through a bailout. That discretion would be applied again and again in future crises.

### Franklin National Bank

Although it was not addressed under the formal OBA power, there was an ad hoc bailout during the mid 1970s of Franklin National Bank of New York (Franklin). The way it became troubled and the approach for dealing with it would be become very familiar in subsequent decades:

> Between 1962 and 1973, Franklin tripled in size as it pursued an aggressive growth strategy. Franklin expanded from its original base on Long Island into New York City and subsequently opened foreign branches in Nassau and London. By 1973, Franklin had over $5 billion of assets and ranked as one of the twenty largest U.S. banks. Many of Franklin's high-risk loans turned sour, and the bank attempted to recover its losses by making speculative trades in the foreign exchange markets. Franklin also increased its reliance on volatile, wholesale funding from the capital markets. In 1974, more than a third of Franklin's liabilities consisted of foreign deposits, uninsured domestic deposits, loans from other banks, and securities repurchase agreements ("repos"). When Franklin publicly disclosed large losses from its nonperforming loans and foreign exchange trading in May 1974, uninsured depositors rapidly withdrew their funds and many banks refused to roll over their interbank loans.[14]

---

13. *Managing the Crisis*, 154. These ranged from $150 million to $1.5 billion in assets. Two of the institutions were in inner-city neighborhoods that lacked other adequate banking services, and so were considered "essential" to provide bank service to their community.
14. Joseph F. Sinkey, Jr., *Problem and Failed Institutions in the Commercial Banking Industry* (Greenwich, CT: JAI Press, Inc., 1979), and Joan E. Spero, *The Failure of Franklin National Bank: Challenge to the International Banking System* (New York: Columbia Uni-

The regulatory agencies, primarily the Office of the Comptroller of the Currency (OCC), the regulator of national banks, came under a great deal of criticism for a regulatory breakdown that allowed Franklin to deteriorate without earlier intervention.[15] Franklin experienced a massive run and lost nearly 25 percent of its deposits in four days when the news of its condition became public in early 1974 and lost 50 percent of its deposits by the time a resolution for the bank was ultimately arranged.[16] The Franklin bank run was not triggered by the typical small depositor who rushed to the local bank to withdraw money in the 1930s. The run on Franklin involved large depositors over the insured limit, including foreign depositors.

At the same time that the run was unfolding, the Federal Reserve propped up Franklin with lender of last resort credit of just over $1 billion starting in May 1974. These borrowings reached nearly $2 billion by October 1974, despite the fact that it was clear that in no sense of the word could Franklin be classified as a "sound" institution deserving of lender of last resort funding. Most likely Franklin was already insolvent in May 1974.[17] In a letter dated October

versity Press, 1980). As summarized in FCIC, "Preliminary Staff Report: Government Rescues of Too Big to Fail Financial Institutions," August 31, 2010, 5.

15. Oversight Hearings Into the Effectiveness of Federal Bank Regulation (Franklin National Bank Failure), Hearings Before a Subcommittee of the Committee on Government Operations—House of Representatives, 94th Congress, 2nd Session, February 10, May 25–6, and June 1, 1976 [hereinafter Franklin Oversight Hearings].

16. Inquiry Into Continental Illinois Corp. and Continental Illinois National Bank, Hearings Before the Subcommittee on Financial Institutions Supervision, Regulation and Insurance of the Committee on Banking, Finance and Urban Affairs, House of Representatives, 98th Congress, 2nd Session, September 18 and 19, 1984, and October 4, 1984, Report 98–111, Testimony of William Isaac, October 4, 1984, 467. Also see Christine M. Bradley, "A Historical Perspective on Deposit Insurance Coverage," *FDIC Banking Review* 13, no. 2 (2000), 16, n. 159 ("By the end of July, FNB had lost 71 percent of its domestic and foreign money-market resources").

17. Franklin Oversight Hearings, 197–200 (on lender of last resort loans); 43 (on solvency) quoting from a *Fortune* magazine article titled "What Really Went Wrong at Franklin National," October 1974 ("The release [issued by the Federal Reserve and Franklin] further stated that the OCC had assured the Federal Reserve that Franklin was a solvent institution and therefore eligible for loans at the Fed's discount window. It is hard to see how the OCC could have offered any such assurances. When [Franklin President] Luftig was informed by telephone of the contents of the [press] release, he called in Edward Lake, the bank examiner from the OCC who had been assigned to the Franklin account. Asked Luftig: 'Are we solvent?' Replied Lake: 'No.'").

1974, the Federal Reserve justified its actions stating that "its emergency credit assistance to Franklin was based on public policy considerations arising from the responsibility of the Federal Reserve System as a lender of last resort and was designed to give Franklin and the Federal banking regulatory agencies concerned a sufficient period to work out a permanent solution to the bank's difficulties."[18]

Franklin was resolved through negotiations over a five-month period beginning in May 1974 among the FDIC, the OCC, the Federal Reserve, and the bidding banks. These negotiations were complicated by the presence of foreign branches and foreign exchange speculation. Franklin was ultimately resolved through a closed-bank purchase and assumption transaction. The FDIC agreed to pay the amount due the Federal Reserve in three years, with periodic payments to be made from liquidation collections.[19] Uninsured creditors and depositors of Franklin were covered and were thus the recipients of a bailout. This was justified by the federal regulators on the basis that to do otherwise would have caused considerable disruption to the banking public in New York and to the international monetary markets and severely damaged the public confidence. However, other than a general statement from the Comptroller of the Currency stating these conclusions, no detailed analysis of this expected disruption has been made publicly available.[20]

In many ways, Franklin was a turning point, indicating a new way for how banks would be resolved and the lengths to which the banking agencies would go in avoiding the least hint of financial instability, with minimal evidence presented of the actual disruptions that would occur absent a bailout. The speed with which events occurred indicated that the concept of a bank run had returned. Franklin was also the first example of intervening in an individual institution that was considered "too big to fail," and the intervention signaled a clear migration to large banks as the focus of bailouts going forward. Franklin was also important because the Federal Reserve funded a transaction to an unsound

---

18. Letter from the Federal Reserve dated October 7, 1974, as quoted in Franklin Oversight Hearings, 200, detailed in Affidavit of James E. Smith, OCC, U.S. District Court of the Eastern District of New York [hereinafter Smith Affidavit], October 8, 1974.
19. FDIC, *The First Fifty Years: A History of the FDIC 1933–1983* (1984). http://www.fdic .gov/bank/analytical/firstfifty/chapter5.html.
20. Franklin Oversight Hearings, Smith Affidavit, 201.

institution, clearly putting at risk public funds.[21] As noted by economist Anna Schwartz, this behavior was "contrary to traditional principles."[22] The bright line between the types of institutions the Federal Reserve and the FDIC assisted was now blurry. Considering these changes, Franklin should have been a red flag for the possibility of similar meltdowns of banks, so that the banking agencies would no longer be caught by surprise from such a collapse. That was not the case.

21. It is not entirely clear whether the FDIC absorbed a cost in resolving Franklin National Bank. No clear statement of the cost is noted on the FDIC's website, although it does note that prior to the 1980s, consistent resolution cost data is not available due to inconsistency of cost methodologies. Sources outside the FDIC have estimated the cost of resolving Franklin at nearly $200 million. The Federal Reserve absorbed interest costs in subsidizing loans to Franklin of approximately $20 million. Anna J. Schwartz, "The Misuse of the Fed's Discount Window," *Federal Reserve Bank of St. Louis Review* 58 (September/October 1992), 64 [hereinafter "Misuse of Discount Window"].

22. "Misuse of Discount Window," 63. Elsewhere in the article Schwartz notes: "Since the 1970s, the Federal Reserve has extended long-term discount window assistance to depository institutions that by objective standards were likely to fail. It has done so in the belief that, in the absence of such assistance, contagious effects would spread from the troubled institutions to sound ones. The belief is particularly entrenched for large troubled intermediaries, reflecting an apprehension that halting the operation of such institutions would have dire, unsettling effects on financial markets." Additionally, Schwartz details the use of the discount window during the 1920s to lend to unsound institutions, a practice "which contravened the ancient injunction to central banks to lend only to illiquid banks, not to insolvent ones."

# 5

## The 1980s Financial Crisis and the Interventions

"**MR. CARPER.** In this country we can't let a major bank like Continental Illinois fail, but having said that we should endeavor to revise the banking system so we can let a major bank like that fail in the future without creating real chaos in our own banking community. Do you concur with that as a reasonable objective? **MR. ISAAC.** I think it is a reasonable objective. We have got to treat large and small banks alike. We have got to find a means to do that." —Colloquy between House Banking Committee member Carper and FDIC Chairman Isaac a few months after the bailout of Continental Illinois, October 4, 1984.[1]

---

**LEGAL SCORECARD:**

- Depository Institutions Deregulation and Monetary Control Act (1980)
- Garn–St. Germain Depository Institutions Act (1982)
- Miscellaneous Revenue Act (1982)
- Competitive Equality Banking Act (1987)
- Agricultural Credit Act (1987)
- Working Group on Financial Markets (1988)

---

1. Inquiry Into Continental Illinois Corp. and Continental Illinois National Bank, Hearings Before the Subcommittee on Financial Institutions Supervision, Regulation and Insurance of the Committee on Banking, Finance and Urban Affairs, House of Representatives, 98th Congress, 2nd Session, September 18 and 19, 1984, and October 4, 1984, Report 98–111, 559 [hereinafter, Inquiry].

DURING THE 1980S, the U.S. financial system experienced its most volatile period since the Depression of the 1930s. The economy suffered through a double-dip recession in the early 1980s. An initial brief recession occurred in the first half of 1980 followed by a more severe recession from mid-1981 to late 1982.[2] Another relatively mild recession occurred during 1990 to 1991, brought on in part by a credit crunch evidenced by negative growth in lending.[3] As in the 1930s, banks tightened up on their willingness to lend. This tightening occurred not only in the early 1980s during the double-dip recession, but also during the 1990 to 1991 recession.[4]

A number of causes can be cited for the turmoil during the 1980s:[5]

- The greatest single cause was the volatility in the macroeconomic environment. Interest rates fluctuated dramatically in large part because of the Federal Reserve's efforts to reduce inflationary expectations and thus inflation. The Federal Reserve displayed its willingness to slow economic activity by increasing short-term rates. Exchange rates were also volatile

---

2. NBER Press Release, "Business Cycle Peaked in January," June 3, 1980, http://www. nber.org/cycles/announcement/june1980.pdf; NBER Press Release, "Business Cycle Trough Last July," July 8, 1981, http://www.nber.org/cycles/announcement/july1981.pdf; NBER Press Release, "Current Recession Began in July," January 6, 1982, http://www .nber.org/cycles/announcement/jan1982.pdf; NBER Press Release, "Recovery Began in November," July 8, 1983, http://www.nber.org/cycles/announcement/july1983.pdf.
3. NBER Press Release, "Business Cycle Dating Committee Determines That Recession Began in July 1990," April 25, 1991, http://www.nber.org/cycles/april1991.html; NBER Press Release, "Determines That Recession Ended in March 1991," December 22, 1992, http://www.nber.org/cycles/march91.html.
4. Stacey L. Shreft and Raymond E. Owens, "Survey Evidence of Tighter Credit Conditions: What Does it Mean?" Working Paper 91–05, Federal Reserve Bank of Richmond, May 15, 1991. This working paper traces the history of the Federal Reserve's Senior Loan Officer Opinion Survey from its beginnings in 1964 through the recessions of the 1960s, 1970s, and 1980s and is meant to put the 1990 to 1991 recession in historical context.
5. Although the article hesitates to argue for a single cause, a good summary of these causes can be found in George Hanc (primary author), "The Banking Crises of the 1980s and Early 1990s: Summary and Implications," *History of the Eighties: Lessons for the Future, Volume I: An Examination of the Banking Crises of the 1980s and Early 1990s*, Federal Deposit Insurance Corporation, 1997, 3–19 [hereinafter *History of the 80s*].

as they were allowed to float after the collapse of the Bretton Woods System in the 1970s, signaling the breakdown of the link between gold and the dollar. Price levels were also volatile due to external shocks and excessive growth in the money supply during the 1970s and early 1980s. For banks, this volatility meant dramatic increases in the risk of imbalances between cost of liabilities and income on assets.

- Partly in response to the macroeconomic changes, there were also changes in the financial marketplace, including dramatic technological innovations in the delivery of financial services. Interstate banking limits were lifted, providing new entrants into markets, and interest rates were deregulated. Financial product innovations, most prominently the development of money market funds, put competitive pressure on banks, as did ongoing changes for thrift institutions, foreign banks, and the commercial paper and junk bond markets. Many banks shifted funds to riskier commercial real estate as well as less-developed-country and leveraged buyout lending, and increased their off-balance-sheet activities.

- Legislative changes included the Depository Institutions Deregulation and Monetary Control Act of 1980 (DIDMCA), which phased out deposit interest-rate ceilings, broadened the powers of thrift institutions, and raised the deposit insurance limit from $40,000 to $100,000, allowing banks to take on more risk funded with insured deposits. Additionally, the Garn–St. Germain Depository Institutions Act of 1982 authorized money-market deposit accounts for banks and thrifts to stem disintermediation; authorized net-worth certificates to implement capital forbearance for thrifts facing insolvency in the short term; and increased the authority of thrifts to invest in commercial loans to strengthen the institutions' viability over the long term.

- Regional economic and financial turmoil was also a factor in the failures. Of the total bank failures during the entire period from 1980 to 1994, nearly 60 percent were in only 5 states. Texas led the way with nearly 600 failures comprising over 40 percent of total banking assets in the state, followed by Oklahoma, California, Louisiana, and Kansas. Sectors of the economy that were concentrated in these regional economies suffered

**Table 5.1.** Failures and Assistance Transactions from 1981 to 1993

| | **Failures and Assistance Transactions** |
|---|---|
| 1981 | 40 |
| 1982 | 119 |
| 1983 | 99 |
| 1984 | 106 |
| 1985 | 180 |
| 1986 | 204 |
| 1987 | 262 |
| 1988 | 470 |
| 1989 | 534 |
| 1990 | 382 |
| 1991 | 271 |
| 1992 | 181 |
| 1993 | 50 |

*Source*: FDIC, http://www2.fdic.gov/hsob/SelectRpt.asp?EntryTyp=30.

during this period leading to failures, oftentimes due to the deflation of asset bubbles in real estate, including farmland.[6]

The response to an increase in troubled financial institutions was a blend of outright closures, the invocation of the FDIC's open bank assistance powers, forbearance, and a variety of what were thought to be one-time, ad hoc bailouts. From 1943 to 1974 the number of failures and assistance transactions never exceeded ten, and for the remainder of the 1970s never exceeded seventeen. But beginning in 1981, the number of failures and assistance transactions started a dramatic rise that lasted well into the early 1990s (Table 5.1). The combined cost of failures and assistance transactions led to a dramatic weakening in the FDIC's financial standing. During the early 1990s the FDIC dipped into insolvency for

---

6. The most obvious example of this is the Texas economy and its dependence on the energy sector that was so dramatically impacted by the drop in the price of oil during this period. Additionally, the changes to the tax code in 1986 also reduced the tax advantages of second homes.

the first time, as its capital level dropped as low as <$7 billion> in 1991. Much of this drop was due to estimates of expected future failures, not all of which materialized as the economy came out of recession.[7]

## Open Bank Assistance

The first use of the Open Bank Assistance (OBA) power during the 1980s also involved by far the largest recipient bank to date, signaling a transition of OBA from a small bank bailout program to a predominantly large bank bailout program.[8] First Pennsylvania Bank, an $8 billion institution, the largest in the city of Philadelphia and the twenty-third largest in the United States at the time, was extended OBA in April 1980. If it had been allowed to fail, it would have been the largest failure in history up to that time. With First Pennsylvania Bank, the banking agencies began to detail what was called a "domino theory" to argue against allowing a large bank to fail, as explained by FDIC Board Member Irvine Sprague:

> Fred Schultz, the Fed deputy chairman, argued in an ever rising voice, that there were no alternatives—we had to save the bank. He said, "Quit wasting time talking about anything else!" Paul Homan of the Comptroller's office was equally intense as he argued for any solution but a failure. The domino theory dominated the discussion—if First Pennsylvania went down, its business connections with other banks would entangle them also and touch off a crisis in confidence that would snowball into other bank failures here and abroad. It would culminate in an international financial crisis. The theory had never been tested.[9]

The legislative history of OBA in 1950 revealed an attempt to justify passage of OBA on the basis that it would involve no cost over a closed bank option. Consistent with that, First Pennsylvania was resolved at a zero cost to the FDIC.

---

7. FDIC, "1990–91 FDIC at a Glance," http://www.fdic.gov/bank/historical/managing/Chron/1991/index.html.

8. Of the OBA transactions completed from 1980 to 1994, roughly three-quarters of the cost of resolution was attributable to banks of $2 billion or more.

9. Irvine H. Sprague, *Bailout* (New York: Basic Books, 1986), 88–89.

In contrast, the next fourteen invocations of OBA authority from 1981 to 1983 were to bail out regional mutual savings banks in New York City and the Northeast, some of which were also large. These were resolved, not at zero cost, but at a rather steep price totaling in the billions.[10]

Continuing the transformation of OBA into a large bank bailout program was the passage of the Garn–St. Germain Depository Institutions Act of 1982, as the legislative focus of OBA was expanded to cover cases "when severe financial conditions exist which threaten the stability of a significant number of insured banks or of insured banks possessing significant financial resources. . . ."[11] Clearly, this language was most applicable in the case of a large, interconnected bank as opposed to a small one whose failure would have relatively less impact. It codified the domino theory of the regulators and broadened the scope for OBA as this language replaced the essentiality clause of the prior legislation. Additionally, the type of actions the FDIC was allowed to undertake was expanded, including the power to "assume the liabilities of, or to make contributions." As a Congressional Research Service analysis during the time points out, Congressman Ron Paul of Texas adamantly opposed the move and raised objections to the broad scope of the changes:

> This conference report is an open-ended guarantee of hyperinflation. . . . Not only is the FDIC given unlimited power to act unilaterally, its actions may include loans, deposits, exchanges, and gifts to any of the 15,000 insured banks that the FDIC chooses. . . . This conference report makes clear exactly what "lender of last resort" means. It means that the Government stands ready to print any amount of paper money or create credit for anyone, at any time, in order to keep a financial institution open. . . . The FDIC has about $11 billion in reserves and insures deposits totaling over $1 trillion. But that is not really important any longer. Last March, the Congress passed House Concurrent Resolution 290, pledging the full faith and credit of the U.S. Government to deposits in

---

10. *Managing the Crisis*, 154–55, 158–60. The mutual savings banks ranged in size up to $3.4 billion and in total cost nearly $2 billion to resolve.
11. United States Code Congressional and Administrative News, 97th Congress, 2nd Session, 1982, Vol. 1, 96 Stat. 1469.

insured institutions. It is not any longer simply a matter of using up $11 or $12 billion. The Government has made a moral obligation to bailout everyone, everywhere, to the tune of $1 trillion.[12]

One restriction added to the OBA provision under Garn–St. Germain was an explicit "cost test" whereby the resolution through OBA needed to, at minimum, be less costly than a liquidation of the bank.[13] There was an exception to this rule for cases where the FDIC determined that the bank was essential to the community.[14]

The Garn–St. Germain changes were made under proposals labeled "Deposit Insurance Flexibility," and then-Chairman William Isaac of the FDIC used the term "flexibility" in his supporting testimony, especially as it related to the use of such powers to provide OBA to savings banks.[15] At the same hearing, the representative of the Reagan Administration Treasury Department supported these changes.[16]

---

12. "Essential in Its Community," 6, citing 128 Cong. Rec. H 8437 (daily edition October 1, 1982).

13. Public Law 97–320 (October 15, 1982), 96 Stat. 1470 ("4(A) No assistance shall be provided under this subsection in an amount in excess of that amount which the Corporation determines to be reasonably necessary to save the cost of liquidating, including paying the insured accounts of, such insured bank, except that such restriction shall not apply in any case in which the Corporation determines that the continued operation of such insured bank is essential to provide adequate banking services in its community").

14. For a detailed discussion of the history of essentiality, see "Essential in Its Community."

15. "Capital Assistance and Deposit Insurance Flexibility Act," Hearings Before the Committee on Banking, Housing, and Urban Affairs, U.S. Senate, 97th Congress, 2nd Session, May 26, 1982 ("The Section 13(c) language is broader as to the form of assistance. Furthermore, it is not limited to any percentage of the bank's previous losses. This combination gives us the flexibility to tailor the aid to meet the needs of a specific institution and provide enough assistance to redirect it on a path to profitability."). Inquiry, 475 ("Chairman St. Germain. Why was an amendment sought? Because there were savings banks in New York City about to fail. . . . Mr. Isaac. The FDIC wanted an amendment to the law in part to take care of the savings bank problem.").

16. "[B]oth agencies have demonstrated due regard for the soundness of management and the long-term viability of troubled institutions, not simply providing wholesale 'bail-outs' for all." This statement refers to the FDIC and FSLIC. Roger W. Mehle, Jr., Assistant Secretary, Domestic Finance, Department of the Treasury, Testimony on S. 2531, the "Capital Assistance Act of 1982," and S. 2532, the "Deposit Insurance Flexibility Act," May 26, 1982.

### Continental Illinois—Circumstances Leading to the Stress

The largest and most high-profile OBA transaction during this period was Continental Illinois of Chicago, which at the time of its resolution was the seventh largest bank in the nation.[17] Continental experienced rapid asset growth throughout the 1970s, including large loan purchases from Penn Square Bank of Oklahoma, which failed in 1982. This growth was in large part funded by volatile and risky short-term liabilities. After Penn Square failed, Continental began to unravel, as problems in its loan portfolio became much more public and its cost of funding increased, much of it funded in the foreign money market. As far back as 1982 the Office of the Comptroller of the Currency (OCC), which was the primary federal regulator of Continental Illinois, had identified problems with the bank's management and overall lending practices, but the OCC apparently did not take effective action.[18] By April of 1984, nonperforming loans had increased to over $2 billion. Continental's stock price plunged to $14 a share after reaching heights of over $40 a share in 1981.[19]

According to the FDIC, the problem it faced in addressing Continental was twofold. One concern was that, because of its interconnected position as a major correspondent bank, a failure of Continental would cause a ripple throughout the banking system, the fabled domino effect.[20] The second concern was that Continental was just too large to take over and sell in the traditional manner that the FDIC used for closing a bank, another case of "too big to fail." That traditional manner involved selling the institution by marketing it over a relatively short period of time and completing a purchase and assumption agreement or a payout of depositors over the course of a weekend. According to the FDIC, it would have taken one to two months to make deposits available to insured depositors, what FDIC Chairman Isaac referred to as the "adminis-

---

17. By almost any measure, Continental Illinois was the largest OBA transaction prior to the 2000s crisis: assets = $34 billion; deposits = $17 billion; cost = $1 billion.

18. Inquiry, 123 ("Mr. Barnard. What you are saying Mr. Kovarick, is as early as 1982—and this is 1984 that the Comptroller's Office was alerted to the deficiencies or to some real criticisms in bank management.").

19. FDIC, "Continental Illinois and Too Big to Fail," Chapter 7, in *History of the 80s,* 243.

20. Inquiry, 456.

trative problem." The FDIC did not have authority to take over such a large or complex institution and sell it over a period of many months.[21]

The FDIC under its own analysis had a limited number of options under law for resolving Continental. It had the choice of closing down Continental outright and allowing a number of the correspondent banks to fail and then going through the mechanics of paying out depositors over a number of months.[22] Or the FDIC could undertake some form of OBA, as it did in the case of First Pennsylvania Bank and others, to inject funds into Continental to stave off its failure.

Rumors began to circulate regarding Continental's condition, triggering a run of uninsured depositors and creditors. Confusing the situation on May 10, 1984, in an effort to instill confidence the OCC, departing from its policy of not commenting on individual banks, issued a statement denying the agency had sought assistance for Continental. It noted that the OCC was unaware of any significant changes in the bank's operations, as reflected in its published financial statements, that would serve as the basis for the rumors about Continental.[23] The day after the Comptroller's statement that all was well, Continental's borrowings from the Federal Reserve reached $3.6 billion. Like Franklin National Bank before it, there is just no argument that Continental at this point was a

---

21. Inquiry, 478. Inquiry, 589 ("Mr. Isaac. Right now we have an administrative problem because the FDIC, candidly, does not have the capacity administratively right now to pay off on a very, very large bank like Continental in a short period of time. With 850,000 accounts, it would take about a month or more to pay off the insured deposits. That is too long. In a small bank that has maybe 10,000 accounts, you are talking about over the weekend and the checks are available on Monday. So administratively, we have a lot we need to do.").

22. There is a real question here of why, as argued by Chairman Isaac, it would take this long to pay depositors. Even during the early 1980s, with short-term contractors at their disposal, it is difficult to believe that this process would have taken so long.

23. Inquiry, 285; Comptroller of the Currency—Administrator of National Bank, "Statement on Continental Illinois," May 10, 1984. Inquiry, 398 ("Chairman St. Germain. Again, this entire process calls for greater openness. It cries out for a greater degree of truthfulness. It does not enhance the confidence of the American people in the Federal regulatory structure to have one of its officials issue misleading statements about the condition of the bank as the Comptroller did during the early stages of the rescue effort.").

sound institution deserving of lender of last resort credit. Its problems had been known for at least two years, and without intervention it was on a clear path to failure. However, then–Federal Reserve Chairman Volcker insisted that this was an appropriate role for the Federal Reserve:

> The operation we are engaged in in lending to these banks—Continental Illinois in this case—is the most basic function of the Federal Reserve. It was why it was founded, to serve as a lender of last resort in times of liquidity pressures of this sort, so that they don't spread through the rest of the system to innocent parties not involved in Continental Illinois at all; we were founded so that there should be that elasticity in the system. That's what a central bank is all about, to provide liquidity in these circumstances. We are just carrying out the most classic function of a central bank.[24]

What Volcker does not make clear is why the Federal Reserve could not lend directly to those "innocent parties not involved in Continental Illinois," such as the banks that were sound who experienced stress because of their connection to Continental.

The Federal Reserve lending facility was followed by an effort by sixteen banks to extend $4.5 billion to Continental Illinois. Neither of these initiatives was enough to stabilize Continental. The FDIC intervened on May 17 with an OBA transaction based on the essentiality test (and thus not on the least cost test), effectively nationalizing Continental with a capital injection, while simultaneously taking an 80 percent government stake and installing new management.[25] The Federal Reserve stated that it would meet any liquidity needs Continental might have, and a group of twenty-four major U.S. banks agreed to provide more than $5.3 billion in funding on an unsecured basis while a perma-

---

24. Hearings Before the Committee on Banking, Housing and Urban Affairs, United States Senate, 98th Congress, July 25 and 31, 1984, 108 [hereinafter Volcker July 1984 Testimony].
25. FDIC, "Continental Illinois and Too Big to Fail," Chapter 7 in *History of the 80s*, 236–47. For details on the essentiality determination for Continental, see Robert V. Shumway, Director of Bank Supervision, "Continental Illinois National Bank and Trust Company of Chicago—Section 13(c)(2) Assistance," Memo to the Board of Directors of the Federal Deposit Insurance Corporation, May 17, 1984.

nent solution was sought. In what was perhaps the most controversial move by the regulators, the FDIC promised to protect all of Continental's depositors and other general creditors, regardless of the $100,000 limit on deposit insurance. The assistance package was to remain in place while the regulators searched for a permanent solution to Continental's problems.[26]

### Continental Illinois—The Justification for Intervention

The Continental Illinois case received a great deal of scrutiny from the Congress. In September and October 1984, just a few weeks before the presidential election and a few months after the rescue, the House Committee on Banking, Finance, and Urban Affairs conducted a set of hearings that acted as a postmortem on the bailout. A wide range of topics was covered including the fairness of the "too big to fail" policy for medium and small banks, the potential fallout of a failure of Continental, and the estimated cost of the OBA transaction, during what were at times very contentious hearings.[27]

The prospect of Continental failing was unprecedented at the time, and at the hearing this possibility was variously described in a range of hyperbolic language:

- C. Todd Conover, Comptroller of the Currency:[28] "In our collective judgment, had Continental failed and been treated in a way in which depositors and creditors were not made whole, we could very well have seen a national, if not an international, financial crisis the dimensions of which were difficult to imagine. None of us wanted to find out."[29]
- Fernand J. St. Germain, Chairman of the Committee on Banking, Finance and Urban Affairs of the House of Representatives: " . . . today we return to this forum faced with what is, for all practical purposes,

---

26. FDIC, "Continental Illinois and Too Big to Fail," Chapter 7 in *History of the 80s*, 244.
27. Inquiry, 470 ("Mr. Isaac. Before we begin, I would really like to say something. Frankly, I'd like to get something off my chest. I took great personal offense at what I witnessed this morning, and I know our staff did, as this agency's intelligence and integrity and mine were called into question, as well as the other bank regulatory agencies.").
28. http://www.occ.treas.gov/conover.htm.
29. Inquiry, 288.

the granddaddy of bank failures, a $44 billion money center bank that rolled into the ditch. . . . Continental presents the greatest multitude of banking question [sic] ever to come before this committee."[30]

- Frank Annunzio, Congressman from Illinois: "I am interested in the 12,000 jobs that would have been lost and the 66 banks that have deposits that have more than 100 percent of their equity capital on deposit in Continental. What would have happened to those banks, and what would have happened to all those employees, and to the banking communities in the Midwest where these 66 banks are located? . . . How much money would have been lost to the corporations in this country, to the individuals in this country, to the individual job holders I described yesterday? I am not interested in upper echelon bankers. I am talking about the cashiers, janitors, clerks and the lower echelon people in all of these institutions throughout Illinois."[31]

- William M. Isaac, FDIC Chairman: "The effects would have been catastrophic. . . . [t]here could have been widespread instability throughout banking, throughout the thrift system, and there would have been massive corporate bankruptcies throughout the Midwest and elsewhere."[32]

As noted in a number of the descriptions above, a primary concern of the banking agencies was the potential contagion that would have flowed from allowing Continental Illinois to fail. In introducing FDIC Chairman Isaac before his testimony, Committee Chairman St. Germain described how this discussion of contagion began with the scary scenario laid out by the banking agencies the night before the bailout of Continental and his thoughts on the dearth of underlying data to support that description.

> All this controversy about numbers—all this confusion in the public's mind about the bailout—might have been avoided had your office done its job up front when the bailout question first came up. . . . I want to give

---

30. Inquiry, 1, 5. It should be noted that because of the provision of OBA, Continental did not ultimately fail.
31. Inquiry, 287–88.
32. Inquiry, 479–80.

you a full right to reply here today, but I'm just sorry you weren't more concerned about numbers and cost analysis a few months ago. Our staff didn't create the problem. They've searched your files and found nothing. They've done the best to try to track what the regulators—what you have been talking about—in those sky-is-falling statements. In that breathless conference call to the Congress the night before the bailout, we all heard the numbers 2,400 and 75—2,400 with relationships with Continental and 75 that would go down the tubes if you didn't let Continental have the money.[33]

During the hearings, Comptroller of the Currency Conover had described this contagion in quite precise detail:

Sixty-six banks, as you know, had deposits in Continental in amounts in excess of the total net worth of the bank. Another 113 banks had deposits in Continental amounting to between 50 and 100 percent of their net worth. If Continental had failed and had been treated as a payoff, certainly those 66 banks would have failed and probably a goodly number of the 113 would have failed, if not immediately thereafter, then certainly within some period of time afterward. So let us say that we could easily have seen another hundred bank failures.[34]

However, what the FDIC and Comptroller of the Currency actually had on hand at the time of the Continental bailout was a very cryptic version of the least cost analysis newly required under law, what one might call a seat-of-the-pants estimate. No written analysis even existed on the assessment of

---

33. Inquiry, 456.

34. Comments of C. Todd Conover, Comptroller of the Currency, Inquiry, 287. Also see Inquiry, 295–6 ("Mr. Conover. It was very clear that the way to deal with Continental was not to do a payoff of insured depositors."); and 353 ("Chairman St. Germain. The FDIC Act requires that the least costly method be utilized, does it not? Mr. Conover. Yes it does. Chairman St. Germain. . . . Now how can you know what the least costly method is that is being utilized unless you perform the actual analyses, rather than just sitting down with a memo pad? Mr. Conover. I agree with that. Chairman St. Germain. Ok. Was that done? Mr. Conover. There were cost analyses that were performed, and they were looked at.").

least cost at that time.[35] As pointed out by Chairman St. Germain, this could not possibly justify the intervention in the case of Continental.[36]

---

35. Inquiry, 472–3 ("Chairman St. Germain. Does your staff have an idea? Mr. Isaac. A rough idea. Chairman St. Germain. A rough idea. We have been looking for the information from them for a long period of time and have gotten absolutely nothing because there was nothing there. Mr. Isaac. We are not about to make the number public because it is not a number that you can place any great degree of confidence in. Chairman St. Germain. Mr. Isaac, we told you we would keep it in confidence if you felt it had to be kept in confidence. Mr. Isaac. I told your staff confidentially the other day about how many would fail. Chairman St. Germain. Based on what? Mr. Isaac. Based upon our analysis. Chairman St. Germain. Which analysis? Mr. Isaac. The analysis of the amount of exposure the banks had in comparison with the condition of those banks. Chairman St. Germain. When was that done? Mr. Isaac. This summer. Chairman St. Germain. When this summer? Mr. Isaac. I don't know. Chairman St. Germain. Well, is it available? Mr. Isaac. If you are asking me whether it was done during the week of May 10, when we were handling the potential failure of Continental, no it was not done. Mr. St. Germain. When approximately was it done? Mr. Isaac. In the months of July or August, I believe. Perhaps September. Chairman St. Germain. Then where are the analyses? Mr. Isaac. There are no written analyses. Chairman St. Germain. There are no written analyses? Mr. Isaac. That is correct. Chairman St. Germain. It was all mental? Mr. Isaac. That is correct. Estimates. Chairman St. Germain. Estimates. Mental estimates? Mr. Isaac. That is correct. Chairman St. Germain. In other words, guesses. Mr. Isaac. That is what this business is. Chairman St. Germain. Educated guesses? Mr. Isaac. That is what this business is, educated guesses. My point is Mr. Chairman the FDIC never represented how many of those 2,300 banks would have failed. Chairman St. Germain. Do you now know as a result of this educated— Mr. Isaac. I know about how many. . . . I would be willing to tell you fewer than 25 would have failed in the first round. . . . Mr. Isaac. At the point when we were doing this it was a totally moot question. Continental had already been taken care of on May 7. We decided on May 17 that the bank would not be permitted to fail. Anything we did in June or July— Chairman St. Germain. Oh, so you made a decision without ever having any written analyses, right? You made the decision without ever having run the numbers. Mr. Isaac. I didn't say that. I said— Chairman St. Germain. That is what you just said. It would have been moot because you said a decision was made on May 17. Mr. Isaac. I told you, Mr. Chairman, that I had some rough numbers that I was given at the time. We could not come up with better numbers. We did not have time. Chairman St. Germain. You said you got those numbers in June or July. Mr. Isaac. No I got the first numbers in May. Chairman St. Germain. In May? Mr. Isaac. Yes. Chairman St. Germain. Those are just rough numbers, right? Mr. Isaac. Very rough.").

36. Inquiry, 455–6 ("Chairman St. Germain. I am shocked that the keeper of the insurance fund did not insist right from the opening gun on a top-to-bottom cost analysis. Perhaps in the final analysis you would have been forced to concede to the other regulators, but I

The 1980s Financial Crisis and the Interventions | 85

In truth and in fact, it appears that the three regulators made their initial decision to assist Continental with little in hand but the broad concept that the bank was "essential" in a global sense. At this point, not even a contrived list of dominoes was in hand and apparently no cost analysis which would have given the regulators a clue as to what route might save the Federal Government money. It appears the decision to bailout was made on high in the early hours without any hard facts or empirical evidence. After that apparently the word went out to the bureaucracy to come up with numbers to rationalize the action for public consumption.[37]

The source of the estimate of 66 bank failures and potentially 113 more banks at risk was not undertaken at the time of the initial intervention, but was compiled as an after-the-fact analysis done by the FDIC about twenty days after the initial assistance program went into effect on May 17.[38] In order to scrutinize the basis of that more detailed after-the-fact analysis, the House Banking Committee recomputed the information from scratch and their conclusion was that about six banks would have probably failed, not 66 as indicated by the Comptroller, and an additional 28 banks had significant exposure and possibly would have failed, not 113 as indicated by the Comptroller.[39] Either because of time pressures

---

would think the man with the fiduciary responsibility would have thrown down the cost analysis in the very first meeting on Continental. It is your responsibility to protect that fund and to place a heavy burden of proof on any one—including your fellow regulators—who wants to tap it. . . . Mr. Isaac, this committee and the public should have had this data months ago. It shouldn't have to be forced out of FDIC in a hearing.")

37. Inquiry, 398.

38. Inquiry, 413 ("Mr. Dugger. Last May Continental Bank's situation reached a point that the FDIC, Comptroller of the Currency and Federal Reserve concluded that a $2 billion temporary assistance program had to be implemented on an emergency basis. The temporary assistance program went into effect on May 17. About 20 days later, as best we can determine, FDIC Chairman Isaac asked his staff to obtain information on the deposit and investment exposure of other banks in Continental. His staff produced two memoranda which appear in the appendix of the staff report, dated June 20 and June 22, about 34 days after implementation of the temporary assistance plan."). Robert Dugger is Deputy Staff Director of the Subcommittee holding the hearing. For copies of the memoranda see Inquiry, 444.

39. It should be noted that such large interbank loans are referred to as concentrations of credit and should have been noted by bank management as part of daily oversight or the regulatory agencies during on-site examinations.

or miscommunication among members of the staff of the FDIC, the FDIC analysis had serious limitations:

- The then-$100,000 of FDIC coverage was not incorporated into the analysis;
- Proceeds from a sale of Continental Bank's assets were not incorporated into the analysis; and
- Deposit and investment data used in the analysis was as of April 30, a date prior to the enormous deposit outflows and public concerns about Continental Bank.[40]

It is not clear why the agencies were not better prepared with a more detailed analysis prior to the time of the bailout given that, as pointed out by Congressman Vento, the problems of Continental had been in the making for about two years prior to the date of the May 17 intervention.[41] Congressman Leach also disputed whether the agencies in fact had any type of plan in place to address a failing bank like Continental: "The plan was to cave. If caving is a plan you had a plan."[42]

The House Banking Committee members showed quite a bit of skepticism over the idea of a contagion effect or a "domino theory" as Chairman St. Germain called it:

[T]he domino theory has been floated, suggesting that 75 or more banks would have failed had the regulators not staffed the bucket brigade. In

---

40. Inquiry, 414.

41. Inquiry, 452 ("Mr. Vento. But the point is that the Comptroller told us and I think it is in the records and the FDIC now that for almost 2 years, that this bank had been in trouble. . . . I mean the idea that this somehow came down quickly, that the pressure of time did not permit them to have this type of information, simply is not an excuse. Into the vacuum moves the idea. The problem, it seems to me, is that this is the main justification that is talked about, that if you make the problem big enough in terms of the issue, then that provides the excuse for extraordinary intervention. It seems to me that the problem, this balloon, this problem which is a problem with regards to Continental Illinois, has a great deal of gaseous substance blown into its body.").

42. Inquiry, 516 ("Mr. Isaac. I would like to maybe comment on a couple of things. One was you said that the regulators could be faulted for not having a plan for dealing with a situation like Continental before it occurred when in fact we did. Mr. Leach. The plan was to cave. If caving is a plan you had a plan.").

fact, the regulators briefed Members of both the House and the Senate in July and used the domino theory as the centerpiece of their contention that 'we had no choice.' . . . Unless they are more incompetent than we suspect, the agencies knew full well that the domino theory was concocted. At most—and this stretches a pessimistic scenario pretty far—maybe a half dozen institutions would have been on the edge of a failure line.[43]

Finally, Chairman Isaac of the FDIC made a definitive statement that: "I have never predicted and this agency has never predicted the number of banks that would have failed as a result of a deposit payoff in Continental. . . . We are not about to make the number public because it is not a number that you can place any great degree of confidence in."[44]

Beyond the analysis of the potential contagion that would or would not flow from a Continental failure, the hearings saw what was likely the start of the widespread use of the phrase "too big to fail":

**Chairman St. Germain.** Mr. Conover, where does Continental Illinois rank in size among the banks of the United States of America? Is it 11th, 10th, 9th, 8th?

**Mr. Conover.** It seems to be moving.

---

43. Inquiry, 396 ("Chairman St. Germain. [T]he domino theory has been floated, suggesting that 75 or more banks would have failed had the regulators not staffed the bucket brigade. In fact, the regulators briefed Members of both the House and the Senate in July and used the domino theory as the centerpiece of their contention that 'we had no choice.' Variations on the theme have been repeated time and again in major publications. Unless one assumes that all the assets of Continental—and they were considerable—would have been vaporized overnight and that the entire support mechanisms of the regulatory system would have disappeared, the numbers are nothing less than absurd. Unless they are more incompetent than we suspect, the agencies knew full well that the domino theory was concocted. At most—and this stretches a pessimistic scenario pretty far—maybe a half dozen institutions would have been on the edge of a failure line."). Inquiry, 446 ("Chairman St. Germain. Your chart indicates how many banks with greater than 99.4 percent of their assets [sic—should be capital] in Continental would have probably failed? Mr. Dugger. The chart indicates that there would be six banks. Chairman St. Germain. As contrasted to the testimony last week of 66. Mr. Dugger. Yes.").
44. Inquiry, 471–73.

**Chairman St. Germain.** Where was it?

**Mr. Conover.** It was eighth, approximately. . . .

**Mr. Wylie.** You have 11 multinationals?

**Mr. Conover.** Right.

**Chairman St. Germain.** All right. Ever see this fellow who is painting himself into that corner? . . . You are painting yourself into a corner because my question now is: Can you foresee, in view of all the reverberations internationally that you described, had Continental Illinois been allowed to fail, and all those people out of work and all those corporations out of money and all those other banks that would have failed, in view of that, can you ever foresee one of the 11 multinational money center banks failing? Can we ever afford to let any of them fail?

**Mr. Conover.** The answer to that, Mr. Chairman, is that we have got to find a way to. In order— . . . to have a viable system . . .

**Mr. McKinney.** Mr. Chairman, let us not bandy words. We have a new kind of bank. It is called "too big to fail." TBTF, and it is a wonderful bank.[45]

## Continental Illinois—Addressing the Policy Issues

The FDIC, the OCC, and the Federal Reserve all misdiagnosed the problems at Continental in identifying it as a crisis of liquidity, as opposed to one of both liquidity and capital weakness, and thus they predicted that there was a low likelihood that the FDIC would sustain a loss. Both Chairman Isaac and Comp-

---

45. Inquiry, 299–300. Inquiry, 575 ("Mr. Patman. Let's go to any of the top 11 largest banks. Mr. Isaac. There is no point in talking about those. Mr. Patman. They are going to be saved because they meet the test of essentiality? Mr. Isaac. I didn't say that. Mr. Patman. Well, I am asking you then. Mr. Isaac. I would not make a prediction on that. Mr. Patman. You wouldn't. Mr. Isaac. No. Mr. Patman. You think there may be one of those 11 banks that would not meet that test, and therefore would not be saved? Mr. Isaac. I didn't say that either. . . . Mr. Patman. We are all concerned that you are letting these large depositors in Seminole, TX [sic] receive only 55 percent of their excess over $100,000; and yet, you are taking the Federal Government and putting it into Continental Illinois and giving all those depositors all of their money back . . . the problem is that some of the depositors in the Nation may get the idea that the only way they can really safely place a deposit of over $100,000 is in one of the large money center banks, such as Continental Illinois. . . .").

troller Conover were confident that the problems at Continental were liquidity-related and not solvency-related.[46] Federal Reserve Board Chairman Volcker in separate testimony also argued that liquidity was at issue, not insolvency, and that Continental was a solvent institution.[47] Continuing with the line of intervention in Franklin National Bank, the lines blurred between the Federal Reserve's funding role and the FDIC's. Chairman Isaac pointed out that it was possible that the Continental rescue effort would earn the FDIC a profit, although during testimony he gave a range of estimated costs that recognized the possibility that there could be a loss.[48] Alternatively, the Congressional Budget Office (CBO) estimated a much higher likelihood of a loss in resolving Continental, with possibilities ranging from a gain of $200 million to a loss of $3.8 billion. The final loss on Continental was ultimately totaled at $1.1 billion, which was slightly higher than the range offered by Chairman Isaac and within the wider range of the CBO estimate.[49] This fact shows that Continental was in fact insolvent. Although this is a singular estimate of bank resolution costs, what it reveals is

46. Inquiry, 298 ("Mr. Hubbard. Was Continental solvent? Mr. Conover. It was and is."). Inquiry, 479 ("Mr. Isaac. The bank is not broke. It was not then; it is not now."). Inquiry, 396 ("Chairman St. Germain. At times, the multibillion dollar bailout has been described as virtually cost-free.").

47. Hearings Before the Committee on Banking, Housing, and Urban Affairs, United States Senate, 98th Congress, July 25 and 31, 1984, 120 [hereinafter Volcker July 1984 Testimony] ("Normally, a high value is placed on maintaining banking services regardless of the size of the bank, consistent with minimizing the cost to the insurance fund. Continental, however, was not insolvent and the shareholders maintain an equity investment with a book value of about $800 million.").

48. FDIC Chairman Isaac predicted that the ultimate cost of resolving Continental Illinois would be between a gain of $1 billion and a loss of $1 billion with the most likely scenario that the FDIC would break even, while the comparative cost of a liquidation was $500 million. Inquiry, 570, 572. However, these estimates were not fully documented. See Inquiry, 573. Inquiry, 595. Letter from William Isaac, Chairman FDIC to Chalmers Wylie, Ranking Minority Member, October 12, 1984 ("Indeed, as I pointed out at last week's hearing, it is possible that the FDIC will earn a profit from the Continental rescue effort").

49. Inquiry, 400 (CBO Estimate). Also see Inquiry, 570. Inquiry, 397 ("Chairman St. Germain. Unfortunately, FDIC's liquidation and bailout estimates often have a way of growing after the initial optimistic projections."). FDIC, "Continental Illinois and Too Big to Fail," Chapter 7 in *History of the 80s*, 245.

that the agencies that are responsible for overseeing a bank may be conflicted in making an estimate of its ultimate costs, whereas a more independent source, such as the CBO, might be a better source for such cost estimates. What it also reveals is the slow transformation of OBA from a program that predominantly resolved small banks at a zero cost to the FDIC to a program that resolved large banks at a great cost to the FDIC.

Closely related to the issue of the cost of resolving Continental is the issue of how long the process would take to pass the bank back into the private sector. Comptroller Conover argued that the intent was to pass Continental back to the private sector as soon as possible, but he speculated that the bank could be disposed of within a couple of years once it returned to profitability.[50] Again, the prediction at the hearing was optimistic, as Continental returned to status as a fully privately owned bank in 1991, a full seven years after the resolution plan was put in place in 1984. In August 1994 Bank of America bought Continental.

Another policy challenge presented by Continental, and an issue that ultimately was the focus of further hearings in the early 1990s, was the notion that a bank could be "too big to fail." In particular, the hearing focused on the inequities of bailing out a large, international bank like Continental through OBA, while at the same time allowing smaller banks to be resolved through closed bank transactions. This sentiment was best summarized by Congressman Leach in questioning Comptroller Conover:

> But the question remains whether there is any justice in it. Can you, as
> Comptroller of the Currency, tell us explicitly whether in your view the

---

50. Inquiry, 311 ("Mr. Vento. How long will it be before the nationalization of this bank is concluded? How many years into the future are we going to have this 80 percent stock in this bank? Mr. Conover. It is hard to say. Here is what I think has to happen. First of all, obviously, the stockholders need to approve the deal. Then the bank has to get back on its feet in a way that will attract the marketplace back to it. It has to start reporting quarter to quarter profits. It ought to be positioned to do that because we positioned that way. Then it is a question of how many quarters of profitable operations have to pass until it makes sense. . . . The intent is to return the bank to private ownership as soon as possible. Mr. Vento. Can you give us any type of timeframe at all, Mr. Conover? Mr. Conover. I think you are going to get different judgments on this. You ought to ask Bill Isaac for his and Paul Volcker for his. As far as I am concerned, I think we are looking at a couple of years of reported profits before it would make any sense. . . .").

big, as well as the small, have the right to fail, whether there are absolute guarantees that exist today for big banks that don't apply to small? And don't you see irony in the notion that, if a big bank gets into trouble and oversteps itself, punishment will be in the form of Federal aid to compete against rivals as a quasi-nationalized entity?

Conover, as well as Isaac in separate testimony, assured questioners that the system had to be changed to let a large bank like Continental fail.[51]

Flowing from the issue of "too big to fail" is the uncertainty created in the marketplace as market participants try to guess which institutions will be granted a bailout and which institutions will not. Congressman Patman summarized this uncertainty in asking a question of FDIC Chairman Isaac as he compared the decision to bail out Continental with all those other decisions regarding problem banks, including a bank failure he cited in his home state of Texas: "Do you see the problem that people have in wondering what your decision is going to be the next time and how to protect themselves and be prudent investors? . . . Will you provide us with any objective test you can think of that the committee or the Congress, or anyone else, could apply to banks of various sizes in determining which banks would likely be subject to being bailed out as Continental Illinois was bailed out, as opposed to what happened in Seminole [a small bank in Texas that failed]?" Isaac responded: "Sure, I think there is a perception that big banks are safer for uninsured depositors than smaller banks. And I think that this is something that we have got to deal with. We have got to change that perception, and we have offered some suggestions on how we might do that."[52]

---

51. Inquiry, 293, 297, 299, 305. ("Mr. Conover. Is there equity today between small and large banks? Mr. Leach. Yes. Mr. Conover. I have said I think that there ought to be, which I think implies that there probably isn't at present. Mr. Leach. Second, are you implying that a large bank does not have the right to fail? That the repercussions are too great? . . . As you know, this Congress and this committee had major jurisdiction over a lot of this, funded legislation to bailout Lockheed, Chrysler, New York City. . . . Do you see any irony or unseemliness in the fact that the only approval required for the regulator's approach is a formal vote of the shareholders of the bank to be saved rather than from the taxpayers and their representatives in Congress who may have to foot the bill."). Inquiry, 559.
52. Inquiry, 587.

The Congress and the agencies grappled with additional policy issues, many of which they are still grappling with today, as will be evident in the later discussion of the 2000s crisis.

One issue was a suggested solution by Congressman Leach of subjecting the larger, multinational banks to higher capital ratios: "Regulators clearly missed the mark. If Continental had had the same capital ratios as the superintendent of Iowa Banking requires for Iowa banks, that is, about 9 percent, and if the bank had been forced to write off loans as rigorously as the superintendent of Iowa banks requires of Iowa banks, this problem would not have existed. The way you solve the solvency problem is with more capital and this committee certainly feels very strongly that the private sector solution is better than the public and that is that the regulators simply demand that banks have a stronger capital base."[53] Capital requirements were ultimately amended as part of the Federal Deposit Insurance Corporation Improvement Act of 1991.

Another issue was a focus on the extent that foreign banks were benefited in the process of paying off Continental creditors as noted in the comments of Comptroller Conover regarding the potential for an "international financial crisis" and that funding had been provided "from the Far East through Europe."[54] Half of deposits of Continental were foreign-based.[55]

A third issue was the potential for moral hazard and a lack of market discipline and what it meant for future financial crises. Obviously, the cost estimates discussed previously did not take into account any moral hazard costs flowing from the interventions:

---

53. Inquiry, 306–7. See also Representative Jim Leach, "Statement Before the Subcommittee on Financial Institutions, Supervision, Regulation and Insurance," September 18, 1984, 3, cited in Inquiry, 87.

54. Inquiry, 288, 291.

55. Inquiry, 287 ("Mr. Vento. Yes, OK. I just would like to know for the record, Mr. Conover, how many foreign banks were involved and what percentage of assets were affected by the actions taken in terms of the agreement? That is a question I asked yesterday and your examiners couldn't answer it. So I want to again state it for the record."). Responses were provided for the record, Inquiry 365 (34.7 percent average foreign loans as a percent of average total loans; 49.5% average foreign deposits as a percent of average total deposits as of March 31, 1984; average number of foreign banks with deposits in Continental, May 1984, was 461).

**Mr. Patman.** What market discipline will investors of over $100,000 in Continental Illinois experience?

**Mr. Isaac.** None.

**Mr. Patman.** Regardless of the amount of their deposits.

**Mr. Isaac.** That is right.[56]

Fourth, some members of the Committee considered the compensation packages for Continental executives as excessive. At one point, Chairman St. Germain derisively referred to the "fellow at Continental, [who] is making a half million."[57]

Finally, in testimony a few weeks after the bailout of Continental, Paul Volcker, then-chairman of the Federal Reserve, had this telling exchange with Senator Riegle about the potential for creating an infinite "safety net" of government guarantees:

> **Sen. Riegle:** I just hope that we don't leave the impression that the safety net is infinite in size and we can take any number of failures at once, because I don't think you believe that and I know I don't believe that and that's what I'm trying to get at. That's the question: the degree to which we are finding ourselves with an overall buildup of pressures on the structure which we'd better pay attention to and which we would be well advised to eliminate rather than gloss over them.
>
> **Chairman Volcker:** To the best of my knowledge, there were characteristics of the Continental Illinois Bank that were unique.[58]

---

56. Inquiry, 513.

57. Inquiry, 377. The reference is apparently to chairman Roger A. Anderson, who was one of the highest-paid bankers in the United States during the early 1980s ("Chairman St. Germain. On page 7 of your statement, you say, 'This is easy. Continental management announced its decision in 1976 to become one of the top three banks lending to corporate America.' For the record, I wish you could tell me what motivates these people to want to be the top 10 or top 5 or top 3? You know go, go, go. Is there something hyper about these people that they want to be the biggest? I talked to some of the English bankers. The fellow who heads up Barkleys [sic], a big institution, he makes I think maybe $80,000 a year. He is underpaid, like you. The fellow at Continental, he is making a half million. Maybe that is one of the motivations.").

58. Volcker July 1984 testimony, 111.

### Continental Illinois—The Immediate Legislative Response

The short-term legislative response after the Continental hearings was to address what Chairman Isaac of the FDIC called the "administrative problem." In the Competitive Equality Banking Act of 1987, the FDIC sought and received the power to create a so-called "bridge bank."[59] This gave the FDIC power to address a Continental-size institution (one of great size or complexity) by allowing it to fail and creating a bridge bank to hold its good assets and a portion of its liabilities until it could be sold off or paid out in a more orderly manner.[60] This would allow the FDIC to "bridge the gap between the failed bank and a satisfactory purchase-and-assumption or other transaction,"[61] precisely what was needed in the Continental situation. The FDIC could use this power when the cost of a bridge bank was less than the cost of liquidating, when the operation of the bank was essential, or when it was in the best interest of the depositors of the failed bank and the public.[62]

### Other OBA and Bailout Transactions

Beyond the Continental case that received so much attention, the broadened authority of the OBA power from Garn–St. Germain allowed the FDIC to provide OBA to 129 banks from 1982 to 1992, most of them in the BancTexas and First City Bancorporation transactions.[63] The assistance provided for those two bank groups was particularly troublesome, as shortly after both received assistance, the projections to return the banks to viability were too optimistic, as they faltered again and ultimately failed and were resolved on a closed-bank basis. Bank of New England was another very large institution resolved, and

---

59. Jack Reidhill, Lee Davison, and Elizabeth Williams, "The History of Bridge Banks in the United States," FDIC, 2005, 12–13, 15–17.
60. FDIC, "Continental Illinois and Too Big to Fail," Chapter 7 in *History of the 80s*, 254. United States Code Congressional and Administrative News, 100th Congress, 1st Session, 1987, Vol. I, 101 Stat. 623.
61. United States Code Congressional and Administrative News, 100th Congress, 1st Session, 1987, Vol. II, 550 (Senate Report No. 100–19, 60).
62. Section 503(a)(3)(i)(1), Competitive Equality Banking Act.
63. *Managing the Crisis*, 153.

at the urging of the Federal Reserve and the Treasury Department, the FDIC bailed out uninsured depositors and most creditors. This treatment caused a backlash in Congress, and ultimately limits were placed on similar efforts going forward.[64]

After the wave of OBA transactions during the 1980s, those inside and outside the FDIC came to scrutinize the downsides of its use. After Chairman Isaac's term came to an end, he began to have second thoughts about the resolution of Continental: "I wonder if we might not be better off today if we had decided to let Continental fail, because many of the large banks that I was concerned might fail have failed anyway. And they probably are costing the FDIC more money by being allowed to continue several more years than they would have had they failed in 1984."[65] FDIC staff also had their own critiques that OBA:

- was primarily used to resolve larger institutions, so owners and creditors of smaller institutions resented the lack of a level playing field;
- allowed weak institutions to remain open and compete with non-assisted institutions;
- increased moral hazard, because if a bank believes it will be bailed out when it gets into trouble, it will take on more risk than if OBA is not available;
- often benefited shareholders and uninsured creditors of the institution over a closed-bank approach, thus reducing market discipline;
- may be more costly than envisioned if projections are optimistic, losses are recurring, and a closed-bank transaction is ultimately needed, resulting in a long and difficult process for completing the transaction; and
- was twinned with significant tax benefits to acquirers at a cost to taxpayers that appeared to exceed any financial benefit received by the government.[66]

---

64. Robert DeYoung and Jack Reidhill, "A Theory of Bank Resolution: Political Economics and Technological Change," January 31, 2008, 26.

65. Robert Trigaux, "Isaac Reassesses Continental Bailout," *American Banker*, July 31, 1989, p. 6.

66. These weaknesses have been cited in FDIC documents, including FDIC, "Open Bank Assistance Transactions," Chapter 5 in *Resolution Handbook* (1998), 54–5; also FDIC, Managing the Crisis, pp. 165–66; and Rosalind L. Bennett, "Failure Resolution and Asset Liquidation: Results of an International Survey of Deposit Insurers," *FDIC Banking Review*

## Government-Sponsored Enterprises

Government-sponsored enterprises (GSEs) are quasi-government entities that are privately owned, but possess certain powers or exemptions that are intended to encourage select economic activity and have the implied backing of the U.S. government. For example, Fannie Mae and Freddie Mac, the mortgage GSEs, were created to encourage mortgage lending. The implied backing means GSEs can borrow at more attractive rates than fully private entities.[67]

During the 1970s, Fannie Mae was able to leverage its low cost of funds, which resulted from its status as a GSE, to maintain profitability. Consistent with its mission, Fannie Mae borrowed short term in the debt market and used the funds to purchase long-term mortgages. Starting in 1979, short-term borrowing costs rose dramatically and, by 1981, Fannie Mae had a negative market-value net worth of $10.8 billion, which prompted a bailout to restore its financial standing. In response to the weakness, the Congress and Fannie Mae's regulator the Department of Housing and Urban Development provided limited tax relief and regulatory forbearance in the form of relaxed capital requirements, without making dramatic changes in management.[68] The Miscellaneous Revenue Act of 1982 addressed the Fannie Mae situation by adjusting its tax treatment. HUD also modified the capital ratio for Fannie Mae, allowing them to move from a 15-to-1 capital ratio as prescribed under law to a 30-to-1 capital ratio. These two actions in combination allowed Fannie to overcome their insolvent status over

---

*(footnote 66 continued)* 14, no. 1 (Fall 2001), 12. Examples of banks that were provided OBA and had recurring losses that led to a closed-bank transaction include BancTexas Group Inc. (1987 OBA and closed in 1990), Alaska Mutual Bank and United Bank of Alaska (1988 OBA and closed in 1989), and First City Bancorporation of Texas (1988 OBA and closed in 1992). For more information see FDIC, *Managing the Crisis*, 161–63. For a detailed critique of the First City Bancorporation transaction, see General Accounting Office (GAO), "Failing Banks: Lessons Learned from Resolving First City Bancorporation of Texas," GAO/GGD 95–37 (March 1995).

67. Thomas H. Stanton, *A State of Risk—Will Government-Sponsored Enterprises Be the Next Financial Crisis?* (New York: HarperCollins Publishers, 1991), 161.

68. GAO, "Federal Housing Enterprises: OFHEO Faces Challenges in Implementing a Comprehensive Oversight Program," GAO/GGP 98–6 (October 1997), 21.

time.[69] Freddie Mac, which held relatively fewer of its mortgages in portfolio, did not experience the same financial difficulties as Fannie Mae.

Another area of credit turmoil during the 1980s was the agricultural sector, and the GSE in that industry, the Farm Credit System (FCS), also saw its financial position deteriorate dramatically during the 1980s, leading to another bailout of a GSE. FCS faced problems brought on by the farm price bubble that inflated during the 1970s, in part through the lending programs and encouragement of the FCS. When the bubble burst, prices dropped by more than 50 percent from 1981 to 1986 in many agricultural states such as Iowa, Nebraska, and Minnesota. The Agricultural Credit Act of 1987 created the Farm Credit System Financial Assistance Corporation. This corporation was authorized to issue up to $6 billion of taxpayer-funded bonds to provide capital assistance to prevent the failure of Farm Credit System institutions weakened by losses arising from collapsing farmland prices. Bonds totaling $1.261 billion were issued with 15-year maturities.[70] The legislation was justified based on the "continuing depression in agriculture that began in the early 1980s, but whose costs originated in the inflationary period in the late 1960s and 1970s."[71]

## Forbearance

As noted in the introduction to this section, part of the financial-sector turmoil during this period was due to the many structural changes in the economy

69. Miscellaneous Revenue Act of 1982, Public Law 97–362, Section 102, "Adjustment to Net Operating Loss Carryback Rules for Federal National Mortgage Association." 47 FR 58044. The underlying legislation allows a ratio of 15-to-1, but it allowed amendment to a higher fixed ratio by the Secretary of Housing and Urban Development. The Secretary in 1968 had fixed a ratio of 20-to-1 and in 1969 a ratio of 25-to-1.

70. United States Code Congressional and Administrative News, 100th Congress, 1st Session, 1987, Vol. 5, 2723 (House Report No. 100–295). Bert Ely, "The Farm Credit System—Reinvented and Mission Challenged," American Bankers Association (November 2002), 5. James Bovard, "Farm Credit Quagmire," Cato Policy Analysis no. 122, July 27, 1989.

71. House of Representatives, *Agricultural Credit Act of 1987*, 100th Congress, 1st session, August 28, 1987, H. Rep. 100–295, 53.

and how banks operated. For example, there was a transition from a heavily regulated environment of limits on interest rates paid on bank deposits (Regulation Q) to a more liberalized environment. Additionally, farm-sector problems placed stress on financial institutions. Forbearance was used to get institutions through a difficult period that some argued was caused by circumstances beyond the banks' control. For this reason, management was generally left in place.[72] This is considered a bailout because in the absence of such forbearance institutions would otherwise be declared insolvent and forced to be resolved through closed-bank means. The primary forbearance programs were the net-worth certificate program, capital forbearance program, and income maintenance agreements.[73] Forbearance ultimately increased the cost of the savings and loan crisis because action on closing institutions was deferred. In some cases, institutions were ultimately resolved at greater costs than if they had been closed initially,

---

72. Much of the material in this section is drawn from FDIC, "Other Resolution Alternatives," Chapter 6, in *Resolution Handbook*, 57–62. For information on forbearance regarding savings and loan institutions through the Federal Savings and Loan Insurance Corporation, see Alane Moysich (primary author), "The Savings and Loan Crisis and Its Relationship to Banking," Chapter 4, *History of the 80s*, 167.

73. The net-worth certificate program was passed as part of the Garn–St. Germain Act (Title II). It was developed in the wake of the deregulation of deposit rates. Institutions that lent on a long-term basis for mortgages or long-term bonds in an inflationary environment suddenly had to pay higher rates for deposits in the more volatile interest-rate environment brought about by inflation. Such institutions were allowed to apply for capital assistance. It was primarily for thrift institutions, but banks with thrift-like portfolios could also participate. The FDIC bought the net-worth certificates from participating institutions, but no cash was exchanged. The net-worth certificates were considered capital for regulatory purposes and amortized over a set period of years. See also William M. Isaac, "A Better Way to Aid Banks," *Washington Post*, September 27, 2008. The capital forbearance program applied to institutions with deteriorated capital positions that were otherwise defined as well-managed institutions whose position was not the result of mismanagement, excessive operating expenses, or excessive dividends. Those institutions with concentrations of 25 percent or more in agricultural or energy loans were temporarily exempted from regulatory capital requirements, either by the regulators or through mandates contained in CEBA regarding agricultural banks. Income maintenance agreements were developed to adjust for the effect on large savings banks of deregulation of interest rates. Again, these were institutions that primarily lent out on low-yielding, long-term mortgage loans whose credit quality of the collateral was not a problem.

before forbearance was granted. Given this fact, many have discredited the use of forbearance.[74]

## Turmoil in the Securities Markets

Although there were no bailouts of a major investment bank during the 1980s and early 1990s, there certainly were points of turbulence. The greatest turbulence occurred during the stock market crash of October 1987, known as Black Monday. The Board of Governors responded swiftly to the crash, providing liquidity to the broader financial system, and they did so very publicly in order to support market confidence.[75] This action was a clear indication that the Federal Reserve System had taken on a role in maintaining overall financial stability, beyond the parameters of the banking system. Another response to the crash was the creation through Executive Order of the Working Group on Financial Markets (WGFM).[76] The WGFM was formed to enhance integrity, efficiency, orderliness, and competitiveness of the financial markets and maintain investor confidence.[77] Representatives on the WGFM included the Secretary of the Treasury, who acted as Chairman of the Working Group; the Chairman of the Board of Governors of the Federal Reserve; the Chairman of the Securities and Exchange Commission; and the Chairman of the Commodity Futures Trading Commission.[78] In early testimony shortly after its creation, a

---

74. George J. Benston and George G. Kaufman, "FDICIA After Five Years: A Review and Evaluation," Federal Reserve Bank of Chicago Working Paper 97–1 (June 11, 1997), 7. Emile J. Brinkman, Paul M. Horvitz, and Ying-Lin Huang, "Forbearance: An Empirical Analysis," *Journal of Financial Services Research* 10 (March 1996): 27–41. Congressional Budget Office Staff Memorandum, "The Cost of Forbearance During the Thrift Crisis," June 1991.

75. Mark Carlson, "A Brief History of the 1987 Stock Market Crash With a Discussion of the Federal Reserve Response," Finance and Economics Discussion Series–Division of Research and Statistics and Monetary Affairs, Federal Reserve Board, Vol. 2007–13, November 2006, 17.

76. Executive Order 12631 (March 18, 1988). Some refer to this as the "President's Working Group on Financial Markets."

77. Section 2, Executive Order 12631.

78. Section 1, Executive Order 12631.

representative from the Treasury Department noted that the Working Group viewed "its primary mission as taking collective safety and soundness actions now which would substantially lessen possible systemic dangers to the U.S. financial system if we were again to encounter a severe stock market decline. Consequently, the Working Group's recommendations are key ingredients to prevent stock market declines from degenerating into self-feeding panics."[79]

Another point of turmoil was the failure in 1990 of Drexel Burnham Lambert (DBL), which was one of the most profitable and largest investment banks during the 1980s. DBL pled guilty to felony charges and paid hundreds of millions of dollars in fines while at the same time suffering through a plunge in the junk bond market. The SEC Chairman at the time, Richard Breeden, argued that no investment bank should be considered "too big to fail," and DBL ultimately filed for Chapter 11 bankruptcy after more than 150 years in business, at the time the biggest failure in the history of Wall Street.[80] A bailout was not seriously

---

79. George D. Gould, Under Secretary for Finance, Department of the Treasury, "The Conclusions and Recommendations of the President's 'Working Group on Financial Markets,'" Hearing Before the Committee on Banking, Housing and Urban Affairs, United States Senate, 100th Congress, 2nd Session, May 24, 1988, 18. See also "Review of the Findings of the President's Working Group on Financial Markets; And the Use of Stock Index Futures and Other Recent Market Developments," Hearings Before the Committee on Agriculture, House of Representatives, 100th Congress, 2nd Session, June 14, 1988, and July 13, 1988.

80. For a recent discussion of the SEC's approach during that time see Richard C. Breeden, Former Chairman—Securities and Exchange Commission, Before the Senate Committee on Banking, Housing and Urban Affairs, March 26, 2009, 17 ("As SEC Chairman, I handled the 1990 closure and bankruptcy filing of Drexel Burnham Lambert, then one of the largest U.S. securities firms. We were able to prevent any losses to Drexel customers without cost to the taxpayers in our closure of Drexel. We froze and then sold the firm's regulated broker dealer, transferring customer funds and accounts to a new owner without loss. Having protected the regulated entity and its customers, we refused to provide assistance to the holding company parent that had a large 'unregulated' portfolio of junk bonds financed by sophisticated investors (including several foreign central banks that were doing gold repos with Drexel's holding company parent). Though there were those who wanted us to bail Drexel out, we forced the holding company into Chapter 11 instead, and let the courts sort out the claims. A similar approach would work today for AIG and its unregulated derivative products unit, which could be left to sort out its claims from swaps customers in bankruptcy without taxpayer financing. This approach of stopping

considered, but one DBL executive noted that "What we needed was a pittance, and the Government decided just to let the company go. With a little nudge from the Government, the banks would have put a package together."[81]

---

the safety net at regulated subsidiaries can be very helpful in unwinding failed firms where there are both regulated and unregulated entities at less cost and less damage to market disciplines than excessively broad bailouts."), http://banking.senate.gov/public/index.cfm?FuseAction=Hearings.Testimony&Hearing_ID=081fbcf6–953b-4701-ba03-e354ec6e8514&Witness_ID=32372767–9708–4e65–8575-dccf42243056, and also see "Fighting Geithnerism," CNBC, March 27, 2009, http://www.cnbc.com/id/15840232?video=1075662755. James Freeman, "Fighting Geithnerism," *Wall Street Journal*, March 28, 2009.
81. "Predator's Fall," *Time,* February 26, 1990.

# 6

## After the 1980s Financial Crisis

"They reckoned that the Continental precedent would force us
to cover all company debtors, including them, because we had
no other way to handle such a large institution and would recoil
from closing it down and risking the panic and huge losses that
might occur in the weakened Texas economy. Some of course
argued that no such panic would have occurred, but most public
officials operate under the banner of 'not on my watch' and do
not care to gamble with such possibilities."

—FDIC Chairman L. William Seidman explaining the
"not on my watch" attitude of public officials who avoid a
large bank failure at all costs during their time in office.[1]

---

1. L. William Seidman, *Full Faith and Credit: The Great S&L Debacle and Other Washington Sagas* (Beard Books, New York, 1993), 144 ("The bondholders and creditors of the First City Holding Company were required to agree to take a substantial 'hit.' Requiring bondholders in the bank holding company to reduce their debt holding became the most difficult part of the deal. In Continental Illinois' failure, the bondholders had been protected, even though they were not insured. Most of First City's bonds had been dumped as its troubles became public, and they had been purchased for a few cents on the dollar by Wall Street arbitrageurs. These individuals from the fast-buck society bought the bonds in a bet that they could hold out for nearly full payment on their cheaply bought debt. They knew that if the FDIC failed to meet their price, we might have to close all of First City's sixty-two banks. They reckoned that the Continental precedent would force us to cover all company debtors, including them, because we had no other way to handle such a large institution and would recoil from closing it down and risking the panic and huge losses that might occur in the weakened Texas economy. Some of course argued that no such panic would have occurred, but most public officials operate under the banner of 'not on my watch' and do not care to gamble with such possibilities.").

LEGAL SCORECARD
- Federal Deposit Insurance Corporation Improvement Act (1991)
- Housing and Community Development Act (1992)

THE LATE 1980S and early 1990s witnessed a transition from the reflexive response of bailouts and forbearance. The FDIC took a dimmer view concerning the interests of banks' owners and bondholders than was taken in the days of Continental. As then–FDIC Chairman Seidman put it, "we decided not to be as solicitous of the interests of the bank's owners and bondholders as we had been in the past." This reference to the past was directed to the treatment of Continental's bondholders.[2] The FDIC showed much less of a willingness to use OBA; after using it in 1988 to resolve First City Bancorporation (which was resolved as a closed bank a few years later), the FDIC only used OBA a handful of times to resolve very small institutions. Alternatively, the new bridge bank authority was used to resolve most of the very large failures in the ensuing years, including First Republic Bank in 1988; MCorp in 1989; Bank of New England in 1991;[3] and First City Bancorporation when it failed as a closed bank in 1992.[4] Legislation was passed in 1989 to resolve the hundreds of savings and loans that had failed under the old Federal Savings and Loan Insurance Corporation, and over the course of five years more than 700 institutions were resolved by the Resolution Trust Corporation without resort to bailouts. The advice of the Clinton Administration and former U.S. bank regulators to Japan during its crisis in the late 1990s was to shutter big insolvent banks.[5]

---

2. *History of the 80s*, 254. Also see note 1.

3. Although, as noted previously, uninsured depositors and creditors were bailed out in the case of Bank of New England.

4. For a good summary, see Jack Reidhill, Lee Davison, and Elizabeth Williams, "The History of Bridge Banks in the United States," FDIC, 2005.

5. James Baker, "How Washington Can Prevent Zombie Banks," *Financial Times*, March 1, 2009. David E. Sanger, "U.S. Sees New Villain in Asia Crisis: Tokyo's Leadership," *New York Times*, February 22, 1998.

Failures of banks and savings and loans peaked in 1989, with failures drifting lower on into the early 1990s.[6] After the brief 1990–91 recession, the economy and the financial system slowly began to turn the corner on many of the problems of the prior decade. It was the beginning of what would be the longest economic expansion in U.S. recorded history, lasting a full decade.[7]

## Open Bank Assistance—The Systemic Risk Exception

The legislative follow-through to the 1980s crisis occurred over a number of years, with some of the changes having an impact immediately, such as the creation of bridge bank authority. From the industry, the post-crisis conclusion regarding the bailouts was that the safety net had been broadened too much and that the doctrine of "too big to fail" (TBTF) had to be reversed. One area of particular focus was the inequity of the policy between the treatment of very large institutions, which were often bailed out, and smaller institutions, which were, more likely than not, summarily closed down.

As the Congress began to consider reform of TBTF, Thomas Labrecque, the president of Chase Manhattan Corporation, testified on behalf of a wide range of financial industry stakeholders, including the American Bankers Association, the Association of Bank Holding Companies, the Association of Reserve City Bankers, the Bank Capital Markets Association, the Consumer Bankers Association, and the Coalition for Regional Banks before the Senate Committee on Banking, Housing, and Urban Affairs:

> We must eliminate the notion of the so-called "too big to fail" policy under which the very largest banks are given de facto 100 percent protection of all deposits. Such a policy is inconsistent with the original intent of deposit insurance and is unfair to smaller banks. Furthermore, big bankers neither want it nor need it. We should allow insurance only of deposits up to $100,000. The original law was designed to protect the

6. FDIC, Failures and Assistance Transactions, Number of Institutions, United States and Other Areas, 1934–2009. See Table 6.1.; *History of the 80s*, vol. 1, 445.

7. NBER, "The Business-Cycle Peak of March 2001," November 26, 2001, http://www.nber.org/cycles/november2001/.

core deposits of the average American, not multiple $100,000 deposits of huge institutions. . . . It would introduce an element of discipline to a system that has become unnecessarily costly and burdensome. It would reduce insurance costs to U.S. banks making them more competitive with foreign and nonbank competitors. Most importantly, it would reduce the contingent liability that U.S. taxpayers would be forced to pay if the system went awry.[8]

During that same hearing, in questioning by Senator Sasser, Labrecque addressed the issue of affiliations between insured depository institutions and securities firms, and emphasized how positive a signal it was that the recently failed Drexel Burnham Lambert (DBL) was allowed to go down without a bailout:

> **Senator Sasser.** What if Drexel Burnham had owned a bank? Would the Fed have rescued the entire company? And I know that, at least in principle, the FDIC only stands behind the bank itself. But, wouldn't there have been an enormous temptation there and a lot of pressure to move in and save the whole structure?
>
> **Mr. Labrecque.** Senator, I would argue that the performance of the Fed and the SEC is very relevant in this situation, because the Fed did have a significant interest here. In this case, it was through the government securities firm. But I think the record shows they didn't bail them out. The record shows that both the Fed and the SEC stood on the sidelines and were willing to let this thing unwind. . . . I think the evidence in Drexel was that the Fed won't jump in. And I think there's more evi-

---

8. Hearing before the Senate Committee on Banking, Housing, and Urban Affairs, Deposit Insurance Reform and Financial Modernization, 101st Congress, 2nd session, Senate Hearing 101–973, April 3, 1990, 54 [hereinafter Deposit Insurance Reform Hearing]. In his prepared remarks, 74 of the same document, Labrecque added: "For market discipline to work, the current 'too-big-to-fail' policy must be renounced. No bank—large or small—should be too big to fail, and no large uninsured depositor should be granted full coverage if the FDIC suffers any losses in resolving the failure. The biggest obstacle to implementing a system incorporating market discipline in the past has been the lack of a resolution framework capable of handling a large bank insolvency in a timely and orderly manner without causing severe disruptions to the financial system. Development of such a framework is a difficult problem—it can now be done. Many of the current difficulties involved in handling a large bank failure are administrative and technological."

dence that too big to fail policy is not a policy that should be maintained and that the system can take it—and did.[9]

Much of the private sector and some in the Congress recognized the need to eliminate TBTF. The government's actions during the late 1980s and early 1990s, allowing large bank failures and DBL to fail outright, showed signs of moving away from TBTF and toward greater market discipline. Given the flaws in OBA, the House of Representatives took particular aim at the FDIC's power of open bank assistance, which granted the discretion to save TBTF institutions. House Banking Committee Chairman Henry Gonzalez sponsored a legislative proposal to bring to an end the TBTF policy.[10]

However, the first President Bush's Treasury Department and the various supervisory agencies were still not willing to entirely jettison the power to intervene when a large institution was on the brink of failure. They seemed to agree generally with the critiques of TBTF, but argued for leaving the option in place to bail out institutions in extreme circumstances. Representing the Bush Treasury, Under Secretary Robert Glauber responded that adjustments were needed, but TBTF had to be preserved in order to protect the financial system and give the agencies "flexibility" to act, using the same term Chairman Isaac of the FDIC had used a decade earlier:

> It is a pleasure to explain the administration's proposal to roll back the Federal Deposit Insurance Corporation's too-big-to-fail policy, which currently results in the protection of all uninsured deposits in most bank failures, particularly large ones. This broad expansion of the Federal Deposit Insurance guarantee has greatly increased taxpayer exposure. It is also unfair to those smaller banks that do not receive this blanket de facto protection. . . . Let me acknowledge at the outset that the administration's proposal preserves the flexibility of the government to protect the Nation's financial system in times of crisis. In rare cases this may result in the protection of uninsured depositors in bank failures. These rare occasions will no doubt raise some of the same questions of

---

9. Deposit Insurance Reform Hearing, 95–96.
10. H.R. 2094 included a proposal to prohibit the FDIC from protecting uninsured depositors beginning in 1995.

unfairness and taxpayer exposure as today's policy of routinely protecting most uninsured deposits. But a policy that risks our financial system to avoid an exceptional case of "unfairness," would be dangerous and irresponsible, in my view.[11]

As detailed in Under Secretary Glauber's testimony, the proposed new approach would only allow TBTF-type interventions under the so-called "systemic risk exception" (SRE). Glauber argued that the dramatic increase in accompanying transparency and accountability that would be a mandate for such an invocation of the SRE would assure that the power would be used only in the rarest of circumstances:

> While systemic risk could still be used as a reason to protect uninsured depositors, the Administration's proposal includes new procedures to make this a much more visible and accountable determination—which we believe will help limit its use to rare instances of genuine systemic risk. The FDIC would not be permitted to factor systemic risk into its selection of a resolution method. Rather, the determination of systemic risk would be reserved to the Federal Reserve Board and the Treasury Department acting jointly, but in consultation with the Office of Management and Budget and the FDIC. Upon such a determination, these agencies could direct the FDIC to provide insurance coverage for all depositors or take other appropriate action to lessen risk to the system. The Federal Reserve is responsible for financial market stability, and because government action could require Federal Reserve discount window loans, it ought to be formally involved in systemic risk decisions. Also, since the Administration is directly accountable to the taxpayer, the Treasury and OMB have a legitimate role to play in this determination. By broadening the decision-making in this way, both government flexibility and accountability can be achieved. Furthermore, we think that lodging this decision at the highest levels of government with high

---

11. "Economic Implications of the 'Too Big to Fail' Policy, Hearing Before the Subcommittee on Economic Stabilization of the Committee on Banking, Finance and Urban Affairs, House of Representatives," 102nd Congress, 1st Session, May 9, 1991, Serial No. 102–31 [hereinafter TBTF Hearing], 6–7.

visibility will mean that uninsured depositors are protected much less often.[12]

Testifying alongside Glauber, FDIC Chairman Seidman showed clear skepticism that such an approach would be much different from the then-existing system and the most recently concluded round of bailouts, including Continental Illinois: "I don't think the proposals that are now before you in the administration bill are going to make any difference in 'too big to fail.' . . . So in my view, the proposals before you insofar as the fears of the small banks are concerned cannot be very comforting."[13] As highlighted by Seidman during his testimony, the changes inherent in such an approval process were not very different from the past circumstances, as the Board of Governors of the Federal Reserve and the Department of the Treasury were in agreement on past OBA interventions, so it was difficult to argue that such a mandate would somehow materially address the TBTF problem. Seidman argued for the creation of a "fund available which they can use" and argued for "constructive ambiguity as to who will be too big to fail" and that "too big to fail should be administered and paid for by the administration in power, after consultation with other regulators."[14] The other bank regulators testifying at the hearing, Comptroller of the Currency Robert Clarke and Governor John LaWare of the Board of

---

12. Testimony of the Honorable Robert R. Glauber, Under Secretary of the Treasury, Before the Subcommittee on Economic Stabilization of the Committee on Banking, Finance, and Urban Affairs, May 9, 1991, 6. Also, TBTF Hearing, 107.

13. TBTF Hearing, 19 ("I have been there all four times. I have spoken with all the other —well, Mr. Clarke is on our board and has been a part of it. We have always spoken with the Fed. They have attended the meetings, they have supported it all four times. We have spoken to the Treasury about it, although they have not necessarily given us their OK. I can tell you that in the last one, the Bank of New England, I told the Treasury that if the administration believed that we should not support the Bank of New England with coverage of uninsured depositors, I would vote for that because I thought it was a public policy question that ought to be decided by the administration.") TBTF Hearing, 35 ("I don't see how it makes too-big-to-fail decisions different than they have been. It makes it easier because the decision is made by the Fed and Treasury, but they can charge it to the FDIC, whereas, if we make the decision, we have to pay for it. I find it difficult to see how in practice it will be more difficult. Beyond that those two organizations have participated in every one of these transactions.").

14. TBTF Hearing, 4, 19.

Governors of the Federal Reserve, argued in support of the Bush Administration's proposal.[15] The GAO representative echoed these comments.[16]

During a hearing panel after the Treasury, FDIC, Fed, OCC, and GAO testified, George Kaufman questioned the logic of the agencies' arguments that systemic risk was evident from recent runs on banks:

> I document that systemic risk is today a phantom issue. It is a scare tactic. . . . The runs on Continental Bank in 1984, the large Texas banks in 1987–1989, and the Bank of New England in 1990–1991 were rational runs on economically insolvent institutions that moved funds not into currency to start systemic risk, but to safer banks. The delayed resolutions by the regulators did little more than increase FDIC losses substantially. The small depositors are the only ones you need to worry about because they are the only ones who could run into currency. The big depositors can't. The only way that systemic risk, if there is such a thing, can occur

---

15. TBTF Hearing, 5, 9–11. Clarke called the Treasury proposal "a reasoned and balanced approach to the issue in a legislative package that would narrow the circumstances under which coverage of uninsured depositors would be provided, in large part by strengthening supervisory standards and by stressing the importance of equity capital." It should be noted that the Office of the Comptroller is a bureau of the Treasury Department. LaWare testified that "it is appropriate to invoke too big to fail only in cases of clear systemic risk." He further clarified that "[b]y systemic risk, I mean the possibility that financial difficulties at a single very large bank or even a small number of banks could spill over to many more financial institutions. Practical situations representing true systemic risk are rare. Unfortunately, the specific considerations relevant to such determinations vary over time with, for example, the underlying strength of the financial system itself. The board endorses reforms that would foster a stronger and more resilient banking system. The goal should be a system in which even if a very large bank failed, the strength of other institutions would be sufficient to limit the potential for systemic risk." Finally, he added that "[t]he board believes that it should have a role in determining when systemic risk exists. As the nation's central bank, The Federal Reserve has responsibilities for the health of the domestic and international payments and financial systems. Thus, the Federal Reserve has both the perspective and the expertise that are useful for evaluating the systemic risk implications of a given crisis or imminent bank failure."

16. TBTF Hearing, 39 ("I think we have to maintain the too-big-to-fail policy under certain circumstances. A problem with the bill as we see it, therefore, is that it seems to repeal too-big-to-fail altogether. We support a lot of the comments that the regulators made in terms of concerns that they had with the bill.").

is if there is a run on all banks into currency. So you have to worry about the small depositors.[17]

Unlike during the Depression, where there was evidence of a dramatic drop in bank deposits and a flight to currency, no evidence was presented of a similar effect during the 1980s that would justify bailing out the largest financial institutions.

### Open Bank Assistance—Federal Deposit Insurance Corporation Improvement Act

The ultimate legislative product that came from the debates over TBTF was the Federal Deposit Insurance Corporation Improvement Act (FDICIA). Efforts led by House Democrats continued to push toward eliminating TBTF:

> The provisions of this legislation that require regulators to take action before a bank becomes insolvent, and then to resolve failed institutions at the least possible cost would eliminate the "too big to fail" policy that is currently being followed by the FDIC. Since large banks are not necessarily healthier than their smaller counterparts, the Committee believes the FDIC should not use insurance funds to keep them open simply because of their size. . . . The current cost test contains an exception where the FDIC "determines that the continued operation of such insured depository institution is essential to provide adequate depository services in the community." The FDIC has cited this clause as the legal basis for its too-big-to-fail policy. The Committee deliberately deleted this clause and strongly intends that the too big-to-fail policy is hereby abolished.[18]

However, the final bill that was passed into law was the Senate bill and the changes to the TBTF policy were not materially different from those proposed by the Bush Administration that left TBTF in place:

---

17. TBTF Hearing, 53, 58.
18. United States Code Congressional and Administrative News, 102nd Congress, 1st Session, 1991, Vol. 3, 1909, 1917 (House Report 102–330).

[FDICIA] addresses the too-big-to-fail problem in several ways. First, the prompt corrective action system described above requires bank regulators to act before an institution is in imminent danger of failing at the expense of the deposit insurance system. Second, [FDICIA] requires the FDIC to follow the least cost resolution approach to resolving failed depository institutions. The bill provides a narrow systemic risk exception for those rare instances in which the failure of an institution could threaten the entire financial system. Third, the bill limits the likelihood of such a systemic risk by limiting banks' credit and other exposures to one another. Finally, title II restricts the Federal Reserve Board's ability to keep failing institutions afloat through discount window advances.[19]

To invoke the noted SRE required the agreement of two-thirds of the FDIC Board of Directors, two-thirds of the Board of Governors of the Federal Reserve, and the secretary of the Treasury in consultation with the president. Additionally, the secretary of the Treasury has to document the determination, and the GAO has to review the decision and report to Congress on the basis, purpose, and likely effect of the decision.[20]

---

19. "Comprehensive Deposit Insurance Reform and Taxpayer Protection Act of 1991," Report of the Committee on Banking, Housing, and Urban Affairs, United States Senate to Accompany S.543 together with additional views, 102nd Congress, 1st Session, Report 102–167, October 1, 1991, 45. Change aimed at limiting interbank liabilities, 46 ("Limiting interbank liabilities—Current law permits insured depository institutions to extend credit representing significant portions of their capital to one another. Such interbank transactions create the possibility that the failure of one institution can imperil other institutions—a form of systemic risk. To limit such risks, [FDICIA] requires the Federal Reserve Board, the agency most familiar with the overall state of the payments system, to devise limits on the amount a bank may lend to or deposit with other banks. This provision does not affect the Federal Reserve banks' authority to lend to institutions experiencing liquidity problems."). See 12 USC 371b-2 and 12 CFR 206 (Regulation F).
20. See 12 U.S.C. 1823(c)(4)(G): (G) SYSTEMIC RISK.—(i) Emergency determination by secretary of the treasury.—Notwithstanding subparagraphs (A) and (E), if, upon the written recommendation of the Board of Directors (upon a vote of not less than two-thirds of the members of the Board of Directors) and the Board of Governors of the Federal Reserve System (upon a vote of not less than two-thirds of the members of such Board), the Secretary of the Treasury (in consultation with the President) determines that—(I) the Corporation's compliance with subparagraphs (A) and (E) with respect to an insured depository institution would have serious adverse effects on economic condi-

The parallel implementation of a system of prompt corrective action (PCA) was proposed "to resolve the problems of insured depository institutions at the least possible long-term loss to the Deposit Insurance Fund."[21] PCA was intended to be a framework for early intervention by the regulatory agencies, as it established five capital categories for banks and set forth a laundry list of mandatory and discretionary actions that the regulators are to take as an institution's financial condition deteriorates as reflected in declining capital ratios. As a bank's capital level falls, regulators are supposed to increase the restrictions, supervision, sanctions, and penalties that are applied to a bank and its owners. Ultimately this would work to turn banks around before they became insolvent and limit the exposure of the FDIC to losses from future bank failures.[22]

---

tions or financial stability; and (II) any action or assistance under this subparagraph would avoid or mitigate such adverse effects, the Corporation may take other action or provide assistance under this section as necessary to avoid or mitigate such effects. (ii) REPAYMENT OF LOSS.—The Corporation shall recover the loss to the Deposit Insurance Fund arising from any action taken or assistance provided with respect to an insured depository institution under clause (i) expeditiously from 1 or more emergency special assessments on insured depository institutions equal to the product of—(I) an assessment rate established by the Corporation; and (II) the amount of each insured depository institution's average total assets during the assessment period, minus the sum of the amount of the institution's average total tangible equity and the amount of the institution's average total subordinated debt. (iii) DOCUMENTATION REQUIRED.—The Secretary of the Treasury shall—(I) document any determination under clause (i); and (II) retain the documentation for review under clause (iv). (iv) GAO REVIEW.—The Comptroller General of the United States shall review and report to the Congress on any determination under clause (i), including—(I) the basis for the determination; (II) the purpose for which any action was taken pursuant to such clause; and (III) the likely effect of the determination and such action on the incentives and conduct of insured depository institutions and uninsured depositors. (v) NOTICE.—(I) IN GENERAL.—The Secretary of the Treasury shall provide written notice of any determination under clause (i) to the Committee on Banking, Housing, and Urban Affairs of the Senate and the Committee on Banking, Finance, and Urban Affairs of the House of Representatives. (II) DESCRIPTION OF BASIS OF DETERMINATION.—The notice under subclause (I) shall include a description of the basis for any determination under clause (i).
21. 12 USC 1831o(a)(1).
22. John A. Buchman, "Expensive Bank Failures and Their Implications for Regulatory Reform," paper presented at the ABA Banking Law Committee's fall meeting in November 2009, 4 [hereinafter "Expensive Bank Failures"], http://www.abanet.org/buslaw/committees/CL130000pub/materials/2009/fall/02.pdf.

The changes to FDICIA did nothing to stop the expansion of the safety net, and in fact allowed regulators to follow the same shortsighted decision-making path that had been followed in the past. As predicted by Former Treasury official Richard Carnell after the passage of FDICIA, the lack of substantive change in the FDICIA amendments actually assured future instability rather than limiting it with regard to large institutions as he noted that regulators

> face perverse incentives to forbear and extend the federal safety net. Forbearance means failing to take timely and appropriate action to re-duce the risk an unhealthy institution poses to the deposit insurance fund (e.g., by limiting dividends, restricting excessive risk-taking, or requiring recapitalization). By overextending the safety net, I mean need-lessly shielding an insured depository institution from market discipline (whether by treating the institution as too big to fail or using Federal Reserve discount-window loans to keep it open when it is economically insolvent). . . . The benefits of forbearance (and the costs of stringency) are short-term and easily identifiable. The costs of forbearance (and the benefits of stringency) are long-term and less obvious. . . . Perverse in-centives similar to those fostering forbearance encourage regulators to overextend the Federal safety net. By assuming risks better left to private parties the government heightens moral hazard and the potential for future instability. But those costs are long-term and diffuse, and appear in no reckoning of the government's obligations. Extending the safety net confers immediate benefits concentrated in large financial institutions.[23]

## Unusual and Exigent Circumstances

Under FDICIA there was also a little-noticed amendment to Section 13(3) of the Federal Reserve Act and the power granted back during the 1930s to lend under "unusual and exigent circumstances" to "any individual, partnership or corporation" when it "is unable to secure adequate credit accommodations

---

23. Richard Scott Carnell, "A Partial Antidote to Perverse Incentives: The FDIC Improve-ment Act of 1991," *Annual Review of Banking Law* 12 (1993): 322–23. Richard Carnell is a former Assistant Secretary of the Treasury.

from other banking institutions."[24] This change to the provision, which had not been invoked since the 1930s, was inserted by Senator Christopher Dodd and was adopted without extensive discussion or debate reportedly at the urging of Goldman Sachs lobbyists. The intention of the change was to allow fully secured Federal Reserve lending to securities firms in the aftermath of the 1987 stock market crash:[25]

> [The Senate version of FDICIA] also includes a provision I offered to give the Federal Reserve greater flexibility to respond in instances in which the overall financial system threatens to collapse. My provision allows the Fed more power to provide liquidity by enabling it to make fully secured loans to securities firms in instances similar to the 1987 stock market crash.

### Government-Sponsored Enterprises

In the aftermath of the savings and loan (S&L) crisis and the resulting insolvency of the S&L industry's deposit insurance fund, the Federal Savings

---

24. Section 473 of FDICIA deleted the italicized text as codified under 12 U.S.C. 343: "In unusual and exigent circumstances, the Board of Governors of the Federal Reserve System, by the affirmative vote of not less than five members, may authorize any Federal reserve bank, during such periods as the said board may determine, at rates established in accordance with the provisions of section 14, subdivision (d), of this Act, to discount for any individual, partnership, or corporation, notes, drafts, and bills of exchange *of the kinds and maturities made eligible for discount for member banks under other provisions of this Act* when such notes, drafts, and bills of exchange are indorsed or otherwise secured to the satisfaction of the Federal Reserve bank."

25. Congressional Record, vol. 137, pt. 24, 36129 (November 27, 1991). This comment did not elicit a comment or discussion and the section in the final Act was in a title on "Miscellaneous Provisions" under a subtitle on "Other Miscellaneous Provisions." Also see Senate Committee on Banking, Housing, and Urban Affairs, Comprehensive Deposit Insurance Reform and Taxpayer Protection Act of 1991, 102nd Congress, 1st session, S. Rep. 167, 202: "This clarifies that access to liquidity in special circumstances can be made available directly to a securities dealer to help preserve market liquidity and avoid market disruption." Congress did not invoke this power in what was the first opportunity to act in this regard with the private sector–led intervention of hedge fund Long Term Capital Management in 1998, a process to which the Federal Reserve Bank of New York provided input. The issue of Goldman Sachs lobbyists is noted in *In Fed We Trust*, 161.

and Loan Insurance Corporation, the Congress became concerned about similar contingent liabilities for the government that could be lurking about in the financial industry. This fact, combined with the bailouts of Fannie Mae and the Farm Credit System during the 1980s, led to heightened scrutiny of the GSEs.[26] As in the case of the FDIC's OBA, the entire structure of the mortgage GSEs, from their supervision to their capital requirements and the allowable leverage due to their implicit guarantee, came under scrutiny during a series of hearings in 1991.[27] Some lawmakers and key players in the Bush Administration recognized the enormous potential contingent liability that existed if one or both of these mortgage giants became insolvent:

> **Chairman Riegle.** Debt securities issued and guaranteed by GSE's now amount to $1 trillion. There is little question that taxpayers would ultimately have to stand behind that debt if any GSE were to ever become insolvent. And, in fact, that's exactly what happened 4 years ago when parts of the Farm Credit System did fall apart. . . . Given the Govern-

26. "Legislative Proposals to Ensure the Safety and Soundness of Government-Sponsored Enterprises," Friday, May 10, 1991, Senate Hearing 102–390, 3 [hereinafter "GSE Safety and Soundness Hearing"]. ("Senator Garn. The problem is that, if one of the GSE's gets into trouble, we might not be able to afford to fix it. These aren't unfounded fears. As recently as 1987, we had to provide $4 billion to bail out the Farm Credit System. And, in the early 1980's, Fannie Mae was insolvent on a market basis and losing $1 million per day."). "Government-Sponsored Enterprises," Hearing Before the Subcommittee on the Committee on Ways and Means, House of Representatives, 102nd Congress, 1st Session, May 22, 1991, Hearing 102–22, 4 [hereinafter "House GSE Hearing"] ("Chairman Pickle. It is reassuring that the current analysis indicates that the GSEs pose no imminent threat, and we would like to emphasize that the GSEs pose no imminent threat and we would like to emphasize that. . . . But I need not remind anyone that this condition can change. In the light of the recent multi-billion dollar bailout of the Farm Credit System, the Federal Savings and Loan Insurance Corporation and the Federal Deposit Insurance Corporation it ill behooves this administration or Congress to be complacent with regard to the GSEs. The safety and soundness of financial institutions requires constant vigilance.").
27. GSE Safety and Soundness Hearing, 5 ("Mr. Glauber. Greater leverage results not only in higher returns to the GSE shareholders, but also in potentially greater taxpayer exposure if a GSE experiences financial difficulty."). House GSE Hearing, 5 ("Mr. Russo. The marketplace recognizes that there is an implicit guarantee on these loans and each GSE has a Federal line of credit which it can use if it is in trouble.").

ment's implicit guarantee, it is essential that we have an effective regulatory structure in place to protect taxpayers.[28]

Others who naively or in their own political self-interest saw the GSE structure as a "free lunch" expressed great skepticism that much needed to be done regarding the GSE structure:

> **Senator D'Amato.** In light of these positive reports, I would have expected the Treasury Department to come to Congress to praise the GSE's, not to bury them with legislation that is wrapped in redtape [sic]. It seems as though the Treasury has the solution in search of a problem. Mr. Chairman, our GSE's administer our country's most successful housing programs. Instead of a taxpayer bailout, our housing GSE's bail out taxpayers because they operate without a dime of Government funds. In fact, as taxpayers, GSE's are even paying money into the Treasury. GSE's have been a win/win situation for homeowners and taxpayers alike. Congress should be very careful not to snatch defeat out of the jaws of victory. Now if I might refer to an old adage: "If it ain't broke, don't fix it."[29]

Ultimately, the Congress passed the Housing and Community Development Act of 1992, which had an entire title within it committed to GSEs.[30] The Act set forth a number of findings regarding the status of the GSEs (here defined as Fannie Mae and Freddie Mac), emphasizing that:

- the GSEs have a public mission;
- more effective federal regulation is needed to reduce risk of failure of the GSEs;
- the GSEs currently pose low financial risk of insolvency;
- neither of the GSEs nor their obligations are backed by the full faith and credit of the United States;

---

28. GSE Safety and Soundness Hearing, 2. GSE Safety and Soundness Hearing, 5 ("Mr. Glauber. [T]he Federal Government's potential risk exposure from GSE's, rather than being disbursed across many thousands of institutions, is dependent on the managerial abilities of the officers of a relatively small group of entities.").
29. GSE Safety and Soundness Hearing, 165.
30. See Title XIII, Public Law 102–550. United States Code Congressional and Administrative News, 102nd Congress, Second Session, 1992, Vol. 3, 106 Stat. 3941.

- an entity regulating the GSEs should have sufficient autonomy;
- an entity regulating the GSEs should establish capital standards, require financial disclosure, and conduct examinations; and
- the GSEs have an obligation to facilitate financing of affordable housing.[31]

The Office of Federal House Enterprise Oversight (OFHEO) was created to ensure that Fannie Mae and Freddie Mac stayed adequately capitalized and operated safely. The legislation also addressed the possibility of a failure of Fannie Mae and Freddie Mac as it gave the power to the Director of OFHEO to appoint a conservator for an Enterprise that fell below the standards in the Act.[32] The only exception, as in the case of the OBA systemic risk exception, was for serious adverse effects on economic conditions of national financial markets or on the financial stability of the housing finance market; or if the public interest would be better served by taking some other enforcement action.[33]

31. Title XIII, Section 1302.
32. Sections 1366 to 1369.
33. Section 1367(2).

# 7

## The 2000s Crisis:
## The Fed and Treasury Intervene

"Even if you don't have the authorities—and frankly I didn't have the authorities for anything—if you take charge, people will follow. Someone has to pull it all together."
　　　　　　—Treasury Secretary Henry Paulson, November 19, 2008[1]

"On the administrative side, I served seven years as the chair of the Princeton economics department, where I had responsibility for major policy decisions such as whether to serve bagels or doughnuts at the department coffee hour."
　　　　　　—Federal Reserve Governor Ben S. Bernanke, January 7, 2005[2]

---

**LEGAL SCORECARD**
- Housing and Economic Recovery Act of 2008

---

LIKE THE BOOMING economy of the 1920s before it, the period from the mid-1980s to the mid-2000s was considered an era of economic stability. The consensus was that steady growth would continue. There had been two recessions during this period—1990–1991 and 2001—but they were both mild,

---

1. David Cho, "A Skeptical Outsider Becomes Bush's Wartime General," *Washington Post*, November 19, 2008.
2. Remarks by Governor Ben S. Bernanke, "Panel Discussion: The Transition from Academic to Policymaker," at the Annual Meeting of the American Economic Association, January 7, 2005. http://www.federalreserve.gov/boarddocs/speeches/2005/20050107/default.htm.

lasting a mere eight months each.[3] Then–Governor of the Federal Reserve Ben Bernanke commented on this period of economic stability in a 2004 speech called "The Great Moderation," and he detailed many of the benefits from the newfound stability. In that speech, Bernanke gave much of the credit for this stability to the conduct of monetary policy during the period and he voiced his opinion that the state of monetary policy "makes me optimistic for the future."[4]

Chairman Bernanke held this optimistic view for many years thereafter, despite a number of emerging problems in the economy. In July 2005, when he was serving as the chairman of the Council of Economic Advisers, he was asked about the housing bubble and he noted that the "fundamentals are also very strong" and that "it is fair to say that much of what has happened is supported by the strength of the economy." In response to a question about a "worst-case scenario" with regard to a substantial drop in housing prices, he simply held to the conventional wisdom in noting that "I don't buy your premise, it's a pretty unlikely possibility, we've never had a decline in house prices on a nationwide basis" and "I don't think it's going to drive the economy from its full employment path" and finally that he had "confidence that bank regulators will pay close attention to the loans that are being made."[5]

After he became chairman of the Board of Governors of the Federal Reserve in 2006, Bernanke maintained his optimism and as late as May 2007, in a speech on the subprime-mortgage market, Bernanke proclaimed that "[i]mportantly, we see no serious broader spillover to banks or thrift institutions from the problems in the subprime market; the troubled lenders, for the most part, have not been institutions with federally insured deposits. . . . All that said, given the fundamental factors in place that should support the demand for housing, we believe the effect of the troubles in the subprime sector on the

---

3. NBER, http://www.nber.org/cycles/cyclesmain.html.

4. Remarks by Governor Ben S. Bernanke, "The Great Moderation" (speech presented at the meetings of the Eastern Economic Association, Washington, DC, February 20, 2004).

5. Ben Bernanke in separate interviews with Mark Haines and Maria Bartiromo, CNBC Anchors, July 2005. See transcript at http://findarticles.com/p/news-articles/analyst-wire /mi_8077/is_20050708/economic-analysis/ai_n50527592/. For video see: Ben Bernanke interview with Mark Haines and Maria Bartiromo, CNBC Anchors, July 8, 2005. http:// www.youtube.com/watch?feature=player_embedded&v=9QpD64GUoXw.

broader housing market will likely be limited, and we do not expect significant spillovers from the subprime market to the rest of the economy or to the financial system."[6]

Treasury Secretary Paulson echoed these comments when, in mid-2007, in response to a question on the meltdown in the subprime mortgage market, he noted definitively that "I don't think it poses any threat to the overall economy."[7] Paulson has also begrudgingly recounted a statement he made on several occasions about that time that subprime mortgage problems were "largely contained" and he later admitted with regard to that statement that "[w]e were just plain wrong."[8] With regard to the broader economy, Paulson's analysis was equally flawed. After a $150 billion economic stimulus package was signed into law in February 2008, he believed that it would solve many of the economy's problems and that the United States was looking at a V-shaped recession with an underlying assumption that the economy would bottom out in mid-2008.[9]

Notwithstanding the confident predictions of Secretary Paulson and Chairman Bernanke, the financial system and the economy continued to deteriorate and a recession began in December 2007.[10] The recovery was not a V-shaped recovery, but instead has been one of the longest and deepest recessions since the 1930s, with a very weak recovery. As in the case of the crisis during the 1980s, the crisis that began in 2007 was also many years if not decades in the making. The lead-up to the crisis was a combination of many factors, most of which can be linked to government policy:

- Systematic encouragement of imprudent borrowing and lending, the most obvious of which was overinvestment in housing (through incentives in the tax code, Fannie Mae and Freddie Mac, government agencies such as Housing and Urban Development and the Federal Housing

---

6. Ben S. Bernanke, "The Subprime Mortgage Market" (statement at the Federal Reserve Bank of Chicago's 43rd Annual Conference on Bank Structure and Competition, Chicago, Illinois, May 17, 2007).

7. Kevin Carmichael and Peter Cook, "Paulson Says Subprime Rout Doesn't Threaten Economy," Bloomberg.com, July 26, 2007, http://www.bloomberg.com/apps/news?pid=newsarchive&sid=arhcov9ThQM8.

8. *On the Brink*, 66.

9. *On the Brink*, 87.

10. NBER, http://ww.nber.org/cycles/dec2008.html.

Authority and programs like the Community Reinvestment Act).[11] The most dramatic gauge of this was the effort to increase homeownership, which had stayed in the range of 62 percent to 65 percent for nearly three decades before the extraordinary government efforts from 1993 to 2007 which pushed this level to nearly 70 percent (see Figure 7.1). After the financial crisis this rate has gone back down to 66.5 percent, which is more in line with its former levels;[12]

- Loose monetary policy after the bursting of the technology bubble and the September 11, 2001, attacks, which saw the federal funds rate drop dramatically from more than 6 percent to 1 percent from 2000 to 2004;[13]
- Incentives to become TBTF as demonstrated in the government response to Franklin National Bank, First Pennsylvania Bank, and Continental Illinois in the preceding decades, which led to consolidation in the commercial banking industry leaving a few so-called "megabanks" (Wachovia, Citigroup, Bank of America) to dominate the industry;[14]
- Wide-scale regulatory breakdowns in meeting the goals of the FDICIA and other efforts regarding timely prompt corrective action. These breakdowns range from OFHEO and its oversight of Fannie Mae and Freddie Mac; to the Office of Thrift Supervision and its oversight of IndyMac, Washington Mutual, and the thrift holding company of AIG;

---

11. For an extensive review of this phenomenon with poker analogies throughout see Russell Roberts, "Gambling With Other People's Money," Mercatus Center–George Mason University, May 2010 http://mercatus.org/sites/default/files/publication/RUSS-final.pdf.
12. Dawn Wotapka, "Boom's Home-Ownership Gains Lost," *Wall Street Journal*, February 1, 2011 ("In the fourth quarter of 2010, 66.5% of Americans owned homes, down from 67.2% a year earlier and the lowest rate since the end of 1998, according to the Census Bureau. During the boom, when easy credit made mortgages available with less regard for income or ability to pay, the ownership rate surged to a record 69.2% in 2004's second and fourth quarters and stayed near that level until the recession deepened."). Dawn Wotapka, "Home Ownership Rate Drops to 1998 Level," *Wall Street Journal*, April 27, 2011.
13. John B. Taylor, *Getting Off Track* (Stanford, CA: Hoover Institute Press, 2009) [hereinafter Getting Off Track].
14. See Kenneth D. Jones and Tim Critchfield, "Consolidation in the U.S. Banking Industry: Is the 'Long, Strange Trip' About to End?" FDIC Banking Review 17, no. 4 (2005), 31–61; Edward J. Kane, "Incentives for Banking Megamergers: What Motives Might Regulators Infer from Event-Study Evidence?" *Journal of Money, Credit, and Banking*, vol. 32, No. 3, Aug. 2003, January 25, 2000, 9.

**Figure 7.1.** Homeownership Rate 1960 to 2005

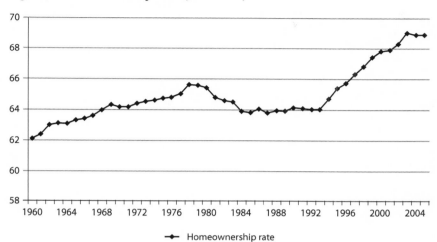

to the oversight of the Federal Reserve over bank holding companies and the oversight of the Office of the Comptroller over banks in the cases of Wachovia, Citigroup, and Bank of America; to the SEC in its oversight of two of the largest institutions that approached failure during the crisis, Bear Stearns and Lehman Brothers; and to the incapacity of coordinating groups like the Working Group on Financial Markets (WGFM) to respond to problem signs in the economy; and

- Panic, overreaction, and inconsistencies in implementation of bailouts by government policymakers concerned that another depression was on the horizon.

Bank failures also increased dramatically in 2008 (Table 7.1). Even as the number of bank failures rose in 2008 and a large failure at IndyMac depleted the deposit insurance fund by $11 billion, in the summer of 2008 Chairman Bair of the FDIC expressed confidence that institutions on the brink of failure would be limited to relatively small institutions:

> **Judy Woodruff:** Are you confident you've got enough to cover the coming big losses?
> **Sheila Bair:** Well, I am. I think—I would be very surprised if institutions approaching the size of IndyMac or bigger than IndyMac would

**Table 7.1.** Failures and Assistance 2008 to 2010

|      | Failures and Assistance |
| :---: | :---: |
| 2008 | 30 |
| 2009 | 148 |
| 2010 | 157 |
| 2011 | 45 |

Data for 2011 is as of mid-June 2011.
*Source*: FDIC, http://www2.fdic.gov/hsob/SelectRpt.asp?EntryTyp=30.

fail. I think we're looking more at the smaller institutions. Again, the number is going to go up, but it's historically going to be very low.[15]

By 2009 the FDIC Fund dipped into insolvency just as it had done during the early 1990s, this time to the tune of nearly <$21> billion.[16] The FDIC had entered a cycle of building up its capital during times of economic recovery and mild recession and then plunging into insolvency during severe financial crises.

A bursting of the housing bubble led to a realignment of market values and a reassessment of the credit environment. Starting in July 2007, the Federal Reserve's Senior Loan Officer Survey revealed what would become a dramatic tightening of lending standards. The Federal Reserve asks survey respondents whether they had tightened lending standards over the most recent quarterly period. The responses reveal either on balance a net tightening or a net loosening of standards for lending. By October 2008 an extraordinary 85 percent of survey respondents noted they had tightened standards for lending since the prior survey. This tightening of lending standards was evident for commercial real estate lending even earlier, as the net tightening responses began in mid-2006.[17]

---

15. "FDIC Chief: Most Banks Will Survive Credit Crunch" (transcript), Online News-Hour with Judy Woodruff, July 28, 2008, http://www.pbs.org/newshour/bb/business/july-dec08/banking_07–28.html.
16. FDIC, FDIC 2009 Annual Report, 74, http://www.fdic.gov/about/strategic/report/2009annualreport/AR09section4.pdf
17. For the quarterly surveys of senior loan officers see http://www.federalreserve.gov/boarddocs/snloansurvey/.

Chairman Bernanke of the Federal Reserve, Treasury Secretary Paulson, and FDIC Chairman Bair did not anticipate the problems that were on the horizon, but their response was not unlike that of policymakers in the 1980s. They responded with a blend of bank closings (predominantly for small institutions) and an unprecedented number of ad hoc bailouts (predominantly for large institutions, including the government-sponsored enterprises). The Federal Reserve advanced the intellectual case for the bailouts as it took the lead in the first of these bailouts, Bear Stearns, and put forth the most effort in justifying those bailouts that followed. Treasury supported the efforts of the Federal Reserve and took the intellectual lead in the instances that required new legislation: the bailout of Fannie Mae and Freddie Mac and the Troubled Asset Relief Program (TARP). The FDIC held out against bailouts despite apparent pressure for quite some time, but ultimately "acquiesced," in Bair's words, to the bailout consensus in late September 2008 after the bankruptcy of Lehman Brothers and the bailout of AIG. This was despite the fact that the FDIC is self-styled as an "independent" agency that should have exercised its own judgment on interventions, whether they were bailouts or plain vanilla bank closings.[18]

The Federal Reserve also took the lead in developing approaches in responding to the crisis. Beyond the familiar individual financial institution bailouts that received the greatest attention, no fewer than nine novel, broad-based approaches were implemented, including the Agency Mortgage Backed Securities Program; the Term Auction Facility; the Primary Dealer Credit Facility; the Term Securities Lending Facility and Term Securities Lending Facility Options Program; the Asset-Backed Commercial Paper Money Market Mutual Fund Liquidity Facility; the Commercial Paper Funding Facility; the Term Asset-Backed Securities Loan Facility; and the Money Market Investor Funding Facility.[19] An initial question with these creative interventions is which programs are bailouts. As applied throughout this analysis, in the case of a lender of last resort facility that provides funding to a sound institution on good collateral with essentially no

---

18. FDIC, "Who Is the FDIC?" http://www.fdic.gov/about/learn/symbol/index.html ("An independent agency of the federal government, the FDIC was created in 1933 in response to the thousands of bank failures that occurred in the 1920s and early 1930s").
19. Board of Governors of the Federal Reserve, "Usage of Federal Reserve Credit and Liquidity Facilities," December 1, 2010, http://www.federalreserve.gov/newsevents/reform_transaction.htm.

risk or subsidy the programs are not considered bailouts. Alternatively, a program involving extension of funding to an unsound institution is obviously a bailout. Additionally, it is also a bailout if the program involves a sound institution, where either the funding is at risk due to questionable collateral at the time of the initiation of the facility or where a subsidy is involved.

The Federal Reserve also took the lead in enabling and justifying the high level of secrecy involved in the bailouts. Chairman Bernanke is well known as an expert on the history of the Great Depression and he has authored a number of books and studies on it. However, the focus of his research has primarily been on the macroeconomic aspects of the downturn as demonstrated by his description of the Great Depression as "the Holy Grail of macroeconomics."[20] Bernanke has not addressed in detail in his writings the Reconstruction Finance Corporation (RFC), the primary bailout of that period, but sad to say the key lesson he seems to have drawn from its activities is that the government was too transparent in disclosing details about the RFC's operations.[21] This likely explains his secretive tendencies during the bailouts regarding disclosure of the underlying details of the Federal Reserve's transactions. The primary justification offered by the Federal Reserve for this secrecy has been to avoid the supposed stigma that would accompany disclosure of the names of individual financial institutions. So goes the argument, the lender of last resort should be advancing funds freely to institutions during a financial crisis and if there is a stigma attached to such borrowings it will inhibit their willingness to engage in such transactions.[22] However, on this matter the Federal Reserve has only itself to blame. The reason that there is any stigma at all to lender of last resort

---

20. Ben S. Bernanke, *Essays on the Great Depression* (Princeton, NJ: Princeton University Press, 2000), 1.

21. Bernanke's justification during the 2000s crisis for not disclosing the names of borrowers from the Federal Reserve is that the history of the Reconstruction Finance Corporation reveals the stigma attached to public disclosure. Michael Grunwald, "Person of the Year 2009: Ben Bernanke," *Time*, December 16, 2009 ("He's also fighting proposals to identify Fed borrowers, pointing out that during the Depression, borrowers turned down Reconstruction Finance Corporation dollars to avoid the stigma of disclosure.").

22. Olivier Armantier, Eric Ghysels, Asani Sarkur, and Jeffrey Shrader, "Stigma in the Financial Markets: Evidence from Liquidity Auctions and Discount Window Borrowing During the Crisis" (unpublished paper, March 15, 2010), http://www.unc.edu/~eghysels/papers/TAF_DW_stigma_AFA_Mar_15_10.pdf.

transactions is that the Federal Reserve has made the choice to extend financing to institutions that were unsound, thus tainting all those accepting such financing.

## Unusual and Exigent Circumstances— The False Narratives

The first in the string of significant bailouts saw the use of the power of the Federal Reserve to intervene in the case of unusual and exigent circumstances (UEC). This power was nominally used during the Depression, but then lay dormant for more than seven decades. In each instance that the UEC power was either used or considered, a false narrative developed that was inconsistent with the available record.

### Bear Stearns—The New Precedent (March 2008)

> "We're not going to do a bailout, are we?"
> —President George W. Bush two days before the Bear Stearns bailout[23]

> **False narrative:** The clear evidence is that a contagion would have resulted if Bear Stearns was allowed to file bankruptcy.

One of the standing precedents for addressing the pending failure of an investment bank was Drexel Burnham Lambert (DBL), which failed in 1990 just prior to the legislative changes of FDICIA broadening the scope of the Federal Reserve's lending facilities. In the case of DBL, the decision was made to allow it to fail and to unwind it through the bankruptcy laws.

Another precedent was Long Term Capital Management (LTCM), which approached failure in 1998. LTCM was a highly leveraged and very large hedge fund that lost nearly 90 percent of its capital from January to September 1998. However, the leverage of LTCM was not out of line with the leverage of similar financial institutions at that time (see Table 7.2). Supposedly, the failure

---

23. Comment made on March 12, 2008. *On the Brink*, 92.

**Table 7.2.** LTCM, Major Securities and Futures Firms Leverage—1998

| Institution | Leverage Ratio |
| --- | --- |
| LTCM | 28-to-1 |
| Goldman Sachs | 34-to-1 |
| Merrill Lynch & Co., Inc. | 30-to-1 |
| Lehman Brothers Holdings, Inc. | 28-to-1 |
| Morgan Stanley Dean Witter | 22-to-1 |

Ratio of assets to equity capital.

*Source*: GAO, "Long Term Capital Management: Regulators Need to Focus Greater Attention on Systemic Risk," GAO/GGD-00–3, October 1999, 7.

of LTCM posed a systemic risk given the potential adverse impact on other financial institutions. In a refrain that would become a template for scare tactics during the 2000s crisis, Chairman Greenspan set out a dark scenario of what would have happened if LTCM were not rescued:

> It was the judgment of officials at the Federal Reserve Bank of New York, who were monitoring the situation on an ongoing basis, that the act of unwinding LTCM's portfolio in a forced liquidation would not only have a significant distorting impact on market prices but also in the process could produce large losses, or worse, for a number of creditors and counterparties, and for other market participants who were not directly involved with LTCM. In that environment, it was the FRBNY's judgment that it was to the advantage of all parties—including the creditors and other market participants—to engender if at all possible an orderly resolution rather than let the firm go into disorderly fire-sale liquidation following a set of cascading cross defaults.[24]

24. Chairman Alan Greenspan, "Private-sector Refinancing of the Large Hedge Fund, Long-Term Capital Management," prepared testimony before the House Committee on Banking and Financial Services, 105th Congress, 2nd Session, October 1, 1998, http://www.federalreserve.gov/boarddocs/testimony/1998/19981001.htm. Chairman Greenspan's testimony does not cite any details for the FRBNY's estimation of the systemic fallout. The FRBNY is not subject to the Freedom of Information Act.

Banks, securities firms, and futures firms that were LTCM creditors and counterparties failed to enforce their own risk management standards in assessing LTCM's position. They appear to have done this because of the reputation of LTCM's principals and the fact that standards were loosened during what was a record period of economic recovery. The GAO criticized federal regulators for not recognizing the potential systemic threat posed by LTCM. The Federal Reserve determined that rapid liquidation of LTCM's trading positions and related positions of other market participants might pose a significant threat to already unsettled global financial markets reeling from the Russian financial crisis. The Federal Reserve facilitated a private sector recapitalization to prevent LTCM's collapse. Ironically, Bear Stearns was the only Wall Street firm that refused to help rescue LTCM in 1998.[25] In facilitating this transaction, the Federal Reserve took on a role as de facto systemic risk regulator, filling the role because of the existence of what was called at the time a "regulatory gap."[26] This involvement in the late 1990s raises the question of why the Federal Reserve did not maintain this role of de facto systemic risk regulator going forward, either directly or through its role on the WGFM.

### Circumstances Leading to the Stress

As in the case of prior crises, banks that found themselves on the brink of insolvency had taken risks that turned out for the worst. Bear Stearns and Lehman Brothers were major players in the subprime market, and when that

---

25. *On the Brink*, 94.

26. See GAO, "Long Term Capital Management: Regulators Need to Focus Greater Attention on Systemic Risk," GAO/GGD-00-3, October 1999, 3–8 ("Although SEC and [the Commodity Futures Trading Commission] regulate registered broker-dealers and futures commission merchants (FCMs) they do not have the authority to regulate unregistered affiliates of broker-dealers and FCMs except for limited authority to gather certain information. This lack of authority, or regulatory 'gap,' has become more significant as the percentage of assets held outside the regulated entities has grown. . . . It was in this financial environment that Federal Reserve officials deemed the rapid liquidation of LTCM's worldwide trading positions and those of others in the market a potential systemic threat to markets worldwide. As a result, the Federal Reserve facilitated the private sector recapitalization of LTCM by its largest creditors and counterparties (the Consortium)."). ("The Federal Reserve, the lender of last resort for banks and other financial institutions, also has an additional objective of ensuring the overall stability of the U.S. financial system.").

market turned sour Bear Stearns found itself in the midst of a liquidity squeeze. As Treasury Secretary Paulson described it, "Bear Stearns's plight was not a surprise. It was the smallest of the big five investment banks, after Goldman Sachs, Morgan Stanley, Merrill Lynch, and Lehman Brothers. And while Bear hadn't posted the massive losses of some of its rivals, its huge exposure to bonds and mortgages made it vulnerable."[27]

The narrative of the collapse of Bear Stearns in the first chapter revealed a number of themes that would be evident through the 2000s financial crisis:

- Regulatory and supervisory breakdowns;
- A lack of consideration regarding available legal authority;
- Speculation about potential market fallout from failure with no apparent basis;
- Vague public explanatory statements;
- Key unreleased documents;
- Seat-of-the-pants analysis;
- The rubber-stamping of actions by the Board of the relevant agency.

Since Bear Stearns was a securities trading and brokerage firm rather than a depository institution or a bank holding company, it reported to and was supervised by the SEC, not the FDIC, the Federal Reserve, or the OCC.[28] The SEC's supervisory framework is focused on enforcing the federal securities law and regulating the securities industry under a mandated disclosure regime. The SEC also sets mandated capital requirements for broker-dealers.[29] This regime differs from the supervisory framework for banks, which is much more focused on the safety and soundness of commercial banks. The line between the role of the Federal Reserve and the SEC was blurred somewhat by the passage of the Gramm-Leach-Bliley Act in 1999, but other than its presence on the WGFM,

---

27. *On the Brink*, 94.
28. Bear Stearns was supervised by the SEC as part of the Consolidated Supervised Entity Program. "Declaration of Margaret Celia Winter," January 21, 2010, Civil Action No. 09–1263 ESH. at ¶ 10–11.
29. For example, SEC, Final Rule: Alternative Net Capital Requirements for Broker Dealers That Are Part of Consolidated Supervised Entities, August 20, 2004, http://www.sec.gov/rules/final/34–49830.htm.

the Federal Reserve had not previously had a major role in the oversight of investment banks.

### Assessing the Magnitude of the Problem

In the case of Bear Stearns, the Federal Reserve determined that the problems were severe enough that they had become a systemic risk to the financial system. The Federal Reserve judged that this systemic risk was much more serious than in the case of DBL and that explicit government intervention was needed. FRBNY President Geithner noted that the focus of the SEC was on Bear Stearns's operations rather than on the systemic impact of potential bankruptcy: "[The SEC was] trying to catch up and figure out if things were as bad as they seemed, and Thursday afternoon we had our one call and they said, 'We need to wait till the end of the day numbers and see what our numbers are. We'll call you after the numbers.'"[30] At the same time, the FRBNY was independently tracking the financial position of Bear Stearns and its impact on the broader financial system. They were particularly interested in the impact on Bear Stearns's counterparties, especially those classified as large financial institutions (LFIs).[31] This concern about large institutions is in clear contrast to the concern in the case of Continental Illinois about small financial institutions that were connected through the bank's correspondent banking network.

It is not clear precisely what form the systemic risk presented by the failure of Bear Stearns would have taken. Like Continental nearly twenty-five years earlier, which had 2,000 correspondent banks, Bear Stearns also had a network of financial relationships as a clearing unit for many broker-dealers. It had open trades with 5,000 other firms and was a party to 750,000 derivatives contracts.[32] So it is obvious that there may have been losses spread through this interconnected

---

30. *House of Cards,* 59.

31. *McKinley v. Board of Governors,* Bates No. 000008, 000017. Bates numbers are the identifying numbers used by FRBNY in classifying emails under request, in this case at the request of the COP.

32. Harvey Rosenblum, Danielle DiMartino, Jessica J. Renier, and Richard Alm, "Fed Intervention: Managing Moral Hazard in Financial Crises," Economic Letter, Federal Reserve Bank of Dallas 3, no. 10 (October 2008), 8. The Bear Stearns Companies, Inc., Form 10-K, November 30, 2007, 80.

network, but as in the case of Continental, the mere fact that there were interconnections did not necessarily translate to devastating losses if the chain of events played out. At the time of the bailout of Bear Stearns and in the period shortly after, the Federal Reserve publicly referred to the supposed systemic risk, but only in vague and speculative terms (see Table 7.3).

The Federal Reserve has been resistant to provide details about either the specific institutions at risk or its analysis of precisely what would have happened if Bear Stearns were allowed to fail. Given that it has been over three years since these events occurred, it is not at all clear why they are unwilling to release the details. What information the Board of Governors has been compelled to release focuses on:[33]

- The impact on the credit default swaps (CDS) market. Buyers of CDS are willing to pay a premium for effectively insuring against a debt default. The buyer of CDS receives a lump sum payment if the debt instrument defaults. Governor Randall Kroszner and a senior staff member from the Board of Governors emphasized that beyond the direct exposures of financial institutions, there was a concern about the turmoil in the entire CDS market if Bear Stearns were allowed to fail given that these types of contracts hadn't really been tested in a crisis previously.[34]

---

33. One issue that should be highlighted is that Bear Stearns was a clearing unit for broker-dealers. This function is not noted in the discussions regarding the systemic risk presented by a failure of Bear Stearns.

34. Deborah P. Bailey, "Re: BS Update," March 13, 2008, 8:52 p.m. ("I do have some of the counterparty numbers and will either send around our [sic] try to walk folks through the numbers. The bigger problem is what would happen to the CDS [credit default swaps] market."); Randall S. Kroszner, "Re: BS Update," email to Donald Kohn, Brian Madigan, Deborah P. Bailey, Roger Cole, and Scott Alvarez, March 13, 2008, 10:14 p.m. ("What will be the impact on the cds market if they file?"); Randall S. Kroszner, "Re: BS Update," email to Donald Kohn, Brian Madigan, Deborah P. Bailey, Roger Cole, and Scott Alvarez, March 13, 2008, 10:57 p.m. ("I think it is not just the direct exposure to BS but the turmoil that this could cause in the entire cds market. These contracts haven't really been tested and the uncertaintu [sic] generated by a filing by a major player could have extreme consequences."); Coryann Stefansson, "Cds," March 14, 2008, 7:39 a.m. ("Top 25 commercial banks held cds worth 14 trillion at 3q07 up 2 trillion from the previous quarter. . . . To my point regarding the perversity of the numbers there are roughly 15 trillion of cds against a 5.7 trillion corporate bond market at the end of 2006. Problem is all buyers and sellers must settle.").

**Table 7.3.** Federal Reserve Description of Systemic Consequences Flowing from Bear Stearns's Failure and Justification for Intervention[1]

"prevent a disorderly failure of Bear Stearns and the unpredictable but likely severe consequences for market functioning and the broader economy"

"likely would have led to a chaotic unwinding of positions in those markets and could have severely shaken confidence"[2]

"a sudden, disorderly failure of Bear would have brought with it unpredictable but severe consequences for the functioning of the broader financial system and the broader economy"[3]

"would have forced Bear's secured creditors and counterparties to liquidate the underlying collateral and, given the illiquidity of markets, those creditors and counterparties might well have sustained losses. If they responded to losses or the unexpected illiquidity of their holdings by pulling back from providing secured financing to other firms, a much broader liquidity crisis would have ensued."[4]

"fragile condition of the financial markets at the time"

"prominent position of Bear Stearns in those markets"

"expected contagion that would result from the immediate failure"[5]

1. General statements consistent and in some cases word for word as detailed in the public statements at the time or shortly after the Bear Stearns failure are contained in Declaration of Coryann Stefansson in support of the motion for summary judgment of the Board of Governors of the Federal Reserve, January 29, 2010, http://www.scribd.com/doc/26302616/Board-of-Governors-of-the-Federal-Reserve-Summary-Judgment-Motion ("Given the prominent position of Bear Stearns in various financial markets, and the vulnerability of those markets in March 2008, the announcement of a Bear Stearns bankruptcy posed the potential for a chaotic unwinding of positions in those markets.").
2. Ben S. Bernanke, testimony before the Senate Committee on Banking, Housing, and Urban Affairs (April 3, 2008).
3. "Key Bear Deal Players Speak Out–Timothy F. Geithner," CNNMoney.com, April 3, 2008, http://money.cnn.com/galleries/2008/news/0804/gallery.bear_stearns_hearing/5.html.
4. Ben S. Bernanke, "Liquidity Provision by the Federal Reserve," Federal Reserve Bank of Atlanta Financial Markets Conference, Sea Island, Georgia, May 13, 2008.
5. Board of Governors of the Federal Reserve System, "Minutes of the Board of Governors of the Federal Reserve System," March 14, 2008 [hereinafter Bear Stearns Minutes].

- The potential exposure of large financial institutions and mutual funds to Bear Stearns, in particular the impact on the market for repurchases, or repos.[35] Repo market borrowing involves selling debt securities such as Treasuries or mortgage backed securities with a promise to repurchase them later, paying interest on the cash that in effect had been borrowed. Investment banks and very large commercial banks are active borrowers in the repo market. The information reveals concern by the Federal Reserve about Bear Stearns's access to repo funding, the consequences to lenders in the repo market if Bear Stearns were to default on a repo and the potential for disorder in that market as a result of a large player's bankruptcy.[36]
- The impact, if Bear Stearns filed bankruptcy, on two commercial bank affiliates and whether they would also fail, one in New Jersey and one in Ireland.[37]

---

35. Deborah P. Bailey, "Bear Sterns Update," email to Board of Governors and Senior Board Staff, March 13, 2008, 2:33 p.m. ("[Bear Sterns] management has indicated that some large mutual fund complexes are expressing concern regarding their exposure to the company via overnight secured funding"); Roberto Perli, "Banks' exposure to Bear Stearns," emails to Brian Madigan, William B. English, and James A. Clouse, March 13, 2008, 6:38 p.m. and 6:35 p.m. ("Coryann Stefansson just called and said that this is the info (still preliminary and probably not super accurate but kind of in the ball park at least) that she has about the exposure of major banks to Bear. The biggest appears to be [xxREDACTEDxx]. Then the major ones are [xxREDACTEDxx] for progressively smaller amounts. She also said that [xxREDACTEDxx] should be on the list, but nobody could confirm it.").

36. See Declaration of Jean Helwege, Exhibit C, in support of Plaintiff Vern McKinley's memorandum of law in opposition to the motion of summary judgment of defendant Board of Governors of the Federal Reserve, 3–6, http://www.scribd.com/doc/28065047 /Exhibit-C-Helwege-Declaration-to-Support-Opposition.

37. Scott Alvarez, "Re: BS Update," email to Deborah P. Bailey, March 13, 2008, 9:01 p.m. ("What about the bank? Can the bank survive its affiliate failing?"). Presumably this reference is to Custodial Trust Corporation, a New Jersey state-chartered bank that was an affiliate of Bear Stearns and is now owned by JPMorgan. Deborah P. Bailey, "Re: BS Update," email response to Scott Alvarez, March 13, 2008, 9:03 p.m. ("Not sure. Will need to look. I did not talk with the FDIC on the bank. do [sic] you know if the SEC did or anyone?"); Deborah P. Bailey, "Re: BS Update," email to Donald Kohn, Brian Madigan, Frederic Mishkin, Kevin Warsh, Randall Kroszner, Rita Proctor, Roger Cole,

Table 7.3 includes a description of a contagion, which brings the analysis back full circle to the analogous case of commercial bank failures during the Depression. Also at that time, the argument was made that contagion would sweep up both well-managed and poorly managed banks. During the Depression, the high level of bank failures led to a dramatic drop in the stock of money. Despite the conclusion that a bankruptcy filing by Bear Stearns would have caused a contagion spreading throughout the financial system, little evidence has been publicly presented to that effect, notwithstanding the fears of the members of the Board of Governors, Board senior staff, and FRBNY staff. As for the market for CDS, contrary to the comments the market actually had been tested. One example of that is in the case of Delta Airlines, and there have been other cases of an unwinding through bankruptcy that did not reveal a mad scramble as envisioned by the Federal Reserve.[38]

As for similar turmoil in the repo market, there is even less of an argument to support that proposition as the underlying collateral can always be sold, and so there is less potential credit risk than in the case of the CDS market. Given the harried circumstances in the days leading up to the Bear Stearns bailout, very little analysis was even undertaken of this issue by the FRBNY. This fact was highlighted in later discussions of the repo activity at Lehman just before the firm filed bankruptcy when FRBNY staff noted that the details of the repo book at Bear Stearns were not even investigated, though a rough estimate made in September 2008 of the size of the repo book placed it between $50 and $80 billion.[39]

---

and Scott Alvarez ("Based on BS global operations, do you know if anyone has talked with the FSA in London? BS also has a bank in Ireland.").

38. For a discussion of bankruptcies for firms that have involvement in the CDS market, see Jean Helwege, Samuel Maurer, Asani Sarkar, and Yuan Wang, "Credit Default Swap Auctions," *Federal Reserve Bank of New York Staff Reports*, 19–21. See http://papers .ssrn.com/sol3/papers.cfm?abstract_id=1407272.

39. Financial Crisis Inquiry Commission (FCIC) Bates No. 155643–47. Email from Meg McConnell "Meeting Tomorrow at 9:00" with attachments dated September 8, 2008. The document notes: "What do we know about conditions in the triparty repo market in September 2008 that we either did not know or that has changed since the situation in March 2008? We didn't/don't know much about Bear's triparty repo book; it was probably about $50–$80 billion, depending on who was talking; it was probably weighted heavily towards MBSs. We know much more about Lehman's triparty repo book; size much larger than Bear."

*Reviewing the Options*

In summary, there is no public record of the deliberations that the Board of Governors went through to choose the option it did, other than a very curt reference in the Board meeting summary: "Board members agreed that, given the fragile condition of the financial markets at the time, the prominent position of Bear Stearns in those markets, and the expected contagion that would result from the immediate failure of Bear Stearns, the best alternative available was to provide temporary emergency financing to Bear Stearns through an arrangement with JPMorgan Chase & Co., also in New York."[40] No other public announcement or testimony shed further clarity on the process.

In the case of Continental Illinois, the FDIC developed an after-the-fact justification in the form of internal estimates of how there would be a domino effect of losses at correspondent banking institutions. There was a similar effort with regard to the FRBNY and Bear Stearns. The key difference is that in the case of the Bear Stearns justification, the summary has not been released by the Federal Reserve.

*The Final Deal*

Although the Board of Governors and FRBNY developed the policy justification for intervention during that singular week beginning March 10, the drama at Bear Stearns was not quite over. The initial structure of the facility was a twenty-eight-day facility, and Bear Stearns's management assumed that they had a few weeks to negotiate a sale of the firm as explained by one Bear Stearns executive: "We're going to get all the money we need. We've got a month to figure out what we want to do next." However, market events on Friday after the announcement of the Board vote were different than expected. After an initial positive burst, the market concluded that the need for the Federal Reserve to intervene was evidence of how bad the situation was. Standard and Poor's, Moody's, and Fitch all downgraded Bear Stearns, and the price of credit default insurance on the firm ballooned. Rather than provide certainty, discussions about the details of the Federal Reserve facility raised new questions. That same Friday, Paulson and Geithner informed Bear Stearns that they had to find

---

40. Board of Governors of the Federal Reserve System, "Minutes of the Board of Governors of the Federal Reserve System," March 14, 2008.

a long-term solution by Sunday night before the markets opened in Asia. Sam Molinaro, Bear Stearns CFO, speculated that all along it was the Federal Reserve's and Treasury's intention to push Bear Stearns into the arms of JPMorgan for the good of the financial system.[41] Secretary Paulson, never one to overstate the case, explained why he was distracted that Friday night at a showing of a National Geographic documentary on the ivory-billed woodpecker: "I'm worried about the world falling apart."[42]

After a weekend of working with JPMorgan, the final terms of the bailout consisted of a $29 billion credit guarantee issued by the FRBNY on a nonrecourse basis, collateralized by mortgage debt, and a subsequent Federal Reserve–facilitated acquisition of Bear Stearns by the commercial bank JPMorgan Chase. The agreement also called for JPMorgan Chase to bear the first $1 billion of any losses associated with Bear Stearns assets.[43] On March 16, 2008, JPMorgan acquired Bear Stearns.[44] The transaction was structured through a vehicle called Maiden Lane.[45] After an initial set of discussions valuing the firm at $2 per share, shareholders ultimately received $10 per share and, as Secretary Paulson correctly summarized it, "The only reason the company had any value at all was because the government stepped in and saved it."[46]

The legal authority for the Bear Stearns transaction came from the expansion of authority under FDICIA as codified in Section 13(3) of the Federal Reserve

---

41. *House of Cards,* 79, 84, 88–89, 98–99.

42. *On the Brink,* 106.

43. FRBNY, "Summary of Terms and Conditions Regarding the JPMorgan Chase Facility," March 24, 2008. JPMorgan Chase, "JPMorgan Chase and Bear Stearns Announce Amended Agreement," March 24, 2008.

44. *McKinley v. Board of Governors,* Case No. 1:09–CV 1263 (ESH) Memorandum in Support of Summary Judgment Motion of Defendant Board of the Federal Reserve System, February 1, 2010, at 4 n.1.

45. In connection with and to facilitate the merger of The Bear Stearns Companies Inc. ("Bear Stearns") and JPMorgan Chase & Co. ("JPMC"), the FRBNY extended credit to Maiden Lane LLC ("ML") in June 2008. ML is a Delaware limited liability company formed by the FRBNY to acquire certain assets of Bear Stearns and to manage those assets over time, in order to maximize the potential for the repayment of the credit extended to ML and to minimize disruption to the financial markets. Federal Reserve Banks Combined Financial Statements, 2009. Also see http://www.newyorkfed.org/markets/maiden lane.html#.

46. *On the Brink,* 118.

Act. That section allows Federal Reserve Banks "in unusual and exigent circumstances," and when authorized by the Board of Governors of the Federal Reserve System, to discount "for any individual, partnership, or corporation" when it "is unable to secure adequate credit accommodations from other banking institutions." Prior to its use in the Bear Stearns case, the powers under Section 13(3) had not been used for an individual institution since the Great Depression in 1936, although their use was considered in the case of New York City in 1975, among others. The practical effect of this provision was to shift a portion of the risk of loss from creditors onto the Reserve Banks and indirectly onto the taxpayer.[47]

### The Aftermath

A few weeks after the Bear Stearns bailout, the Senate Banking Committee held a hearing with invitations extended to Secretary Paulson, Chairman Bernanke of the Board of Governors, FRBNY President Geithner, and Chairman Cox of the SEC. Secretary Paulson was traveling, so his deputy Robert Steel testified in his absence. Senator Dodd started off the hearing in dramatic fashion when he noted the decisions were made during a brief period of "96 hours" during which the major agencies "took dramatic and unprecedented actions to stabilize our markets." Then he transitioned into a more populist tone: "Was this a justified rescue to prevent a systemic collapse of financial markets, or a $30 billion taxpayer bailout as someone called it, for a Wall Street firm while people on Main Street struggle to pay their mortgages?"[48]

Much of the hearing focused on the perceived swiftness of the fall of Bear Stearns; the unprecedented action in broadening the safety net to bail out an investment bank; the expectations in the marketplace going forward for future bailouts; and the use of the legal authority codified in Section 13(3) that had not been utilized in more than seventy years. Citing no specific analysis or evidence, then–FRBNY President Geithner set the tone of the hearing, laying

---

47. Walker F. Todd, "FDICIA's Emergency Liquidity Provisions," *Reserve Bank of Cleveland Economic Review* 29, no. 3 (1993, 3rd quarter), 18–20.
48. C-Span, "U.S. Financial Markets and Sale of Bear Stearns," Senate Committee on Banking, Housing and Urban Affairs, April 3, 2008, Senate Banking Hearing [hereinafter April 3 hearing].

out a gloom-and-doom scenario that he said would have prevailed had he and his fellow regulators allowed a Bear Stearns bankruptcy filing to come to pass:

> A failure to act would have added to the risk that Americans would face lower incomes, lower home values, higher borrowing costs for housing, education, other living expenses, lower retirement savings and rising unemployment.[49]

From a public relations standpoint, this description makes more sense than to say the failure may have put brokers with regional securities firms out of work, which was closer to the truth.

As one observer noted, "[f]or the most part, the Fed, Treasury and the SEC held their own against the Banking Committee's interrogation. But they did so largely by defending the Bear Bailout as a once-in-a-lifetime act of extreme desperation, not as the expression of a nascent policy."[50] Many of the members of the Senate Banking Committee, even before the hearing, seemed to have already determined that they would give the Treasury, Federal Reserve, and SEC a passing grade for their actions on Bear Stearns, even without clear evidence of what might have happened in the case of a Bear Stearns bankruptcy.

On June 27, 2008, the Board released the minutes of its March 14, 2008, meeting. Four months after the Board had acted, the minutes only disclose, as set forth above, that a contagion was expected given the position of Bear in the market. Among other necessary findings, the minutes summarily state only that the Board had concluded that "unusual and exigent circumstances existed," and "Bear Stearns, and possibly other primary securities dealers, were unable to secure adequate credit accommodations elsewhere."[51] Nowhere did the Board identify the specific evidence it considered or how it analyzed that evidence.

Another important development in the aftermath of Bear Stearns was the creation of a new facility implemented through the FRBNY, also under the authority of Section 13(3) of the Federal Reserve Act: the primary dealer credit facility (PDCF). Primary dealers serve as trading partners of the FRBNY in

---

49. April 3 hearing, 49:00.
50. Sorkin, *Too Big to Fail*, 70.
51. Bear Stearns Minutes at 2, 3.

its implementation of monetary policy and the list of such dealers includes a number of major investment banks.[52] The PDCF allowed primary dealers to borrow from the FRBNY on a collateralized basis during times of market stress, especially in the repo market. The PDCF operated as a tri-party repo contract between the primary dealer as borrower, a clearing bank as manager of pricing and margins, and the FRBNY as lender. Primary dealers communicated a demand for overnight funds to a clearing bank, usually Bank of New York or JPMorgan Chase. The clearing bank then verified that a sufficient amount of eligible collateral had been pledged and then notified the FRBNY accordingly. Then the FRBNY transferred the amount of the loan to the clearing bank for credit to the primary dealer.[53]

The debate rages on in the aftermath of Bear Stearns whether the institution suffered from a liquidity crisis or a capital solvency crisis. The Federal Reserve still argues that it was a liquidity crisis as it continues to estimate that they will not incur a loss on the transaction to bail out Bear Stearns.[54] During 2010 Chairman Bernanke justified the intervention on that basis:

> [T]o prevent potentially catastrophic effects on the U.S. financial system and economy, and with the support of the Treasury Department, the Federal Reserve also used its emergency lending powers to help avoid the disorderly failure of two systemically important financial institutions,

52. FRBNY, "Primary Dealers List," November 2, 2010. The current list includes BNP Paribas Securities Corp., Barclays Capital Inc., Cantor Fitzgerald & Co., Citigroup Global Markets Inc., Credit Suisse Securities (USA) LLC, Daiwa Capital Markets America Inc., Deutsche Bank Securities Inc., Goldman, Sachs & Co., HSBC Securities (USA) Inc., Jefferies & Company Inc., J.P. Morgan Securities LLC, Merrill Lynch, Pierce, Fenner & Smith Incorporated, Mizuho Securities USA Inc., Morgan Stanley & Co. Incorporated, Nomura Securities International, Inc., RBC Capital Markets, LLC, RBS Securities Inc., and UBS Securities LLC. Lehman Brothers, Bear Stearns, and Merrill Lynch were all deleted from the list during 2008. See FRBNY, "Primary Dealers List—Changes to Primary Dealers List," November 2, 2010.

53. For a detailed discussion, see Tobias Adrian, Christopher R. Burke, and James J. McAndrews, "The Federal Reserve's Primary Dealer Credit Facility," Federal Reserve Bank of New York—Current Issues in Economics and Finance 15, no. 4 (August 2009), 1–11.

54. Floyd Norris, "The Regulatory Failure Behind the Bear Stearns Debacle," *New York Times,* April 4, 2008.

Bear Stearns and American International Group. Credit extended under these arrangements currently totals about \$116 billion, or about 5 percent of the Federal Reserve's balance sheet. The Federal Reserve expects these exposures to decline gradually over time. The Board continues to anticipate that the Federal Reserve will ultimately incur no loss on these loans as well. These loans were made with great reluctance under extreme conditions and in the absence of an appropriate alternative legal framework.[55]

However, the Federal Reserve's own 2009 annual report had an estimate of \$2.2 billion for the ultimate loss on the Bear Stearns transaction which would point to a capital solvency issue.[56] Since the early days of the Bear Stearns transaction, there has been an estimated loss of \$2 billion or more for the intervention in Bear Stearns.[57] That estimate will change over time, but we will not get the final determination on this accounting cost for many years to come.[58] Even if in an accounting sense the Bear Stearns transaction is ultimately presented as

---

55. Chairman Ben S. Bernanke, "Federal Reserve's Exit Strategy," Before the Committee on Financial Services, U.S. House of Representatives, February 10, 2010, http://www .federalreserve.gov/newsevents/testimony/bernanke20100210a.htm.

56. This estimate was not easy to find. It is buried within the nearly 600-page annual report and is not contained in the audited financial statements, but is instead in a table referred to as "Key Financial Data for Limited Liability Companies (LLCs)." Board of Governors of the Federal Reserve System, 96th Annual Report—2009, 190, [hereinafter Fed 2009 Annual Report]. The estimate is described as "the allocation of the change in net assets and liabilities of the consolidated LLCs that are available for repayment of the loans extended by the FRBNY and the other beneficiaries of the consolidated LLCs. The differences between the fair value of the net assets available and the face value of the loans (including accrued interest) are indicative of gains or losses that would be incurred by the beneficiaries if the assets had been fully liquidated at prices equal to the fair value." JPMorgan Chase also absorbed an estimated \$1.2 billion of loss on the Bear Stearns transaction as per the initial agreement on allocation of losses.

57. "The Fed Takes a Writedown," *Wall Street Journal*, October 28, 2008 ("The Federal Reserve—or shall we say, the taxpayer—bet on Bear Stearns' mortgage portfolio is now officially underwater. Last Thursday, the Fed wrote down the value of the portfolio of mortgage debt to \$26.8 billion as of September 30, from \$29.5 billion in June. . . . As of the Fed's latest estimate of value of the portfolio, taxpayers are in for losses of \$2.2 billion.")

58. The equivalent data for year end 2010 just released in June 2011 reveals an estimate of zero cost for Bear Stearns. JPMorgan's loss is estimated at \$114 million. See Board of Governors of the Federal Reserve System, 97th Annual Report—2010, "Key financial data for Consolidated Limited Liability Companies," 133 [hereinafter Fed 2010 Annual Report].

a zero cost transaction, given the circumstances in March 2008 it is clear that it was insolvent during those harried weeks in March 2008.[59] In other words, it cannot be said that Bear Stearns was a sound institution that the Federal Reserve should have offered funding to through its lender of last resort powers.

An important consideration in making the decision to intervene in the Bear Stearns case was whether any thought was given to the impact of the decision on cases of future financial institutions under similar stress, what is often called moral hazard. The accounting approach noted above completely ignores any such moral hazard costs. Peter Wallison, a member of a commission investigating the causes of the financial crisis, described the potential for moral hazard in questioning of Scott Alvarez, General Counsel of the Board of Governors of the Federal Reserve, and Robert Steel of the Treasury Department:

> To me [Bear Stearns] was in effect the original sin, because everything changed after Bear Stearns was rescued. Among other things, participants in the market thought all large firms, at least larger than Bear Stearns, would be rescued. Companies probably did not believe they had to raise as much capital as they might have needed because they probably thought they didn't have to dilute their shareholders because the government would ultimately rescue them, and fewer creditors were going to be worried about their capitalization. The Reserve Fund probably did not think it had to eliminate from its balance sheet the commercial paper it held in Lehman because it thought Lehman would probably be rescued and it wouldn't have to suffer that loss. Potential buyers of, say, Lehman probably thought they were entitled to get some government support, since the buyer of Bear Stearns, JPMorgan Chase, got government support. And finally, Lehman itself has said, Fuld has said that he thought Lehman would be rescued. And so he was likely to drive a much harder bargain with potential buyers. So the decision on Bear Stearns was exceedingly important in analyzing this entire process.[60]

---

59. The reason that Bear Stearns was able to transform itself from an insolvent entity to a seemingly solvent entity was because the government support that was wrapped around Bear Stearns essentially acted as a capital injection that added value to the firm.

60. FCIC, "Hearing on Too Big to Fail: Expectations and Impact of Extraordinary Government Intervention and the Role of Systemic Risk in the Financial Crisis," Official Transcript, September 1, 2010, 119–20.

In response, Alvarez insisted that moral hazard was a consideration in the form of assessing the "cost to the system" of intervening. When Wallison followed up with Alvarez regarding the calculation of the cost, Alvarez admitted the lack of specificity to such an analysis: "There's no single number, or even a series of numbers that you can add up and be certain about. There's a lot of judgment involved."[61]

The Bear Stearns intervention became the precedent that would be drawn upon again and again to justify all manner of interventions. As noted by *Wall Street Journal* reporter David Wessel, Bear Stearns changed the way financial market players assessed the likelihood of a bailout: "In the Great Panic, there will always be Before Bear Stearns and After Bear Stearns."

> ***After Bear Stearns,*** potential buyers of any failing financial institution—Lehman Brothers, Wachovia—would ask the Fed not whether it would lend, but how much it was willing to kick in.
>
> ***After Bear Stearns,*** the debate would not be *whether* the Great Panic would require government bailouts but would instead be *who* would be bailed out and on what terms.
>
> ***After Bear Stearns,*** the line between Fed-protected, deposit-taking Main Street banks and less tightly regulated, more leveraged Wall Street investment banks was obliterated.
>
> ***After Bear Stearns,*** the Fed's elastic interpretation of its power to lend to almost anyone in "unusual and exigent circumstances" would lead the Bush Administration to see the Fed as the lender of *first* resort, rather than its traditional role as lender of *last* resort.
>
> ***After Bear Stearns,*** although not immediately, many members of Congress would realize for the very first time just how much power Ben Bernanke wielded and how much money was at his disposal.[62]

The Bear Stearns bailout also marked the crossing of a line of demarcation between the Federal Reserve's focus on monetary policy and the domain of fiscal policy that had been historically left to more political segments of the

---

61. FCIC Transcript, 120–3.

62. David Wessel, *In Fed We Trust: Ben Bernanke's War on the Great Panic* (Crown Business: New York, 2009), 147–48 [hereinafter *In Fed We Trust*]. Wessel's reference to the "Great Panic" is to the 2000s crisis that began in 2007.

government, such as the Treasury Department. In crossing that line and injecting itself into fiscal matters, the decision had the effect of politicizing the Federal Reserve's operations, which would have a lingering impact throughout the remainder of the crisis.[63]

## Lehman Brothers—The "Disorderly" Bankruptcy (September 2008)

> "The inconsistency of federal government decisions in not rescuing Lehman after having rescued Bear Stearns and the GSEs, and immediately before rescuing AIG, added to uncertainty and panic in the financial markets."
> —Financial Crisis Inquiry Commission summary of Lehman bankruptcy.[64]

---

**False narrative:** The big mistake during the financial crisis was to let Lehman Brothers file bankruptcy.

---

After the Bear Stearns intervention, the precedent was set that the government stood ready to intervene in the case of a firm that, like Bear Stearns, was large, interconnected, and whose failure might cause unpredictable systemic consequences, or as the Federal Reserve described it, a "contagion." Most of the policy analysis regarding Bear Stearns focused on what happened in the lead-up to its liquidity crisis: the funding sources drying up that week in mid-March; the Federal Reserve inserting itself into the rescue effort even though it was not the primary supervisor of Bear Stearns; and the arrival on the scene of

---

63. Walker F. Todd, "FDICIA's Emergency Liquidity Provisions," *Federal Reserve Bank of Cleveland Economic Review* 29, no. 3 (1993, 3rd quarter), 17, 19. Maxwell Fry, "The Fiscal Abuse of Central Banks," International Monetary Fund, Working Paper 93–58, July 1993.

64. Financial Crisis Inquiry Commission, *The Financial Crisis Inquiry Report: Final Report of the National Commission on the Causes of the Financial and Economic Crisis in the United States,* February 2011, 343 [hereinafter *Financial Crisis Inquiry Commission Report*].

JPMorgan Chase as a white knight. In contrast, most of the policy analysis of Lehman Brothers has focused on what happened after its failure: the response of investors, financial institutions, and government policymakers to the bankruptcy filing.[65] Based largely on that aftermath, many have concluded that the decision to allow Lehman Brothers to file for bankruptcy was a mistake. Although Lehman Brothers was not ultimately bailed out under Section 13(3) as Bear Stearns was and thus its failure cannot fit into the narrative of the structure and form of the bailouts, it is still important in assessing the decision-making regarding the bailouts and the overall response of the government to the stress faced by financial institutions.

### Circumstances Leading to the Stress

When Bear Stearns's difficulties were revealed in March 2008, investors immediately began to review the portfolios of institutions that were also susceptible to a liquidity squeeze. Lehman Brothers logically came under scrutiny as the next potential investment bank to fail, sending its stock price down dramatically.[66] As Treasury Secretary Paulson put it, "[Lehman] had the same profile of sky-high leverage and inadequate liquidity combined with heavy exposure to real estate and mortgages, that had helped bring down Bear Stearns." Paulson pressed Lehman's chairman and CEO Dick Fuld in late March for the firm to recognize its losses, raise equity from the private sector, and strengthen its liquidity. Fuld had in mind a number of potential private investors he planned to follow up with, including General Electric and Berkshire Hathaway.[67]

---

65. See *In Fed We Trust,* 2–3, 21–6, 188–9. Wessel's focus is on the aftermath of the bankruptcy filing to the exclusion of assessing the circumstances leading up to it: "The government-sanctioned bankruptcy of a Wall Street firm founded before the Civil War marked a new phase in the Great Panic, a moment when financial markets went from bad to awful," 2.

66. "After Bear Stearns Is Lehman Next?" ABC News/Money, March 17, 2008, http://abc news.go.com/Business/Economy/story?id=4464095&page=1 (online version has March 10, 2008, date, but this is obviously in error as the article mentions in the past tense the fall of Bear Stearns). David Bogoslaw, "Is Lehman Liquid Enough," *Businessweek,* March 18, 2008, http://www.businessweek.com/investor/content/mar2008/pi20080317_703353 .htm?chan=top+news_top+news_index_top+story.

67. *On the Brink,* 123–24.

In contrast to Bear Stearns, where government scrutiny from outside the SEC was applied to the liquidity standing of the firm only days before its collapse, Lehman Brothers was under scrutiny for months prior to its bankruptcy filing. As early as April 2008, staff from the Treasury Department began meetings with large investment banks like Lehman Brothers to solicit their thoughts on the regulatory and supervisory environment needed in the aftermath of Bear Stearns.[68] In a meeting later that month with Treasury officials, Lehman Chief Legal Officer Tom Russo supported the idea of Federal Reserve discount window access for individual investment banks on a market-wide basis in order to avoid any stigma associated with discount window borrowing.[69] The PDCF program that was implemented in the aftermath of Bear Stearns provided support to primary dealers such as Lehman Brothers, and as Bill Dudley of the FRBNY described it, without it "Lehman might have experienced a full blown liquidity crisis."[70]

In June 2008, evidence began to build of serious liquidity problems at Lehman Brothers. A number of its counterparties began to pull back on funding, and an FRBNY liquidity stress analysis revealed a funding gap of $15 billion over a four-week time horizon driven by the firm's heavy exposure to overnight funding sources.[71] That same month, Vice Chairman of the Board of Governors Kohn relayed a prediction to Chairman Bernanke from the industry that turned out to be prescient: "One of the hedge fund types on Cape Cod told me that his colleagues think Lehman can't survive—the question is when and how they go out of business not whether. He claimed this was a widely shared view on the Street."[72] By early July 2008, Lehman was under the regular scrutiny not only

---

68. FCIC Bates No. UST-FCIC 0029516–17. Email from Treasury Assistant Secretary for Financial Institutions David Nason to Lehman Chief Legal Officer Tom Russo, April 18, 2008.

69. FCIC Bates No. UST-FCIC 0029512–4. Email from Mario Ugoletti of the Treasury Department to Jeremiah Norton, Deputy Assistant Secretary for Financial Institutions Policy, April 29, 2008.

70. FCIC Bates No. FCIC 154463–4. Email from Dudley to Chairman Bernanke, Brian Madigan, Don Kohn, and Timothy Geithner, June 17, 2008.

71. FCIC Bates No. FCIC 155450–2. Email from Kirsten Harlow to various FRBNY staff on June 19, 2008. FRBNY, "Primary Dealer Monitoring: Liquidity Stress Analysis," June 25, 2008, 2–5.

72. FRB to LEH Examiner 000781–2. Email from Don Kohn to Chairman Bernanke, June 13, 2008.

of the FRBNY but also the Board of Governors in Washington, and communication was initiated regarding "contingency planning options for Lehman."[73] About that same time, Secretary Paulson assigned one of his senior advisors to start contingency planning with the Federal Reserve and SEC regarding Lehman. As part of this contingency planning, Bob Hoyt, the Treasury's general counsel, determined that Treasury had no authority to bail out Lehman. Meanwhile, Congressman Frank, chairman of the House Committee on Financial Services, encouraged the Fed and Treasury to broadly interpret their powers.[74]

During the efforts to resolve Lehman Brothers, there began a troubling trend of heavy-handed interventions in facilitating shotgun marriages of financial institutions, a banking version of *Deal or No Deal*. During 2008, the government began preemptive efforts to push together potential banking partners in order to strengthen a weak institution before it reached the point of a meltdown. Applying pressure to chosen merger partners took the LTCM precedent of facilitating a private sector transaction one step further.

The justification advanced a few months earlier for bringing Bear Stearns together with JPMorgan Chase was the potential systemic impact and the level of government assistance involved. In the case of Lehman Brothers, given its similarities with Bear Stearns, it was highly likely that it would experience a similar liquidity crisis. According to Secretary Paulson, the preferred partner for Lehman Brothers was Bank of America as he forcefully pushed a merger to avoid a bankruptcy filing.[75] Paulson even went so far as to tell Lewis to put on his "imagination hat" in order to come up with a structure of a deal that

---

73. *McKinley v. Board of Governors* BOG–FOIA 10–267–000090. Email from Vice Chairman Don Kohn to Governor Kevin Warsh and Patrick Parkinson titled "calls," July 14, 2008 ("Tim [Geithner] would like to keep that call short and reassemble to talk about contingencies for LEH"). On July 10, a number of senior officials at the Board of Governors began to communicate with one another regarding updates on and such contingency planning options for Lehman. See *McKinley v. Board of Governors* BOG–FOIA 10–267–000001–6, http://www.scribd.com/doc/42413488/Defendant-Federal-Reserve-Document-Production-Lehman-Part-I-summer-2008-heavy-redactions-Lawsuit-3.
74. *On the Brink*, 138–39.
75. *On the Brink*, 177 ("I told [Ken Lewis] that we wanted him to seriously consider buying [Lehman].")

would work.[76] This process was the beginning of a far-reaching effort of picking winners and losers, not just for Lehman Brothers but for all of the dwindling number of financial institutions.[77] As part of these efforts, Secretary Paulson even raised the possibility to President Bush of speaking with China's President Hu Jintao about one of the potential merger transactions.[78]

It should not be surprising that Secretary Paulson, a dealmaker from his days at Goldman Sachs, would instinctively contemplate such mergers. However, FRBNY President Geithner was also heavily involved in the deal making, even though as someone who spent most of his career in the government he had very little experience in this area. He pushed these deals so forcefully that some CEOs referred to him as "eHarmony," after the online dating service.[79] Besides trying to match Bank of America and Lehman Brothers these efforts included proposed marriages of

- Morgan Stanley and Citigroup;[80]
- JPMorgan Chase and Morgan Stanley;[81]
- Mitsubishi UFJ and Morgan Stanley;[82]
- China Investment Corporation and Morgan Stanley;[83]
- Goldman Sachs and Citigroup;[84]
- Goldman Sachs and Wachovia;[85]

---

76. *Financial Crisis Inquiry Commission Report*, 332. Based on an interview by the FCIC with Ken Lewis on October 22, 2010.

77. On the international front, similar pressure was applied to Barclays. ("We are not going to import your cancer.") Mark Kleinman, "Hank Paulson begs banks to rescue Lehman Brothers," Telegraph.co.uk, September 14, 2008, http://www.telegraph.co.uk /finance/newsbysector/banksandfinance/4676607/Hank-Paulson-begs-banks-to-rescue -Lehman-Brothers.html. *In Fed We Trust*, 12–13.

78. *On the Brink*, 271. *Too Big to Fail*, 445. The effort was related to China Investment Corporation and a potential deal regarding Morgan Stanley.

79. *Too Big to Fail*, 480.

80. *Too Big to Fail*, 456.

81. *On the Brink*, 275. *Too Big to Fail*, 437, 459, 478, 480, 481.

82. *On the Brink*, 277, 347, 360. *Too Big to Fail*, 474, 480, 482.

83. *On the Brink*, 271. *Too Big to Fail*, 445.

84. *On the Brink*, 275. *Too Big to Fail*, 456, 457, 462.

85. *On the Brink*, 272. *Too Big to Fail*, 472, 475, 491.

- Morgan Stanley and Merrill Lynch;[86]
- Bank of America and Merrill Lynch;[87]
- Citigroup and Wachovia;[88] and
- Morgan Stanley and Wachovia.[89]

In hindsight, many of these proposed mergers reveal very questionable judgment regarding the efficacy of the combination, not to mention the fact that when you push together two behemoths you make the "too big to fail" conundrum even worse. The underlying basis for suggesting such mergers was unclear and the process of picking the chosen partners was lacking in transparency. For example, the extent of due diligence performed by these policymakers before these mergers were suggested is unclear. In most cases there seemed to be no more basis for pushing together the two institutions than some vague notion of how the combination would work, given the complementary strengths and weaknesses of each. Finally, these efforts were rife with potential conflicts of interest, especially where the Federal Reserve was involved given its role as supervisor of bank holding companies. Although Secretary Paulson and FRBNY President Geithner were shameless in their efforts to push such deals, Chairman Bernanke seemed to recognize the potential conflict as manifested by his awkwardness in being asked to push for a merger between JPMorgan Chase and Morgan Stanley.[90]

Ultimately efforts at attracting investors for Lehman were not successful. Discussions with Buffett did not get very far as the renowned investor just had too many questions regarding the firm upon a review of a 10-K report.[91] Efforts to spin off bad assets in a so-called "good bank, bad bank" structure also fell flat.[92] Despite the encouragement of the government dealmakers, overtures from financial institutions including Bank of America, Barclays, Goldman

---

86. *On the Brink*, 203–4.

87. *In Fed We Trust*, 260.

88. *In Fed We Trust*, 226. *Too Big to Fail*, 496.

89. *Too Big to Fail*, 450, 491.

90. *Too Big to Fail*, 480 ("Bernanke, who was usually remote and silent in such situations, cleared his throat and added, 'You don't see what we see. We're trying to keep the system safe. We really need you to do a deal.'").

91. *Too Big to Fail*, 54–57.

92. *Too Big to Fail*, 230–58.

Sachs, and the Korea Development Bank failed to materialize into a capital injection or other transaction to bolster the capital and liquidity of Lehman.[93]

### Assessing the Magnitude of the Problem

From looking at the data, the predicted fallout from a Lehman Brothers failure would have been worse than Bear Stearns's given Lehman was so much larger. With roughly $600 billion in assets, Lehman was bigger and even more interconnected.[94] Bear Stearns had 750,000 derivatives contracts, while the comparable figure for Lehman was approximately 1.2 million derivatives contracts.[95] Just days before Lehman filed bankruptcy, Chairman Bernanke received a high-level briefing that focused on such raw numbers without much detail or analysis: "In many ways, if Lehman were to fail, it would be a much more complex proposition to unwind their positions than it would have been to unwind the positions held by Bear Stearns. At the end of 2007, Lehman's net positions in derivatives measured approximately $54 billion or nearly twice the size of Bear Stearns at that time. While Lehman's management has taken significant steps to reduce these positions and de-risk Lehman's balance sheets, it is likely that a failure by Lehman would be significant."[96]

As early as August 2008, the Federal Reserve focused on two sources of systemic risk presented by the possible failure of an investment bank like Lehman Brothers: tri-party repo borrowing and over-the-counter (OTC) derivatives activities. Although their analysis of systemic risk was intended to address these problems generically and not in relation to any particular institution, a meeting with Lehman Brothers in August caused a stir when it was revealed that the

---

93. *Too Big to Fail*, 306–7, 314, 319–20, 322, 329 (Bank of America); 94–95, 258–59, 261–62, 264–65, 269–71, 323–25, 336–37 (Barclays); 237–38, 245, 252, 264, 112–16, 186, 205–6, 209–10, 212–16, 231 (Korea Development Bank).

94. *On the Brink*, 181.

95. "The Unwinding of Lehman Brothers," CNBC interview of Bryan Marsal on July 6, 2009, at the 2:40 mark, http://video.nytimes.com/video/2009/07/06/business/1194841374907/the-unwinding-of-lehman-brothers.html. A separate analysis showed 1.3 million for Lehman as of May 30, 2008. FCIC Bates No. 155641, in "External Trade Count," an attachment from an email from Meg McConnell sent to various staff at the FRBNY on September 9, 2008.

96. FCIC Bates No. 154787. Email from Jason Miu of the FRBNY, "Financial Markets Conference Call 9/11/08," September 11, 2008.

FRBNY was meeting with Lehman but not any of the other investment banks. The primary concerns regarding systemic risk were the possibility of a fire sale of tri-party repo collateral in a bankruptcy and the closeout of OTC derivatives transactions with counterparties. The FRBNY and Board of Governors knew little about over-the-counter derivatives activities at Lehman and other investment banks. Their disclosures detailed the number of contracts, the total exposure, and their estimated market value, but did not disclose the terms of the contracts or the counterparties.[97] To that end, a Default Management Group (DMG) was proposed to bring together representatives of major market participants to anticipate issues flowing from a default of a major counterparty.[98] Coordinated by the FRBNY, a DMG made up of counterparties in derivatives, swaps, and repo transactions was constituted for Lehman on September 11. The group was responsible for coordinating a wind down and netting of their exposures with Lehman.[99] Additionally, in order to analyze the unwinding of these positions and the risks to the counterparties, Secretary Paulson requested the development of a "playbook" for an investment bank failure that would address the tri-party repos, OTC derivatives, and also obligations to various clearing entities. However, it does not appear that the playbook was completed before the Lehman bankruptcy filing.[100]

Going through the projected consequences of allowing Bear Stearns to fail cited by the Board of Governors and the FRBNY, the same conditions existed for Lehman. In a number of cases, the conditions in the market had actually worsened and the financial system was arguably even more fragile than in March 2008 (Table 7.4).

Even with these enumerated criteria in mind, Chairman Bernanke gave mixed signals regarding the extent of systemic risk, as at times he downplayed the

---

97. *Financial Crisis Inquiry Commission Report*, 329.

98. FCIC Bates No. 156050–3. Email from Pat Parkinson to Steve Shafran and Laurie Schaffer of the Treasury Department and numerous FRBNY staff, August 8, 2008.

99. FCIC Bates No. 154818–20. Email from Jamie McAndrew of the FRBNY, "Default Management Group 9 Sep 2008," September 11, 2008.

100. FCIC Bates No. 156055 draft email from Pat Parkinson to Steve Shafran, September 5, 2008. It is not clear the playbook was ever developed in time for the Lehman bankruptcy as FRBNY President Geithner asked for a draft of the playbook to be completed by September 15, which was the day Lehman filed bankruptcy.

**Table 7.4.** Comparison of Bear Stearns Criteria versus Lehman Brothers Criteria

| Comments Regarding Bear Stearns to Justify Intervention | Lehman Brothers |
|---|:---:|
| "unpredictable but likely severe consequences" | √ |
| "chaotic unwinding of positions" | √ |
| "would have forced Bear's creditors and counterparties to liquidate the underlying collateral" | √ |
| "If they responded to losses or the unexpected illiquidity of their holdings by pulling back from providing secured financing to other firms, a much broader liquidity crisis would have ensued" | √ |
| "prominent position of Bear Stearns in those markets" | √ |
| "fragile condition of the financial markets at the time" | √ |
| "expected contagion that would result from the immediate failure" | √ |

*Source*: See Table 7.3.

potential fallout from a Lehman bankruptcy. In testimony very soon after the failure of Lehman Brothers, Bernanke focused on investor and counterpart capacity to respond to risk and implied that actions taken by investors and counterparties had minimized the systemic impact:

> Government assistance should be given with the greatest of reluctance and only when the stability of the financial system, and, consequently, the health of the broader economy, is at risk. . . . In the case of Lehman Brothers, a major investment bank, the Federal Reserve and the Treasury declined to commit public funds to support the institution. The failure of Lehman posed risks. But the troubles at Lehman had been well known for some time, and investors clearly recognized—as evidenced, for example, by the high cost of insuring Lehman's debt in the market for credit default swaps—that the failure of the firm was a significant possibility. Thus, we judged that investors and counterparties had had time to take precautionary measures.[101]

---

101. Ben S. Bernanke, "Economic Outlook," testimony before the Joint Economic Committee of the U.S. Congress, September 24, 2008.

In later testimony before the Financial Crisis Inquiry Commission (FCIC), a body set up to investigate the causes of the financial crisis, Bernanke explained this confused line of testimony: "I regret not being more straightforward there, because clearly it has supported the mistaken impression that in fact we could have done something. We could not have done anything."[102] Chairman Bernanke's statement about the precautionary measures taken by investors is not supported by the factual record. Little evidence has been presented that market participants expected a Lehman bankruptcy and adjusted their positions accordingly. In fact, the available evidence reveals the unintended consequences and moral hazard implications of the Bear Stearns bailout. Expectations were that another bailout would be made available for Lehman. For example, the bankruptcy specialist responsible for unwinding Lehman Brothers has detailed how the firm's board was surprised by the Lehman filing, in part because they assumed that a Bear Stearns–style transaction was forthcoming.[103]

Secretary Paulson also cites one example of a built-in expectation of a bailout. In referring to Lehman, he observed that "[o]ne of the biggest issues was that the firm did not appear to have taken seriously the possibility of having to file for bankruptcy until the last minute." The actual bankruptcy petition was filed on September 15, and the prospect of filing was not even taken seriously the day before: "A Lehman team, accompanied by their counsel Harvey Miller of Weil, Gotshal and Manges, would not arrive at the New York Fed to discuss bankruptcy options until early Sunday evening [September 14], and even then Lehman appeared to have no immediate intention of filing."[104] While the argument for intervention was that the bailout was necessary because of all the adverse consequences that would flow from a Lehman Brothers bankruptcy filing, Lehman Brothers had absolutely no incentive to reduce those adverse consequences by lifting a finger to prepare for that filing.

---

102. FCIC, "Too Big to Fail: Expectations and Impact of Extraordinary Government Intervention and the Role of Systemic Risk in the Financial Crisis," September 2, 2010 [hereinafter FCIC TBTF Hearing], 19 (Angelides reference to testimony), 25 (Bernanke quote).
103. "The Unwinding of Lehman Brothers," CNBC interview of Bryan Marsal on July 6, 2009. 20:54 run time, http://video.nytimes.com/video/2009/07/06/business/1194841374 907/the-unwinding-of-lehman-brothers.html.
104. *On the Brink,* 216.

Another indicator of market participants' expectation of a bankruptcy filing was the price of insurance on Lehman's obligations before it filed for bankruptcy. The price did not begin to rise until very shortly before Lehman filed for bankruptcy. The fact that prices for CDS on Lehman stayed so stable in the summer and early fall of 2008, despite widespread perceptions that Lehman was financially precarious, strongly suggests that market participants expected the government to prop Lehman up if necessary, so that the CDS would not be triggered.[105] These are just three examples of the expectations of stakeholders of Lehman and the distorted incentives that flowed from the precedent of a Bear Stearns bailout.

The evidence of systemic risk in both the Bear Stearns and Lehman examples was weak. In neither case could intervention be justified on the basis of institution-specific circumstances. A more detailed analysis of the counterparty positions should have been undertaken. Although major commercial banks and broker-dealers such as Deutsche Bank, Mizuho International, Calyon (Credit Agricole), JPMorgan Chase, and Morgan Stanley do appear on the list of the top twenty-five counterparties, their exposures were relatively small and total in the hundreds of millions, certainly nothing that would, on their own, put the firms at risk (Table 7.5).[106]

With regard to tri-party repos as well, Lehman's involvement was quite a bit larger than that of Bear Stearns, with Lehman's book of repos at $182 billion, while Bear's book was estimated at $50 to $80 billion. The top eleven counterparties provided 80 percent of the repo financing.[107] But as discussed in the case

---

105. David Skeel, *The New Financial Deal: Understanding the Dodd-Frank Act and Its (Unintended) Consequences* (Hoboken, New Jersey: Wiley, 2011), 28–29 [hereinafter *New Financial Deal*].

106. FCIC Bates No. 155640 in "Top 25 Counterparties by Current Exposure (to Lehman)," an attachment from an email from Meg McConnell sent to various staff at the FRBNY on September 9, 2008. The column for the "Counterparty Credit Exposure (CCE)" for these five major financial institutions totaled $283 million, $260 million, $225 million, $213 million, and $173 million, respectively. Other counterparties on the list with larger exposure included Ministry of Finance of Italy = $2.9 billion, BH Finance LLC = $1.4 billion, Pyxis ABS CDO = $1.1 billion, Libra CDO = $0.9 billion, MKP Vela CBO = $0.9 billion, and Central Bank of Norway = $0.5 billion.

107. *McKinley v. Board of Governors,* BOG–FOIA 10–267–000070 in email titled "LB Triparty Repo Followup" from Lucinda Brickler to various staff of FRBNY dated

**Table 7.5.** Abbreviated List—Major Lehman Derivatives Counterparties

| Counterparty | Credit Exposure |
| --- | --- |
| Deutsche Bank | $283 million |
| Mizuho International | 260 million |
| Calyon (Credit Agricole) | 225 million |
| JPMorgan Chase | 213 million |
| Morgan Stanley | 173 million |

*Source*: FCIC Bates No. 155640 in "Top 25 Counterparties by Current Exposure
(to Lehman)." Note: The list above is limited to major commercial banks
and broker-dealers out of the list of top 25 counterparties.

of Bear Stearns, the underlying collateral can always be sold and so there is less
potential credit risk than in the case of the derivatives market.

*Reviewing the Options*

Although the analysis regarding systemic risk posed by Lehman was off the
mark, the Treasury and the Federal Reserve did recognize the problems with
Lehman early on and concluded that it was highly likely that Lehman Brothers
would have a funding crisis similar to Bear Stearns's. Staff from these agencies
looked at numerous options to avoid a bankruptcy filing. As in the case of Bear
Stearns, the Board of Governors and FRBNY were struggling with the intrica-
cies of an investment bank and how to structure potential funding options.
Rather than being able to rely on published analysis of their own, FRBNY staff
circulated amongst themselves a 2001 manual developed by the Basel Committee on Banking Supervision in Switzerland on the winding down of large and
complex financial institutions.[108]

---

September 9, 2008. FCIC Bates No. 155646–7 in untitled two-page document, an
attachment from an email from Meg McConnell sent to various staff at the FRBNY on
September 9, 2008.
108. *McKinley v. Board of Governors,* Bates No. BOG–FOIA 10–267–000669–718.
Document sent September 11, 2008. J. Brockmeijer, "Report from the Task Force on
the Winding Down of Large and Complex Financial Institutions," Basel Committee
on Banking Supervision.

Not unlike Bear Stearns, the working assumption was that liquidity, and not capital solvency, was the only issue for Lehman.[109] Initial plans regarding intervention focused on providing liquidity to Lehman using the PDCF through a tri-party arrangement to step into the shoes of the clearing bank, JPMorgan Chase, if it no longer wanted to take on the risk. Pat Parkinson of the Board of Governors described this reasoning: "[T]he biggest difference between today and when Bear lost access to financing is that the PDCF is in place. As long as we judge that [Lehman] is sound we should be willing to lend to it through the PDCF at conservative haircuts. . . . With the PDCF in place there is no need to use JPMC as the intermediary."[110] However, an analysis in mid-July revealed that about $13 billion of Lehman's $200 billion in tri-party borrowings was not PDCF eligible. There was also concern about the vulnerability of borrowings beyond the $200 billion of tri-party borrowings.[111] Although these plans were meant to cover a broad range of possible institutions, the discussions specifically mentioned Lehman and used current data for Lehman as an example of how such an approach might work. An additional option if problems were of a liquidity nature was to have a Section 13(3) loan go directly to a broker-dealer.[112]

Staff from Treasury also explored the possibility regarding Lehman that they might "let the firm fail" and what authorities were available to minimize

---

109. FCIC Bates No. UST-FCIC 0029097. Email from Treasury Assistant General Counsel Laurie Schaffer to Robert Hoyt, Treasury General Counsel, July 10, 2008.

110. FCIC-155510–12. Email from Pat Parkinson titled "another option we should present re: triparty" to various Board of Governors and FRBNY staff, July 11, 2008. Also *McKinley v. Board of Governors,* BOG–FOIA 10–267000030.

111. FCIC-154545. Email from Pat Parkinson to Chairman Bernanke, Kevin Warsh, Scott Alvarez, and Brian Madigan, July 20, 2008. The proposed solution to cover the noneligible collateral was to make the non-PDCF collateral eligible for the PDCF. FCIC-154556 from early September showed tri-party borrowings of about $150 billion with $20 billion not PDCF eligible.

112. FCIC-155482–91. Emails between staff of the Board of Governors and FRBNY and a memo to Timothy Geithner, "Managing a Loss of Confidence in a Major Tri-party Repo Borrower," July 11, 2008, from Lucinda Brickler, William Brodows, Chris McCurdy, and Til Schuermann. Also see references to a 13(3) loan with heavy redactions in *McKinley v. Board of Governors* BOG–FOIA 10–267–000159 email titled "Our Options in the Event of a Run on LB" from Scott Alvarez to Chairman Bernanke, Brian Madigan,

effects on creditors and the system, including a prepackaged bankruptcy or the possibility of Treasury operating the business or having a bankruptcy judge appoint Treasury as receiver.[113] They also started reviewing options in which, unlike Bear Stearns where there was a ready buyer waiting in the form of JPMorgan, there would be no buyer waiting in the wings and any facility would "be a permanent addition to the government's balance sheet." This suggestion provoked one FRBNY staffer to question how deep these investment commitments should go: "The question is whether the government wishes to get into the private equity business—not whether the government wishes to get into the investment banking business."[114] Another option reviewed under a "no buyer" scenario was the so-called "good bank/bad bank" structure. This would have involved transforming Lehman into a commercial banking organization by putting assets into the bank or industrial loan company and possibly having Lehman become a financial holding company.[115] This would have been similar to a Bear Stearns Maiden Lane structure with about $60 billion of illiquid assets supported by $5 billion of Lehman equity and FRBNY backstopping; and $600 billion of other assets supported by $23 billion of Lehman equity, with the FRBNY receiving an equity stake. Bill Dudley of the FRBNY described this as an offer Lehman couldn't refuse: "We could propose it to Lehman as a choice.

Donald Kohn, and Kevin Warsh, July 21, 2008 ("That would be a 13(3) loan. [redacted heavily]"); *McKinley v. Board of Governors* BOG–FOIA 10–267–000163. Email titled "Our Options in the Event of a Run on LB" from Scott Alvarez to Patrick Parkinson and Brian Madigan, July 21, 2008; and *McKinley v. Board of Governors* BOG–FOIA 10–267–000159. Email titled "Our Options in the Event of a Run on LB" from Scott Alvarez to Chairman Bernanke, Brian Madigan, Donald Kohn, and Kevin Warsh, July 21, 2008 ("Not sure we do have legal authority [heavily redacted]").

113. FCIC Bates No. UST-FCIC 0029096. Email from Treasury Assistant General Counsel Laurie Schaffer to Robert Hoyt, Treasury General Counsel, July 11, 2008.

114. FCIC Bates No. 155504–6. Various FRBNY internal emails July 12 and 13, 2008.

115. *McKinley v. Board of Governors,* Bates No. BOG–FOIA 10–267–000084. Email from Mark VanDerWeide to Patrick Parkinson titled "LB Repos," July 14, 2008. For an additional discussion of the bank holding company option, see *Financial Crisis Inquiry Commission Report,* 328. Geithner told Fuld this was "gimmicky" and "[could not] solve a liquidity/capital problem."

Does not have to be coercive. If slide were to continue, what might have looked unattractive might increasing [sic] look attractive relative to the alternatives."[116]

As time went on, it became very clear that the age-old question of whether Lehman Brothers was experiencing a liquidity crisis or an insolvency crisis had a clear answer. It was experiencing an insolvency crisis, as evidenced by "a gaping hole in its balance sheet."[117] After many months of consideration, Bank of America's Gregory Curl informed Secretary Paulson that his bank would need the government to cover $40 billion of losses before they would commit to any deal. He bluntly stated the case against a private, stand-alone deal: "We've been through the books, and they're a mess."[118] Barclays also pulled out of consideration, largely at the urging of its primary supervisory agency in the United Kingdom, the Financial Services Authority, which determined that the underlying risk in Lehman was too great.[119] Just before Lehman filed bankruptcy, in an email Chairman Bernanke commented on the deep insolvency: "How much capital injection would have been needed to keep [Lehman] alive as a going concern? I gather $12 [billion] or so from the private guys together with Fed liquidity support was not enough."[120] Despite this consensus that Lehman Brothers was in fact insolvent, the FRBNY has not publicly released its internal analysis of the collateral Lehman had to support any transaction and it is not entirely clear that such an analysis exists.[121]

---

116. FCIC Bates No. 154477–9. Proposal by Bill Dudley in an email to Donald Kohn, Kevin Warsh, Timothy Geithner, Patrick Parkinson, and various FRBNY staff on July 15, 2008. FCIC Bates No. 0029680. Email from Pat Parkinson to Steven Shafran of Treasury, "now I am on a conf call," dated September 9, 2008 ("What are our options if, unlike BS, no buyer materializes?").

117. *On the Brink*, 199, 209.

118. *Too Big to Fail*, 300.

119. *McKinley v. Board of Governors*, BOG–FOIA 10–267–000726. Email from Matthew Eichner titled "LEH View from UK" to various FRBNY staff and then forwarded to Pat Parkinson, September 12, 2008 ("This is very raw information but represents a significant change in tone."). *On the Brink*, 195. *Too Big to Fail*, 343–46.

120. FCIC Bates No. 155000 untitled email from Chairman Bernanke to Governor Kevin Warsh, September 14, 2008. *McKinley v. Board of Governors*, BOG–FOIA 10–267–001171.

121. In testimony before the FCIC, Chairman Bernanke responded to a question from Chairman Angelides about such an analysis: "That was based on analysis at the Federal Reserve Bank of New York, primarily, which had been going on through the weekend.

In fully assessing options, the next step was to determine precisely what power the Federal Reserve had to intervene with an insolvent investment bank like Lehman Brothers. Secretary Paulson maintains that once it was clear that Lehman Brothers was deeply insolvent, there was absolutely no way the Federal Reserve could invoke its powers to lend in unusual and exigent circumstances, and this fact was made clear to Dick Fuld and Ken Lewis, the chairman of Bank of America.[122] Given that the option of providing anything but short-term funding was off the table, Patricia Mosser of the FRBNY sent a summary of remaining options to Bill Dudley: "(1) find a buyer at any price, (2) wind down Lehman's affairs, or (3) force it into bankruptcy."[123]

There also may have been a political calculation at work in foreclosing the bailout option. Since March 2008 there had been a build-up of criticism regarding the bailout of Bear Stearns, as well as that of Fannie Mae and Freddie Mac during the summer (see page 218 for a discussion of these bailouts). The tide began to turn away from a reflexive reaction to bail out a financial institution that faced bankruptcy. "I'm being called Mr. Bailout. I can't do it again," Secretary Paulson noted.[124] Jim Wilkinson, Secretary Paulson's chief of staff, expressed a similar sentiment regarding the potential political fallout in an email to Treasury colleague Michele Davis: "I just can't stomach us bailing out Lehman. Will be

---

And of course prior to that we had done a lot of analysis based on our presence at Lehman during the summer." Transcript, FCIC TBTF Hearing , 26–27. See also follow-up questioning from Commissioner Peter Wallison about a "study of the collateral that was available," to which Chairman Bernanke responded: "I don't have any—to my knowledge, I don't have a study to hand you. But it was the judgment made by the leadership of the New York Fed and the people who were charged with reviewing the books of Lehman that they were far short of what was needed to get the cash to meet the run. And that was the judgment that was given to me." FCIC TBTF Hearing, 84. Also see *Financial Crisis Inquiry Commission Report*, 341 ("[T]he Fed did not furnish to the FCIC any written analysis to illustrate that Lehman lacked sufficient collateral to secure a loan under 13(3)").

122. *On the Brink,* 173, 177, 196. Also see Lehman Examiner's Interview of Henry M. Paulson, Jr., June 25, 2009, 14–15.

123. *Financial Crisis Inquiry Commission Report,* 331. According to Mosser, Option 1 would involve "minimal temporary support" and Option 3 would be "[a] mess on every level, but fixes the moral hazard problem."

124. *In Fed We Trust,* 14–15.

horrible in the press don't [you] think?"[125] Numerous other comments of Federal Reserve and Treasury officials during this time were consistent with the sentiment of allowing Lehman to file bankruptcy rather than conducting another bailout (see Table 7.6).

By early September it became clear that if something was not done within a matter of days CEO Fuld would have to file bankruptcy. An email from Pat Parkinson of the Board of Governors summarized the reality: "Tim [Geithner] and Cox had been scheduled to call Fuld at 4 pm. . . . They will essentially tell him that if he doesn't raise capital chapter 11 is the alternative, except for U.S. [broker-dealer], which SEC thinks can be liquidated in an orderly manner."[126]

Although Secretary Paulson maintained that a bailout was not an option and no government assistance could be provided to facilitate a Lehman transaction because of a lack of authority, this view was never made public until months after the bankruptcy filing. As noted previously, the initial public position, as outlined by Chairman Bernanke, was that investors and counterparties had had time to take precautionary measures. It was not until a January 2009 interview that Paulson made public the idea that the authority to intervene was lacking: "We were unable to talk about [the idea of government assistance] in a way in which we wanted to talk about it. You're unable to say 'we let [Lehman] go down because we were powerless to do anything about it.' You don't want to say 'the emperor has no clothes.'"[127] Chairman Bernanke has made consistent statements about the need at the time to be less than candid about the true reasons for allowing Lehman to fail.[128]

---

125. FCIC Bates No. 0029964. Email from Jim Wilkinson to Michele Davis, Untitled, September 9, 2008.

126. *McKinley v. Board of Governors*, BOG–FOIA 10–267–000245. Email titled "Lehman Brothers" from Pat Parkinson to Chairman Bernanke, Kevin Warsh, Brian Madigan, and Scott Alvarez, September 9, 2008.

127. *In Fed We Trust*, 24.

128. FCIC TBTF Hearing, 24–5 ("This is my own fault, in a sense, but the reason we didn't make the statement in that testimony, which was only a few days after the failure of Lehman, that we were unable to save it was because it was a judgment at the moment, with the system in tremendous stress and with other financial institutions under threat of run, or panic, that making that statement might have, might have even reduced confidence further and led to further pressure").

**Table 7.6.** Quotes Regarding Lehman Bankruptcy Filing

---

"[C]an't imagine a scenario where we put in [government] money."[1]

Fed Economist Nellie Liang: "[H]ope we don't protect Lehman's sub debt holders."

Federal Reserve Governor Warsh: "I hope we dont [sic] protect anything."[2]

"No way [government] money is coming in. . . . I'm here writing the usg coms plan for orderly unwind. . . . also just did a call with the [White House] and usg is united behind no money. No way in hell Paulson could blink now. . . ."[3]

"Off the record, [Secretary Paulson's] view is that the existing tools should be used as needed. Existing tools include the pdcf."[4]

---

1. FCIC Bates No. 0029418. Email from Jim Wilkinson, Treasury Chief of Staff, to Abby Adlerman, September 12, 2008.
2. FCIC Bates No. 154863. Email between Board of Governors Economist Nellie Liang and Fed Governor Kevin Warsh, September 12, 2008.
3. FCIC Bates No. 0029412. Email untitled from Jim Wilkinson, Treasury Chief of Staff, to Jes Staley, September 14, 2008.
4. FCIC Bates No. 0029177. Email titled "Lehman query" from Michele Davis, Treasury Spokesperson, to Krishna Guha of the *Financial Times*, September 14, 2008.

FRBNY President Geithner may have wanted a bailout for Lehman, but he conceded the countervailing pressures were too great: "There is no political will for a federal bailout."[129] However, as the time of Lehman's bankruptcy filing approached, Paulson and Geithner remained open to the possibility of completely reversing themselves as Paulson has detailed: "Tim [Geithner] expressed concern about my public stand on government aid. He said that if we ended up having to help a Lehman buyer, I would lose credibility. But I was willing to say 'no government assistance' to help us get a deal. If we had to reverse ourselves over the weekend, so be it."[130] In the days leading up to the bankruptcy filing, a number of statements by FRBNY, Board of Governors, and Bush Administration

---

129. Deborah Solomon, Dennis K. Berman, Susanne Craig, and Carrick Mollenkamp, "Ultimatum by Paulson Sparked Frantic End," *Wall Street Journal*, September 15, 2008, http://online.wsj.com/article/SB122143670579134187.html.
130. *On the Brink*, 187.

**Table 7.7.** Eleventh-Hour Quotes on the Possibility of a Lehman Bailout

---

**Wednesday, September 10, 5:17 p.m.:** "At 4:15pm FRBNY/Board call, same three options were laid out once again by Tim [Geithner]. Working groups were directed to spend the next few hours fleshing out how a Fed-assisted BofA acquisition transaction might look. . . . "[1]

**Thursday, September 11, 6:55 a.m.:** "FRBNY financial commitment: . . . We should have in mind a maximum number of how much we are willing to finance before the meeting starts, but not divulge our willingness to do so to the consortium.

Financial capital: How do we best hone in on the monetary figure we think the consortium will have to provide in new capital and the type/maximum amount of any FR financing to support the consortium?"[2]

**Thursday, September 11, 1:46 p.m.:** "[G]et ready for the Lehman bailout."[3]

**Thursday, September 11:** "Geithner's discussions with the Financial Services Authority (the FSA) left open the possibility that there would be Government assistance."[4]

**Friday, September 12:** "Paulson advised the FSA that the FRBNY might be prepared to provide Barclays with regulatory assistance if necessary."[5]

**Friday, September 12, 8:53 a.m.:** "Margie just told me that we may have a Board meeting today about Lehman Brothers."[6]

---

1. FCIC Bates No. 154786. Email from Mark VanDerWeide to Scott Alvarez of Board of Governors, September 10, 2008. *McKinley v. Board of Governors*, BOG–FOIA 10–267–00037.
2. FCIC Bates No. 154768–73. Email with attachment "Liquidation Consortium" (September 10, 2008) to email of Patrick Parkinson of the Board of Governors, September 11, 2008.
3. FCIC Bates No. 0029510. Email untitled from Bryan Corbett, Special Assistant to the President, in an email to David Nason, Treasury Department Assistant Secretary for Financial Institutions.
4. Report of Anton R. Valukas, Bankruptcy Examiner, 617–18 (March 11, 2010).
5. Report of Anton R. Valukas, Bankruptcy Examiner, 618 (March 11, 2010).
6. *McKinley v. Board of Governors*, Bates No. 10–267–000748. Email from Katie J. Ross titled "possible Board meeting today" to Jon Hiratsuka and Natalie Burch, September 12, 2008. Apparently this potential meeting was to consider extension of a possible emergency transaction under Section 13(3) of the Federal Reserve Act. Also see Lehman examiners' interview of Ben S. Bernanke, December 22, 2009, at 9 as cited in the Report of Anton R. Valukas, Bankruptcy Examiner, 618 (March 11, 2010) ("Chairman Bernanke told the Examiner that he remained in Washington, DC during Lehman's final weekend in part because a possibility existed that Bernanke might need to convene a meeting of the Federal Reserve Board to

**Table 7.7.** *continued*

---

*Friday, September 12, 5:12 p.m.:* "All [FRB Presidents] seemed fine with LEH briefing, though I was quized [sic] closely by Fisher on the appetite for Fed/ Gov't involvement beyond liquidity provision. I told him strong predilection against by both Treas. And Fed. . . . but could give no 100% guarantees on what perception of situation would be Sunday evening."[7]

*Friday, September 12, 6:45 p.m.:* "I've also attempted to briefly describe a few things we may need to consider in the event that JPMC refuses to unwind Lehman's positions on Monday—assuming they're still in business, but haven't been rescued—and the policy makers believe an intervention is necessary to protect the market from the fallout of a suddent [sic] default."[8]

*Weekend of September 13–14:* "[D]uring the weekend's negotiations, the Government gave conflicting signals regarding the availability of some form of federal assistance."[9]

---

exercise the Federal Reserve's emergency lending powers under Section 13(3) of the Federal Reserve Act").
7. FCIC Bates No. 154870. Email "RB Presidents" from Donald Kohn to Chairman Bernanke and Governor Kevin Warsh, September 12, 2008.
8. FCIC Bates No. 155903. Email "triparty repo thoughts for this weekend" from Lucinda Brickler, September 12, 2008.
9. Examiner interview of Gregory Curl, Bank of America, September 17, 2009. Report of Anton R. Valukas, Bankruptcy Examiner, 618 (March 11, 2010).

officials also seemed to indicate openness to a Federal Reserve bailout of some sort (Table 7.7).

As the bankruptcy of Lehman Brothers drew near, market participants of the cafeteria capitalist variety were in a panic over the potential of a Lehman bankruptcy and began to desperately lay out possible intervention options for the FRBNY. One example of this was a series of options set out by Louis Bacon, a billionaire hedge fund manager who served on the FRBNY Investor Advisory Committee on Financial Markets:

- "The Fed can cut rates";
- "The Treasury can announce a large GSE [mortgage backed security] purchase program under their GSE support package from this weekend";
- "The Treasury can announce a major expansion of funding to the Federal Home Loan Bank system";

- "Bank regulators can cut risk weightings on GSE-issued [mortgage backed securities] and debt on the basis that the government has backstopped the Agencies";
- "The FRB may also attempt to stabilize or support the [LEH-Lehman Brothers] situation by lending to LEH through the PDCF as a backstop until LEH works out its situation or to LEH's newco/spinco. . . . or they could facilitate a transaction by using the Maiden Lane structure that was set up for [Bear Stearns] in some way";
- "The Fed could also make another innovation it [sic] liquidity facilities— perhaps a major extension in the term, say to three years. . . . .";
- "However, none of the above will fix the fundamental problem, which is too many bad assets that need to get off of too many balance sheets. . . . To me this says that it is time for the government to start seriously considering an RTC2. By RTC2 I mean some sort of vehicle, either pre-funded by the government or backstopped with government money, that would purchase assets for once and for all off bank balance sheets, giving in their place a government recap bond of some sort."[131]

The precise details of the final unwinding of the liquidity position of Lehman are still in dispute focusing on a $5 billion demand for cash made by JPMorgan Chase related to tri-party repo commitments. Severe liquidity problems were present, and Lehman contends that JPMorgan made improper demands for the cash.[132] JPMorgan Chase contends that $5 billion was needed for JPMorgan to continue to support Lehman in as stabilizing a way as possible and that despite JPMorgan's constant efforts to support Lehman and not do anything to frighten the market, a run on the bank eventually ensued for reasons unrelated to JPMorgan.[133] By Wednesday, September 10, JPMorgan Chase had unwound

131. FCIC Bates No. 0029425–28. Email forwarded by Hayley Boesky of the FRBNY titled "Panic" dated September 11, 2008, of an email from Louis Bacon titled "Options for short-circuiting the market," September 11, 2008.

132. *In re: Lehman Brothers Holdings, Inc. et al v. JPMorgan Chase Bank*, Complaint, U.S. Bankruptcy Court, Southern District of New York, 23.

133. Written Testimony of Barry Zubrow, chief risk officer, JPMorgan before the FCIC, September 1, 2010, 7–8.

their entire Lehman book.[134] The book of tri-party repos shrank by $18 billion over the course of the day on Wednesday, September 10, and nearly $4 billion more on September 11.[135] By the evening of Friday, September 12, Lehman's only hope to survive was federal assistance or a merger.[136]

As the option of a bailout was taken off the table and the possibility of a private transaction fell through after Bank of America and Barclays pulled back, the only remaining option to save Lehman, at the suggestion of FRBNY President Geithner, involved a redux of the approach used for LTCM. That earlier deal, which involved a consortium of banks to save LTCM, had also reportedly saved Lehman Brothers indirectly.[137] The idea would be to gather together commercial banks and investment banks that would be most adversely impacted by a Lehman insolvency in order to facilitate a funding mechanism with Bank of America as the acquirer. The group would include JPMorgan Chase, Morgan Stanley, Goldman Sachs, Citigroup, Merrill Lynch, Credit Suisse, Barclays, Bank of New York Mellon, State Street, and Royal Bank of Scotland.[138] Once again, the

---

134. *McKinley v. Board of Governors,* BOG–FOIA 10–267–000730. Email from Pat Parkinson titled "Has JPMC Unwound?" forwarding a message from Brian Begalle of FRBNY to Chairman Bernanke and Don Kohn, September 12, 2008 ("They have unwound the entire Lehman book, per Jon Ciciola").

135. *McKinley v. Board of Governors,* BOG–FOIA 10–267–000439. Email from Brian Begalle titled "Lehman Triparty Summary from Yesterday" to various FRBNY staff, September 11, 2008. *McKinley v. Board of Governors,* BOG–FOIA 10–267–000476. Email from Jan Voigts titled "Lehman Triparty Summary from Yesterday" to various FRBNY staff, September 11, 2008. *McKinley v. Board of Governors* BOG–FOIA 10–267–000802. Email from Brian Begalle titled "LEH Triparty" to various FRBNY staff, September 12, 2008.

136. Report of Anton R. Valukas, Bankruptcy Examiner, 621 (March 11, 2010).

137. *Too Big to Fail,* 301 ("As John Thain's GMC Yukon pulled up to the building [Federal Reserve Bank of New York], he couldn't help but recall the last time he had come there, as a partner at Goldman, in response to another such cataclysmic event, the rescue of Long-Term Capital Management in 1998. For three straight days, he had worked around the clock to come up with a solution. And had they not saved Long-Term Capital, the next domino back in 1998 was clearly Lehman Brothers, which was suffering from a similar crisis of confidence.").

138. FCIC Bates No. 154768. Attachment "Liquidation Consortium" attached to email from Pat Parkinson of the Board of Governors to Don Kohn, Scott Alvarez, and Brian Madigan, September 11, 2008.

obvious question came up of whether the government would be willing to put together a Bear Stearns–type transaction in combination with the consortium's efforts. FRBNY President Geithner cited the poor asset quality of Lehman to deny the possibility and Secretary Paulson cited the inability of the government to fill the capital hole.[139] Significantly this meant that Secretary Paulson, who during the Bear Stearns discussion said he was prepared to do anything if there was a chance of avoiding a failure, now recognized that the government's powers under law were not limitless.[140] A stand-alone deal by the consortium did not come together this time around and Lehman had to file bankruptcy.[141]

FRBNY staff thought through in great detail how the Lehman bankruptcy filing should play out, even getting down to precisely when the filing should occur: mid-afternoon on Sunday, September 14. This timing was intended to allow markets, clearing entities, and counterparties time to react to the filing. The staff analysis also noted the possibility of a mid-morning filing which would minimize disruption in the tri-party repo market as it would occur after the morning unwind of that market. The analysis also addressed which entities would be eligible for bankruptcy protection and the response by U.S. regulators to the filing.[142]

Management of Lehman planned to file bankruptcy on Monday, September 15, but they were given one last hope of being pulled away from bankruptcy. On September 14, the Federal Reserve announced that the collateral eligible to be pledged at the PDCF had been broadened.[143] However, the change was limited to tri-party transactions and was not the lifeline that Lehman had hoped for.[144] The inevitable filing would go forward, as Kevin Warsh noted in an email entitled

---

139. *On the Brink*, 178, 191–93, 196.
140. *On the Brink*, 101.
141. *Too Big to Fail*, 340–50.
142. FCIC Bates No. 154847. Email from Ada Li titled "Bankruptcy.doc," with the attached memo "Decision to File Bankruptcy," September 12, 2008.
143. Board of Governors of the Federal Reserve, Press Release, September 14, 2008, http://www.federalreserve.gov/newsevents/press/monetary/20080914a.htm.
144. FCIC Bates No. 154997. Email titled "Don and I are starting RB president calls" from Donald Kohn to Chairman Bernanke, September 14, 2008 ("LEH heard about the pdcf enlargement and thought it was a lifeline, but they didn't understand it was limited to triparty"). Also see *Financial Crisis Inquiry Commission Report*, 337 ("Lehman's broker-

"Lehman is decided to file" sent to Timothy Geithner just a few hours before the filing: "Another good call TFG. Well done."[145]

### The Aftermath

**John Harvey, FRBNY:** "Currently, there is 100% pullback in the Fed Funds market in conditions similar to August 2007. Market is anticipating massive injections of funding by the Federal Reserve into the funding markets today."

**Coryann Stefansson, Board of Governors:** "This echoes what I hjeard [sic] from european contacts this morning. . . . .fed funds markets r locked. . . . .crisis of confidence amongst major players."[146]

Many argued that the financial system would have been better off had Lehman also been bailed out, and the evidence to support that is that all manner of bad things flowed from the Lehman failure. Typical of those advocating this viewpoint is billionaire Wilbur Ross, who is renowned for restructuring troubled companies: "I do feel it was a tragic mistake, and subsequent events have proven that was the case."[147] However, on the weekend before the Lehman filing, Ross was unwilling to comment on whether or not he thought it was a good move by the Federal Reserve and Treasury. He chose instead to wait out the aftermath of the bankruptcy filing, a luxury that policymakers did not have.[148]

---

dealer affiliate—not the holding company—could borrow against the expanded types of collateral").

145. *McKinley v. Board of Governors,* Bates No. FOIA 10–267–001180. Email titled "Lehman is decided to file" from Kevin Warsh to Timothy Geithner, September 14, 2008.

146. *McKinley v. Board of Governors,* Bates No. BOG–FOIA 10–267–001253. Email titled "DB Treasury Update" from John Harvey to various FRBNY staff and Coryann Stefansson and forwarded to Deborah P. Bailey, dated September 15, 2008. Message forwarded to Brian Madigan, William English, Roger Cole, and Scott Alvarez.

147. "When Wall Street Nearly Collapsed—Wilbur Ross: Lehman's Death a Tragic Mistake," *Fortune,* September 14, 2009 ("I do feel it was a tragic mistake, and subsequent events have proven that was the case"), http://money.cnn.com/galleries/2009/fortune /0909/gallery.witnesses_meltdown.fortune/20.html.

148. "Wilbur Ross Expects 1000 Bank Failures," September 14, 2008, http://www.youtube .com/watch?v=FBvNWuz62zs.

In the aftermath of the Lehman Brothers bankruptcy, a number of events ensued, some of which are interrelated, beyond the direct impact on Lehman shareholders, creditors, and counterparties:[149]

- The "breaking of the buck" of the Reserve Primary Fund, a money market that invested in Lehman Brothers Holding Inc. debt;[150]
- The largest-ever one-day rise in the cost of insurance against bond defaults in the credit-default-swap market;[151]
- Hedge fund withdrawals at Morgan Stanley and Goldman Sachs;[152]
- A dramatic drop in the level of commercial paper outstanding to levels experienced three years earlier;[153]
- Rates on commercial paper increased upwards of 300 basis points or more for certain nonfinancial firms;[154] and
- Spreads between LIBOR and T-bill rates ballooned from 100 basis points to over 400 basis points.[155]

In reviewing the potential fallout from a possible Bear Stearns bankruptcy filing, the phrase "disorderly failure" was used freely and even more so in the aftermath of the bankruptcy of Lehman Brothers. This usage was in keeping with the argument that the big mistake during the crisis was to let Lehman fail. The concept of a disorderly failure was never clearly explained in the context of Bear Stearns, but researchers at the International Monetary Fund (IMF) have attempted to do just that. They posit that during 2008, authorities in the United

---

149. This analysis is drawn from "Bright Lines and Bailouts," 11–12.

150. This left investors unlikely to get back all the cash they put in because the fund failed to maintain assets of at least $1 for every dollar invested. Tim Paradis, "Money Funds 'Break the Buck,' Investors at Risk," Associated Press, September 17, 2008.

151. Carrick Mollenkamp, Mark Whitehouse, Jon Hilsenrath, and Ianthe Jeanne Dugan, "Lehman's Demise Triggered Cash Crunch Around Globe," *Wall Street Journal*, September 29, 2008 [hereinafter "Lehman's Demise"].

152. "Lehman's Demise."

153. V. V. Chari, Lawrence Christiano, and Patrick J. Kehoe, "Facts and Myths about the Financial Crisis of 2008," Working Paper 666, Federal Reserve Bank of Minneapolis Research Department, October 2008 (Figure 6A) [hereinafter "Facts and Myths"].

154. "Facts and Myths."

155. "Facts and Myths."

States were presented with two potential options when a financial institution approached failure: a disorderly bankruptcy as chosen with Lehman, or a bailout as chosen with Bear Stearns (Figure 7.2). According to this theory, the disorderly bankruptcy in the case of Lehman involved low fiscal cost accompanied by high levels of financial instability, while the bailout of Bear Stearns offered high fiscal cost accompanied by low levels of financial instability. The Lehman bankruptcy, under this hypothesis, led to uncertainty and contagious disruption in the financial markets and to a loss of key services. This narrative accepts without any cited evidence that the Lehman failure was the proximate cause of the instability beginning in September 2008. This analysis also takes a very short-run and thus shortsighted view. The bailout option has a number of indirect costs that are not easily measured, not the least of which is the moral hazard that accompanies such a decision. These costs may not manifest themselves until well after the short run and contribute to financial instability in the future. The Continental Illinois bailout clearly had an adverse impact on future financial stability, as the bailout did nothing to address the long-term consequences of TBTF policy. The primary conclusion of the IMF analysis is for the creation of a "special resolution regime" that is structured so that a lower threshold of fiscal cost and financial instability are achieved.[156]

It cannot be denied that losses spilled over to shareholders and creditors in the aftermath of the Lehman Brothers' bankruptcy filing, and it is likely that the fallout was quantitatively worse than the fallout from Bear Stearns would have been given the sheer difference in size between the two investment banks and the fact that Lehman was in a worse financial position. The description of a disorderly bankruptcy evokes images of a chaotic situation of cascading losses, especially as it relates to financial institutions. But the reality of the so-called disorderly bankruptcy can be more clearly revealed by looking at the direct impact of the Lehman bankruptcy filing on the holders of over $600 billion in liabilities detailed in that filing. The largest single Lehman creditor was Aozora Bank of Tokyo, which was owed $463 million. This is a relatively small amount

---

156. Martin Cihak and Erlend Nier, "The Need for Special Resolution Regimes for Financial Institutions—The Case of the European Union," IMF Working Paper, WP/09/200 (September 2009).

**Figure 7.2.** Fiscal Cost and Systemic Impact in Resolution Regimes

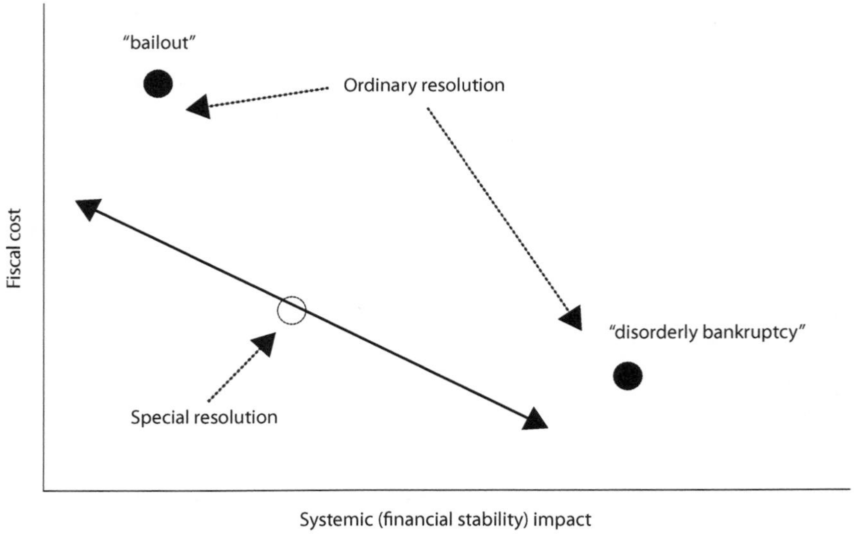

*Source*: Martin Cihak and Erlend Nier, "The Need for Special Resolution Regimes for Financial Institutions—The Case of the European Union," Figure 1, p. 5.

in relation to the bank's $7.4 billion capital base.[157] A few days after the Lehman filing, the bank put out a release that its actual exposure after offsetting hedging and pledged collateral was only a small fraction of that at less than $25 million.[158] Other creditor banks in the largest thirty unsecured claimants, such as Mizuho, BNP Paribas, and Shinsei Bank were not so diligent as to cover their potential exposures. However, not a single firm filed bankruptcy as a result of Lehman's failure.[159] Based on the evidence from the Lehman bankruptcy filing and the list of impacted creditors, some of the creditors properly hedged their

---

157. See Jean Helwege, "Financial Firm Bankruptcy and Systemic Risk," *Journal of International Financial Markets, Institutions & Money* 20 (2010): 6; and the *Regulation Magazine* article of the same name (Summer 2009): 27. Also see U.S. Bankruptcy Court, Southern District of New York, Voluntary Petition, Lehman Brothers Holdings Inc., September 14, 2008, Schedule 1, 30 Largest Unsecured Claims, 2.

158. Reuters, "Aozora Says Net Lehman Exposure May Be Under $25 Mln," September 15, 2008.

159. Jean Helwege, "A New Systemic Risk Regulator and Too Big to Fail," Center for the Study of Financial Regulation (Winter 2010): 3. Also see *Financial Crisis Inquiry Com-*

exposure to Lehman (such as Aozoro), and others did not and took a loss in the hundreds of millions (Mizuho, BNP Paribas, Shinsei Bank). This case study highlights the nature of bailouts and who their primary beneficiaries would have been in the case of Lehman. The banks like Aozora Bank that properly protected themselves by hedging and perfecting of collateral interests would not have benefited very much from a Lehman bailout despite their large exposure. Those companies that were more careless about their risk management, perversely, would have derived a greater benefit from a bailout.

As for the broader impact of the Lehman failure beyond the direct creditors, it is exceedingly difficult to parse out the impact of everything that was going on simultaneously as detailed by economist John Taylor:

> Many commentators have argued that the crisis worsened because the U.S. government (specifically the Treasury and the Federal Reserve) decided not to intervene to prevent the bankruptcy of Lehman Brothers over the weekend of September 13 and 14. It is difficult to bring a rigorous empirical analysis to this important question, but researchers must do so because future policy actions depend on the answer. Perhaps the best empirical analyses we can hope for at this time are event studies that look carefully at reactions in the financial markets to various decisions and events. Such an event study. . . . suggests that the answer is more complicated than the decision not to intervene to prevent the Lehman bankruptcy and, in my view, lies elsewhere.[160]

Taylor plots the commonly cited spread between the three-month London Inter-bank Offered Rate and the three-month overnight index swap (LIBOR-OIS Spread) as an indicator of financial stress (Figure 7.3). This spread rose dramatically as the crisis started in August 2007, going from roughly 0.1 percent to 1.0 percent in the summer of 2007. During and in the aftermath of the Lehman collapse from mid-September to mid-October it rose dramatically again from roughly 1.0 percent to nearly 4.0 percent. Taylor points out that in

---

*mission Report*, 339–40. Although this section discusses the "calamity" in the aftermath of the Lehman bankruptcy, despite the fact that it cites the losses at the Reserve Primary Fund, it cites no financial institutions that failed as a result of Lehman Brothers.
160. *Getting Off Track*, 25–26.

**Figure 7.3.** Taylor Event Study of Post-Lehman Period

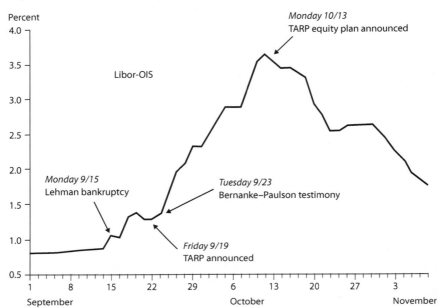

*Source*: *Getting Off Track*

the immediate aftermath of the Lehman bankruptcy during the week that followed the filing, this measure did rise, but it was not far out of line with the events of the prior year. But as the weeks wore on and the government announced a torrent of interventions, not all of which were consistent or clearly articulated, the spread was driven up to its height. Taylor refers to this period as "No Predictable Framework for Interventions."[161] These announcements, nearly all of which were interventions by government that under normal market conditions would have been dominant news, overwhelmed the fallout from Lehman, and there is no clear evidence that its failure had a dramatic effect on financial distress. It is no wonder that this blizzard of activity created enormous uncertainty for market participants (Table 7.8).

---

161. *Getting Off Track*, 28–29.

Yet another way of assessing the broader, indirect impact of the Lehman failure is to compare its immediate aftermath with the immediate aftermath of the bailout of American International Group (AIG) just a few days later. This can be done by comparing a variety of common indices on the day following the bankruptcy of Lehman and the bailout of AIG (Table 7.9). The disorderly bankruptcy theory would predict a dramatic difference. It is hard to argue that the broader market reaction was so significantly different between the two events.

Notwithstanding the characterization of the Lehman Brothers bankruptcy as disorderly, the firm of Alvarez and Marsal, the lead firm on the follow-through, has worked to unwind the firm in an orderly manner.[162] It was obviously a challenge to get the bankruptcy process ramped up, as there was almost no prior preparation—the expectation was that a bailout was imminent. Overall, the bankruptcy process has been smoother and, where needed, faster than almost anyone could have anticipated. When a company files Chapter 11, the managers continue to run the business, and most creditors are subject to the "automatic stay"—a rule that requires creditors to stop trying to collect what they are owed in order to give the company breathing space to begin dealing with the company's financial distress. Lehman and its lawyers—Harvey Miller and Weil, Gotshal—have used this process quite effectively. Three days after filing, Lehman arranged a sale of its North American investment banking business to Barclays, and the sale was quickly approved by the court after a lengthy hearing. Barclays provided a $450 million loan to fund Lehman's operations through the completion of the sale. As is common, the loan agreement required Lehman to appoint a professional turnaround manager to run the company. Its operations in Europe, the Middle East, and Asia were bought by Nomura, a large Japanese brokerage firm. By September 29, Lehman had agreed to sell its investment management business to two private equity firms.[163] It is hard to argue that the wind-up would have been more orderly if the firm had been bailed out by the Federal Reserve, the Treasury Department, or the FDIC.

---

162. "The Unwinding of Lehman Brothers," CNBC interview of Bryan Marsal, 20:54 run time, July 6, 2009, http://video.nytimes.com/video/2009/07/06/business/1194841374907/the-unwinding-of-lehman-brothers.html.

163. *New Financial Deal*, 29–31.

**Table 7.8.** Announcements (Government and Private) after Lehman Brothers' Failure as Rates and Spreads Broadened

| Date | Agency (Government) or Company (Private) | Action |
|---|---|---|
| 9/15/2008 | Bank of America | Announces intent to purchase Merrill Lynch & Co.[1] |
| 9/15/2008 | Lehman Brothers Holdings | Files for Chapter 11 bankruptcy protection[2] |
| 9/16/2008 | Federal Reserve | Authorizes the FRBNY to lend up to $85 billion to AIG[3] |
| 9/16/2008 | Primary Reserve Money Fund | Falls below $1, primarily due to losses on Lehman Brothers investments[4] |
| 9/17/2008 | SEC | Temporary emergency ban on short selling of financial sector stocks[5] |
| 9/18/2008 | Federal Reserve (FOMC) | Expands existing swap lines by $180 billion and authorizes new swap lines[6] |
| 9/19/2008 | Federal Reserve | Announces creation of the Asset-Backed Commercial Paper Mutual Fund[7] |

1. Bank of America Buys Merrill Lynch Creating Unique Financial Services Firm, September 15, 2008, http://newsroom.bankofamerica.com/index.php?s=43&item=8255.

2. Lehman Brothers Holdings Inc. Announces It Intends to File Chapter 11 Bankruptcy Petition, September 15, 2008, http://www.sec.gov/Archives/edgar/data/806085/000110465908059632/a08-22764_4ex99d1.htm.

3. Board of Governors of the Federal Reserve System, Press Release, September 16, 2008, http://www.federalreserve.gov/newsevents/press/other/20080916a.htm.

4. http://www.reservefunds.com/pdfs/Press%20Release%202008_0916.pdf.

5. SEC, "SEC Issues New Rules to Protect Investors Against Naked Short Selling Abuses," September 17, 2008, http://www.sec.gov/news/press/2008/2008-204.htm.

6. Board of Governors of the Federal Reserve System, Press Release, September 18, 2008, http://www.federalreserve.gov/newsevents/press/monetary/20080918a.htm.

7. Board of Governors of the Federal Reserve System, Press Release, September 19, 2008, http://www.federalreserve.gov/newsevents/press/monetary/20080919a.htm.

| Date | Agency (Government) or Company (Private) | Action |
|---|---|---|
| 9/19/2008 | Treasury | Announces temporary guaranty program for money market mutual funds[8] |
| 9/20/2008 | Treasury | Submits draft legislation to Congress for authority to purchase troubled assets[9] |
| 9/21/2008 | Federal Reserve | Approves applications of investment banking companies Goldman Sachs and Morgan Stanley[10] |
| 9/23/2008 | Treasury Federal Reserve Securities and Exchange Com. | Testimony before the Senate on asset purchase plan[11] |
| 9/24/2008 | Federal Reserve (FOMC) | Establishes new swap lines of $30 billion with various central banks[12] |
| 9/24/2008 | President Bush | National speech on financial crisis[13] |
| 9/25/2008 | Treasury (OTS) | Closes Washington Mutual Bank; JPMorgan Chase acquires[14] |

8. U.S. Department of the Treasury, "Treasury Announces Guaranty Program for Money Market Funds," September 19, 2008, http://www.ustreas.gov/press/releases/hp1147.htm.
9. U.S. Department of the Treasury, "Proposed Treasury Authority to Purchase Troubled Assets," September 20, 2008, http://www.ustreas.gov/press/releases/hp1150.htm.
10. Board of Governors of the Federal Reserve System, Press Release, September 21, 2008, http://www.federalreserve.gov/newsevents/press/bcreg/20080921a.htm.
11. See C-Span, "U.S. Credit Markets and Federal Rescue Plan, Senate Committee—Banking, Housing and Urban Affairs," 4:52:00 run time, September 23, 2008.
12. Board of Governors of the Federal Reserve System, Press Release, September 24, 2008, http://www.federalreserve.gov/newsevents/press/monetary/20080924a.htm.
13. TPMTV, "President Bush Addresses Nation on Economic Crisis," September 24, 2008, http://www.youtube.com/watch?v=YsDmPEeurfA&feature=related.
14. Office of Thrift Supervision, "Washington Mutual Acquired by JPMorgan Chase," September 25, 2008, http://www.ots.gov/index.cfm?p=PressReleases&ContentRecord_id =9c306c81–1e0b-8562-eb0c-fed542943a56&ContentType_id=4c12f337-b5b6–4c87-b45c -838958422bf3&MonthDisplay=9&YearDisplay=2008.

Table 7.8. *continued*

| Date | Agency (Government) or Company (Private) | Action |
|---|---|---|
| 9/26/2008 | Federal Reserve (FOMC) | Increases existing swap lines with the European Central Bank and Swiss National Bank[15] |
| 9/29/2008 | Federal Reserve (FOMC) | Authorizes a $330 billion expansion of swap lines with various central banks.[16] |
| 9/29/2008 | Treasury | Opens Temporary Guarantee Program for Money Market Funds[17] |
| 9/29/2008 | FDIC | Announces that Citigroup will purchase the banking operations of Wachovia Corporation[18] |
| 9/29/2008 | U.S. House | Rejects legislation submitted by the Treasury Department requesting authority to purchase troubled assets[19] |
| 10/03/2008 | Wells Fargo | Announces a competing proposal to purchase Wachovia Corporation unassisted by the FDIC[20] |

15. Board of Governors of the Federal Reserve System, Press Release, September 26, 2008, http://www.federalreserve.gov/newsevents/press/monetary/20080926a.htm.
16. Board of Governors of the Federal Reserve System, Press Release, September 29, 2008, http://www.federalreserve.gov/newsevents/press/monetary/20080929a.htm.
17. U.S. Department of Treasury, "Treasury Announces Temporary Guarantee Program for Money Market Funds," September 29, 2008, http://www.ustreas.gov/press/releases/hp1161 .htm.
18. FDIC, "Citigroup Inc. to Acquire Banking Operations of Wachovia," September 29, 2008, http://www.fdic.gov/news/news/press/2008/pr08088.html.
19. U.S. Department of the Treasury, "Statement by Secretary Henry M. Paulson, Jr. on Emergency Economic Stabilization Act Vote," September 29, 2008, http://www.treas.gov/ press/releases/hp1168.htm.
20. Statement by the Board of Governors of the Federal Reserve and the Office of the Comptroller of the Currency, October 3, 2008, http://www.federalreserve.gov/newsevents/press /bcreg/20081003a.htm.

| Date | Agency (Government) or Company (Private) | Action |
| --- | --- | --- |
| 10/03/2008 | U.S. Congress, President Bush | Passes and signs, respectively, the Emergency Economic Stabilization Act of 2008 which establishes TARP[21] |
| 10/06/2008 | Federal Reserve | Announces that it will pay interest on depository institutions' required and excess reserve balances[22] |
| 10/07/2008 | Federal Reserve | Announces the creation of the Commercial Paper Funding Facility (CPFF) to provide a liquidity backstop to commercial paper issuers[23] |
| 10/07/2008 | FDIC | Announces an increase in deposit insurance coverage to $250,000 per depositor as authorized under EESA[24] |
| 10/08/2008 | Federal Reserve | Authorizes FRBNY to borrow up to $37.8 billion in securities from AIG in return for cash collateral[25] |
| 10/08/2008 | Federal Reserve (FOMC) | Votes to reduce its target for the federal funds rate 50 basis points to 1.50 percent[26] |

21. Government Printing Office, Public Law 110–343, October 3, 2008, http://frwebgate.access.gpo.gov/cgi-bin/getdoc.cgi?dbname=110_cong_public_laws&docid=f:publ343.110.pdf.
22. Board of Governors of the Federal Reserve System, Press Release, October 6, 2008, http://www.federalreserve.gov/newsevents/press/monetary/20081006a.htm.
23. Board of Governors of the Federal Reserve System, Press Release, October 7, 2008, http://www.federalreserve.gov/newsevents/press/monetary/20081007c.htm.
24. FDIC, "Emergency Economic Stabilization Act of 2008 Temporarily Increases Basic FDIC Insurance Coverage from $100,000 to $250,000 Per Depositor," October 7, 2008, http://www.fdic.gov/news/news/press/2008/pr08093.html.
25. Board of Governors of the Federal Reserve System, Press Release, October 8, 2008, http://www.federalreserve.gov/newsevents/press/other/20081008a.htm.
26. Board of Governors of the Federal Reserve System, Press Release, October 8, 2008, http://www.federalreserve.gov/newsevents/press/monetary/20081008a.htm.

**Table 7.8.** *continued*

| Date | Agency (Government) or Company (Private) | Action |
|---|---|---|
| 10/12/2008 | Federal Reserve | Announces its approval of application of Wells Fargo to acquire Wachovia[27] |
| 10/13/2008 | Federal Reserve (FOMC) | Increases existing swap lines with foreign central banks[28] |
| 10/14/2008 | Treasury | Announces the TARP will purchase capital in financial institutions. Nine large financial institutions announce intention to subscribe to $125 billion[29] |
| 10/14/2008 | FDIC | Creates a new Temporary Liquidity Guarantee Program to guarantee various debt of all FDIC-insured institutions and their holding companies[30] |

27. Board of Governors of the Federal Reserve System, Press Release, October 12, 2008, http://www.federalreserve.gov/newsevents/press/orders/20081012a.htm.
28. Board of Governors of the Federal Reserve System, Press Release, October 13, 2008, http://www.federalreserve.gov/newsevents/press/monetary/20081013a.htm.
29. U.S. Department of the Treasury, "Treasury Announces TARP Capital Purchase Program Description," October 14, 2008, http://www.ustreas.gov/press/releases/hp1207.htm.
30. Federal Deposit Insurance Corporation, "FDIC Announces Plan to Free Up Bank Liquidity," October 14, 2008, http://www.fdic.gov/news/news/press/2008/pr08100.html.

*Source*: Largely based on the Federal Reserve Bank of St. Louis, "The Financial Crisis: A Timeline of Events and Policy Actions," http://timeline.stlouisfed.org/index.cfm?p=timeline.

**Table 7.9.** One-Day Difference in Indices Post-Lehman and AIG

| Index | Lehman | | | AIG | | |
|---|---|---|---|---|---|---|
| | 12-Sep | 15-Sep | change | 16-Sep | 17-Sep | change |
| S&P 500 | 1251.7 | 1192.7 | −4.71% | 1213.6 | 1156.39 | −4.71% |
| Volatility (VIX) | 25.66 | 31.7 | 23.54% | 30.3 | 36.22 | 19.54% |
| TED spread | 1.35 | 2.01 | 0.66 | 2.19 | 3.02 | 0.84 |
| 13-week treasury bill | 1.46 | 0.81 | −0.65 | 0.86 | 0.02 | −0.84 |

*Source*: Kenneth A. Ayotte and David A. Skeel, Jr. "Bankruptcy or Bailouts," *Journal of Corporation Law* 35 (2010), p. 469, 490.

Despite the efforts to demonize the decision to allow Lehman Brothers to fail, there were actually benefits that flowed from the failure of Lehman Brothers:

- There was an obvious reduction of moral hazard as the government finally demonstrated that it would allow a large financial institution to fail. Unfortunately, any benefits from this were undermined by later actions to undertake multiple bailouts of AIG, Citigroup, Bank of America, and the TARP program.

- Creditors were able to learn about the true fallout from the failure of Lehman Brothers, and it allowed investors and lenders to learn how to protect themselves in the future against failures of large financial institutions. For example, the breaking of the buck example has been cited as an example of the terrible fallout from the Lehman failure, but the loss by the Primary Fund was a mere 3 percent, and this revealed the possibility of losses in such money-market funds.

- As assets were sold off through bankruptcy, the failure led to price discovery, whereby the market moved back into balance aligning the reality of the market to overcome the distortions of previous mal-investment.

- We now have a case study of a bankruptcy filing, and one of the clear benefits of that knowledge is that we know that concerns regarding cascading failures were pure fantasy. No material financial institution bankruptcies flowed from the failure of Lehman Brothers.

- A poorly managed and possibly corrupt investment bank was taken out of the financial system, and those competitors that were able to take business away from Lehman were rightly rewarded for their ability to navigate their way through the crisis.[164]

- Lehman is resolved and no longer hangs over the financial system as an uncertainty, unlike the status of bailed-out, nationalized institutions like AIG, Fannie Mae, and Freddie Mac, which have lingered on for many years after the initial bailout.

### American International Group— The Orderly Resolution? (September 2008)

> "You guys have handed me a bag of sh*t."
> —FRBNY President Geithner displaying his
> displeasure with the OTS's supervision of AIG

> "Without the bailout, AIG's default and collapse could have brought down its counterparties, causing cascading losses throughout the financial system."
> —A speculative conclusion drawn by the FCIC
> which was unsubstantiated by clear evidence in
> the body of the underlying FCIC report.[165]

---

**False narrative:** AIG exploited a huge gap in the supervisory system and new powers are needed for a systemic risk supervisor to fill that gap.

---

164. In March 2010, a report was released by a court-appointed examiner that detailed an accounting procedure, repo 105, which allowed Lehman Brothers to appear to have lower leverage than it in fact did. Jenner and Block, "Lehman Brothers Holding, Inc.: Chapter 11 Proceedings Examiner's Report." Additionally, Ernst and Young is under scrutiny for the quality of its audits of Lehman Brothers. However, it appears that there are no clear cases of criminally prosecutable action that contributed to the Lehman collapse.

165. *Financial Crisis Inquiry Commission Report*, 351–52. The Geithner quote is from an interview with John Reich by the FCIC, May 4, 2010. The speculative comment is contained in a summary of the AIG chapter.

*Circumstances Leading to the Stress*

On the morning of the Lehman Brothers filing, key newspapers highlighted the cash squeeze of AIG.[166] Previously, at the last meeting of the major banks attempting to put together a private sector bailout of Lehman, AIG was already a topic for discussion.[167] AIG experienced liquidity and capital problems driven in large part by losses in a unit separate from its traditional insurance businesses. That financial products unit sold CDS contracts designed to protect investors against defaults on an array of assets, including mortgage-related securities tied to pools of subprime mortgages. As housing values fell and the subprime-mortgage market crumbled, exposure of AIG on the contracts rose, driving $18 billion in losses over the course of three quarters, forcing AIG to put up billions of dollars in collateral.[168] Internal models employed by AIG, as well as those of most other financial institutions and ratings agencies, were fatally flawed as to their assumptions regarding the risk of these assets.[169]

Beginning in July 2008, one fear on the minds of senior management at AIG was a Bear Stearns–like scenario that would be triggered by a ratings downgrade. Management began to analyze their problems and tried to rationalize that they were merely experiencing a liquidity problem, not a solvency problem. They were dumbfounded by the fact that although they thought they had hundreds of billions of dollars' worth of securities and collateral, if their situation worsened a spiral could begin of selling assets quickly at deep discounts. A downgrade could trigger covenants in its debt agreements to post even more collateral, making the spiral even worse.[170] Executives at AIG spent the weekend of September 13 and 14

---

166. Carrick Mollenkamp, Susanne Craig, Serena Ng, and Aaron Lucchetti, "Crisis on Wall Street as Lehman Totters, Merrill Is Sold, AIG Seeks Cash," *Wall Street Journal*, September 15, 2008 [hereinafter, "Crisis on Wall Street"].

167. *On the Brink*, 193. Vikram Pandit of Citigroup asked if the group would talk about AIG. FRBNY President Geithner said in response: "Let's focus on Lehman."

168. Matthew Karnitschnig et al., "U.S. to Take Over AIG in $85 Billion Bailout," *Wall Street Journal*, September 16, 2008 [hereinafter, Matthew Karnitschnig et al.].

169. Carrick Mollenkamp, Serena Ng, Liam Pleven, and Randall Smith, "Behind AIG's Fall, Risk Models Failed to Pass Real-World Test," *Wall Street Journal*, October 31, 2008.

170. Chief Executive Officer Willumstad and Head of Strategy Brian T. Schreiber discussed these issues at length, *Too Big to Fail*, 207.

trying to raise cash, either from asset sales, a capital infusion from private-equity firms, or both. They also met with state regulators to see if they could transfer capital from some of AIG's subsidiaries to the parent holding company.[171] The governor of New York, David Paterson, and the State Insurance Department considered allowing AIG to access $20 billion from its insurance subsidiaries.[172] When credit-rating agencies ultimately downgraded AIG debt on September 15, it led to collateral calls of $14.5 billion.[173]

The standard narrative about ongoing oversight of AIG in the lead-up to this dire financial position was that AIG took advantage of or "gamed" a gap in the regulatory system as argued by Chairman Bernanke in testimony:

> AIG exploited a huge gap in the regulatory system, there was no over-sight of the financial-products division, this was a hedge fund basically that was attached to a large and stable insurance company.[174]

In turn, Chairman Bernanke has advanced the argument that legislative changes were needed to address this gap.[175] Much of the media and many commentators have accepted this same narrative.[176] Chairman Bernanke's comments would lead one to believe that of all the federal financial agencies of the government, none of them had the responsibility for watching over the activities of

---

171. "Crisis on Wall Street."

172. COP AIG Report, 62.

173. David S. Hilzenrath and Glenn Kessler, "U.S. Seizes Control of AIG With $85 Billion Emergency Loan," *Washington Post*, September 17, 2008. Matthew Karnitschnig et al.

174. Craig Torres and Hugh Son, "Bernanke Says Insurer AIG Operated Like a Hedge Fund," Bloomberg.com, March 3, 2009, http://www.bloomberg.com/apps/news?pid=20601110&sid=aon7qoAGB_m4. C-Span, "The Federal Budget and the Economy," Chairman Bernanke testimony before the Senate Budget Committee, 1:56:42 run time, March 3, 2009.

175. "Bernanke Angry About AIG," *Wall Street Journal*, March 3, 2009 ("We have no structure—no legal and regulatory structure—that allows us to resolve in a safe and sound way a large financial international conglomerate," he said. "We're much better off, frankly, trying to resolve it within the context of continued operation than to allow it to fail and allow all the chaos that would occur following a bankruptcy.").

176. *In Fed We Trust*, 190 (". . . the size and reach of the hedge fund that AIG had built without any regulator realizing what it was doing"), and 194 as the Bernanke language is presented without questioning its basis.

AIG, and in particular its financial products division. However, an analysis of the record leads to a different conclusion.

Federal financial agencies implement a range of programs of oversight for financial institutions. The extent of scrutiny applied to institutions varies, but is usually classified as regulation, supervision, or oversight. The distinctions between the three types of scrutiny are that regulations are usually quantitative, rules-based, and inflexible in nature; supervision is more qualitative and flexible relying on first-hand observation combined with the judgment of the supervisor; and oversight is a more detached analysis and less intrusive than supervision.[177]

The holding company for AIG was supervised by and under the oversight of the Office of Thrift Supervision (OTS), which is housed within the Treasury Department. OTS supervises savings associations and their holding companies to maintain their safety, soundness, and compliance with consumer laws. OTS was the consolidated supervisor of AIG, a savings and loan holding company. OTS had the authority to supervise and examine each holding company enterprise and relied on functional regulators for information on specific entities within the holding company.[178] As an example of their supervision, during their

---

177. The distinctions in the following discussion between supervision, regulation, and oversight are cogently summarized in Ernest T. Patrikis, first vice president, Federal Reserve Bank of New York, March 1, 1997 ("While I can describe the differences between oversight, supervision, and regulation by drawing sharp lines, in reality, the lines are not that sharp. Regulation is prescriptive, often quantitative, and generally not very flexible. It may prohibit an activity or prevent it. It may prevent it in a limited way, for example, in proportion to capital. It involves the formulation and issuance of specific rules and regulations, under governing law, for the conduct of business. Supervision is more qualitative. It depends upon the judgment of an examiner or inspector. It involves the safety and soundness of specific institutions, in the light of the general continuous review of the activities of the entire industry to ensure prudent operation and compliance with law and regulation. Oversight is a form of general supervision. It typically is used to refer to the monitoring of a corporate group, as opposed to a specific firm. Oversight is considered much less intrusive than supervision and might be viewed as surveillance, normally conducted at a distance, while supervision involves close, first-hand observation and analysis.").
178. OTS was the consolidated supervisor of AIG due to its status as a savings and loan holding company. Scott Polakoff, acting director, Office of Thrift Supervision, "American International Group: Examining What Went Wrong, Government Intervention, and Implications for Future Regulation," Committee on Banking, Housing, and Urban Affairs, U.S. Senate, March 5, 2009, 6 [hereinafter, Polakoff Testimony].

review of capital adequacy, OTS considered the risk inherent in an enterprise's activities. In extensive detail in early 2009 testimony before the Senate Committee on Banking, Housing, and Urban Affairs, Scott Polakoff, the acting director of OTS, outlined chronologically how the agency and various global functional regulators had supervised and had oversight over the activities of AIG, including its financial products division:

- In 1999 AIG applied to form a federal savings bank, which was approved in 2000 as AIG FSB.
- In 2000, OTS focused on the impact of the holding company on AIG FSB.
- In 2003, as OTS's supervision of holding companies evolved, it took a more enterprise-wide approach to supervising conglomerates like AIG. OTS was responsible for communicating with other functional regulators and supervisors who shared jurisdiction over AIG consistent with the Gramm-Leach-Bliley legislation passed in the late 1990s.
- In 2005, OTS began to convene annual supervisory college meetings with key foreign supervisory agencies and U.S. state insurance regulators. During the part of the meeting devoted to presentations from AIG, supervisors had an opportunity to question the company about supervisory or risk issues. AIG had a multitude of regulators in more than 100 countries. OTS established relationships with these regulators through information-sharing agreements and obtained their assessment of concerns for their segment of AIG.[179]
- In 2005, OTS conducted several targeted, risk-focused reviews of various business lines at AIG, including the financial products division, and made many recommendations to management regarding risk management oversight, financial reporting, and corporate governance. A report was issued to the AIG Board in March 2006 that noted weak-

---

179. Also see *Financial Crisis Inquiry Commission Report*, 350 ("Starting in 2004, the OTS worked to persuade the European Union that it was capable of serving as AIG's 'home country consolidated supervisor.' In 2005, the agency wrote: 'AIG and its subsidiaries are subject to consolidated supervision by OTS . . . as part of its supervision, OTS will conduct continuous on-site reviews of AIG and its subsidiaries.'").

nesses in AIG's management and internal relationships, especially the Corporate Legal Compliance Group and Internal Audit Division.

As to the financial products division, OTS made numerous recommendations regarding weaknesses in documentation of complex transactions, accounting policies and procedures, stress testing, communication of risk tolerances, and lines of authority, as well as credit risk management and measurement.[180]

- In 2006, OTS adopted a risk-focused continuous supervision program and implemented it for AIG through an on-site examination team at headquarters in New York to maintain a contemporaneous understanding of all material parts of AIG, including domestic and cross-border operations. As part of the program, monthly meetings were held with AIG's Regulatory and Compliance Group, Internal Audit Director, and external auditors. Quarterly meetings were held with the chief risk officer, the Treasury Group, and senior management, and annual meetings were held with the Board of Directors.

- In 2007, as the U.S. mortgage market began to deteriorate, OTS increased scrutiny of AIG's financial products division and American General Finance (AGF), a major provider of consumer finance products. A supervisory agreement was also signed by OTS and AIG FSB.

- After a 2007 review of the financial products division, OTS instructed them to revisit their assumptions regarding financial modeling in light of the deterioration in the subprime market.

- In mid 2007, OTS questioned AIG about the evaluation of CDS backed by subprime mortgages.

- In October 2007, OTS took action against AIG on a number of fronts, including regarding weaknesses and deficiencies in risk management and assessment, reporting, and compliance. OTS worked with AIG's external auditor, PwC, on problems related to CDS and a related material weakness reported through an SEC 8K filing.

---

180. AIG's financial products subsidiary lead, Joseph Cassano, felt the OTS did not have the power to examine his subsidiary. See *Financial Crisis Inquiry Commission Report*, 351 ("I overheard one employee saying that Joe Cassano felt that [the OTS was] overreaching our scope by going into FP").

- OTS met with AIG senior management in March 2008 and downgraded their savings and loan holding company supervisory rating (CORE— Capital, Organizational Structure, Relationship, and Earnings).
- OTS sent a letter to AIG's general counsel detailing risk management failures in March 2008.
- In August 2008, OTS reviewed and accepted a final comprehensive remediation plan.
- As AIG's liquidity position became more precarious in September 2008, OTS initiated heightened communications with domestic and international financial regulators. OTS identified the financial products division as the focal point of AIG's problems.[181]

The effort of the OTS and the global functional regulators belies the notion that somehow deregulation or a lack of regulation was the underlying basis for the problems at AIG or more broadly the entire financial crisis. Derivatives and unregulated financial products and practices, including CDS, have been cited as one of the causes of the financial crisis, and AIG use of the product is one of the cases cited to support this notion.[182]

Chairman Bernanke implied that there was an enormous gap in the oversight with regard to AIG. However, as part of his testimony, Scott Polakoff of OTS recognized that a supervisory failure was at the root of the problem and his predecessor as director of the OTS, John Reich, admitted that the OTS had never fully understood the financial products unit and thus could not regulate it. Polakoff admitted his agency did not foresee the extent of the risk concentration in the financial products division of AIG and the potential systemic impact CDS products had. This disagreement between the Federal Reserve and OTS was illustrated in an exchange between Polakoff and Vice Chairman Don Kohn of the Federal Reserve while both were testifying before the Senate Committee. On full display was the spectacle of Polakoff arguing that OTS was responsible for oversight and supervision of AIG, and Kohn of the Federal Reserve arguing

---

181. Polakoff Testimony, 7–16.
182. The FCIC was created in 2009 with the express purpose of examining the causes of the crisis. Of the twenty-two specific areas of inquiry for the FCIC, one is "derivatives and unregulated financial products and practices, including credit default swaps," http://www.fcic.gov/about/.

that no one was responsible for oversight and supervision of AIG.[183] Clearly in light of all the evidence presented by Polakoff, he had the better of the argument.

Beyond the breakdown at the supervisory agency level, the AIG case was a perfect opportunity for the WGFM, created in the aftermath of the stock market crash of 1987, to address the building problems at financial institutions. After all, the WGFM was chaired by the Treasury Department, which had the OTS as one of its constituent offices; had on its membership the Chairman of the Federal Reserve, which takes responsibility for overall financial stability; and also had on its membership the SEC and the Commodity Futures Trading Commission (CFTC), which take responsibility for regulating a variety of financial instruments.[184] The WGFM was structured to coordinate at a high level in just such a situation where collective action was needed to address a potential systemic risk.

Secretary Paulson, the chair of the WGFM, has noted numerous times that he chaired meetings or otherwise held events revolving around the WGFM's work: an initial meeting in August 2006; the release of Treasury's analysis of the financial crisis in March 2008; in the aftermath of the AIG meltdown in September 2008; and just after the passage of the TARP legislation in October 2008. However, he cites a number of problems with the workings of the group both before and during his time as Treasury Secretary, including that the agencies were competitive and did not share information with one another, and that the group was essentially ceremonial and meetings were ad hoc and brief with no

---

183. Polakoff Testimony, 17. C-Span, "Government Intervention and Regulation of AIG," Senate Committee on Banking, Housing, and Urban Affairs, March 5, 2009; minutes 64:00 to 66:00 is where Vice Chairman of the Board of Governors Donald Kohn notes that no one was responsible for the whole company and that the AIGFP was not supervised by anybody, and then Polakoff notes that on this point there is a "slight difference of opinion" and discusses the oversight of the AIG holding company by OTS, consistent with his testimony as summarized in the text above. A similar exchange occurs from minutes 74:00 to 79:00. Also see "Volcker Says States Share AIG Blame," *Wall Street Journal*, February 26, 2010. Volcker did not mention the supervision by OTS in this article, but instead oddly blamed the problem of supervision on state supervisors.

184. For a sample of releases of the WGFM, see U.S. Department of the Treasury, "Remarks by Secretary Henry M. Paulson, Jr. on Recommendations from the President's Working Group on Financial Markets," March 13, 2008, http://www.treas.gov/press/releases/hp872.htm.

staff presentations. He concluded that overall the WGFM was ineffective and as an example he cited a statement issued by the group in October 2008 in the midst of the crisis that was intended to reassure markets, but which instead fell flat.[185]

*Assessing the Magnitude of the Problem*

Throughout the summer of 2008, AIG's management continued their efforts to address building liquidity and capital problems, and they were hopeful that government-backed sources of funding would be made available to the company. In late July, AIG's Chairman Willumstad met with FRBNY President Geithner in an attempt to gain access to the Federal Reserve's discount window, to which many investment banks had received access. In putting off Willumstad, Geithner cited the historic nature of extending this funding source to an insurance company and the difficulty of getting such a move approved.[186]

By August 2008, staff from the FRBNY held what they referred to as a "long sought meeting" with counterpart staff from the OTS, the primary federal supervisor of AIG. The OTS representatives discussed a recent AIG capital raise of $20 billion, which they noted was primarily for liquidity purposes and much of which was used to support AIG financial products. The OTS was generally comfortable with AIG's liquidity position, and they also made clear their confidence that AIG could access the capital markets, noting that AIG had $3 to $5 billion in "excess capital."[187] A summary prepared shortly thereafter by an FRBNY analyst described the condition of AIG as "under increasing capital and liquidity pressure." The report also noted the significant amounts of near-term liabilities coming due, the ratings-based triggers that could result in significant collateral calls of up to $18 billion, and the lack of standby credit facilities to manage sudden cash needs.[188]

---

185. *On the Brink*, 50–52, 90, 235–37, 331–34. At the meeting during the meltdown of AIG, President George W. Bush made the oft-quoted comment that "Someday you guys are going to have to tell me how we ended up with a system like this and what we need to do to fix it."

186. *Too Big to Fail*, 207–9.

187. FCIC Bates No. AIG0015409 email from Kevin Coffey titled "AIG Meeting with OTS" forwarded to various FRBNY staff, August 14, 2008.

188. FCIC Bates No. AIG0015390 report by Kevin Coffey titled "AIG—Summary of Potential Earnings, Capital and Liquidity Issues," August 14, 2008.

Another FRBNY analysis about two weeks later in early September revealed a rapidly deteriorating situation, described the AIG liquidity position as "precarious," and noted that borrowing through the PDCF could potentially allow the firm to unwind its positions in an orderly manner. However, it noted that access to such a facility was not necessary for the survival of the firm. The analysis identified as contributors to this precarious financial position the reliance on volatile funding sources and off-balance-sheet commitments that could lead to collateral calls, contract terminations, and the exercise of put options. In its final paragraph, the report relays the comments of a Goldman Sachs analyst who concluded that AIG management and the rating agencies were in denial over the losses embedded in AIG and that they were ill prepared for the challenges facing the firm.[189] Although these two sets of analysis in August and early September did focus on some of the firm-specific problems at AIG, they did not seriously consider the possibility of an AIG failure or the potential externalities that would result from such a failure.

As the evidence began to build in early September 2008 that AIG's problems were coming to a head, Willumstad again met with FRBNY President Geithner to lobby for a coveted position as the equivalent of a primary dealer.[190] This would allow AIG to have access to the PDCF. Geithner was not responsive this time either, as he was consumed with Lehman Brothers. At that time, Willumstad did not raise a red flag that AIG was facing serious issues.[191] At that

---

189. FCIC Bates No. AIG0016236 report without author cited titled "AIG Liquidity and Access to the PDCF," September 2, 2008.

190. As part of this status the primary dealers are obligated to: (1) participate in the execution of open market operations, and (2) provide the FRBNY's trading desk with market information and analysis helpful in the formulation and implementation of monetary policy. Primary dealers are also required to participate in all auctions of U.S. government debt and to make reasonable markets for the FRBNY when it transacts on behalf of its foreign official account-holders. FRBNY, "Administration of Relationships with Primary Dealers," January 11, 2010.

191. *Too Big to Fail,* 235–37. Congressional Oversight Panel (COP), "June Oversight Report: The AIG Rescue, Its Impact on the Markets, and the Government's Exit Strategy," June 10, 2010, 128. The meeting occurred on September 9, 2008. It appears that the request for access to the discount window was not taken seriously until September 14, when FRBNY President Geithner received a briefing on discount window access. Email from Paul Whynott to various FRBNY staff, "AIG Update," September 14, 2008, 11:54 a.m. (Bates No. FRBNYAIG00459).

September meeting, apparently in an effort to get Geithner to focus on the request, Willumstad gave him a report that detailed AIG's counterparty exposures. The report was part of Willumstad's continuing lobbying effort that AIG was systemic and that Geithner should take notice. The report detailed $2.7 trillion of notional derivative value around the world with 12,000 individual contracts. Most importantly, about $1 trillion of that value was concentrated with twelve major financial institutions. The journalist that uncovered this report concluded that based on this report it pointed to only one conclusion: "You didn't have to be a Harvard MBA to instantly comprehend the significance of that figure. If AIG went under, it could take the entire financial system along with it."[192] But the question is whether a Harvard MBA would jump to such a quick conclusion without digging further into the precise impact of a potential AIG failure.

Only a few days later, on September 12, 2008, another Bear Stearns–like scene began to take shape as staff at the Board of Governors once again went through a seat-of-the-pants analysis to get the most basic information on AIG over just a matter of a few days in order to understand the potential impact of an AIG failure on other financial institutions:

> "I am getting a lot of questions from Investors about AIG. . . . It kinda feels like the market is melting down again for financials."[193]
>
> "Do you guys have an expert on AIG?"[194]
>
> "What do you know about AIG? Have you produced memos on them anytime recently?"[195]
>
> "We don't have an expert on the company, but I do believe we have done some work on their credit exposures."[196]

---

192. *Too Big to Fail,* 236–37.

193. *McKinley v. Board of Governors,* Bates No. BOG–FOIA 10–251–000005 email from unidentified market contact (name redacted) titled "I am getting a lot of questions from Investors about AIG," sent to various FRBNY staff, September 12, 2008, 9:30 a.m.

194. *McKinley v. Board of Governors,* Bates No. BOG–FOIA 10–251–000006 email from William English titled "AIG," sent to Deborah P. Bailey, September 12, 2008.

195. *McKinley v. Board of Governors,* Bates No. BOG–FOIA 10–251–000010 email from William English titled "AIG," sent to Maria Perozek, September 12, 2008.

196. *McKinley v. Board of Governors,* Bates No. BOG–FOIA 10–251–000007 email from Jon Greenlee titled "AIG," sent to William English, September 12, 2008.

"Anyone in your group know much about AIG?"[197]

"Trish Mosser just called. AIG is coming to FRBNY this afternoon. Evidently they have a huge hole and are worried about downgrades, liquidity problems. Source of hole is credit derivatives. She will call later with details."[198]

"NY Fed talked with them. It's not good."[199]

"I've heard. One FRBNY staffer thinks it's in worse shape than [Lehman Brothers]."[200]

"There is a big concern. I did tell the Chairman and vice chairman because the President of AIG said that he was planning to call the Chairman and vice chairman re: 13–3 loan. We are working on background of the Co. AIG is under the OTS."[201]

"You will get an email later. You probably will be invited to a meeting tomorrow.

They are in terrible shape, possibly worse than Lehman! The losses are at the derivative products sub."[202]

"Given how dire the situation with AIG is, Jim and I thought we should probably follow up to get more information on their risk profile, etc. sometime tomorrow."[203]

---

197. *McKinley v. Board of Governors,* Bates No. BOG–FOIA 10–251–000008 email from Jon Greenlee titled "AIG," sent to Sabeth I. Siddique, September 12, 2008.

198. *McKinley v. Board of Governors,* Bates No. BOG–FOIA 10–251–000014 email from Pat Parkinson titled "AIG," sent to Brian Madigan and Michael Gibson, September 12, 2008.

199. *McKinley v. Board of Governors,* Bates No. BOG–FOIA 10–251–000020 email from Deborah P. Bailey titled "AIG," sent to Pat Parkinson, September 12, 2008.

200. *McKinley v. Board of Governors,* Bates No. BOG–FOIA 10–251–000020 email from Pat Parkinson titled "AIG," sent to Deborah P. Bailey, September 12, 2008. This comment raises the question why the Federal Reserve would even consider assisting AIG if the financial position of AIG were worse than that of Lehman Brothers.

201. *McKinley v. Board of Governors,* Bates No. BOG–FOIA 10–251–000020 email from Deborah P. Bailey titled "AIG," sent to Pat Parkinson, Brian Madigan, Scott Alvarez, and Jon Greenlee, September 12, 2008.

202. *McKinley v. Board of Governors,* Bates No. BOG–FOIA 10–251–000020 email from Pat Parkinson titled "AIG," sent to Michael Gibson, September 12, 2008.

203. *McKinley v. Board of Governors,* Bates No. BOG–FOIA 10–251–000029 email from Patricia Mosser titled "followup with AIG," sent to various FRBNY and Board staff, September 12, 2008.

"Moody's report is very recent (mid August), so may be useful background. Here is the important instution [sic] webpage from [Moody's] website."[204]

"I found very little on the derivatives activities of AIG, which is frustrating. They don't seem to say much in the 10-Ks/10-Qs."[205]

"Can one of you guys give me a call so we can coordinate the work on AIG and hopefully reduce overlap?"[206]

"Obvious question is what major bank counterparties think their exposures are. Given market awareness of AIG's problems, I see no reason not to ask the banks."[207]

"Sorry . . . need to get an understanding of lehman bros [sic] exposures at the firm and aig . . . without going to the firm . . . any chance u [sic] all have reports lying around."[208]

"At this point, I need you not to go to your banks regarding AIG or Lehman but rather to go to you [sic] internal MIS to determine the impact of a bankruptcy of Lehman or AIG to your organization."[209]

At about this time, the FRBNY was becoming fully aware of the potential for systemic problems with AIG. Hayley Boesky, the director of market analysis at the FRBNY, sent an email titled "AIG panic." Not unlike the Bear Stearns analysis and the reactions at the Board of Governors, it appeared the FRBNY

---

204. *McKinley v. Board of Governors,* Bates No. BOG–FOIA 10–251–000033 email from William Nelson titled "some additional info on AIG," sent to various Board staff, September 12, 2008.

205. *McKinley v. Board of Governors,* Bates No. BOG–FOIA 10–251–000055 email from William English titled "Background on AIG," sent to Brian Madigan, September 13, 2008.

206. *McKinley v. Board of Governors,* Bates No. BOG–FOIA 10–251–000085 email from Michael Gibson titled "AIG," sent to various FRBNY staff, September 13, 2008.

207. *McKinley v. Board of Governors,* Bates No. BOG–FOIA 10–251–000069 email from Pat Parkinson titled "Update on AIG," sent to Brian Madigan and Deborah P. Bailey, September 13, 2008.

208. *McKinley v. Board of Governors,* Bates No. BOG–FOIA 10–251–000114 email from Coryann Stefansson titled "Lehman, Wamu and AIG restricted," sent to James Barnes, dated September 13, 2008.

209. *McKinley v. Board of Governors,* Bates No. BOG–FOIA 10–251–000290 email from Coryann Stefansson titled "Previous email," sent to various Reserve Bank staff, September 13, 2008.

staff knew very little about AIG as the references were based on secondhand information and contained no independent analysis of the situation:

> "More panic from the [hedge funds]. Now focus is on AIG. I am hearing worse than LEH [Lehman Brothers]. Every bank and dealer has exposure to them. People I heard from worry they can't roll over their funding. Were big writers of GIC and negative basis buyers. Estimate I hear is $2 trillion balance sheet."[210]

The afternoon of September 12, top management of AIG met with staff from the FRBNY and detailed the firm's liquidity problems: They only had five to ten days before they ran out of liquidity; there was a potential for rating agency downgrades; there were problems with counterparties pulling back in the repo markets; and there was difficulty in rolling over commercial paper. AIG proposed a number of possible solutions to the building problems including asset sales and the use of PDCF-eligible collateral. However, they noted that many of the assets were in distressed or illiquid markets or at various insurance subsidiaries that could be under regulatory limitations on asset disposition. AIG staff at the meeting made the same point that Willumstad had made only a few days earlier with Geithner: "Unwinding in event of bankruptcy is likely to be very messy, because derivatives book is large and complex $2.7 trillion, largely of very long-term structure products. $1 trillion is concentrated in 12 large counterparties." The final point of discussion in the meeting was a request for funding: "They explicitly asked about how to obtain an [individuals, partnerships and corporations] 13–3 loan."[211]

Another call followed that night at 8 p.m., as summarized by Brian Madigan at the Board of Governors: "We (NY and Board staff) had a conf call with AIG this evening. The situation seems very serious. I will be filling [Vice Chairman] Don [Kohn] in shortly. Board staff will be meeting at 8 a.m. and then briefing

210. Email from Hayley Boesky to Bill Dudley, Michael Schetzel, Brian Peters, and Meg McConnell, "AIG Panic," September 12, 2008, 6:58 p.m. Bates No. FRBNYAIG00511. The estimate of $2 trillion seems to be wildly overstated as AIG total assets at this time were about half that level.

211. *McKinley v. Board of Governors,* Bates No. BOG–FOIA 10–251–000025 email from Patricia Mosser titled "AIG Meeting this Afternoon," sent to various staff of the FRBNY and Board of Governors, September 12, 2008.

the Chairman."[212] At that meeting, the issue came up again of "the 12 largest international banks (both U.S. and European) across a wide array of product types (bank lines, derivatives, securities lending, etc.) meaning there could be significant counterparty losses to those firms in the event of AIG's failure . . . $2.7 trillion in notional derivatives exposure across all books across 12 major dealers."[213] Madigan then gave a heads-up to Chairman Bernanke: "Staff participated in a call yesterday evening in which AIG further briefed us on the firm's situation. The firm is requesting a loan from the Federal Reserve. We are in the office this morning analyzing the situation. We will brief you soon."[214]

The communications with AIG continued into September 13, and the descriptions became more dramatic and dire as noted in the comments of Vice Chairman Don Kohn:

> Staff has been in contact with AIG (Jacob) this morning. AIG sees this as a liquidity event and has investment bankers looking at assets this weekend but will not sell off core assets and is not seeking a major equity injection or strategic partner. They face the possibility of a multi-grade downgrade ffrom [sic] Moody's on Monday, which would probably be the death knell. They were vague as to what they expected from us except that it sounded like an open ended liquidity facility. . . . AIG will get back to us later this morning with a more specific request for us and a more specific plan for raising cash and capital. they [sic] are talking to the insurance commissioners at 10.[215]

Staff of the Board of Governors and the FRBNY began to circulate spreadsheets with exposure data for banks reminiscent of the analysis taken during

---

212. *McKinley v. Board of Governors,* Bates No. BOG–FOIA 10–251–000051 email from Brian Madigan titled "AIG," sent to Patrick Parkinson, September 12, 2008.

213. *McKinley v. Board of Governors,* Bates No. BOG–FOIA 10–251–000053 email from Meg McConnell to Kevin Warsh titled "Update on AIG," September 13, 2008 forwarding an email from Alejandro LaTorre to various FRBNY staff dated September 12, 2008.

214. *McKinley v. Board of Governors,* Bates No. BOG–FOIA 10–251–000068 email from Brian Madigan to Chairman Ben Bernanke titled "AIG," September 13, 2008.

215. *McKinley v. Board of Governors,* Bates No. BOG–FOIA 10–251–000072 email from Vice Chairman Don Kohn to Chairman Ben Bernanke, Timothy Geithner, and Kevin Warsh titled "AIG," September 13, 2008.

March 2008 as Bear Stearns came close to filing bankruptcy. The data of particular interest was a list of the "Total Exposures to AIG" described as "what firms stand to lose in the event of AIG default" (see Table 7.10). More than forty financial institutions were on the list including Goldman Sachs, Bank of America, Citigroup, Morgan Stanley, and Lehman Brothers.[216]

At first glance, the numbers look quite daunting, with the world's largest banks having a trillion dollars of total value and more than $100 billion that they "stand to lose." However, these numbers are far removed from estimates of expected losses. A deeper analysis of just one of the banks on the list—Goldman Sachs—reveals that the numbers in the table, as well as on Willumstad's list before it, are nearly meaningless. Goldman likely had about $100 billion of total exposure on Willumstad's list given to Geithner and $9 billion of loss exposure in Table 7.10. However, the problem is that the analysis has to be done on a "net" basis, taking into account any offsetting hedges. In fact, Goldman had so heavily hedged their exposure to AIG that Gary Cohn, the firm's co-president and chief operating officer, reportedly boasted that Goldman might actually make $50 million if AIG collapsed.[217] The true exposure is also overstated because the institution likely still has a loan or debt on its books, which may or may not go into default. To do a true analysis of exposure, all such hedging and default scenarios for all of the banks would have to be taken into account. There is no evidence that the FRBNY or the Board staff in Washington undertook that more detailed and accurate analysis.[218]

Based on this available data, the FRBNY has cited three primary justifications for intervening on the basis of systemic risk:[219]

---

216. *McKinley v. Board of Governors,* Bates No. BOG–FOIA 10–251–000099 email from Brandon Hall to bank supervision staff titled "LFI Exposures to AIG," September 13, 2008. Email from Michael Held to Timothy Geithner, "Pros and Cons on AIG Lending," September 14, 2008, 4:44 p.m. Bates Number FRBNYAIG00496.

217. *Too Big to Fail,* 382.

218. There was also an additional analysis of financial system risk undertaken, but it did not look at the individual exposures, but instead used an estimate of "spillover risk" developed at the FRBNY. FCIC-SSI0001367 email from Tobias Adrian titled "AIG's Financial System Risk," sent to various FRBNY staff on September 13, 2008.

219. As set forth in COP AIG Report, 131–33.

**Table 7.10.** Twenty Largest Banks—AIG Loss Exposure
(September 14, 2008)

| Bank Name | Total Exposure to AIG ($s in millions) |
|---|---|
| ABN Amro | $14,683 |
| BNP Paribas | 12,684 |
| Deutsche Bank | 12,670 |
| Barclays | 11,952 |
| Danske | 9,358 |
| Goldman Sachs | 8,927 |
| Calyon | 6,709 |
| Societe Generale | 6,033 |
| UBS | 5,780 |
| Bank of America | 5,695 |
| Citigroup | 5,343 |
| HSBC | 5,103 |
| ING | 4,947 |
| Credit Suisse | 4,850 |
| Morgan Stanley | 4,803 |
| Lehman Brothers | 3,861 |
| Banco Santander | 3,650 |
| JPMorgan | 3,501 |
| Merrill Lynch | 3,277 |
| Dresdner | 2,930 |

*Source*: Email forwarded to Timothy Geithner from Michael Held,
data compiled by Alejandro LaTorre, September 14, 2008.

- Given AIG's role as a large seller of CDS, an AIG failure could have
  exposed its counterparties to large losses and disrupted the operation
  of the payments and settlements system. According to Geithner, if the
  AIG parent holding company had filed for bankruptcy, defaults on more
  than $100 billion of debt and trillions of dollars of derivatives would

have resulted.[220] Another internal analysis of the FRBNY speculated that due to its size, franchise, and the wholesale and retail dimensions of its business, there was significant name risk and potential contagion with a failure of AIG, which would have a greater impact than the failure of Lehman Brothers.[221] A congressional body that analyzed the AIG bailout, the Congressional Oversight Panel (COP), has speculated about a "domino effect" across AIG counterparties and the capital markets, domestically as well as internationally.[222] These included concerns about AIG insurance subsidiaries. However, these analyses appear to be nothing more than idle speculation as the actual projected losses from defaults is never revealed and evidence has never been presented that this contagion would have materialized. AIG insurance subsidiaries were separately capitalized and supervised by state insurance commissioners.[223] Finally, FRBNY and Treasury argued that banks and other counterparties that used AIG's CDS as protection would have suddenly found themselves un-hedged and un-collateralized.[224] However, this analysis completely ignores the possibility of unaccounted-for and offsetting hedges, as in the example previously cited of Goldman Sachs. It also ignores the collateral that Goldman Sachs had received to date from AIG.

---

220. COP AIG Report, p. 131, notes that they came to this conclusion based on a briefing with FRBNY and Treasury officials and various internal FRBNY emails, but no specific quantitative details net of hedging are cited. Written Testimony of Jim Millstein, chief restructuring officer, U.S. Department of the Treasury, before the COP, May 26, 2010 ("In the absence of such assistance, AIG would have then defaulted on more than $2 trillion notional of derivative obligations and on over $100 billion of debt to institutions").

221. Alejandro LaTorre, "Systemic Impact of AIG Bankruptcy," attachment to email September 16, 2008, 3:16 a.m. (FRBNYAIG00479) [hereinafter, "Systemic Impact memo"].

222. COP AIG Report, 157–60. Also see *Financial Crisis Inquiry Commission Report*, 347–350.

223. As to cross-holdings, beyond the insurance subsidiaries, AIGFP had liabilities across AIG, both to the parent and other subsidiaries. AIGFP had "intercompany payables" of $54 billion owed to the parent. FRBNY considered the systemic risk of these obligations to be high, as "the failure of FP to perform on obligations to other AIG entities may create an event of default for the company," and the "[f]ailure of FP may put at risk the financial condition of other AIG operating subsidiaries." COP AIG Report, 50.

224. COP AIG Report, 131.

- An AIG default could have triggered severe disruptions to an already distressed commercial paper market. Once again supporting evidence for this proposition has not been publicly presented and what evidence is available is lacking in substance.[225]
- The Federal Reserve and Treasury feared that an AIG failure could have undermined an already fragile economy by weakening business and investor confidence.[226] On this particular point, the analysis draws on two of the many buzzwords ("fragile" and "confidence") used during the initial Bear Stearns bailout with no supporting details provided.

The COP largely gives the FRBNY and the Treasury a pass on their analysis of systemic risk and their ultimate decision to bail out AIG. Clearly, though, the COP's comments are not a ringing endorsement of the actions taken:

> The Panel concludes, however, that an AIG bankruptcy could have risked such severe financial disruptions that testing its consequences would have been inadvisable. In a time of crisis, FRBNY and Treasury's fundamental decision to provide support was *probably necessary (or at least a reasonable enough conclusion made under great pressure)*; if that support had been provided in the context of a bankruptcy, the outcome for AIG and markets would have been very different.[227]

---

225. Like the prior case of the CDS market, this proposition is cited by Treasury and FRBNY, but again the conclusion is based on a briefing with FRBNY and Treasury officials and various internal FRBNY emails and not quantitative details. One of the emails notes the "significant contagion potential," regarding $20 billion of AIG commercial paper, but then to support this proposition makes the following cryptic reference: "If CP can't be rolled over, issuers draw down on bank lines; credit extension dries up, banks capitalization further deteriorates, rating downgrades ensue." Systemic Impact memo, Bates No. FRBNYAIG00482. Also see COP AIG Report, 156, emphasis of the author in the following passage ("As discussed above, however, AIG had issued $20 billion of commercial paper—four times the amount of Lehman's outstanding commercial paper. *If a Lehman failure could cause* these investment vehicles to begin trading at a discount and result in a wave of investor redemptions in prime funds and the reinvestment of capital into government funds, *it seems quite plausible that* an AIG failure would have further destabilized these investments, reduced or halted credit availability for corporations and financial institutions (even on a short-term basis), and caused higher lending rates.").
226. COP AIG Report, 132.
227. COP AIG Report, 161. Emphasis is that of the author.

The implication of this is that almost any decision was justified by the time pressure. But given the long history and knowledge of the problems at AIG as noted by OTS, time pressure is simply not an excuse.

### Reviewing the Options

As in the case of Bear Stearns and Lehman Brothers, the FRBNY did not directly supervise or regulate AIG, and they had even less knowledge of the insurance industry and less internal capacity to analyze the options available to resolve AIG. One paper that made the rounds of the Board of Governors during this time was an analysis from 2005 that laid out the distinctions between resolving a bank and an insurance company.[228] In referring to the chairman of the board and chief executive officer of AIG, one of the largest financial services companies in the world, Brian Madigan of the Board of Governors was so unfamiliar with Robert Willumstad, the firm's chief executive officer, that he did not even recognize his name when he relayed the details of an upcoming phone call with AIG: "Jacob Frenkel just called. He will call back to my office with someone named Williamson at 11:00 am to discuss their efforts to sell assets."[229] The staff from the FRBNY and Board of Governors had little knowledge of precisely how the complex transactions AIG had structured would be unwound. Chairman Bernanke admitted that "I don't know the insurance business." Further undermining confidence in their analysis of AIG is the comment of Governor Warsh, who desired an analysis through means other than the continuing seat-of-the-pants approach. He argued for a short-term solution to get AIG through their liquidity and solvency problems with a life of thirty days, enough time to seriously examine AIG: "I know it could leave us with open-ended exposure, but

---

228. *McKinley v. Board of Governors,* Bates No. BOG–FOIA 10–251–000204 email from William Nelson to William Walsh of a previously forwarded email from Jon Greenlee to various Board staff titled "Failure of an Insurance Company," September 13, 2008. The circulated study was Report of the National Association of Insurance Commissioners (NAIC) and the Federal Reserve System Joint Troubled Company Subgroup, "A Comparison of the Insurance and Banking Regulatory Frameworks for Identifying and Supervising Companies in Weakened Financial Condition," April 19, 2005. *McKinley v. Board of Governors* BOG–FOIA 10–251–000205 to 000248.

229. *McKinley v. Board of Governors,* Bates No. BOG–FOIA 10–251–000074 email from Brian Madigan titled "AIG," sent to Scott Alvarez and Don Kohn, September 13, 2008.

let's actually figure out what the hell is going on here." Despite all of these very serious questions about the Federal Reserve's ability to assess the potential fallout from an AIG bankruptcy and their uncertainty regarding how to structure a transaction, they pressed on.[230]

Efforts were made to bring together an outside party or a consortium of private financial institutions rather than relying solely on a government bailout. Warren Buffett considered first whether to inject $10 billion of capital and then as the capital situation worsened to inject $25 billion, which he smartly declined to do. Then, as the analysis deepened, the estimate of the required capital injection grew to $40 billion, and as uncertainty increased further in the aftermath of Lehman Brothers and with the slew of government interventions (see Table 7.8), the estimate grew to $60 billion and then to between $80 and $90 billion.[231] Additionally, an unnamed bidder proposed a transaction that the AIG Board rejected, as described by Vice Chairman Donald Kohn:

> "Call from Frankel and Willumsted [sic] tonight renewing request for FR credit. Main points: Expect downgrade tomorrow which will accelerate demand for collateral. Probably enough liquidity to get to Weds., but not much further. Need 50 b liquidity. Have 8, can get 15 more out of insurance subs, but would only be approved if part of plan to get back to health. Board rejected [name redacted] offer, which he described as, in effect, 10b of equity in exchange for 60 percent of the companya nd [sic] conditioned on access to Fed window. (Also would fire board and upper management.) Board voted to authorize sale of subs if necessary to repay FR credit. [sentence redacted] Two asset sales in negotiation for combined 11–13 b, but neither are sure and both would require regulatory approvals and hence take months. [name redacted] talking about 10b equity, but very vague. portrayed access to FR credit as necessary to enable equity raise. Notjhing [sic] to announce tomorrow morning. [sentence redacted] I was completely noncommital—didn't comment at all on request. Simply said I would relay conversation to colleagues. Will-

230. *Too Big to Fail,* 395. *In Fed We Trust,* 193.
231. *Too Big to Fail,* 293–94, 308–9.

ing to talk tonight, Tim [Geithner], if you think it's necessary. Otherwise we should consult tomorrow morning."[232]

Although speculation within the FRBNY and Board of Governors was that AIG's failure would have a systemic impact, as in the case of Lehman, it was also clear that bankruptcy was the only option available under law. AIG was an unsound institution that was illiquid and insolvent. Board of Governors economist William Nelson made this point early on in the ongoing assessment of AIG: "What should we do? If AIG doesn't have collateral they can pledge to us, I just don't think we can lend. It seems like it would have to be the Treasury. If we think the entity is insolvent, can you think of anyway [sic] to make the failure more orderly?"[233] Later that weekend, the analysis of whether AIG was insolvent became even clearer as stated by Vice Chairman Don Kohn: "brief conversation with Jacob [Frenkel]. Tol dhim [sic] we were 'very reluctant' to open up another 13–3 facility for an entity not even an investment bank. And that the market thought it was not only a liquidity problem but also a capital problem."[234]

Another message from Vice Chairman Kohn later that same day summarizing another conversation with Frenkel and Willumstad of AIG emphasized the capital shortfall and the reluctance of the Board of Governors to go forward until the capital problems were addressed: "I told them we were 'very reluctant' to open up our discount window to them when it wasn't clear they had a good plan for getting enough capital into the company and were depending on asset sales over along [sic] period. I said we also were aware that we would begiving

---

232. *McKinley v. Board of Governors,* Bates No. BOG–FOIA 10–251–000447 email from Donald Kohn titled "AIG," sent to Chairman Bernanke, Timothy Geithner, Brian Madigan, Scott Alvarez, and Deborah P. Bailey, September 14, 2008. The deal referred to that was turned down by the AIG Board may have been by JC Flowers and Co. See *Financial Crisis Inquiry Commission Report,* 348–49.
233. *McKinley v. Board of Governors,* Bates No. BOG–FOIA 10–251–000052 email from William Nelson titled "AIG Meeting Notes," sent to Roberto Perli, September 12, 2008.
234. *McKinley v. Board of Governors,* Bates No. BOG–FOIA 10–251–000117 email from Don Kohn titled "Material—As per Alex LaTorre," sent to Scott Alvarez and Brian Madigan, September 12, 2008. The justification offered by Kohn of being reluctant because AIG was not even an investment bank seems inconsistent with the concern for potential systemic risk.

[sic] a whole new class or classes of borrowers under our discount window umbrella. . . . I told them to make plans as if we wouldn't be there for them, but also to keep in touch. They seemed to think they had a week or so—though the next few days would be tough."[235] Governor Warsh weighed in on the capital problems at AIG in a similar dire assessment on September 15, the same day of the Lehman bankruptcy filing: "Received report tonight on capital hole at AIG; far worse than expected; hole too big to be filled, according to [name redacted]. Not good."[236] Chairman Bernanke was not entirely convinced that capital was at issue.[237]

FRBNY President Geithner attempted one last effort at an LTCM-style lending facility. This involved a number of banks and investment banks pulling together, seemingly ignoring any of the potential conflicts of interest that could have been involved with including AIG counterparties, such as Goldman Sachs, in the discussions.[238] As these discussions continued, the conflicts became even more obvious and unseemly.[239] The COP succinctly summarized the issue of conflicts in the structuring of the AIG resolution strategy:

---

235. *McKinley v. Board of Governors,* Bates No. BOG–FOIA 10–251–000117 email from Don Kohn titled "AIG," sent to Chairman Bernanke, Timothy Geithner, Kevin Warsh, Scott Alvarez, and Brian Madigan, September 13, 2008.

236. *McKinley v. Board of Governors,* Bates No. BOG–FOIA 10–251–000847 email from Kevin Warsh titled "AIG," sent to Chairman Bernanke, Donald Kohn, and Michelle Smith, September 15, 2008. The name of the institution Governor Warsh is referring to was redacted citing exemption 4 of the Freedom of Information Act (see Appendix 1).

237. *Financial Crisis Inquiry Commission Report,* 349 ("The Federal Open Market Committee was briefed about AIG. Members were told that AIG faced a liquidity crisis but that it was unclear if there were also solvency issues.") This comment is based on Ben Bernanke letter to FCIC Chairman Phil Angelides, December 21, 2010.

238. *Too Big to Fail,* 316, 364, 375–76, 391 ("A look of horror came over Braunstein's face, raising his voice. Where the hell did Goldman Sachs come from? Don't they have a conflict? I mean, look at their exposure to AIG. They're a huge counterparty." Braunstein was head of investment banking for JPMorgan.).

239. *Too Big to Fail,* 391 ("Winkelried of Goldman then jumped in. 'Let me just say there is a huge systemic risk to letting this institution fail. I don't need to tell you the number of counterparties that would be exposed.'"), 392 ("When Geithner was satisfied that everyone had complied, he posed a question for which no one in the group had been prepared. 'What would it look like if we said the Fed was going to do this?' . . . Goldman's Winkelreid could not hide a slight smile.").

The rescue of AIG illustrates the tangled nature of relationships on Wall Street. People from the same small group of law firms, investment banks, and regulators appear in the AIG saga (and many other aspects of the financial crisis) in many roles, and sometimes representing different and conflicting interests. The lawyers who represented banks trying to put together a rescue package for AIG became lawyers to FRBNY, shifting sides in a matter of minutes. Those same banks appear first as advisors, then potential rescuers, then as counterparties to several different kinds of agreements with AIG, and ultimately as the direct and indirect beneficiaries of the government rescue. Many of the regulators and government officials (in both Administrations) are former employees of the entities they oversee or that benefit from the rescue.[240]

All the while, FRBNY and Board of Governors staff heard from market players about how the government just had to intervene, more examples of cafeteria capitalism. This approach is clearly expressed by an unnamed market player in a screed sent to Board of Governors' economist James Clouse:

> It seems many in the market were not at all prepared for Lehman to go under. Most expected some form of takeover or bail out (maybe not the most irrational of beliefs given Bear Stearns and the potential for serious systemic risk). A lot of funds facing Lehman have seen significant losses incurred on collateral on repo's, swaps, etc. There are also many with uncertain overall positions as a result of uncertainty over current trades with Lehman. Given that the U.S. has now showed a willingness to let a major institution fail, there is widespread concern about many other names, and an increasing unwillingness to lend or trade with other counterparties. I have heard a number of funds raise concerns about whether the Merrill/BoA deal with [sic] conclude (people who've just incurred serious losses on Lehman exposures are inclined to take a negative view of things). Similarly AIG is causing high concern—the extent of losses which would be transmitted to the banking system through a failure is seen as a very high risk. The money markets and FX forward

---

240. COP AIG Report, 234.

markets are becoming increasingly dislocated–U.S.$ overnight rates being quoted somewhere between 10+20% at present. Credit spreads across the board are continuing to blow out, and liquidity is extremely poor. The very very high risk decision to let Lehman fail seems to be triggering a loss of confidence in policy makers [sic] ability to understand or fix the current problems (at least in the U.S.). If this runs much further or there are other major defaults this situation could be difficult to pull back. I would not rule out the need for the U.S. or even G7 to issue a generalized guarantee on all senior bank obligations if this situation gets further out of hand to prevent a major systemic breakdown in the banking and payments system.[241]

The Board of Governors' Director of International Affairs, Nathan Sheets, was subject to a similar lobbying effort:

I really think you have a major problem here. Lehman failure has set of [sic] a huge set of chain reactions across markets causing leverage to unwind in a disorderly manner. Many funds/corporates/hedge funds can't work out their positions and are scrambling to replace naked exposures created by the failure. There seem to be differences in treatment for the unwind depending on instruments, etc causing chaos for market exposures. The ETF market is being shut down by the AIG problems. The U.S. senior bank debt market is collapsing due to the collapse in recovery rate assumptions as more failures are considered. Most important is the collapse in confidence in the policymaker community among market participants. It was a choice to let Lehman fail and trigger this situation. The market is very close to seizing. Many market participants are close to a moving towards short dated government bonds and avoiding bank exposure (in every way a major run on the banking system). There may well be a need to issue a general guarantee on bank obliga-

---

241. *McKinley v. Board of Governors,* Bates No. BOG–FOIA 10–251–000867. Email from unnamed market participant to James Clouse, titled "Few things," September 16, 2008. The email was then forwarded to Governor Warsh by Margaret Owens. BOG–FOIA 10–251–000876.

tions in the manner the Scandanavian's [sic] did in 2002 and the UK did for a short period during Northern Rock's collapse to prevent the payments system collapsing in the next few hours.[242]

All throughout the efforts to raise funds for AIG the position of the FRBNY, the Board of Governors, and the Treasury Department was clearly stated and unchanged. Just as in the case of Lehman Brothers, AIG was insolvent or on the brink thereof and there was no buyer, so there would be no bailout. Bankruptcy was the only option, unless a white knight came along to rescue AIG. This description of the positions is consistent with what we know of the private meetings and emails, as well as public statements (see Table 7.11). The focus was on the private efforts, and the consistent approach was that if these private efforts failed, then AIG's parent would be allowed to fail and there would be no contribution by the FRBNY to facilitate a restructuring of AIG.

Unfortunately the paper trail ends early morning on September 16, 2008, and the Board of Governors met later that day to make a decision on AIG. However, in an interview with the COP, Thomas Baxter, Jr., FRBNY's general counsel, recounted the substance of a conference call that morning. Also on the call were FRBNY President Geithner, Secretary Paulson, Chairman Bernanke, and Governors Kevin Warsh and Elizabeth Duke. The participants seemingly turned on a dime regarding whether the consequences of a bankruptcy were far worse than those that would come from providing funding to AIG.[243] Secretary Paulson did not detail the reasons for the reversal, but merely noted that "we could not let AIG go down."[244] The FRBNY and in particular President Geithner reversed the no bailout policy demonstrated with Lehman Brothers that lasted just a few days because, according to him: "I just changed my mind, and I wasn't alone in changing my mind." Geithner described what had caused him to change his mind: the realization that AIG had become more than a big insurance company; it was now a company that had made financial promises

---

242. *McKinley v. Board of Governors,* Bates No. BOG–FOIA 10–251–000874–875. Email from unnamed market participant to Nathan Sheets, titled "problem," September 16, 2008.

243. COP AIG Report, 70.

244. *On the Brink,* 229. Paulson mentions two calls that morning, but it is not clear which call Baxter was on.

**Table 7.11.** Comments Regarding a Federal Reserve Bailout of AIG

| What Was Said | Who Said It, When, and Where |
|---|---|
| "[AIG] should not be particularly optimistic [on the Fed providing financing] given the hurtles [sic] and history of 13–3 lending."[1] | *September 13, 2008; 11 a.m.:* Scott Alvarez, General Counsel of the Board of Governors in a meeting with AIG Senior Management |
| "We noted that 13–3 borrowing from the Fed would send a negative signal to the market."[2] | *September 13, 2008; 11 a.m.:* Scott Alvarez and Brian Madigan, Board of Governors; Trish Mosser and Rich Charlton, FRBNY in the summary of a meeting with AIG management |
| "Tim [Geithner] said that the Fed was not prepared to lend to AIG and that the company should get a consortium of private lenders to make a bridge loan."[3] | *September 14, 2008:* Secretary Paulson referencing a conversation with Geithner and Robert Willumstad, CEO of AIG |
| "We also knew AIG was highly vulnerable. Nonetheless even with those new complications, it still seemed inconceivable that the Federal Reserve could or should play any role in preventing AIG's collapse."[4] | *September 14, 2008:* FRBNY President Geithner in summary testimony recounting the intent regarding a possible bailout of AIG as of September 14 |

1. *McKinley v. Board of Governors*, Bates No. BOG–FOIA 10–251–000096 email, Bates No. FRBNYAIG00508. Email from Patricia Mosser to FRBNY and Board of Governors Staff, "AIG/Board Call," September 13, 2008, 12:54 p.m. The email summarized the meeting held at 11 a.m., September 13.
2. Bates No. FRBNYAIG00508. Email from Patricia Mosser to FRBNY and Board of Governors Staff, "AIG/Board Call," September 13, 2008, 12:54 p.m. The email summarized the meeting held at 11 a.m., September 13.
3. *On the Brink*, 218.
4. U.S. Department of the Treasury, "Secretary Written Testimony Before the House Committee on Oversight and Government Reform," January 27, 2010.

| What Was Said | Who Said It, When, and Where |
|---|---|
| "Liesman wonders if he can say that the fed thinks aig shd [sic] pursue all other options before coming to us. Is that too explosive? Seems reasonable but maybe not reasonable for us to say or for steve [sic] to hype."[5] | *September 14, 2008, 11:31 p.m.:* Michelle Smith in an email to Governor Kevin Warsh regarding inquiries from CNBC Analyst Steve Liesman about a Federal Reserve AIG loan |
| "We also believe that the private sector is and should be actively working on a resolution, and that based on our earlier dimensioning work, that AIG has options (albeit unpleasant) to solve this themselves."[6] | *September 15, 2008, 10:24 a.m.:* Brian Peters, senior vice president–Risk Management, FRBNY, in an internal email message |
| "Kevin [Warsh] sounded sceptical [sic] on extending credit to AIG—I wondered if this was the result of being exhausted after a mad weekend or a fair reflection of the stance at this juncture."[7] | *September 15, 2008, 11:13 a.m.:* *Financial Times* reporter making an apparent reference to a prior conversation with Federal Reserve Governor Warsh |
| "There's no government money for this."[8] | *September 15, 2008:* FRBNY President Geithner on the availability of government funding in a meeting with potential consortium members of a loan for AIG |

5. *McKinley v. Board of Governors*, Bates No. BOG–FOIA 10–251–000495 email from Michelle Smith to Kevin Warsh, titled "Liesman wonders if he can say," September 14, 2008, 12:54 p.m.
6. Email from Brian Peters to various staff of the FRBNY, "AIG Important," September 15, 2008, 10:24 a.m.
7. *McKinley v. Board of Governors*, Bates No. BOG–FOIA 10–251–000620 email from Krishna Guha to Michelle Smith, titled "trying to reach you . . . (sorry)," September 15, 2008.
8. *Too Big to Fail*, 388.

Table 7.11. *(continued)*

| What Was Said | Who Said It, When, and Where |
| --- | --- |
| "Let me say, what is going on right now in New York has got nothing to do with any bridge loan from the government. What's going on in New York is a private sector effort, again focused on dealing with an important issue that is, I think, important that the financial system work on right now."[9] | *September 15, 2008, 1:42 p.m.:* Treasury Secretary Paulson in a press briefing at the White House |
| "Attached is a proposal to allow the parent [of AIG] to fail while insuring against the negative retail dynamics."[10] | *September 16, 2008, 1:44 a.m.:* Alejandro LaTorre, assistant vice president, FRBNY, in an email to Timothy Geithner, Brian Peters, William Rutledge, Patricia Mosser, and Tanshel Pointer |

9. The White House, "Press Briefing by Dana Perino and Secretary of the Treasury Henry Paulson," September 15, 2008, 1:42 p.m., http://georgewbush-whitehouse.archives.gov/news /releases/2008/09/20080915–8.html.

10. Email from Alejandro LaTorre to Timothy Geithner, Brian Peters, William Rutledge, Patricia Mosser, and Tanshel Pointer, "Proposal to Insulate Retail Impact of AIGFP Failure," September 16, 2008, 1:44 a.m.

on which hundreds of financial firms around the world depended. According to him, a disorderly disintegration had to be avoided.[245] Confident of his acceptance of Geithner's view of the facts on AIG, Chairman Bernanke noted, "If there's been any doubt about the power of financial stress to affect the real economy, I hope that it's been removed at this point."[246]

In the case of Bear Stearns, it was very clear that documents existed that might shed light on some of the last-minute decision-making, and that is clearly also the case with regard to AIG. The Board of Governors has acknowledged the existence of documents, but thus far they have been unwilling to dis-

245. *In Fed We Trust*, 191–92.
246. "Bernanke Angry About AIG," *Wall Street Journal*, March 3, 2009, http://blogs .wsj.com/economics/2009/03/03/bernanke-angry-about-aig/tab/article/.

close the content of those documents. One set of emails directly addresses the issue of the solvency of AIG.[247] Another set of emails and documents exchanged between the Treasury Department and the Board of Governors addresses in detail the authority of the Board of Governors to provide a bailout to AIG.[248] Another document, focused on the possible use of Section 13(3) to bail out AIG, was requested by former Senator Bunning and is also the subject of a Freedom of Information request by the *Wall Street Journal*.[249] Finally, a document named "Background for Decision to Lend to AIG" was finalized after the Board of Governors approved the bailout of AIG.[250]

After the bailout decision had been made that morning, the Federal Reserve began "looking for someone else's money," but the Treasury and the FDIC saw no clear way that they could contribute to the effort to bail out AIG.[251] So

---

247. *McKinley v. Board of Governors,* Bates No. BOG–FOIA 10–251–000092, 098, 103, 104, emails from Adam Ashcraft to various FRBNY and Board staff titled "AIG solvency," September 13, 2008. *McKinley v. Board of Governors,* Bates No. BOG–FOIA 10–251–000286, email from Brian Madigan to various Board of Governors staff, titled "Partial memo draft," September 14, 2008.

248. *McKinley v. Board of Governors,* Bates No. BOG–FOIA 10–251–000865, 891, 895, 940, 956, emails from Robert Hoyt of Treasury to Dan Jester, Jeremiah Norton, Neel Kashkari, David McCormick, and Tony Ryan of Treasury; Scott Alvarez of the Board of Governors; and Timothy Geitner of the FRBNY titled "Use of Existing Authority," September 16, 2008.

249. *McKinley v. Board of Governors,* Bates No. BOG–FOIA 10–251–000171–180, email from William Nelson to various staff of the Board of Governors titled "aig ipc draft," September 13, 2008. Senator Bunning requested a memo "Issues Related to Possible IPC Lending to American International Group" presented to the Board of Governors for approval of lending to AIG, dated September 15, 2008 [sb-aig-01000092 to sb-aig-01000125]. Review and Outlook, "Systemic Risk Stonewall," *Wall Street Journal,* September 1, 2010 ("In February, we sent a FOIA request to the Fed for an internal memo titled 'Issues Related to Possible IPC Lending to American International Group' and an email from Chairman Bernanke that included a draft of the proposal that he would soon present to the Fed Board of Governors to approve lending to AIG. Yesterday a Fed spokeswoman told us it is still reviewing the request."), http://online.wsj.com/article/SB10001424052748703467004575463781244452958.html.

250. *McKinley v. Board of Governors,* Bates No. BOG–FOIA 10–251–001115–116, email from Brian Madigan to Michelle Smith titled "Background for decision to lend to AIG," September 16, 2008. In the email Madigan notes that "This could use some further work."

251. *In Fed We Trust,* 193.

in between the morning call and the afternoon board meeting later that day, AIG had to provide the FRBNY with sufficient collateral to lend on a secured basis consistent with Section 13(3) of the Federal Reserve Act. FRBNY security personnel went to AIG's headquarters in lower Manhattan, and, after collecting stock certificates representing billions of dollars' worth of AIG's equity stakes in its insurance subsidiaries, walked back to the FRBNY.[252] AIG, whose liquidity position was reportedly so strained that it could not produce any collateral acceptable enough to back funding from the private markets, nonetheless produced collateral acceptable to the FRBNY. In the case of Lehman Brothers, the decision was that sufficient collateral was not available to support a transaction. In the case of AIG, the opposite conclusion was reached. However, no public record is available of the collateral review undertaken by the FRBNY in either of these cases.

The Board of Governors approved the bailout about 3 p.m. on September 16 as noted by Michelle Smith: "It was just approved by the board. Terms are going to aig now. Aig has a board mtg at 5."[253] In the public description of its reasoning, the Board of Governors reverted back to the disorderly-failure language in determining that "the disorderly failure of AIG was likely to have a systemic effect on financial markets that were already experiencing a significant level of fragility and that the best alternative available was to lend to AIG to assist it in meeting its obligations in an orderly manner as they came due." The Board members also agreed that the terms of the transaction should best protect the interests of the U.S. government and taxpayers.[254] According to the COP, "through internal discussions and a dialogue with AIG and its state insurance

---

252. COP AIG Report, 70.

253. *McKinley v. Board of Governors,* Bates No. BOG–FOIA 10–251–001114, email from Michelle Smith to Calvin Mitchell, titled "Where do we stand," September 16, 2008.

254. The Federal Reserve Board, "Government in the Sunshine Meeting Notice," Matters Considered: Discussion on Financial Markets, September 17, 2008. It is assumed that this is the meeting at which the AIG bailout was approved, although this is not certain. The matter considered is labeled "Discussion on Financial Markets." Separately, the Federal Reserve Board issued minutes of the meeting in a release titled "Extension of Credit to American International Group, Inc.," but those minutes are not time stamped. Additionally, these minutes were not issued until March 11, 2009.

regulators, the Board and FRBNY ultimately chose to provide AIG with assistance after identifying the systemic risks associated with the company and contemplating the consequences of an AIG bankruptcy or partial rescue." However, the precise details of those discussions have not been publicly released.[255]

Throughout the efforts to structure a bailout of AIG, Secretary Paulson held to the view that "the Fed felt it could make a loan to help AIG because we were dealing with a liquidity, not a capital problem."[256] This contradicts the internal comments at the Federal Reserve that indicated AIG was insolvent. The best indicator of the state of AIG was the lack of willingness of private parties to provide funding, described by Vice Chairman Kohn as that the market determined that the problem was one of insolvency. If these private parties were confident in the capital standing of AIG, they would have provided funding, but they declined just as they had done for Lehman Brothers. The record is clear that in the absence of outside funding AIG would have been insolvent by the end of the day on September 16, 2008.[257]

Once the possibility of a fully private deal fell through, the FRBNY and Treasury characterized their options as a "binary choice" between allowing AIG to fail and rescuing the entire institution, including all of its business partners. A review by the COP rejected this reasoning as simplistic and pointed out that there was a range of options. The COP concluded that once the initial effort by a consortium fell through no further efforts were made to pursue a private sector solution or to pursue a mixed FRBNY–private sector solution. It highlighted the fact that the government put the rescue in the hands of only two banks and that these banks had severe conflicts of interest given they would have been the beneficiaries of a bailout. In interviews with the COP, the FRBNY and Treasury questioned whether there was enough time to work through all these possible options.[258]

---

255. COP AIG Report, 129. The COP cites FRBNY and Treasury briefings with the COP in this regard, but refuses to release details regarding such meetings.
256. *On the Brink*, 229.
257. COP AIG Report, 233.
258. COP AIG Report, 143–45, 231–33.

## The Final Deal

The Federal Reserve Board authorized the creation of a twenty-four-month facility that could be drawn upon for up to $85 billion, collateralized by all the assets of both AIG and its primary unregulated subsidiaries. In exchange, the U.S. government received a 79.9 percent equity interest in AIG along with the right to veto the payment of dividends to common and preferred shareholders.[259] AIG's chief executive officer was asked to step aside.[260] The 80 percent ownership stake and management changes were the precise response to the near failure of Continental twenty-five years earlier. These details were taken from the term sheet of the private consortium that ultimately fell apart at the last minute. In that proposal a $75 billion figure was agreed upon and the FRBNY added $10 billion as a cushion. The cost of the package had gone from $20 billion to $85 billion in a matter of a few days.[261] As in the case of Bear Stearns, the legal authority for the AIG transaction was also from Section 13(3) of the Federal Reserve Act.

It was very clear within weeks of the transaction that it was unworkable in the long run, and it may have actually exacerbated the financial squeeze at AIG. In other words, it probably would have been better to allow AIG to file bankruptcy.[262] Ultimately, the initial transaction was reworked in November 2008, which included Treasury providing $40 billion of TARP funding, increasing the term of the transaction to five years from the original two years, and lowering the interest rate and fees charged. The facility was reworked again in April 2009.[263] As part of these restructurings, a number of AIG counterparties were taken out 100 percent on their exposures, despite the fact that these counter-

---

259. Board of Governors of the Federal Reserve (press release, September 16, 2008).
260. Karnitschnig et al.
261. COP AIG Report, 71.
262. Carol D. Leonnig, "Effectiveness of AIG's $143 Billion Rescue Questioned," *Washington Post*, November 3, 2008. Office of the Special Inspector General for the Troubled Asset Relief Program, "Factors Affecting Efforts to Limit Payments to AIG Counterparties," November 17, 2009, 12 [hereinafter, SIGTARP Report].
263. COP AIG Report, 86–87. The TARP funding later grew to $49 billion made up of the original $40 billion, plus $1.6 billion in unpaid dividends, plus $7.54 billion of drawdowns on a facility extended in April 2009.

parties likely would not have received similar payments under bankruptcy.[264] The fact that the counterparties were aware that AIG was deemed a systemic institution left the FRBNY with little leverage to negotiate a cramdown of losses onto the counterparties.[265] When asked by Representative John Campbell why he "chose to pay all the counterparties 100 cents on the dollar," Secretary Geithner responded: "If you default on those commitments, then you will end up defaulting on all commitments and the firm will come collapsing down and fail." It is no wonder that such comments have become fodder for comedians commenting on the inane justifications for the bailouts.[266]

### The Aftermath

There is probably no better description of the uncertainty caused by the changes in policy direction of the Federal Reserve and the Treasury during that week in mid-September than the summary by Elizabeth Warren, the head of the COP:

> So the big mistake is to say, "North 90 miles an hour," and then go south 140 miles an hour. Confidence that these guys have a clue drops to zero. So the way I measure this is not what happens in the 48 hours between [the collapse of] Lehman and AIG. It's how it is that Treasury and Fed articulates [sic] two of the most diametrically opposed policies within literally hours of each other, and then the kind of chaos we end up in. . . . You can't go north and south at the same time without destroying everyone's confidence.[267]

Secretary Paulson seemed perplexed that the actions by the Federal Reserve to save AIG did not receive a better response: "Tuesday was bad, but Wednesday

264. SIGTARP Report, 30.
265. SIGTARP Report, 18–19.
266. "January 12, 2010: Clusterf#@k to the Poor House—Wall Street Bonuses," *Daily Show with Jon Stewart,* http://www.thedailyshow.com/watch/tue-january-12-2010/cluster f--k-to-the-poor-house---wall-street-bonuses, at the 3:40 mark, 4:47 run time.
267. "Breaking the Bank," *Frontline,* interview with Elizabeth Warren, Chair, TARP COP, http://www.pbs.org/wgbh/pages/frontline/breakingthebank/interviews/warren .html.

[the day after the AIG announcement] was worse. Our intervention with AIG didn't calm the markets—if anything, it aggravated the situation."[268] Shortly after becoming Treasury Secretary, Timothy Geithner came to accept the idea that "[a]s the crisis intensified and more dramatic government action was required, the emergency actions meant to provide confidence and reassurance too often added to public anxiety and to investor uncertainty."[269]

Dick Fuld, the CEO of Lehman Brothers, justifiably had his own take on the bailout of AIG. Just a few days earlier, he was told that because there was no buyer for Lehman there was no deal for the Federal Reserve to support, so his firm had to file bankruptcy. Here was AIG with no buyer, yet the Federal Reserve acted on its own to prop them up. In a conversation the day after the AIG announcement Fuld pleaded with Secretary Paulson: "I see you bailed out AIG. Hank, what you need to do now is let the Fed come into Lehman Brothers. Have the government come in and guarantee it. Give me my company back. I can get all the people back. We will have Lehman Brothers again."[270]

As time went on the story of why there was intervention morphed from "the exposures are large so we have a problem" to "we don't know what the exposures are." A few days after the bailout of AIG, Chairman Bernanke came to the conclusion that "Since nobody really knew the exposures of specific banks to AIG, confidence in the entire banking system would have plummeted, putting the whole system at risk."[271]

The question of the final resolution cost of AIG still lingers. As was the case with Bear Stearns, the Federal Reserve argues that they will not incur a loss on the transaction to bail out AIG.[272] The 2009 Annual Report of the Federal Re-

---

268. *On the Brink*, 242.

269. U.S. Department of the Treasury, "Secretary Geithner Introduces Financial Stability Plan," February 10, 2009, http://www.ustreas.gov/press/releases/tg18.htm.

270. *On the Brink*, 243.

271. *In Fed We Trust*, 26. Sorkin concludes that because we knew the exposures and they seemed to be big, it meant AIG would take down the entire financial system. David Wessel quotes Bernanke concluding that, because we didn't know the exposures, that fact put the entire financial system at risk. Whether we know the exposure of financial institutions to AIG or we don't know the exposures, both instances lead to the conclusion that intervention was necessary.

272. Chairman Ben S. Bernanke, "Federal Reserve's Exit Strategy," February 10, 2010, http://www.federalreserve.gov/newsevents/testimony/bernanke20100210a.htm.

serve System has a very small estimate of less than $100 million for the ultimate loss on AIG and the 2010 report actually shows a gain.[273] But this estimate is not a good indicator of the cost of resolving AIG. As noted previously regarding the restructuring of the AIG transactions, the bulk of the losses on AIG are reflected in the cost of the TARP, as the TARP funding took out much of the Federal Reserve's facility. The cost estimate for AIG has varied and as of early 2010 stood at $45.2 billion.[274] The Treasury Department has now restructured the AIG transaction in an effort to expeditiously dispose of the government's stake in the institution and now estimates that it will make a small profit on AIG. However, the special inspector general for the TARP has questioned the underlying methodology that leads to this conclusion and notes that the projections are subject to a great degree of uncertainty.[275] It will likely take at least until 2012 for Treasury to ultimately dispose of this stake by slowly selling its stock and only at that time will they be able to finalize the loss estimate for AIG. The Treasury Department will have to balance how fast they can sell their stake in AIG with how much value they can get over time.[276]

Although much of the aftermath from AIG focused on the payment of extraordinary pay and bonuses to its employees, which ultimately led to the appointment of a "compensation czar" to oversee compensation at large bailed-out institutions, other more substantive topics were also scrutinized.[277] In hearings that cast a light on the transactions flowing from the AIG bailout, one area of

---

273. *Fed 2009 Annual Report,* 190–191. *Fed 2010 Annual Report,* 133.

274. U.S. Treasury Department, Office of Financial Stability, "Summary Table of TARP Investments," March 31, 2010, http://www.financialstability.gov/docs/TARP%20Cost% 20Estimates%20-%20March%2031%202010.pdf.

275. Jeffrey Sparshott and Kevin Kingsbury, "AIG Rescue Will Prove Profitable, Treasury Says," *Wall Street Journal,* November 2, 2010. SIGTARP, "Quarterly Report to Congress," October 26, 2010, 7–9. Treasury Department Office of Financial Stability, "Statement by the U.S. Treasury Department on AIG Exit Plan," September 30, 2010, http://www.financialstability.gov/latest/pr_09302010.html. U.S. Treasury Department, Office of Financial Stability, "Troubled Asset Relief Program: Two Year Retrospective," October 2010, 4. The current estimate is that the AIG stake from TARP will yield $5 billion in surplus to the Treasury Department.

276. Serena Ng, Deborah Solomon, and Joann S. Lublin, "AIG, U.S. Agree on an Exit Deal: Making It Work Will Be Tougher," *Wall Street Journal,* October 1, 2010.

277. Stephen Labaton, "Treasury to Set Executives' Pay at 7 Ailing Firms," *New York Times,* June 10, 2009.

focus was payments to counterparties and to what ends those payments of tens of billions of dollars to counterparties such as Societe Generale, Goldman Sachs, Merrill Lynch, and Deutsche Bank were made. In response to questions from Senator Mark Warner, Vice Chairman of the Board of Governors Kohn set forth a very strained and what Senator Warner later referred to as "amorphous" explanation for making the payments to counterparties:

> If we impose losses on the counterparties for AIG, not so much worried about those particular counterparties, actually don't know what the list is, but my guess is many of them can handle it themselves, I am worried about the *knock-on effects* in the financial markets, so now would other people be willing to do business with other U.S. financial institutions, forget A.I.G., forget the counterparties, think about the systemic risk here if they thought that in a crisis like this they might have to take some losses. There is huge moral hazard here, we have made those credit counterparties whole in ways that will reduce their incentive to be careful in the future.[278]

At the same hearing, Kohn refused to release the names of the recipients of the counterparty payments.[279] AIG released the names of the counterparties just a few days later and no adverse impact flowed from this disclosure.

Kohn's line of argument is consistent with similar exchanges with officials defending the various bailouts, that somehow the beneficiaries of the bailouts were not the owners or creditors of the financial institutions that avoided the harsh treatment accorded in bankruptcy, not the counterparties who were generally big institutional investors, but that somehow the target of the billions in bailouts was the little guy, those hurt by the so-called "knock-on effects." Similarly, never straying from his tone after the Bear Stearns bailout, then–Treasury Secretary Geithner repeated his oft-repeated refrain at a January 2010 hearing

---

278. Emphasis is the author's. C-Span, "Government Intervention and Regulation of AIG," Senate Committee on Banking, Housing, and Urban Affairs, March 5, 2009. The exchange between Senator Warner and Vice Chairman Kohn is from the 104:40 mark to 115:00, total run time 2:23:18 [hereinafter, Kohn Testimony].

279. Kohn Testimony, 47:00 mark. Eric Dinallo also used this uncommon reference to knock-on effects at the 38:00 mark of the video.

that were it not for the bailout of AIG "[t]housands of more factories would have closed their doors, millions more Americans would have lost their jobs, the value of American's houses and savings would have fallen even further than they did at that time. People would have rushed to take their money out of banks. It would have brought about utter collapse."[280] But it is not clear from any of the information that has been released by the Board of Governors or the FRBNY before or after the bailout that there was any substantive analysis taken of these so-called "knock-on" effects.

As in the case of Lehman, the public explanation for the AIG bailout changed significantly in subsequent months. In the Board minutes at the time of the initial bailout, the justification was primarily the systemic effect on financial markets, which had become a familiar rationale for intervention, while the insurance operations were described as sound. However, in the months that followed, the Federal Reserve and Treasury publicly introduced the idea that disruptions to the insurance company subsidiaries and the potential seizure of regulated insurance company subsidiaries were also a factor in the decision-making. The COP questioned whether these changes in emphasis might have been in response to public displeasure with the AIG bailout in order to present to the public more sympathetic beneficiaries of their decision to intervene in AIG, including policyholders, state and local governments that invested in AIG, and retirement plans that purchase insurance from AIG. An example of this more populist tone was starkly laid out in January 2010 by then–former Treasury Secretary Paulson in one final gasp of fear-mongering to justify the AIG intervention as he was leaving his post:

> If AIG had gone down, I believe that we would have had a situation
> where main street companies, industrial companies of all sizes wouldn't
> have been able to raise money for their basic funding. And they wouldn't
> have been able to pay their employees. They would have had to let them
> go. Employees would not have paid their bills. This would have rippled

---

280. C-Span, "Secretary Geithner on Government Assistance for AIG," House Committee on Oversight and Government Reform, January 27, 2010, at 51:25 mark, total run time 2:23:41.

through the economy . . . . [W]e have, after everything that was done, all the resources, we have 10 percent unemployment. I believe we easily would have had 25 percent unemployment.[281]

## The Other Federal Reserve Bailouts

The Bear Stearns and AIG transactions were bailouts, as they involved transactions with unsound institutions. From the standpoint of the FRBNY, the repayment of these facilities was clearly at risk. There were also numerous other facilities implemented by the Federal Reserve where repayment was at risk or where there was a subsidy involved in the transaction (Table 7.12). The Dodd-Frank legislation compelled the Board of Governors to post to their website the underlying details of these various programs, and these first appeared on December 1, 2010.[282]

## Government Sponsored Enterprises

> "We thought that after we stabilized Fannie and Freddie that we bought ourselves some time. Maybe a month, maybe three months." —Former Treasury Assistant Secretary Neel Kashkari, FCIC Interview. The following week Lehman Brothers filed bankruptcy and AIG was bailed out.

*Circumstances Leading to the Stress*

The government sponsored enterprises (GSEs) faltered during the 2000s crisis to a much greater extent than during the 1980s crisis. During that crisis, Fannie Mae and Freddie Mac were not the significant players that they would later become. During the interim years between the creation of Office of Federal Housing Enterprise Oversight (OFHEO) as the regulatory authority for Fannie Mae and Freddie Mac in 1992 and the 2000s crisis, the GSEs continued to

---

281. COP AIG Report, 134–7. "Geithner Defends AIG Bailout at Fiery Hearing," *PBS Newshour,* January 27, 2010, at 5:30 of 6:45 total run time, http://www.pbs.org/newshour /bb/politics/jan-june10/aig_01-27.html.
282. The details are set out on http://www.federalreserve.gov/newsevents/reform_trans action.htm.

**Table 7.12.** Non-Systemic Federal Reserve Support Programs

| Program | Inception Date | Subsidy |
|---|---|---|
| Term Asset-Backed Securities Loan Facility (TALF) | March 3, 2009 | $13 billion (subsidy) |
| Commercial Paper Funding Facility | October 27, 2008 | $2 billion (subsidy) |
| Asset-Backed Commercial Paper Money Market Fund Liquidity Facility | September 22, 2008 | $2 billion (subsidy) |

*Source*: Congressional Budget Office, "The Budgetary Impact and Subsidy Costs of the Federal Reserve's Actions During the Financial Crisis," May 2010, p. 8, Table 1.

grow rapidly, continued to expand the scope of their authority and forcefully reacted against any efforts to limit the breadth of their operations. Throughout the Clinton years, the GSEs were given a mandate to increase their affordable-housing goals and expand their presence in the financial system, and this continued largely unabated during the Bush Administration years that followed. As early as the mid-1990s, the GSEs began to move into the subprime-mortgage market.[283] Executives at the GSEs were well aware of the risks that their push into subprime and Alt-A mortgages exposed them to, but they likely also felt pressure from Congress to push into this market to fulfill affordable-housing goals.[284]

For the other bailouts discussed thus far, they were cases of fully private companies that were at risk. In contrast, Fannie Mae and Freddie Mac were privately owned companies, but they had a public mission giving them a quasi-government status. Years before they experienced their financial problems, many observers concluded that Fannie and Freddie had the implicit backing of the government, notwithstanding the vehement arguments of those who argued

---

283. Vern McKinley, "The Mounting Case for Privatizing Fannie Mae and Freddie Mac," Cato Institute Policy Analysis no. 293, December 29, 1997 (see note 75 and related text) [hereinafter "Privatizing Fannie Mae and Freddie Mac"].
284. James R. Hagerty, "Fannie, Freddie Executives Knew of Risks," *Wall Street Journal*, December 10, 2008. Alt-A mortgages either have limited supporting documentation or display some other weakness.

there was no implied backing.[285] This implied backing exposed the U.S. government to an enormous contingent liability if Fannie Mae and Freddie Mac were to become insolvent.[286] As the mortgage market deteriorated in 2007, the response of many private market players was to pull back on their investment in the sector. Perversely, the response of the GSEs was "full speed ahead" as summarized by Treasury Secretary Paulson: "[T]he key here to getting through the crisis was to limit the decline in housing and the more effective thing you could do was to make sure there was funding [available] for mortgages. . . . [S]o they [Fannie and Freddie] were the game in town. The only game in town." In fact, constraints on the GSEs were actually loosened during the early stages of the crisis, likely digging a deeper hole for the GSEs.[287]

The question of the insolvency of the GSEs became more than a theoretical exercise when financial problems of the GSEs were revealed, and in July 2008 a report estimated that Fannie Mae and Freddie Mac might need as much as $75 billion in additional capital. The stock of both enterprises fell by nearly 20 percent in one day.[288]

In 1984, banking regulator C. Todd Conover gave public assurances of Continental's stability days before its demise. Early in 2008, the SEC observed that Bear Stearns's capital position was "fine" days before it melted down. As the stock price of Fannie Mae and Freddie Mac deteriorated dramatically in the summer

---

285. Thomas Stanton, Peter Wallison, and Bert Ely are three of the most well known of those that emphasized that there was an implied guarantee. The three published a book in 2004 titled *Privatizing Fannie Mae, Freddie Mac and the Federal Home Loan Banks: Why and How* (American Enterprise Institute for Public Policy Research, Washington, DC, 2009).

286. "Privatizing Fannie Mae and Freddie Mac" (see notes 62 and 63 and related text). During March 2008, an FRBNY executive vice president pushed Robert Steel of the Treasury to "harden" or make explicit the government guarantee. Steel responded that "I do not like that . . . I view that as a very significant move, way above my pay grade to double the size of the U.S. debt in one fell swoop." *Financial Crisis Inquiry Commission Report*, 314.

287. Henry Paulson, interview by FCIC (April 2, 2010), 3. *Financial Crisis Inquiry Commission Report*, 310–315. There were constraints on how many loans the GSEs could fund, limits on the loans and securities they could hold on their books, and a 30 percent capital surplus requirement. James Lockhart, Director of OFHEO, referred to this as a "tightrope with no safety net."

288. *On the Brink,* 142.

of 2008, James Lockhart, the head of the OFHEO, which supervised Fannie Mae and Freddie Mac, had his chance to make a similarly doomed and ill-timed statement. When asked in an interview on business channel CNBC about the existence of an implied government guarantee for Fannie Mae and Freddie Mac and if worst came to worst they were to fail, he tried to calm the markets in responding:

> Both of these companies are adequately capitalized, which is our highest criteria. Both of these companies are managing through these issues, they have tested management teams and as a regulator we have been in constant contact with them.[289]

Treasury Secretary Paulson repeated this reference to capital a week later at a hearing before the Senate Banking Committee, and he also added that he considered the GSEs "very viable" and had "no intent to nationalize" them.[290] Chairman Bernanke had highlighted the "well capitalized" status of the GSEs just a few days before.[291] Meanwhile, the Board of Governors of the Federal Reserve did make available the discount window lending facility to Fannie Mae and Freddie Mac, citing a "possible systemic threat to financial stability."[292] This was yet another case of invoking the Federal Reserve's lender of last resort authority to support an unsound institution.

In response to the continuing deterioration of the GSEs, Secretary Paulson shepherded passage of the Housing and Economic Recovery Act of 2008 (HERA),[293] which was the first significant legislation passed during the crisis.

---

289. Reuters and AP, "Fannie, Freddie Adequately Capitalized: Lockhart," CNBC, July 8, 2008 http://www.cnbc.com/id/25584136/Fannie_Freddie_Adequately_Capitalized_Lockhart.

290. C-Span, "Financial Market Regulation," Senate Committee on Banking, Housing, and Urban Affairs Hearing, July 15, 2008, at 45:20 (very viable); 94:05 (no intent to nationalize), and 13:45 (not prompted by any sudden deterioration) of 2:25:20 total run time.

291. See C-Span, "Transformation of Financial Markets," House Committee on Financial Services, July 10, 2008, at the 1:47:50 mark, total run time 3:16:00.

292. Board of Governors of the Federal Reserve, "Discount Window Lending—Proposal to Lend to Fannie Mae and Freddie Mac through Advances Secured by Obligations of the United States or any U.S. Agency," July 13, 2008. *On the Brink*, 147. Also see Timothy P. Clark and Scott Alvarez, interview by FCIC, February 23, 2010.

293. Public Law 110–289.

The act granted the treasury secretary the power to "purchase any obligations and other securities issued on such terms and conditions as the Secretary may determine and in such amounts as the Secretary may determine" and also transformed the OFHEO into the Federal Housing Finance Agency (FHFA).[294] Before deploying the power to intervene in the GSEs' operations, the secretary had to first determine that it was "necessary to (i) provide stability to the financial markets; (ii) prevent disruptions in the availability of mortgage finance; and (iii) protect the taxpayer."[295] Secretary Paulson famously referred to the unlikely use of this power saying: "If you have got a bazooka in your pocket and people know you've got it, you may not have to take it out, you're not likely to take it out."[296] After passage of the powers he summarized exactly how strong that bazooka was in citing the vast powers granted to him:

> The legislation gave us broad discretion to provide financial support to the GSEs as we saw fit. The terms and conditions of the support were left almost entirely to the discretion of the Treasury secretary, giving us ample flexibility to structure investments and loans in any way that made sense. The legislation did not impose any limitations on the amount of that support, except that it would not be exempt from the debt ceiling and that we would need the GSEs to approve any equity investment we made in them. All told, it was perhaps the most expansive power to commit funds ever given to the Treasury secretary.[297]

The power seemed to go to Paulson's head as he described a subsequent meeting between Secretary Paulson, Chairman Bernanke, and the leadership of Fannie Mae and Freddie Mac: "I didn't think they completely recognized the awesome power of the government and what it would mean for Ben [Bernanke]

---

294. Section 1117 of the Housing and Economic Recovery Act of 2008, codified as 12 U.S.C. 1455 and 1719.

295. Housing and Economic Recovery Act of 2008, Section 1117, codified as 12 U.S.C. 1719 and 1455.

296. C-Span, "Financial Market Regulation," Senate Committee on Banking, Housing, and Urban Affairs, July 15, 2008 testimony, at the 65:45 mark, total run time 2:25:20 ("If you've got a squirt gun in your pocket, you may have to take it out, if you have got a bazooka and people know you've got it, you may not have to take it out, you're not likely to take it out").

297. *On the Brink*, 155.

and me to sit across from the boards of Fannie Mae and Freddie Mac and tell them what we thought was necessary for them to do."[298]

But, the passage of the HERA legislation during July 2008 did not have the intended effect of calming investor fears. Foreign investors, primarily governments in Japan, China, and Russia, held $1 trillion of the debt issued or guaranteed by the GSEs, and they were getting nervous and putting pressure on the Treasury Department to make clear their commitment to bail out the GSEs if necessary. They bought these securities in the belief that the GSEs were backed by the U.S. government.[299] The reality of the problems at Fannie Mae and Freddie Mac overwhelmed the hopeful statements of Director Lockhart of the GSEs' supervisor, Chairman Bernanke and Secretary Paulson. Like so many actions during 2008, the passage of the legislation may even have made things worse by creating confusion about precisely what this new authority meant and essentially confirming just how fragile Fannie Mae and Freddie Mac were.[300]

The volatile cocktail of high leverage, the political strong-arming that accompanied maintaining and expanding the GSE structure, and the political incentives of expanding homeownership combined with the GSEs' off-budget status led to the financial spiral that brought the GSEs near capital insolvency. The Federal Reserve, the Office of the Comptroller of the Currency, Morgan Stanley, and Blackrock, a New York money manager, reviewed the financial position of Fannie Mae and Freddie Mac. Each had capital holes amounting to tens of billions of dollars, and an estimate of the amount of capital needed to fill that hole for the two GSEs through late 2009 was $110 billion.[301]

One challenge in ultimately resolving Fannie Mae and Freddie Mac was in developing sufficient supporting documentation to detail this capital shortfall. The FHFA and its predecessor the OFHEO had not made the case that Fannie Mae and Freddie Mac had any capital difficulties. In another case of a regulatory breakdown, the extent of problems in the GSEs had caught FHFA completely off guard, as the most recent regulatory examinations conducted by the agency had not cited any capital deficiencies at all. As late as August 22,

---

298. *On the Brink*, 167.
299. *On the Brink*, 159. *Too Big to Fail*, 222.
300. *Too Big to Fail*, 199. *On the Brink*, 147, 158.
301. *On the Brink*, 162.

2008, just weeks before the takeover of the GSEs, FHFA had sent out letters to them reviewing their June 30 financial statements, noting that the enterprises were "adequately capitalized."[302]

### Assessing the Magnitude of the Problem

The OFHEO, the regulator of Fannie Mae and Freddie Mac up until 2008, actually undertook some early analysis of the potential systemic risk posed by the GSEs in a study published in 2003. The agency presciently identified the relevant factors in the mortgage market that could make Fannie Mae and Freddie Mac vulnerable to an adverse shock, which is exactly what they were experiencing during the summer of 2008:

- high levels of interdependencies among financial institutions;
- high leverage of such institutions;
- the presence of bubbles in the prices of real and financial assets;
- underpricing of the financial safety net;
- weak market discipline of institutions covered by the safety net;
- lax safety and soundness regulation and poor public disclosure; and
- the presence of macroeconomic problems.[303]

Back then, the OFHEO also recognized the rapid pace of growth in the GSEs and that at least in part this growth was facilitated by the benefits of government sponsorship.[304]

As part of the study, the OFHEO also ran various potential scenarios that assumed deterioration in the housing finance market that could impact the housing sector and the aggregate economy. In one of those scenarios, a single

---

302. FHFA—Letter from Christopher Dickerson to Daniel Mudd, "Notice of Proposed Capital Classification," August 22, 2008. FHFA—Letter from Christopher Dickerson to Richard F. Syron, "Notice of Proposed Capital Classification," August 22, 2008. *On the Brink*, 163–65, 169. Secretary Paulson refers to these letters as draft letters, but "Draft" does not appear on the letters. The letters did note a caveat that the FHFA had the authority to change the assessment contained therein.
303. OFHEO, "Systemic Risk: Fannie Mae, Freddie Mac and the Role of OFHEO," February 2003, 13 [hereinafter, OFHEO Systemic Risk Study].
304. OFHEO Systemic Risk Study, 54.

GSE suffers large losses, which results in widespread selling of its debt and a large decline in the market price of its mortgage backed securities. In this scenario, the point was made that such a systemic threat was not present a decade or two before as in the early 1980s, when the failure of Fannie Mae or Freddie Mac would have posed a much smaller systemic threat to the U.S. economy. When Fannie Mae became insolvent at year-end 1981, it had less than $60 billion in outstanding debt and $3 billion in guaranteed mortgage backed securities. That failure would have imposed losses on investors, mortgage lenders, and related firms, but probably would not have seriously threatened a collapse of the housing finance system or a disruption of financial markets generally.[305]

The rapid growth since the early 1980s, facilitated by the duopoly structure and other characteristics inherent in government sponsorship, brought about that possibility of systemic risk. The dominance of Fannie Mae and Freddie Mac is very clear from the fact that as of 2008 they had unsecured debt and mortgage guarantees of over $5 trillion compared to the $12 trillion mortgage market.[306] The conventional argument is that large financial institutions should not be allowed to fail because of the direct negative impact on lending. With the GSEs, the impact is more indirect. If Fannie Mae and Freddie Mac were allowed to fail outright, they would no longer be able to play their traditional role in purchasing loans from primary market lenders in the secondary market.

The analysis by the OFHEO also noted that the likelihood of Fannie Mae or Freddie Mac becoming illiquid or insolvent was a remote possibility, at least in part because of the OFHEO's oversight of the two GSEs. The scenario analysis also set forth all the tools that were available to the OFHEO to address potential problems if they were to arise: a written agreement or cease-and-desist order with a GSE; or placement of a GSE in conservatorship; or some combination of these options. Finally, the scenarios assessed the possibility that both GSEs would

305. OFHEO Systemic Risk Study, 92–105.
306. Dawn Kopecki, "U.S. Considers Bringing Fannie, Freddie on to Budget," Bloomberg.com, September 11, 2008, http://www.bloomberg.com/apps/news?pid=20601109 &sid=adr.czwVm3ws&refer=home. "Fannie Mae and Freddie Mac Alert for Investors," Bloomberg.com, September 9, 2009, http://www.bloomberg.com/apps/news?pid=conews story&tkr=FNM%3AUS&sid=akgiQ6J1.oGw.

become financially troubled. The study concluded with the recommendation that Congress should grant receivership authority to the OFHEO, an authority that was granted as part of the HERA legislation but never invoked.[307]

As their financial problems mounted, Secretary Paulson was hesitant to even talk publicly about the systemic risk to the financial system from Fannie Mae and Freddie Mac. In response to a question in a hearing on financial markets in July 2008 from Congressman Dennis Moore regarding the systemic risk posed by the GSEs, Secretary Paulson declined to give a direct response: "In today's world I don't think it is helpful to speculate about any financial institution and systemic risk. I'm dealing with the here and now, and the important role that they're playing and other financial institutions are playing."[308] This comment was in keeping with the approach of the WGFM, the coordinating body chaired by Secretary Paulson, with representatives from the Federal Reserve, the SEC, and the CFTC. In an indication of the ongoing tension between secrecy and transparency of the bailouts, the WGFM avoided confronting the possibility of the systemic risk inherent in the failure of Fannie Mae and Freddie Mac. In preparation for WGFM meetings, Treasury staff planned to conduct tabletop exercises on the failure of one of the GSEs, but decided against executing such an analysis for fear that word might leak out to the press, leading the public to believe that such worst-case scenarios were imminent.[309]

As the GSEs approached failure in September 2008, Chairman Bernanke detailed in a meeting with the boards of Fannie Mae and Freddie Mac "the catastrophe that would occur if we did not take these actions."[310] This catastrophe scenario has not been detailed publicly. Although the original statement from Treasury and the Federal Housing Finance Agency (FHFA, successor to OFHEO) announcing an intervention in the operations of Fannie Mae and Freddie Mac addressed their systemic risk, it did not state any factors in this determination of systemic risk other than the sheer size of the GSEs.[311]

---

307. OFHEO Systemic Risk Study, 90, 99, 102, 103, 114.
308. C-Span, "Transformation of Financial Markets," House Committee on Financial Services, July 10, 2008, at the 1:48 mark.
309. *On the Brink*, 52.
310. *On the Brink*, 16. The actions referred to were intervention and placement into conservatorship.
311. U.S. Department of the Treasury, "Statement on Treasury and Federal Housing Finance Agency Action to Protect Financial Markets and Taxpayers," September 7, 2008

*Reviewing the Options*

Given the advanced stage of the capital problems of the GSEs in September 2008, under law the two primary options for addressing the capital problems with Fannie Mae and Freddie Mac were conservatorship and receivership. Conservatorship was originally provided for in the 1992 legislation addressing the GSEs, and receivership was added as part of HERA in 2008. Conservatorship is a process to put a weak financial institution in a safe and sound condition and preserve and conserve assets, and receivership is intended to be a liquidation procedure executed through asset sales and payment of claimants.[312]

Secretary Paulson initially concluded that the best option for Fannie Mae and Freddie Mac would be to have the FHFA place them into receivership. This would have allowed for downsizing the GSEs and addressing their long-term position in the market. However, upon getting advice from the New York law firm of Wachtell, Lipton, Rosen, and Katz (hereinafter, Wachtell), there was a change in direction. According to Secretary Paulson, they determined that going the receivership route would be disruptive to the GSEs' business and difficult to implement in a short period of time. There would also have been a risk of a court challenge and early termination of Fannie Mae and Freddie Mac's derivative contracts. Wachtell recommended conservatorship because it allowed for a rapidly implemented "time out" not unlike Chapter 11 bankruptcy, so that Fannie Mae and Freddie Mac could avoid defaulting on their debts.[313] As the Treasury Department refuses to release the Wachtell report, it is not possible to know the balancing of the options undertaken by the firm.[314] It took three weeks to convince Lockhart and the FHFA that conservatorship was the best option and that was followed by a difficult period in convincing the GSEs, especially given the limited prior notification of capital solvency problems.[315] The choice of conservatorship was clearly very shortsighted, as what was contemplated as a "time out" in late 2008 has lingered on and as of midyear 2011 has not been resolved. There has been no clear resolution of the status of the GSEs, leading

---

[Hereinafter, Treasury Statement] ("Then, to address systemic risk, in 2010 their portfolios will begin to be gradually reduced at the rate of 10 percent per year, largely through natural run off, eventually stabilizing at a lower, less risky size.").

312. 12 USC 4617 details the powers and duties of FHFA as conservator and receiver.

313. *On the Brink,* 162–66.

314. Judicial Watch has requested the Wachtell report, and their request has been denied.

315. *Financial Crisis Inquiry Commission Report,* 318–20.

to continued uncertainty in the mortgage market, and the choice to place them in conservatorship was no doubt accomplished at a higher fiscal cost than the receivership option. Pursuant to the Dodd-Frank legislation, the Obama Administration did release a report on options for Fannie Mae and Freddie Mac in early 2011.[316]

In the original announcement of the placement of Fannie Mae and Freddie Mac into conservatorship, the Treasury Department and the FHFA declined to detail exactly why they chose conservatorship over receivership other than to note the desire to avoid an automatic triggering of receivership.[317] Presumably, the justification for placing Fannie Mae and Freddie Mac in conservatorship over receivership had something to do with the perceived systemic impact of the receivership option. But as with so many of the decisions during the crisis, the details of this analysis have not been publicly released, and the FHFA has refused to release internal documents in this regard.[318] The FHFA admits it has documents that detail the answers to the important deliberative questions on Fannie Mae and Freddie Mac: why they chose conservatorship over receivership and if there were other options; the public perception of and reaction to each of the options; analysis of the potential for judicial review; and the expected response of Fannie Mae and Freddie Mac management to the actions of the FHFA. But they cite exemptions regarding protection of their deliberative process, attorney-client privilege, and attorney work product to shield them from public scrutiny.[319]

---

316. U.S. Department of the Treasury, U.S. Department of Housing and Urban Development, "Reforming America's Housing Finance Market—A Report to Congress," February 2011.

317. Treasury Statement ("This commitment will eliminate any mandatory triggering of receivership and will ensure that the conserved entities have the ability to fulfill their financial obligations").

318. See FHFA, "Questions and Answers on Conservatorship," undated ("The goals of the conservatorship are to help restore confidence in the Company, enhance its capacity to fulfill its mission, and mitigate the systemic risk that has contributed directly to the instability in the current market"). The author filed Freedom of Information Requests with the FHFA and has also filed a suit after they refused to release relevant documents.

319. *McKinley v. FHFA,* No. 10–01165 (D.D.C.), "Preliminary Vaughn Index," September 3, 2010.

*The Final Deal*

By September 2008, as the condition of Fannie Mae and Freddie Mac continued to deteriorate, the two were placed into conservatorship by the Director of the FHFA, the agency responsible for the oversight of Fannie Mae and Freddie Mac.[320] In a joint announcement with the FHFA Director, Treasury Secretary Paulson appeared to absolve the management of the GSEs when he noted that "I attribute the need for today's action primarily to the inherent conflict and flawed business model embedded in the GSE structure, and to the ongoing housing correction. GSE management and their Boards are responsible for neither."[321]

Despite that statement regarding management of the GSEs, new CEOs supported by new non-executive chairmen took over management of the two GSEs. The Treasury used its power to purchase obligations and invest up to $200 billion ($100 billion for each GSE) in preferred stock, while warrants were issued to the Treasury representing an ownership share of 79.9 percent. The preferred stock is particularly important:

> The Senior Preferred Stock Purchase Agreements are the cornerstone of the financial support that the U.S. Treasury is providing to Fannie Mae and Freddie Mac. The SPSPAs effectively provide a very long-term federal guarantee to existing and future debt holders. Each SPSA commits the Treasury to purchase up to $100 billion in senior preferred shares. That commitment protects the credit interests of all holders of the Enterprises' senior and subordinated debt and MBS [mortgage-backed securities].[322]

---

320. U.S. Department of the Treasury, "Statement by Secretary Henry M. Paulson Jr. on Treasury and Federal Housing Finance Agency Action to Protect Financial Markets and Taxpayers," September 7, 2008. The power to place Fannie Mae and Freddie Mac in conservatorship is derived from 12 U.S.C. 4617, which gives the director the discretionary power to place a critically undercapitalized enterprise in conservatorship, a procedure that is also detailed in §4617.

321. Paulson, "Statement on Treasury and Federal Housing Finance Agency Action."

322. Senior Preferred Stock Purchase Agreement executed between Treasury and Fannie Mae and Treasury and Freddie Mac, September 26, 2008 (see "maximum amount," 3, and "warrant," 4).

## The Aftermath

Secretary Paulson characterized himself as "naive" to believe that the intervention would halt the crisis-believing that it "would put a floor under the housing market decline, and provide confidence to the market." Others at Treasury thought it would buy them some time, possibly up to three months. But it was clear within a few days that they were wrong when Lehman filed bankruptcy and AIG was bailed out.[323]

The initial limit of $100 billion for each of the GSEs was raised to $200 billion, and then on Christmas Eve 2009 this structure was amended again to allow an unlimited financial backstop to Fannie Mae and Freddie Mac through 2012.[324]

Beyond the fiscal uncertainty about the limits to the federal commitment to the GSEs, there continues to be uncertainty regarding how to address Fannie Mae and Freddie Mac in the long term. During the summer of 2008 and the development of an approach to deal with the GSEs, Secretary Paulson made his intentions clear to resolve the issue during his tenure and not kick the can down the road: "I want to address the issue. I don't want to leave the problem unsolved."[325] However, that is exactly what he ended up doing, and the status of Fannie Mae and Freddie Mac, and more importantly the parameters of the government commitment as a consequence of their initial bailout, have still not been addressed. Because the approach to wind down the government commitment regarding the GSEs has not been clarified, the final cost of the intervention is in a similar state of uncertainty. The Obama Administration has released a summary of three potential options to wind down the two GSEs.[326]

---

323. *Financial Crisis Inquiry Commission Report*, 321.

324. James R. Hagerty and Jessica Holzer, "U.S. Move to Cover Fannie, Freddie Losses Stirs Controversy," *Wall Street Journal*, December 28, 2009; Zachary A. Goldfarb, "U.S. Promises Unlimited Financial Assistance to Fannie Mae, Freddie Mac," *Washington Post*, December 27, 2009.

325. *Too Big to Fail*, 211.

326. U.S. Department of the Treasury, U.S. Department of Housing and Urban Development, "Reforming America's Housing Finance Market—A Report to Congress," February 2011.

The FHFA has released projections regarding the ultimate cost of resolving Fannie Mae and Freddie Mac. As of the date of those projections, the GSEs had drawn $148 billion. Under the three scenarios utilized by FHFA, the GSEs will ultimately draw between $221 billion and $363 billion.[327]

---

327. Federal Housing Finance Agency, "FHFA Releases Projections Showing Range of Potential Draws for Fannie Mae and Freddie Mac," October 21, 2010.

# 8

## The 2000s Crisis:
## The FDIC Intervenes

"I'm not completely comfortable with [the option to bail out
Wachovia] but we need to move forward with **something**,
clearly because this institution is in a tenuous situation."
—Sheila C. Bair, chairman of the FDIC, in deciding
among options to resolve Wachovia Bank[1]

---

**LEGAL SCORECARD**
- Helping Families Save Their Homes Act of 2009

---

THE POLICY CHALLENGES posed by "too big to fail" that
so clearly manifested themselves in the case of open bank assistance (OBA)
for Continental Illinois and other institutions were never fully resolved. FDIC
Chairman Isaac noted the two problems presented by the bank: (1) the administrative problem and (2) the domino theory problem. The administrative
problem was taken care of by granting the FDIC the power to create a bridge
bank.[2] If a very large or complex bank was on the brink of failure, a bridge bank
could bridge the gap until the FDIC could either find a buyer or resolve the bank
through other means. The domino theory problem was supposed to be addressed
through the systemic risk exception for "those rare instances in which the failure

---

1. FDIC, Board of Directors—Meeting Closed Session, Transcript, September 29, 2008,
22. Emphasis of the author.
2. For savings institutions this is referred to as a conservatorship. For background see
Gibson, Dunn, and Crutcher, "Overview of the FDIC as Conservator or Receiver," September 26, 2008, http://blogs.law.harvard.edu/corpgov/files/2008/10/092608-overview-
fdicasconservator-receiver.pdf.

of an institution could threaten the entire financial system" and also through limits on interbank exposures.[3] But even the FDIC recognized the uncertainty of what the systemic risk exception meant, as evidenced by speculation in an FDIC document from the late 1990s regarding the potential for another Continental-sized problem: "[T]he problem of systemic risk remains, as does the question of how regulators would respond today to a dilemma similar to the one they confronted in May 1984."[4]

That uncertainty flowed from the systemic risk exception in FDICIA, which was an ill-advised legislative compromise after the 1980s crisis. The intention in putting in place the exception was to reserve the use of OBA for only the rarest of circumstances. However, the legislative language was open-ended, as it did not prescribe the parameters of its use, did not provide a definition of systemic risk, and did not address how commitments under it should be structured. It only contained the vague description that it should be invoked to avoid "serious adverse effects on economic conditions or financial stability."[5] The FDIC had discretion to invoke it upon approval of two-thirds of the FDIC Board of Directors, two-thirds of the Board of Governors of the Federal Reserve, and the secretary of the Treasury in consultation with the president, with an after-the-fact review by the GAO to assess the decision. So the idea was to transparently place scrutiny of the decision at very high levels within the government.

In the years since that amendment as part of FDICIA, consolidation in the industry accelerated and so called megabanks proliferated (see Table 8.1).[6] In fact, some argue that the incentives to become TBTF in the wake of Continental were a large driving force behind the consolidation.[7] In 2004, just a few

---

3. Senate Committee on Banking, Housing, and Urban Affairs, Comprehensive Deposit Insurance Reform and Taxpayer Protection Act of 1991, 102nd Congress, 1st Session, S. Rep. 167, 45.

4. *History of the 80s*, p. 254 (1997).

5. Section 13(c) of the Federal Deposit Insurance Act after the amendment under FDICIA of 1991.

6. See Kenneth D. Jones and Tim Critchfield, "Consolidation in the U.S. Banking Industry: Is the 'Long, Strange Trip' About to End?" *FDIC Banking Review* 17, no. 4 (2005).

7. Edward J. Kane, "Incentives for Banking Megamergers: What Motives Might Regulators Infer From Event-Study Evidence?" *Journal of Money, Credit, and Banking*, Vol. 32, No. 3, January 25, 2000, 6.

**Table 8.1.** Concentration of Commercial Banking (1990 to 2005)

| Percent of Assets and Deposits in the Top 10 Commercial Banks | | |
|---|---|---|
| | **Percent of Assets** | **Percent of Deposits** |
| 1990 | 25 | 17 |
| 2005 | 55 | 45 |

*Source*: Kenneth D. Jones and Robert C. Oshinsky, "The Effect of Industry Consolidation and Deposit Insurance Reform on the Resiliency of the U.S. Bank Insurance Fund," April 25, 2007.

years before the onset of the financial crisis, an FDIC analysis warned that this consolidation phenomenon actually increased systemic risk in the U.S. banking and financial system, and that losses associated with a single megabank failure had the potential to be catastrophic to the Bank Insurance Fund (BIF), which represents the capital position of the FDIC.[8]

Large and small bank failures throughout 2008 put pressure on the FDIC's BIF. Legislative changes in response to the crisis included a temporary increase in deposit insurance coverage to $250,000, which was extended until 2013 under the Helping Families Save Their Homes Act of 2009. This act also permanently increased the FDIC's borrowing authority from Treasury from $30 billion to $100 billion and, if necessary, up to $500 billion.[9]

The most expensive of the bank failures was IndyMac FSB, which failed on a closed-bank basis in July 2008 at a cost to the FDIC of nearly $11 billion, the highest cost to resolve an institution in FDIC history.[10] Uninsured depositors and other creditors also suffered losses. Citing yet another regulatory breakdown, the Treasury Department's inspector general (IG) noted that the OTS continued to give IndyMac high ratings right up until shortly before it failed in 2008.

---

8. Kenneth D. Jones and Chau Nguyen, "Increased Concentration in Banking: Megabanks and Their Implications for Deposit Insurance," June 2004.

9. The temporary increase was under the Emergency Economic Stabilization Act of 2008, Public Law 110–343. This was extended under the Helping Families Save Their Homes Act, Public Law 111–22. Dodd, "Helping Families Save Their Homes Act" (2009), http://banking.senate.gov/public/_files/050609_HelpingFamiliesSummary.pdf.

10. Information for IndyMac Bank, F.S.B., and IndyMac Federal Bank, F.S.B., Pasadena, CA, http://www.fdic.gov/bank/individual/failed/IndyMac.html.

OTS had at times as many as forty bank examiners involved in the supervision of IndyMac. However, the examination results did not reflect the serious risks associated with IndyMac's business model and practices. Finally, the IG report noted that OTS did not issue any type of enforcement action, either informal or formal, to put a limit on IndyMac operations until June 2008, just weeks before the institution's failure.[11]

## Open Bank Assistance

FDIC Chairman Bair reportedly felt pressure from FRBNY President Geithner to invoke the systemic risk exception and use OBA in the case of Washington Mutual (WaMu).[12] WaMu was a large $300 billion financial institution that approached failure in September 2008. About $16 billion or 9 percent of its deposits fled the institution as its financial standing deteriorated.[13] Those that likely ran from the bank were uninsured depositors who, as in the case of IndyMac, were exposed if they did not move fast to get their deposits under the insured limit. Chairman Bair resisted the pressure from Geithner to succumb to the "not on my watch" mentality of avoiding a large bank failure. After the bank's charter was withdrawn by the OTS on September 25, the FDIC Board decided to have

---

11. Treasury Department—Office of Inspector General, "Material Loss Review of Indy-Mac Bank FSB," February 26, 2009.

12. *In Fed We Trust*, 219–21 ("Geithner strongly objected to Bair's reasoning. . . . Geithner first complained directly to Bair, who would not be moved. He then called Don Kohn, who had been mediating between the FDIC and the Office of Thrift Supervision. And he lobbied John Dugan, the comptroller of the currency and regulator of national banks, the ones most vulnerable if the terms of the WaMu deal undermined investor confidence. Geithner was beginning to sound like a shill for the banks. He knew that. But in the midst of the Great Panic, the government couldn't sweat such details. Bernanke, on the other hand, wasn't as worried as Geithner. He was reluctant to pull the 'systemic risk' emergency cord—especially since JPMorgan Chase was willing to take over all of WaMu's operations and stand behind all the bets it had made in financial markets. Ultimately, Geithner and WaMu debt holders lost. The latter group was left waiting to see if any money would fall their way in a bankruptcy proceeding against WaMu's parent, but there wasn't much.").

13. "JP Morgan Buys Washington Mutual," *Morning Edition*, National Public Radio, September 26, 2008, http://www.npr.org/templates/transcript/transcript.php?storyId=95076157.

WaMu fail on a closed bank basis, the largest financial institution closure in U.S. history, leading to losses not only for the shareholders, but also creditors.[14]

The resolution caused a rare split in opinion among the bailout agencies. FDIC Chairman Bair characterized the sale of WaMu as "successful" and rightly noted that "WaMu was not a well-run institution" deserving of a bailout. The FDIC never contemplated using funds to protect unsecured creditors. Scott Alvarez, General Counsel of the Board of Governors, agreed that "there should not have been intervention in WaMu." However, Treasury's Neel Kashkari sarcastically and hysterically disagreed: "We were saying that's great, we can all be tough, and we can be so tough that we plunge the financial system into the Great Depression. And so, I think, in my judgment that was a mistake."[15] According to an analysis by the Treasury Department, senior and subordinated debt holders of the WaMu holding company and its insured depository subsidiaries suffered large losses.[16]

This disparate treatment highlights the inconsistent treatment of similarly situated creditors during the crisis. WaMu and IndyMac creditors rightly took a large loss on their investments in FDIC receivership, which is roughly the equivalent of a bankruptcy proceeding, but in the cases of bailed-out institutions such as Bear Stearns, AIG, Fannie Mae, and Freddie Mac, creditors avoided losses.

## Wachovia

### *Circumstances Leading to the Stress*

The time for the FDIC to justify the first invocation of the OBA power came just a few days later on September 29 in the case of Wachovia, a top-ten financial institution on par with Continental Illinois in its rank among the largest financial institutions in the United States. Like many of the investment banks,

---

14. WaMu was resolved through purchase and assumption by JPMorgan Chase. FDIC, "JPMorgan Chase Acquires Banking Operations of Washington Mutual," September 25, 2008. The author has filed a Freedom of Information Act (FOIA) request with the FDIC regarding any consideration of OBA for WaMu.

15. *Financial Crisis Inquiry Commission Report*, 365–66.

16. GAO, "Federal Deposit Insurance Act: Regulators' Use of Systemic Risk Exception Raises Moral Hazard Concerns and Opportunities Exist to Clarify the Provision," GAO-10–100 (April 2010), 13 [hereinafter, GAO SRE report].

mortgage GSEs, and AIG, Wachovia suffered massive losses from its mortgage-related investments, including a $100 billion portfolio of option-adjustable-rate mortgages (ARMs) inherited from its acquisition of Golden West Financial Corporation in California in 2006. Simultaneously, Wachovia pushed aggressively into commercial real estate. A new chief executive officer, Robert Steel, who was a deputy to Treasury Secretary Paulson, was brought in to restructure Wachovia, but by September 2008 it was clear Wachovia was on the brink of failure.[17] However, the FDIC was not informed of the extent of the problems at Wachovia until the weekend of its ultimate collapse.[18] The lateness in notifying the FDIC can be traced to a regulatory breakdown at the Office of the Comptroller and the Federal Reserve Bank of Richmond, as both gave Wachovia passing grades on operations just weeks before closure.[19] In a single day on Friday, September 26, 2008:

- Wachovia lost $5.7 billion of deposits and $1.1 billion of commercial paper and repos;
- Worried creditors had asked Wachovia to repay $50 to $60 billion, or roughly half of all of its long-term debt;
- Wachovia's 10-year bonds fell in value from 73 cents to 29 cents on the dollar; and
- The annual cost of buying protection on $10 million of Wachovia debt jumped from $571,000 to almost $1,400,000.[20]

### Assessing the Magnitude of the Problem

The FDIC put Wachovia up for bid and received separate offers from Wachovia management, Citigroup, and Wells Fargo. Chairman Bair reportedly

---

17. Dan Fitzpatrick and Diya Gullapalli, "Storm of Fear Enveloped Wachovia," *Wall Street Journal*, September 30, 2008.

18. Statement of John Corston, Acting Deputy Director, Complex Financial Institutions Branch, FDIC, September 1, 2010, 11.

19. Federal Reserve Bank of Richmond, Supervisory Assessment of Wachovia Corporation, July 22, 2008. Office of the Comptroller of the Currency, Letter and Examination on Wachovia Bank, August 4, 2008, http://www.fcic.gov/hearings/pdfs/2010−0901 -Wachovia-Package.pdf.

20. *Financial Crisis Inquiry Commission Report*, 367.

had a desire to follow the same approach as with WaMu's to apply a haircut to shareholders and creditors: "I don't think that the small banks should have to pay for the sins of the big banks."[21] Surprisingly, as the FDIC announced the resolution, the transaction was in the form of an OBA transaction for Wachovia with Citigroup as the winning bidder. There was no hint of the precise reason for invoking the exception, or an indication why the exception was used for Wachovia but not for WaMu a few days earlier. It would have been logical for the FDIC to explain this complete turnaround in its approach for the initial invocation of the OBA power. It would have been logical to address questions like what the fallout from a Wachovia failure would have been in the announcement of the bailout. But FDIC Chairman Bair's public explanation noted in terms that could have been used to describe any of the previous bailouts that the "decision was made under extraordinary circumstances with significant consultation among the regulators and Treasury," and that "this action was necessary to maintain confidence in the banking industry given current financial market conditions."[22]

Efforts in the aftermath of the Wachovia approval to compel the disclosure of a justification for the approval were met with the resistance of the FDIC. The response from the FDIC to these requests came in the form of heavily redacted minutes of relevant meetings and related memos.[23] Legal disputes over disclosure of government documents are decided under the Freedom of Information Act

---

21. *In Fed We Trust,* 222.

22. FDIC, "Citigroup Inc. to Acquire Banking Operations of Wachovia," September 29, 2008. Ultimately, the OBA transaction was not consummated because Wells Fargo bid for Wachovia in an unassisted merger a few days later. David Enrich and Dan Fitzpatrick, "Wachovia Chooses Wells Fargo, Spurns Citi," *Wall Street Journal,* October 4, 2008. Damian Paletta, "Affidavit Suggests Wachovia Neared Failure," *Wall Street Journal,* October 5, 2008. Dan Fitzpatrick, "On Crisis Stage, FDIC Plays the Tough," *Wall Street Journal,* November 3, 2008.

23. The author submitted an FOIA request to the FDIC for details supporting the determination on the Wachovia proposed OBA transaction (filed on November 18, 2008). These deliberations by the FDIC were undertaken in closed board meetings as defined under the Government in the Sunshine Act (5 U.S.C. 552(b)), and full access to the information had been denied by the FDIC, which cited numerous sections of the act. The request for information on Wachovia was appealed internally with the FDIC's General Counsel under the administrative procedures of the FDIC regarding FOIA requests. In February 2009,

(FOIA). A good standard to follow regarding justifications for withholding documents under FOIA was set forth by the Obama Justice Department in January 2009:

- The government should not keep information confidential merely because public officials might be embarrassed by disclosure;
- Or because errors and failures might be revealed;
- Or because of speculative or abstract fears.[24]

The FDIC fought disclosure of the details of the Wachovia intervention for nearly two years. After a *Wall Street Journal* editorial in September 2010 detailed the efforts of the FDIC to prevent disclosure,[25] the Financial Crisis Inquiry Commission (FCIC), which had responsibility for investigating the causes of the crisis, released in full the minutes and transcripts of the FDIC Board Meeting where the Wachovia transaction was approved. They also released a supporting memo drafted by the FDIC. All of the elements cited by the Justice Department can be found with regard to the withheld Wachovia documents.

The supporting memo by FDIC staff recommending OBA to the FDIC Board was a mix of general statements about the troubled economy and conclusory statements and rampant speculation about the potential impact of a Wachovia failure (see Table 8.2). Speculative and abstract fears are elements

---

*(footnote 23 continued)* the FDIC released a heavily redacted version of the relevant board minutes, with minimal new information released. In July 2009 suit was filed in the Federal District Court in Washington, DC, *McKinley v. Federal Deposit Insurance Corporation, et al.*, Civil Action No. 09–1263 ESH. After the filing the FDIC released a previously undisclosed Board Memorandum which should have been released earlier, but was not. The memorandum had a section entitled "Systemic Risk Exception" but the section, which ran a full two-and-a-half pages, was completely whited out. See a copy of the memo in Appendix 1 with redaction and fully unredacted.

24. The White House—President Barack Obama, "Memorandum for the Heads of Executive Departments and Agencies—Freedom of Information Act," January 21, 2009, http://www.whitehouse.gov/the_press_office/FreedomofInformationAct/. U.S. Department of Justice—Office of Information Policy, "President Obama's FOIA Memorandum and Attorney General Holder's Guidelines—Creating a New Era of Open Government," January 21, 2009.

25. Review and Outlook, "Systemic Risk Stonewall," *Wall Street Journal*, September 1, 2010. http://online.wsj.com/article/SB10001424052748703467004575463781244452958.html.

**Table 8.2.** FDIC Evidence Wachovia Was Systemic (September 2008)

". . . significant adverse effects on economic conditions and the financial markets."

"Term funding markets have been under considerable stress for more than a year. . . ."

"LIBOR rates have increased more than 100 basis points since early September, commercial paper rates have also risen dramatically and the volume of financial paper has risen dramatically."

"Concerns about actual and potential losses on financial institutions' obligations have caused outflows from prime money market mutual funds totaling nearly $400 billion . . ."

". . . investors appear to have become more concerned about the outlook of a number of U.S. banking organizations, putting downward pressure on their stock prices and upward pressure on their collateralized debt security spreads."

". . . a least cost resolution would be expected to have significant systemic consequences."

". . . would intensify liquidity pressures on other U.S. banks, which are extremely vulnerable to a loss of confidence by wholesale suppliers of fund."

"Investors would likely be concerned about direct exposures of other financial firms to Wachovia . . ."

". . . failure of Wachovia would lead investors to doubt the financial strength of other institutions that might be seen as similarly situated."

". . . lead investors to reassess the risk in U.S. commercial banks more broadly, particularly given the current fragility of financial markets generally and the term funding markets for financial institutions."

". . . a least cost resolution did not support foreign depositors; the resolution could imperil this significant source of funding for other U.S. financial institutions."

". . . global liquidity pressures could increase and confidence in the dollar could decline."

" . . . could lead more money market mutual funds to 'break the buck,' accelerating runs on those and other money funds."

". . . might well lead short-term funding markets to virtually cease."

*(Table 8.2 continued on the next page)*

**Table 8.2.** (*continued*)

| |
|---|
| ". . . the individuals and businesses whose deposits have been swept into non-deposit investments or foreign deposits (e.g. at a Cayman branch) would find all or part of their funds unavailable and likely face losses." |
| ". . . likely cause investors to sharply raise their assessment of the risks of investing in similar (albeit smaller) regional banks, making it much less likely that those institutions would be able to raise capital and other funding." |
| ". . . the consequences of a least-cost resolution could extend to the broader economy." |
| ". . . would further undermine business and household confidence." |
| ". . . would almost surely have systemic effects." |

*Source*: FDIC, Memo to the Board of Directors, Wachovia Bank, September 29, 2008, 9–11 ("Systemic Risk" Section). Subject of litigation in *McKinley v. FDIC*, Case 1:10-cv -00420.

cited by the Obama Justice Department. The description of possible systemic fallout from the failure of Wachovia was devoid of a precise linkage between the failure of Wachovia and a variety of potential adverse systemic events.

It is unclear how much of this very general analysis can even be attributed to the FDIC. The FCIC noted that the presentation to the FDIC Board by the agency's staff largely relied on an analysis of systemic risk by the Federal Reserve Bank of Richmond. That analysis stated generally that mutual funds held $66 billion of Wachovia debt, but beyond that it did not state any specific financial institutions (or dominos) that were at risk if Wachovia failed.[26]

### Reviewing the Options

Another element of the Justice Department analysis of inappropriate reasons for withholding documents under FOIA is that embarrassing revelations might be disclosed. One such revelation was the disclosure that the Treasury

---

26. *Financial Crisis Inquiry Commission Report*, 368–89 ("FDIC Associate Director Miguel Browne hewed closely to the analysis prepared by the Richmond Fed"). The noted analysis is John A. Beebe, "Wachovia Large Fund Providers," Federal Reserve Bank of Richmond interoffice memo to Jennifer Burns, September 27, 2008.

Department agreed that if there were any losses in the Wachovia transaction, Treasury would separately fund those.[27] At the time, Treasury did not clearly have the power to fund such losses, and Secretary Paulson made clear many times in the lead-up to the Lehman bankruptcy that this was the case. Another embarrassing disclosure is that the chairman of the FDIC admitted that she "acquiesced" to the pressure of the Treasury Department, which was "vigorously pushing this" proposal, even though the FDIC is an independent agency that should not succumb to pressure from the politically driven Treasury Department.[28] White House chief of staff Josh Bolten also applied pressure as he called Bair the day before the FDIC vote on Wachovia to express support for the systemic risk exception.[29] Beyond the pressure applied by the Treasury and the White House, other sources of information reveal that Chairman Bair was also pressured by FRBNY President Geithner to invoke the systemic risk exception. In response to the FDIC's original inclination to allow Wachovia to be closed, "Geithner blew up. Wachovia has to open on Monday, he argued. It must be sold this weekend, the buyer needs government assistance, and the debt holders need to be protected. It has to be this way. . . . The policy of the U.S. government is that there will be no more WaMu's."[30]

The final element of the Justice Department analysis is withholding information on errors and failures by the agency involved. The FDIC staff memo on Wachovia did not even give the FDIC Board any clear options other than open bank assistance. For example, they did not offer the option of a bridge bank. This was a power granted to the FDIC in the wake of Continental Illinois, designed specifically for cases where a large or complex institution is approaching failure. Clearly this would have been an option that would have allowed the FDIC to take over the bank and get its operations under control, without the need to provide OBA. Little discussion took place on the available options, as one of the FDIC Board members, John Reich, admitted in response to a call for questions from Chairman Bair: "There's a lot that I don't know, unfortunately."[31]

---

27. Minutes of the Board of Directors meeting of the FDIC, September 29, 2008, 56404.

28. FDIC Wachovia Transcript, 18, 19, 21.

29. Sheila Bair, interview by FCIC, August 18, 2010.

30. *In Fed We Trust*, 222–23.

31. FDIC, Board of Directors—Meeting Closed Session, Transcript, September 29, 2008, 15 [hereinafter FDIC Wachovia Transcript].

Even with this lack of information, the FDIC Board did not take the opportunity to ask many questions of the FDIC staff and the Board meeting lasted a mere 30 minutes.[32] In reviewing the option of Citigroup as a potential bidder, no one asked about the financial capacity of Citigroup to absorb Wachovia. As a result of a recent bank examination Citicorp was placed under a Memorandum of Understanding (MoU) by its bank regulator (the Office of the Comptroller in June 2008) and the holding company regulator (the Federal Reserve in May 2008). An MoU is an agreement between a regulator and a financial institution that identifies weaknesses and outlines suggested corrective action. The two MoUs addressed weaknesses in risk management, corporate governance, management information systems, and loan loss reserves.[33] Normally, the Federal Reserve would have reviewed the application of Citigroup to buy Wachovia under the Change in Bank Control Act, which would have required an investigation of the competence, experience, integrity, and financial ability of Citigroup management.[34] No reference to the availability of such a review is noted in the FDIC Board memo or meeting minutes. As will be discussed later in this chapter, Citigroup itself was on the brink of failure just a few weeks later.[35]

---

32. *Financial Crisis Inquiry Commission Report*, 369.

33. FDIC, Memo to the Board of Directors, "Citigroup, N.A.," November 23, 2008, 7. Special Inspector General for the Troubled Asset Relief Program, "Extraordinary Financial Assistance Provided to Citigroup, Inc.," January 13, 2011, 23. Chairman Bair also expressed concern about Citigroup after the fact. See *Financial Crisis Inquiry Commission Report*, 370. ("[Bair] also told the FCIC that she had concerns about Citigroup's own viability if it acquired Wachovia for that price. 'In reality, we didn't know how unstable Citigroup was at that point.'")

34. 12 USC 1817(j). It is not clear that a full review by the Federal Reserve was completed given the time pressure involved.

35. FDIC Chairman Bair explained the situation in later testimony in September 2010 before the FCIC. The question asked on the Wachovia/Citigroup deal was: "We have Citi that's already weak and in trouble. They are being asked now to merge with an organization that I think you thought might be insolvent, or on its way to insolvency—," to which Chairman Bair responded: "I think at the time, based on information we had, we thought that Citi was the stronger institution. And obviously later they ran into their own set of problems. But at that point, I think it was the collective decision of everyone that this would stabilize the situation; that this would stabilize the situation that Citi was, even though it perhaps had its own problems, was the stronger institution than Wachovia and that would stabilize the situation. We had to do *something*. I mean, I think we had— we had to do *something*." Emphasis is that of the author.

## The Aftermath

A review of the Wachovia transaction by the GAO was mandated under the changes in FDICIA. This requirement was originally intended to place scrutiny on the decision-making process behind OBA. Although two years had elapsed after the bailout before the review was published, the final product shed little further light on the basis for intervention.[36] The GAO did not seriously question the underlying details of the potential fallout from a Wachovia failure and essentially accepted the FDIC's, the Treasury's, and the Federal Reserve's justifications for intervention at face value. However, GAO did make clear throughout its discussion of the Wachovia transaction that the statements of the FDIC, Treasury, and Federal Reserve described potential consequences, not necessarily likely or probable consequences:[37]

- FDIC protection against large losses on Wachovia assets was intended to facilitate an orderly sale to Citigroup and avert a resolution with *potentially* systemic consequences.
- In recommending a systemic risk determination, the Federal Reserve and FDIC described the extent of Wachovia's interdependencies and the *potential* for disruptions to markets in which it played a significant role.
- Treasury, the FDIC, and the Federal Reserve concluded that FDIC assistance under the systemic risk exception could avert the *potential* systemic consequences of a least cost resolution of Wachovia's bank and thrift subsidiaries. In particular, they determined that authorizing FDIC guarantees to protect against losses to Wachovia's uninsured creditors would avoid or mitigate the *potential* for serious adverse effects on the financial system and the economy by facilitating the acquisition of Wachovia's banking operations by Citigroup.
- Although the loss-sharing agreement never took effect, the announcement of the Citigroup acquisition and loss-sharing agreement may have helped to avert a Wachovia failure with *potential* systemic consequences.[38]

---

36. GAO SRE report.

37. GAO SRE report, 12–16.

38. This quotation highlights the fact that the Citigroup purchase of Wachovia was never completed, as Wells Fargo made a later bid for Wachovia. See David Enrich and Dan

The arguments by the GAO and by the FDIC for intervening in the case of Wachovia are not at all convincing, and like so many of the bailouts before Wachovia, there was no quantifiable evidence that the fallout from allowing the institution to fail would have been damaging other than to the creditors directly exposed at the institutions in question.

A few weeks after the Wachovia approval, in October 2008 the G-7 Finance Ministers issued the following statement of policy, which was later endorsed by the Central Bank Governors of the International Monetary and Financial Committee of the Board of Governors of the IMF: "Take decisive action and use all available tools to support systemically important financial institutions and prevent their failure."[39]

This statement codified a growing worldwide mentality of reflexively bailing out large institutions, even though there was little actual evidence of systemic fallout. Beyond the sacrifice of sovereignty involved in such a move, this endorsed action by the G-7 and the IMF had an obviously questionable policy basis. To verify that fact, one need look no further than a working paper issued by the IMF that same month on the topic of systemic banking crises. The working paper did not provide evidence that preventing the failure of such systemically important financial institutions is the best approach to a financial crisis. In fact, with regard to bailing out or supporting such institutions, a process referred to in the working paper as "providing assistance," it clearly highlighted the problems with that approach:

> Existing empirical research has shown that providing assistance to banks and their borrowers can be *counterproductive*, resulting in increased losses to banks, which often abuse forbearance to take unproductive risks at government expense. . . . Further, a lack of attention to incentive problems when designing specific rules governing financial assistance *can*

---

*(footnote 38 continued)* Fitzpatrick, "Wachovia Chooses Wells Fargo, Spurns Citi," *Wall Street Journal*, October 4, 2008. Damian Paletta, "Affidavit Suggests Wachovia Neared Failure," *Wall Street Journal*, October 5, 2008. Dan Fitzpatrick, "On Crisis Stage, FDIC Plays the Tough," *Wall Street Journal*, November 3, 2008.

39. U.S. Department of the Treasury, "G-7 Finance Ministers and Central Bank Governors Plan of Action," October 10, 2008, HP-1195; Communiqué of the International Monetary and Financial Committee of the Board of Governors of the International Monetary Fund, October 11, 2008.

*aggravate moral hazard problems*, especially in environments where these institutions are weak, unnecessarily raising the costs of resolution.[40]

After the October announcement, numerous countries have acted consistently with this prescriptive measure of the G-7 and the IMF.[41] More recently, the IMF has seemed to reverse itself on this matter, as Dominique Strauss-Kahn, the former Managing Director of the IMF, has commented that new banking crises should be prevented in ways other than recapitalization of banks by the state.[42]

## The Temporary Liquidity Guarantee Program

### Circumstances Leading to the Stress

Despite the lack of clear evidence to support the game plan of the G-7 and the IMF, back in the U.S. the FDIC, Federal Reserve, and Treasury went forward with two additional invocations of the OBA power: the multi-bank application of the systemic risk exception for the Temporary Liquidity Guarantee Program (TLGP), which applied to a broad swath of banks; and then individually for Citigroup. The TLGP was developed by the FDIC after a number of institutions, such as WaMu and Wachovia, experienced large outflows of uninsured deposits. Throughout September 2008, a number of private individuals had called for a "general guarantee on bank obligations," and that is essentially what was called for under the TLGP.

### Assessing the Magnitude of the Problem

In their presentation to the FDIC Board of Directors, the FDIC staff cites an internal study on the effect of a run on uninsured deposits on economic

---

40. Luc Laeven and Fabian Valencia, "Systemic Banking Crises: A New Database," IMF Working Paper WP/08/224, October 2008, 4. Bolded words are the emphasis of the author.
41. For example, Belgium, Germany, Sweden, Ukraine, Latvia, and Kazakhstan are all examples of governments that since that time have bailed out so-called systemic financial institutions.
42. "International Monetary Fund: Recapitalization is a One-Time Measure," *Kyiv Post*, October 4, 2010.

activity. The study indicated that a 5 percent run would reduce GDP growth by over 1 percent per annum in a normal economy while the same run on a stressed economy would decrease GDP growth by as much as 2 percent.[43] Based in part on that study, the FDIC concluded that "there is ample evidence over the last few months that there have been and continue to be, rapid and substantial outflows of uninsured deposits, from institutions that are perceived to be under stress."[44] But the mere fact that there were outflows of uninsured deposits at banks means little, and similar to the efforts in Wachovia to stop disclosure of key documents, the FDIC has refused to expose the internal study for outside scrutiny.[45] The GAO, in its review of the TLGP, was skeptical of the underlying basis for these conclusions, noting that the FDIC did not track the outflows, but their conclusion was based on anecdotal reports from institutions and regulators serving as their primary supervisors.[46]

The FDIC also invoked the oft-cited disruption to money markets after the failure of Lehman Brothers.[47] However, despite all of these recitations, there was no clear showing of a contagion that would have justified such a broad-based program of bank guarantees. The Federal Reserve, in its analysis of the TLGP, also came up with a rather novel justification for going forward with the program, an undefined concept known as "unexpected losses," which might be

---

43. Minutes of the Board of Directors meeting of the FDIC, October 13, 2008, 56470.

44. Minutes of the Board of Directors meeting of the FDIC, October 13, 2008, 56470. Mitchell Glassman, Memorandum to the Board of Directors of the FDIC, "FDIC Guarantee of Bank Debt," October 13, 2008, 3.

45. The author argues that the study falls under an FOIA request at issue in *McKinley v. FDIC*, Case 1:10-cv-00420-EGS (D. District of Columbia filed March 15, 2010), opinion at http://docs.justia.com/cases/federal/district-courts/district-of-columbia/dcdce/1:2010cv00420/141205/17/. After the suit was initiated, the FDIC provided redacted versions of the relevant board minutes and staff memo. About a year after the original request the FDIC provided unredacted versions of the relevant board minutes and staff memo. The litigation is ongoing and one of the disputed documents is the internal FDIC study on deposit outflows.

46. GAO SRE report, 16–17 ("According to FDIC officials with whom we spoke, they were not tracking outflows of these deposits, but relied on anecdotal reports from institutions and the regulators serving as their primary supervisors").

47. *McKinley v. FDIC*, Case 1:10-cv-00420-EGS (D. District of Columbia filed March 15, 2010). Minutes of the Board of Directors meeting of the FDIC, October 13, 2008, 56471.

imposed on investors.[48] The directive of the G-7 was also cited as a justification for approving the TLGP.[49]

### The Final Deal

Based on that rather thin reed of anecdotal evidence, the FDIC embarked on an extraordinary expansion of its powers. TLGP allowed the FDIC to go well beyond its traditional role of insuring deposits within the prescribed limit under law to extending coverage to a broad range of creditors. FDIC Director Curry, as part of his statement accompanying his vote to support the TLGP, noted that it was "a major expansion of the FDIC's business beyond deposit insurance and beyond depository institutions."[50] It did so through two programs: the Debt Guarantee Program (DGP), which guaranteed newly issued unsecured debt of financial institutions and their holding companies; and the Transaction Account Guarantee Program (TAGP), which extended an unlimited deposit guarantee to non–interest bearing transaction accounts.[51]

Not only was the TLGP an expansion of the types of instruments that could be covered by the FDIC, but it was also an expansion of the type of intervention that OBA could be used for. From the time of its inception when the power was granted to the FDIC in 1950, it was always applicable to either an individual institution or a group of institutions held within a single ownership structure,

---

48. GAO SRE report, 17 ("The Federal Reserve reasoned, among other things, that the failures and least-cost resolutions of a number of institutions could impose unexpected losses on investors and further undermine confidence in the banking system, which already was under extreme stress").

49. GAO SRE report, p. 18 ("In a memorandum describing the basis for TLGP determination, Treasury explained the need for emergency actions in the context of a recent agreement among the United States and its G7 colleagues to implement a comprehensive action plan to provide liquidity to markets and prevent the failure of any systemically important institution, among other objectives. To implement the G7 plan, several countries had already announced programs to guarantee retail deposits and new debt issued by financial institutions. Treasury noted that if the United States did not take similar actions, global market participants might turn to institutions and markets in countries where the perceived protections were the greatest.").

50. *McKinley v. FDIC*, Case 1:10-cv-00420-EGS (D. District of Columbia filed March 15, 2010). Minutes of the Board of Directors meeting of the FDIC, October 13, 2008, 56477.

51. GAO SRE report, 19–21.

such as a holding company. Even during the development of FDICIA, this limitation was clear as noted in the debate at that time that its use should be limited to "those rare instances in which the failure of an institution could threaten the entire financial system."[52] The TLGP was a system-wide program that was not so limited to an individual institution or ownership group, applying an expansive interpretation of the systemic risk exception. Although no court has ruled on when or how the TLGP may be used, the GAO raised a number of questions regarding the program as part of its review. The OBA power has also always been reserved for troubled institutions, those institutions on the brink of failure. There was no such limit on the TLGP as it applied to the full range of institutions, and in fact it was directed specifically to viable institutions.[53]

### The Aftermath

In early 2009, Edward Yingling of the American Bankers Association summarized the transformation of the FDIC: "While a creative approach was certainly required in this difficult environment, the programs announced have taken the FDIC well beyond its chartered responsibilities to protect insured depositors in the event of a bank failure."[54] As the TLGP has been utilized, the primary financial institutions accessing it have been medium and large institutions as over 90 percent of institutions with more than $10 billion in assets opted into the two programs.[55] The program cost of the TLGP has been estimated at $4 billion, but more recent FDIC testimony details that the cost will be less than that.[56]

---

52. Senate Committee on Banking, Housing, and Urban Affairs, Comprehensive Deposit Insurance Reform and Taxpayer Protection Act of 1991, 102nd Congress, 1st Session, S. Rep. 167, 45.

53. GAO SRE report, 18, and appendix II to the report, 43–57 ("However, while seeking to encourage broad participation, TLGP was not intended to prop up nonviable institutions, according to FDIC officials").

54. Edward Yingling, On Behalf of the American Bankers Association, Committee on Financial Services, U.S. House of Representatives, February 3, 2009.

55. GAO SRE report, 20.

56. Alan S. Blinder and Mark Zandi, "How We Ended the Great Recession," July 27, 2010, Table 1, 3, Statement of Jason C. Cave, "Temporary Liquidity Guarantee Program," Before the Congressional Oversight Panel, March 4, 2011. Neither of these analyses detail the methodology for the cost estimates. http://www.economy.com/mark-zandi/documents/End-of-Great-Recession.pdf

## Citigroup

### Circumstances Leading to the Stress

Shortly after the creation of the TLGP, the OBA reverted back to an individual institution/banking group basis in the case of Citigroup in November 2008. Only a few weeks earlier, Citigroup was approved to acquire Wachovia through an OBA transaction, but that acquisition was never consummated. Citigroup was hurt not only by tens of billions of dollars in write-downs of mortgage-related securities, but also by a lack of cohesion in implementing its business model as a global financial conglomerate. The company failed to turn a profit during 2008 and announced plans to slash tens of thousands of jobs. In late November 2008, its share value plummeted nearly 60 percent during one week.[57] The failure of Citigroup's proposed acquisition of Wachovia triggered further uncertainty about Citigroup's place in the future financial landscape. As Secretary Paulson put it: "The sprawling New York–based giant, built through multiple acquisitions, struggled with an unwieldy organizational structure and lacked a single unifying culture or clear business strategy. I'd long believed it had become almost too complex to manage."[58] As the troubles mounted for the banking group in November 2008, Citigroup and Citibank, the lead banking subsidiary of Citigroup, were well on the way to becoming wards of the state, as evidenced by obligations from a range of government and government-sponsored entities:

- $84 billion from the Federal Home Loan Banks;
- $25 billion from the Troubled Asset Relief Program (TARP); and
- $24 billion from the Federal Reserve's collateralized liquidity programs.[59]

### Assessing the Magnitude of the Problem

Building on its prior analysis of outflows during the TLGP approval, the FDIC and the Federal Reserve noted their concern about Citigroup's ability to

---

57. Ben White and Vikas Bajaj, "Woes at Citigroup Began With Failed Bid for Wachovia," *New York Times*, November 21, 2008. Eric Dash and Julie Creswell, "The Reckoning: Citigroup Saw No Red Flags Even as It Made Bolder Bets," *New York Times*, November 22, 2008.

58. *On the Brink*, 403.

59. *Financial Crisis Inquiry Commission*, 381.

meet its funding obligations and expected deposit outflows and concluded that Citigroup would not be able to withstand this funding pressure. Repeating the analysis applied in the prior case of Wachovia, comments from the Treasury, FDIC, and Federal Reserve regarding Citigroup were a mix of general statements about the economy and financial industry combined with conclusory statements about the potential impact of a Citigroup failure that it:

- had systemic implications due to its interconnectedness;
- would further undermine confidence in the banking system by imposing significant losses on Citigroup's creditors and uninsured depositors;
- would lead to investor concern about direct exposures of other financial firms to Citigroup and the willingness of U.S. policymakers to support systemically important institutions;
- would lead to losses for banking organizations with the largest exposures to Citigroup, estimating that the most exposed institution could suffer a loss equal to about 2.6 percent of its Tier 1 regulatory capital;
- could lead investors to reassess the riskiness of U.S. commercial banks more broadly;
- could intensify global liquidity pressures and increase funding pressures on other institutions given Citigroup's substantial international presence and imposition of losses on foreign depositors; and
- would disrupt other markets in which Citigroup was a major participant, such as payment, settlement, and counterparty arrangements.[60]

Also consistent with the Wachovia OBA, the FDIC staff memo on the Citigroup OBA transaction committed a section to systemic risk. The only part of that section that addressed systemic risk was another vague statement of potential harm if Citigroup were allowed to fail, so much so it seemed that the FDIC had not even undertaken its own independent analysis:

> It appears likely that any transaction implemented by the FDIC under a least-cost framework would have significant adverse effects on economic conditions and the financial markets based on Citigroup's size and the markets in which it operates. Given Citigroup's significant international

---

60. GAO SRE report, 24–26.

presence, effects on money market liquidity could be expected on a global basis. Term funding markets remain under stress.[61]

Not surprisingly, Chairman Bair later admitted "[w]e were told by the New York Fed that problems would occur in the global markets if Citi were to fail. We didn't have our own information to verify this statement, so I didn't want to dispute that with them."[62] The FDIC staff, seemingly groping for a profound analysis to conclude its Board memo and Board presentation with, stated the obvious: "In creating the systemic risk exception, Congress clearly envisioned that circumstances could arise in which the exception should be used."[63] The FDIC Board unanimously voted to support the invocation of the systemic risk exception. FDIC Director Reich expressed concern that there had been "some selective creativity exercised in the determination of what is systemic and what's not," and that there "has been a high degree of pressure exerted in certain situations, and not in others, and I'm concerned about parity."[64]

Despite the fact that there was almost no analysis that went behind the conclusion, Citigroup was labeled as systemic. Secretary Paulson stated the case as a conclusion: "If Citi isn't systemic, I don't know what is."[65] Chairman Bernanke sounded absolutely hysterical, stating that he believed that a Citigroup failure had the potential to block access to ATMs and halt the issuing of paychecks.[66]

---

61. Disclosure in dispute in *McKinley v. FDIC*, Case 1:10-cv-00420-EGS (D. District of Columbia filed March 15, 2010). Minutes of the Board of Directors meeting of the FDIC, November 23, 2008, 56622. James Wigand and Herbert Held, Memo to the FDIC Board of Directors, October 13, 2008, 8–9 [hereinafter, Citi Board Memo]. Although the heading was labeled "Systemic Risk," the remainder of the section discussed issues that were not systemic, but specifically related to Citigroup as an individual institution.

62. SIGTARP Citi Report, 42.

63. *McKinley v. FDIC*, Case 1:10-cv-00420-EGS. Minutes of the Board of Directors meeting of the FDIC, November 23, 2008, 56623. Citi Board memo, 10.

64. *McKinley v. FDIC*, Case 1:10-cv-00420-EGS. Minutes of the Board of Directors meeting of the FDIC, November 23, 2008, 56627. SIGTARP, "Extraordinary Financial Assistance Provided to Citigroup, Inc." January 13, 2011, 15 [hereinafter, SIGTARP Citi Report].

65. SIGTARP Citi Report, 15.

66. SIGTARP Citi Report, 14. It is not clear that any evidence was cited for this fear. The bridge bank structure, created in the aftermath of the Continental Illinois failure, could have been utilized to assure continued operation of the payment system.

### Reviewing the Options

Citigroup proposed a bailout plan at 3:36 a.m. on Saturday, November 22, 2008. Incredibly, the proposal requested that the government guarantee 100 percent of the value of a $306 billion pool of troubled assets.[67] In exchange, Citigroup would issue the government $20 billion in preferred stock.[68] A number of other options were considered during that weekend by the troika of the Treasury Department, the Federal Reserve, and the FDIC including:

- Creating a conservatorship similar to those for Fannie Mae and Freddie Mac. This was rejected because the Government did not want the market to perceive that the Government had nationalized Citigroup;
- Creating a special purpose vehicle to purchase troubled assets from Citigroup with government funds;
- Creating a public-private investment fund to buy troubled assets or toxic assets from the bank; and
- Providing for an additional capital injection which was described by one FRBNY official as "throwing cash at it."[69]

### The Final Deal

The Treasury Department, the Federal Reserve, and the FDIC took a much more unified approach to the Citigroup transaction than in the earlier cases of OBA and unusual and exigent circumstances. The transaction was a blend of funding and guaranty powers of the Treasury, the FDIC, and the Federal Reserve. The Citigroup transaction was structured with loss sharing among Citigroup, the Treasury, the FDIC, and the Federal Reserve as follows:

- **Size:** Up to $306 billion in assets to be guaranteed, so called "ring-fencing."
- **Term of Guarantee:** Guarantee in place for ten years for residential assets, five years for nonresidential assets.

---

67. Bradley Keoun and Donal Griffin, "Citigroup Executives Griped About Taxpayer's 'Take-It-Or-Leave-It' Bailout," Bloomberg.com, January 14, 2011.
68. SIGTARP Citi Report, 17, 24.
69. SIGTARP Citi Report, 18. The reference to conservatorship may be a reference to the FDIC's bridge bank authority, although in the context it is not entirely clear.

- **Deductible:** Citigroup absorbs all the losses in the portfolio up to $39.5 billion (in addition to existing reserves).
- **Any losses** in portfolio in excess of that amount shared between the U.S. government (90 percent) and Citigroup (10 percent) with government share to be allocated as follows:
  - Treasury second loss up to $5 billion;
  - FDIC takes the third loss up to $10 billion.
- **Financing:** Federal Reserve Bank of New York funds the remaining pool of assets with a nonrecourse loan, subject to the institution's 10 percent loss sharing and interest payments with recourse to Citigroup.
- **Preferred Stock:** Citigroup issued the FDIC and the Treasury approximately $3 billion and $4 billion of preferred stock respectively for bearing the risk associated with the guarantees.[70]

Ultimately, further restructuring led to de facto nationalization of Citigroup in June 2009, with the government holding approximately 35 percent of common equity stock.[71] The stake and related warrants were disposed of in 2011 at what is reported as a profit, but the estimated subsidy of providing the assistance package was $2 billion.[72]

### The Aftermath

As in the case of the Wachovia approval, the GAO did not seriously question the underlying details of these justifications for the potential fallout from a Citigroup failure and essentially accepted the FDIC's, the Treasury's, and

---

70. Treasury, Federal Reserve, and FDIC, Summary of Terms, November 23, 2008, http://www.fdic.gov/news/news/press/2008/pr08125a.pdf.
71. GAO SRE report, 26.
72. Tom Barkley, "Profit on Citigroup: $12.3 Billion," *Wall Street Journal*, January 26, 2011. Randall Smith, Aaron Lucchetti, and Michael Crittenden, "U.S. Unloads Citi Stake for a $12 Billion Profit," *Wall Street Journal*, December 7, 2010. Bradley Keoun and Donal Griffin, "Citigroup Stake Sold by Government for $10.5 Billion," *Washington Post*, December 6, 2010. Subsidy information was estimated by the Congressional Budget Office on the Federal Reserve's intervention. Congressional Budget Office, "The Budgetary Impact and Subsidy Costs of the Federal Reserve's Actions During the Financial Crisis," May 2010, 8, Table 1 [hereinafter, CBO Subsidy Study].

the Federal Reserve's justifications at face value. Additionally, as part of the oversight program of the Special Inspector General for the Troubled Asset Relief Program (SIGTARP) and to respond to a request from former Congressman Alan Grayson, SIGTARP performed a review of the decision to provide funding and asset guarantees to Citigroup. The SIGTARP analysis was marginally more hard-hitting than the GAO report, noting that the decision that Citigroup had to be saved was "strikingly ad hoc" and that the "consensus appeared to be based as much on gut instinct and fear of the unknown as on objective criteria." But in fact, every one of the bailouts—Bear Stearns, AIG, Wachovia, Fannie Mae, and Freddie Mac—could be characterized in this way. Strangely enough, the SIGTARP report contains the ultimate conclusion that there was "no evidence that the determination was incorrect."[73]

There were two additional proposed OBA transactions, one for Bank of America and one for the Public-Private Investment Program (PPIP). However, neither of these two proposed transactions resulted in a systemic risk determination by the Treasury as in the cases of Wachovia, TLGP, and Citigroup.[74] The Bank of America transaction would have been structured very similarly to the Citigroup transaction with a ring-fencing of specific assets combined with commitments from the FDIC, the Treasury Department, and the Federal Reserve regarding guarantees or absorption of losses. Again, the FDIC did little independent analysis but largely relied on the analysis of the other agencies.[75] The estimated subsidy of the Bank of America transaction was $1 billion.[76]

---

73. SIGTARP Citi Report, p. 42.
74. GAO SRE report, p. 2, 10.
75. *McKinley v. FDIC*, Case 1:10-cv-00420-EGS (D. District of Columbia filed March 15, 2010). Minutes of the Board of Directors meeting of the FDIC, January 15, 2009, 56747. Mitchell Glassman, Sandra Thompson, Arthur Murton, John Thomas, Memo to the FDIC Board of Directors, January 15, 2009. Press release by FDIC, Treasury, and Fed.
76. CBO Subsidy Study, 8.

# 9

## The 2000s Crisis:
## TARP

"Tell the Hill we're fixing to have a meltdown."
> —President George W. Bush[1]

"The trouble, however, was not merely the new policies that were implemented but also the threat of additional, unknown policies. Fear froze the economy, but that uncertainty itself might have a cost was something the young experimenters simply did not consider." —Amity Shlaes, *The Forgotten Man: A New History of the Great Depression.*[2]

---

**LEGAL SCORECARD**
- Emergency Economic Stabilization Act of 2008

---

AS EARLY AS April 2008, plans were in the works for a broad-based government response to a possible worst-case scenario of large bank failures and loss of confidence. Neel Kashkari, an assistant Treasury secretary, and one of his colleagues, Phillip Swagel, developed an emergency contingency plan, the so-called "Break the Glass Bank Recapitalization Plan" (BTG).[3] The heading

---

1. *On the Brink*, 257.

2. *The Forgotten Man: A New History of the Great Depression* (New York: Harper Perennial, 2007), 9.

3. Break the Glass Bank Recapitalization Plan, 1. http://www.scribd.com/doc/23788612/Break-the-Glass-Plan-for-the-US-Treasury-Dept-by-Neel-Kashkari, http://www.andrewrosssorkin.com/?p=368 [hereinafter, Break the Glass]. *Too Big to Fail*, 83, 90–93. *In Fed We Trust*, 176–77.

of the plan described it as a "plan for the [U.S. government] to recapitalize the banking sector by purchasing illiquid mortgage-related assets." This description also noted that it was "designed to help banks resume lending and help stabilize the housing and mortgage markets."[4] The major elements of the plan gave Treasury the power to:

- Purchase $500 billion of mortgage backed securities from financial institutions via an auction mechanism;
- Compensate bidders with newly issued Treasury securities rather than cash;
- Hire private asset managers to maximize value for taxpayers and unwind the position over time (up to ten years);
- Purchase assets of U.S.-headquartered banks, broker-dealers, and thrifts in asset categories of residential and commercial mortgage backed securities; and
- Receive compensation of at least 10 percent equity in the institution for purchasing the assets.

The plan also set forth pros and cons for the plan, two of the most prominent of which were interlinked: the pro that it would free banks to resume lending and the con that there was no guarantee that the banks would actually resume lending.[5]

## Circumstances Leading to the Stress

Even before the Lehman bankruptcy filing, there was already talk of going to the Congress for more powers. Chairman Bernanke noted these conversations on the weekend prior to the Monday bankruptcy filing, although the effort did not seem to be an initiative of the Federal Reserve: "I have learned that we may want to discuss some broader issues, e.g. should we go to Congress to ask for other authorities."[6] Additionally, there were also legislative proposals

---

4. Break the Glass, 1.
5. Break the Glass, 4.
6. FCIC Bates No. 154949 email from Chairman Bernanke to Scott Alvarez, Kevin Warsh, Michelle Smith, and Donald Kohn, September 13, 2008.

circulating between the Board of Governors and the FRBNY in the midst of the meltdown of AIG.[7]

Representatives from the Treasury and the Federal Reserve began to rethink the approach that Neel Kashkari, assistant secretary to Paulson, candidly described: "So there is no one metric I can point to. Ultimately, it's the combined judgment of Treasury and the Fed that made those decisions."[8] The inconsistencies in this ad hoc approach of many months of bailouts were obvious. Vincent Reinhart, former director of Monetary Affairs at the Board of Governors of the Federal Reserve, summarized the prior interventions:

> Until now, the responses of government officials have been inconsistent and improvisational. Their first impulse was to extend the federal safety net to investment banks. Thus, in March, the Federal Reserve rescued Bear Stearns, breaking a 60-year-old precedent by lending to a non-depository. That set in motion an uneven process of failure and intervention. The private sector lost its incentive to pump capital into troubled firms and gained an incentive to pick among the winners and losers of the government intervention lottery. Lehman Brothers or AIG? Washington Mutual or Wachovia? Rather than forecasting underlying values, financial markets were predicting government intentions. We should not be here, but we are.[9]

### Assessing the Magnitude of the Problem

By September 2008, the Treasury Department began to think about breaking the glass on the BTG plan. Secretary Paulson lobbied for new powers, noting

7. *McKinley v. Board of Governors*, BOG–FOIA 10–251–000885–888, email from Donald Kohn to Chairman Bernanke, Governor Warsh, Timothy Geithner, Brian Madigan, and Scott Alvarez titled "legislative agenda," September 16, 2008. The attached document "Possible Legislative Proposals.doc" had reportedly been deleted.

8. "One on One with Neel Kashkari, Interview," May 27, 2009. This comment is at the 4:00 mark, total run time 19:36. http://knowledge.wharton.upenn.edu/article.cfm?articleid =2246.

9. Vincent R. Reinhart, "A Bill That Deserved to Pass," American.com, October 6, 2008, http://www.american.com/archive/2008/october-10–08/a-bill-that-deserved-to-pass.

that "our tool kit is substantial, but insufficient."[10] However, the description by the Treasury Department of the plan was that given the magnitude of the problem assets on the books of banks it would be analogous in approach to the Resolution Trust Corporation (RTC). This was the agency that resolved more than 700 savings and loans during the prior 1980s crisis.[11] Various former government officials also prominently noted the possibility of resurrecting the RTC to address the building problems in the financial sector.[12] However, these comparisons were flawed and reveal a fundamental misunderstanding by the Treasury Department and others of the circumstances and structure of the RTC. The RTC acquired and disposed of assets from mortgage-related financial institutions. But a key point is that the institutions under the responsibility of the RTC were all closed financial institutions under government control.

In contrast, the proposed BTG plan involved buying assets from viable, open financial institutions. So those managing a BTG plan would have to decide which assets to purchase from which institutions and, most importantly, at what prices. The BTG plan itself acknowledged the difficulties regarding the pricing on the "buy side."[13] These three difficult buy-side decisions were a given for the RTC because it handled all of the assets of the failed institutions other than those sold to acquirers at resolution. As a result, RTC had a much clearer mandate and it was a more straightforward exercise to meet that mandate. The "sell side" transaction for the BTG approach would involve holding assets until maturity or until the secretary of the Treasury determined that an asset sale was "optimal."[14] The RTC was directed to maximize the value of

---

10. U.S. Department of the Treasury, "Statement by Secretary Henry M. Paulson Jr. on Emergency Economic Stabilization Act Vote," September 29, 2008.

11. Reuters, "Paulson Raised RTC-style Concept With Congress: Source," September 18, 2008. CNBC, "Paulson's RTC-Type Solution," September 18, 2008, total run time 5:13 http://www.cnbc.com/id/15840232?video=860094402#. *Too Big to Fail*, 429.

12. Nicholas F. Brady, Eugene A. Ludwig, and Paul A. Volcker, "Resurrect the Resolution Trust Corporation," *Wall Street Journal*, September 17, 2008. Michael R. Crittenden and Patrick Yoest, "Resolution Trust Plan is Floated," *Wall Street Journal*, September 18, 2008. L. William Seidman and David C. Cooke, "What We Learned From Resolution Trust," *Wall Street Journal*, September 25, 2008.

13. Break the Glass, 2 ("Determining what prices to pay for heterogeneous securities would be a key challenge").

14. Emergency Economic Stabilization Act, §113(a)(2)(A).

assets, minimize the impact of transactions, make efficient use of funds, and minimize losses—which generally meant a swift disposition to avoid holding costs.[15] The differences in these two approaches made the proposed BTG purchase of assets an entirely unworkable concept in comparison. So even though the Treasury Department should be given credit for being prescient about how bad the problems in the mortgage industry would get, they also have to be held up to criticism for proposing and passing under law such an unworkable plan.

The proposed BTG plan was truly unprecedented given the fact that bailouts were never previously focused on so-called "viable" institutions.[16] Kashkari emphasized that it was "a healthy bank program" and that "banks must be deemed viable without government assistance to be eligible for the program."[17] The reason for this focus was to target healthy institutions that would be in a

---

15. The relevant wording of the statute is "(i) maximizes the net present value return from the sale or other disposition of institutions . . . or the assets of such institutions; (ii) minimizes the impact of such transactions on local real estate and financial markets; and (iii) makes efficient use of funds obtained from the Funding Corporation or from the Treasury; (iv) minimizes the amount of any loss realized in the resolution of cases; and (v) maximizes the preservation of the availability and affordability of residential real property for low- and moderate-income individuals." (Section 501 of the Financial Institutions Reform, Recovery, and Enforcement Act of 1989 as amended.)

16. So-called is the operative phrase, as some institutions, such as CIT, ultimately failed even though they were deemed to be viable. Also, Citigroup within a short period of time after it was deemed "viable" was on the brink of failure and received FDIC open bank assistance. AIG also ultimately received funding under the program.

17. Assistant Treasury Secretary Neel Kashkari, in a speech at the Brookings Institution, January 8, 2009, said: "We said this is a healthy bank program. We want healthy banks across the country to apply to the program. . . . Banks must be deemed viable without government assistance to be eligible for the program." On the C-SPAN video, this question-and-answer is from the time segment 27:15 to 31:00, http://www.cspan.org/Watch/watch.aspx?MediaId=HP-A-14161. Kashkari previously emphasized this limitation under questioning from Congressman Dennis Kucinich regarding the government's unwillingness to provide TARP funding to National City Corporation of Ohio, a troubled bank: "The regulators do go to some banks they think are not solvent institutions and discourage them from applying to the program [TARP]. . . . Congressman, we review applications that the regulators submit to us with their recommendation. If a regulator does not submit an application to Treasury because a regulator deems a financial institution is going to fail, we can't review it. And I don't think it's a good use of taxpayer money to put taxpayer capital into an institution that's going to fail." C-Span, "Treasury Use of Bailout Funds—Panel 1," November 14, 2008, at the 1:27:45 mark of total run time 2:19:55.

position to lend once the asset purchases were consummated. Viable institutions were not the primary focus during the Depression with the RFC.[18] They were not the primary focus during the 1980s with the cases of OBA like Continental Illinois or the GSEs like Fannie Mae and the Farm Credit System. They had not been the focus during the 2000s with the cases of Bear Stearns, AIG, Fannie Mae, and Freddie Mac.

Secretary Paulson and Chairman Bernanke approached the Congress after concluding that Treasury was going to need a large amount of funding and was going to need it immediately. The original BTG plan had a price tag of $500 billion, but a new number of $700 billion became the focus for what would become the TARP, what many people think of today when they hear the term "bailout." There was little quantitative support for this request. As a Treasury spokeswoman noted, the development of the new number was more seat-of-the-pants analysis: "It's not based on any particular data point. We just wanted to choose a really large number."[19] Secretary Paulson and Chairman Bernanke frantically argued that the legislation had to be passed within days, reminiscent of the rush to passage of the 1933 RFC powers that were introduced and acted upon within a day. In a hearing during this period, Senator Menendez highlighted the ridiculousness of such a deadline: "Now we have been told that we have less than seven days to make our choices and eight minutes to ask questions, so you will forgive me if I am not signing right away on the bottom line."[20] Senator Tester sounded a similar sentiment in laying out yet another breakdown attributable to the banking agencies: "Why do we have one week to determine $700 billion that has to be appropriated or this country's financial system goes down the pipes. Wasn't there some opportunity sometime down the line where we could have been informed of how serious this crisis was so we could have taken some preventative steps before this got to this point."[21]

---

18. As detailed in the earlier discussion on the RFC, there were isolated cases of strong institutions receiving RFC funding.

19. Brian Wingfield and Josh Zumbrun, "Bad News for the Bailout," Forbes.com, September 23, 2008, http://www.forbes.com/home/2008/09/23/bailout-paulson-congress-biz-beltway-cx_jz_bw_0923bailout.html.

20. C-Span, "U.S. Credit Markets and Federal Rescue Plan," September 23, 2008, at the 46:20 mark, total run time 4:52:40 [hereinafter C-Span TARP Hearing].

21. C-Span TARP Hearing at the 1:53:00 mark.

FRBNY President Geithner highlighted how fragile a situation Paulson and Bernanke had created: "You cannot go out and talk about big numbers with regard to capital needs for banks without inviting a run. If you don't get the authority I'm certain you'll spark a freaking panic. You have to be careful about not going public until you know you're going to get it."[22]

## Reviewing the Options

In what is likely the most troublesome decision and also the most damaging to confidence in the run-up to passage of legislation, Assistant Secretary Kashkari had a different approach in mind than Geithner about how to explain the options to the Congress. A number of actions taken in the ensuing weeks brought on the precise reaction of panic that Geithner had cautioned against. Not unlike the case of Continental Illinois and "the scary scenario" laid out before the Congress in 1984, Kashkari's approach in explaining the options to the Congress was clear: "We've got to scare the shit out of the staff." Rather than focus on the legislation and the details, he wanted to focus on the potentially devastating problems they all would face if the Congress chose not to pass the legislation.[23]

Secretary Paulson seemed to take Kashkari's advice to heart, too. He reportedly warned Senator James Inhofe and others on a conference call that the situation would be far worse than the Great Depression if Treasury was not given the authority to buy assets from banks.[24] He also tried to scare the members with the potential political ramifications: "I'm doing this for you as much for me. If we don't do this, it's coming down on all our heads." Senator Christopher J. Dodd said the looming threats to the U.S. economy outlined by Paulson had galvanized lawmakers, noting that "I've been here 28 years. I've never been in a more sobering moment."[25] President Bush was also called in to continue the "scare the shit out of them" approach with a nationally televised address:

---

22. *Too Big to Fail*, 419–20.

23. *Too Big to Fail*, 492.

24. Jeff Poor, "Inhofe: Paulson Used Scare Tactics to Force Bailout Legislation," Business and Media Institute, November 19, 2008, http://www.businessandmedia.org/articles/2008/20081119073313.aspx.

25. Greg Hitt, "Congress Pledges Action," *Wall Street Journal*, September 20, 2008.

The government's top economic experts warn that without immediate action by Congress, America could slip into a financial panic and a distressing scenario could unfold. More banks could fail, including some in your community. The stock market would drop even more which would reduce the value of your retirement account. The value of your house could plummet, foreclosures would rise dramatically and if you own a business or a farm you would find it harder and more expensive to get credit. More businesses would close their doors and millions of Americans could lose their jobs. Even if you have good credit history, it would be more difficult for you to get the loans you need to buy a car or send your children to college and ultimately our country could experience a long and painful recession. Fellow citizens, we must not let this happen.[26]

During testimony that same week, Bernanke and Paulson stumbled in their efforts to explain the option they were recommending.[27] As might be expected, they had the greatest difficulty in responding to questions on the issue of the prices to be paid for the assets.[28] Both Bernanke and Paulson also emphasized how they had reviewed all of the options and that the purchase of assets was the best approach. They said other approaches, such as placing preferred stock into the financial institutions, were more appropriate for a failing bank scenario as opposed to the open institutions that were the target of TARP, a position that they would dramatically reverse a few weeks later.[29] The initial efforts at passage failed and the market panicked as Geithner had warned, not necessarily as an indicator of support for the underlying policy approach of TARP, but because of the uncertainty and lack of confidence in Secretary Paulson and Chairman Bernanke.

---

26. TPMTV, "President Bush Addresses Nation on Economic Crisis," September 24, 2008, http://www.youtube.com/watch?v=YsDmPEeurfA&feature=related.
27. See generally C-Span TARP Hearing.
28. For example, see C-Span TARP Hearing and Senator Enzi questioning how the government would be able to structure "market" transactions at the 2:36:00 mark.
29. C-Span TARP Hearing, at 2:04:15 to 2:07:45. Senator Corker described the presentation as a "deer in the headlights mentality" and "being done on the fly," at the 1:15:12 mark.

## The Final Deal

What ultimately passed after the Congress added some fiscal sweeteners to the bill was the Emergency Economic Stabilization Act of 2008 (EESA),[30] which granted the Treasury secretary authority to purchase troubled assets in an amount up to $700 billion outstanding at any one time.[31] The purpose of EESA was to restore liquidity and stability to the financial system, which the Treasury interpreted to include stimulating lending.[32] These purchases would be made from financial institutions—including banks, savings associations, credit unions, security brokers and dealers, and insurance companies.[33]

## The Aftermath

Within weeks of passage of the EESA, there was an oft-noted change of direction in the focus of the TARP, which further increased the level of uncertainty.[34] Even before ultimate passage of TARP, there was a developing realization that the plan to buy toxic assets was entirely unworkable. Some of the staff of the Treasury Department surreptitiously began to look at alternatives, even as the push continued to pass a final, modified version of the TARP.[35] Initially, problem assets were going to be purchased from financial institutions, and the program was sold to Congress and taxpayers on that basis. The shift was caused

---

30. EESA, Public Law 110–343.

31. EESA, §115(a)(3).

32. EESA, §2. U.S. Department of the Treasury, Frequently Asked Questions, Capital Purchase Program Q&A, October 15, 2008.

33. EESA, §§3(5) and 101(a)(1).

34. U.S. Department of the Treasury, "Treasury Announces TARP Capital Purchase Program Description," http://www.ustreas.gov/press/releases/hp1207.htm. Ruthie Ackerman, "TARP Changes Colors," *Forbes*, November 12, 2008. "Treasury Prepares for a TARP-and-Switch," *Time*, October 8, 2008.

35. It appears that about the time of the voting down of TARP on September 29, 2008, there was a move afoot to change strategies away from the purchase of assets. *Too Big to Fail*, 500 ("Dan Jester and Jeremiah Norton had their own ideas about the problem Paulson was facing. They had convinced themselves that the concept of buying up toxic assets was never going to work; the only way the government could truly make a difference would be to invest directly in the banks themselves. 'This is crazy,' Norton said of the TARP proposal as he walked into David Nason's office. 'Do we really think this is the

in part by the many challenges faced in getting the originally envisioned asset-purchase program up and running, as Treasury had overpromised what could be delivered. Then the focus turned to capital injections into banks—or what was called the Capital Purchase Program (CPP), an approach not unlike that used in the 1930s with the Reconstruction Finance Corporation (RFC). Consistent with the asset purchase approach, the CPP was undertaken with the goal of stimulating lending.[36] The big difference was that the RFC focused on troubled institutions trying to shore up their capital, and TARP was focused on "viable" institutions. These investments were allowed, given the broad definition of "troubled asset" under the law.[37] This change in strategy to capital injections took place after the United Kingdom took the same approach.[38]

The first nine purchases of equity occurred on October 28 after a meeting between Paulson, Bernanke, and representatives from nine of the nation's largest banks.[39]

Not unlike Roosevelt's encouragement to partake in the RFC, Paulson reportedly required participation by the nation's largest banks, regardless of their

---

(*footnote 35 continued*) right approach?' Jester and Norton had made the case to Paulson before, but the politics of using government money to buy stakes in private enterprises, he knew, had gotten in the way. And once Paulson had gone public with his current plan it seemed as if it would be difficult for him to reverse course. . . . The next day Jester and Norton went to visit with Paulson. They laid out their case: Buying the toxic assets was too difficult; even if they ever figured out how to implement the program, it was unclear whether it would work.").

36. U.S. Department of the Treasury, "Frequently Asked Questions: Capital Purchase Program Q&A," Question #1, October 15, 2008.

37. EESA, §3(9), which included the phrase "any other financial instrument that the Secretary, after consultation with the Chairman of the Board of Governors of the Federal Reserve System, determines is necessary to promote financial market stability." The Congressional Oversight Board Panel also notes the shifting strategies of the TARP between September and November 2008, from (1) buying mortgage-related assets and (2) purchasing preferred stocks and warrants, to (3) not buying mortgage-related assets, (4) participation in the Federal Reserve's Term Asset-Backed Securities Loan Facility, and (5) other strategies. The Congressional Oversight Board Panel, "Questions About the $700 Billion Emergency Economic Stabilization Funds," December 10, 2008, 12–13.

38. Dana Cimilluca, Sara Schaeffer Muñoz, and Carrick Mollenkamp, "UK Plans to Buy Into Banks in Bold Move," *Wall Street Journal*, October 8, 2008.

39. Damian Paletta, Jon Hilsenrath, and Deborah Solomon, "At Moment of Truth, U.S. Forced Big Bankers to Blink," *Wall Street Journal*, October 15, 2008.

financial condition, in order to avoid a stigma from being attached to recipients of the government capital injections.[40] Before long, funding from the TARP was not only used for financial institutions, but also for a broader range of interests, including automakers, not unlike the expansion in purpose and authority of the RFC during the 1930s.[41] Upon Paulson's departure in January 2009, many Bush Administration holdovers remained in the early months of the Obama Administration to follow through on implementation of TARP.

Notwithstanding the nostalgic choice of RFC-style capital injections, data from the Federal Reserve's own Senior Loan Officer Opinion Survey, as well as data on lending during the 2008 and 2009 time period, undermines the case for capital injections as a means to stimulate lending. There was a near universal tightening of credit that began in mid-2007 and continued to get worse through October 2008, when an extraordinary 85 percent of survey respondents noted they had tightened standards for lending since the prior survey. As detailed in the Senior Loan Officer Opinion Survey, it was very clear why the banks were not lending during the latter half of 2008. They feared the uncertain economic outlook, which led them to a reduced tolerance for risk, especially with regard to industry-specific lending such as mortgage lending. The responses of survey participants stayed steady throughout 2008 and well into 2009. Fears of deterioration in the capital standing of the institution, presumably a justification for altering TARP's focus to capital injections, were very far down the list of reasons for the banks to tighten their credit (Table 9.1).

Available lending data verifies the idea that there were many other reasons behind the tightness of lending and that the capital injections would not address the problem of tight lending standards. As an assessment of whether the TARP capital injections had their intended impact, the COP for TARP undertook an analysis of whether those banks that received TARP funding actually increased their lending once they received funding:

> The data show that lending by the largest [Capital Purchase Program] recipients, those with assets over $100 billion, and recipients of 81 percent

---

40. William Poole, "Treasury Has No Authority to Coerce Banks," *Wall Street Journal,* October 17, 2008. Poole is former president and chief executive officer of the Federal Reserve Bank of St. Louis.

41. Congressional Oversight Panel, "An Update on TARP Support for the Domestic Automotive Industry," January 13, 2011.

**Table 9.1.** Reasons for Bank Tightening of Credit Standards

| Reasons for Tightening Credit Standards | Oct. 2008 | Jan. 2009 | Apr. 2009 |
|---|---|---|---|
| Uncertain economic outlook | 98.2% | 100.0% | 97.7% |
| Reduced tolerance for risk | 86.8% | 85.7% | 81.4% |
| Industry-specific problems | 80.8% | 91.8% | 88.1% |
| Decreased liquidity in secondary market | 56.6% | 44.9% | 46.5% |
| Less aggressive competition | 49.1% | 55.1% | 44.2% |
| Increase in defaults public debt market | 45.3% | 42.9% | 34.9% |
| Deterioration in bank's capital position | 38.5% | 26.5% | 32.6% |
| Deterioration in bank's liquidity position | 36.5% | 12.2% | 18.7% |

*Note*: Stated reason is considered very or somewhat important by the respondents.
Period is three months, ending October 2008 and January and April 2009, respectively.
*Source*: Board of Governors of the Federal Reserve System, Division of Monetary Affairs,
"October 2008 Senior Loan Officer Opinion Survey on Bank Lending Practices,"
November 3, 2008. Idem, "January 2009 Senior Loan Officer Opinion Survey on
Bank Lending Practices," February 2, 2009. Idem, "April 2009 Senior Loan Officer
Opinion Survey on Bank Lending Practices," May 4, 2009.

of the funds disbursed under the CPP—declined, a decrease that is all
the more stark given that lending appears to have increased at medium-
sized banks, those with assets between $10 and $100 billion, although
those received only 11.4 percent of CPP funds.[42]

The proponents of TARP predictably argue that the lending situation would
have been worse without the availability of the TARP funding, but as the COP
report also notes, there was no data to either support or challenge this asser-
tion.[43] Based on the evidence of the decrease in lending at large banks, this
means the TARP involved the borrowing of hundreds of billions of dollars by
the federal government to provide liquidity and capital primarily to very large

---

42. COP, "May Oversight Report: The Small Business Credit Crunch and the Impact of the
TARP," May 13, 2010, 26 [hereinafter, COP lending analysis], http://cybercemetery.unt.
edu/archive/cop/20110402035902/http://cop.senate.gov/documents/cop-051310-report
.pdf.
43. COP lending analysis, 26.

**Figure 9.1.** Cash as a Percentage of Total Assets

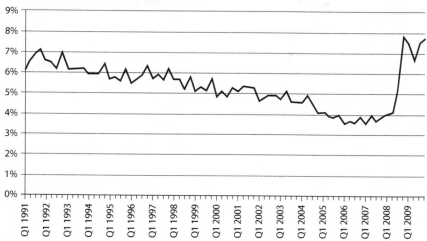

*Source*: Friedman Billings and Ramsey Capital Markets, as cited in the Congressional
Oversight Panel Report.

banks that simply sat on the funds throughout 2008 and 2009.[44] Probably the
starkest indicator of the resulting cash hoarding is a time series of cash as a percentage of total assets at banks. Notwithstanding the TARP capital injections,
during 2008 the holding of cash spiked and has stayed within a relatively tight
band ever since (see Figure 9.1).

During and after the passage of TARP, there was a great deal of criticism of
Secretary Paulson and his inability to explain TARP as a necessary government
program, whether it was his halting and convoluted responses or his swigging
of Dasani water while on live television. So this argument goes, it was not the
substantive policy that was wrong, but the communication of that message.[45]

---

44. The COP's implication that the TARP should have mandated that the money should
be lent is ill advised, as this would have been an extraordinary exercise in government
credit allocation.

45. In the book *In Fed We Trust* this was referred to as getting the "theater" right as
contrasted with getting the "substance" right, 7–8. See 243 ("The markets provided no
relief: a situation that was unsettled at best had received another blow from Paulson's
bumbled communications. A week after the presidential election, Paulson delivered a
speech to a few dozen reporters and a half dozen television cameras in the Treasury's

But that argument is flawed as it fails to sufficiently question the substantive policy basis of the decisions that were made. As supported by the lack of significant changes in lending, the TARP approach was just bad policy.

An important question is what drove Secretary Paulson in his decision-making during the financial crisis. His descriptions are telling in this regard. First of all, he argues that he is a devotee of the free market:

- "I am a firm believer in free markets, and I certainly hadn't come to Washington planning to do anything to inject the government into the private sector."[46]
- "More than any other president, Ronald Reagan represented the free-market principles I had long believed in."[47]

However, Paulson's brand of interventionism in no way represented free-market policy. He was driven by an idea that he had to do whatever "the market" demanded and would respond to, and that clearly is a very different thing. Additionally, he often characterized the market as having one voice and one opinion, when there were clearly participants in "the market" who would have benefited from the opposite action he recommended.[48] All throughout the interventions

---

*(footnote 45 continued)* fourth-floor 'media room.' Swigging from a bottle of Dasani water while on live television, Paulson once again screwed up the theater. He made explicit that he was abandoning the very strategy he had used to sell Congress on approving his request for $700 billion: The Treasury wouldn't be buying toxic mortgage assets from the banks because that was no longer 'the most effective way' to use the money. . . . But it wasn't the substance of the decision that hurt; there were after all, arguments for and against buying assets. As Paulson put it later, there was virtue in being 'pragmatic enough to change plans when facts and conditions change.' Instead the speech was another one in a series of Paulson's abrupt changes in course. This appearance of inconsistency destroyed any lingering credibility Paulson had. The final impression he would leave is of the balding former college football player lurching from one approach to another without a game plan.") For another example of this, see *In Fed We Trust*, 183–84, regarding Fannie Mae and Freddie Mac and his oft-quoted bazooka comment.

46. *On the Brink*, 3.
47. *On the Brink*, 408.
48. See generally Michael Lewis, *The Big Short: Inside the Doomsday Machine* (New York: W.W. Norton & Company, Inc., 2010).

of 2008, if the market wanted it, Paulson would provide it, even if it involved absolute and complete distortions of the "free market":[49]

- "The market expected a Bear rescue. If there wasn't one, all hell would break loose. . . . "[50]
- "We hoped the market would be comforted by the perception that the investment banks had come under the Fed umbrella." [Primary Dealer Credit Facility][51]
- "We had announced a transaction that the market initially wouldn't accept because it wanted certainty and wanted it quickly." [Bear Stearns][52]
- "Having an unlimited capacity—we used the term *unspecified*—would be more reassuring to the markets." [Fannie Mae and Freddie Mac][53]
- "The market believed that its problem was liquidity, not capital." [AIG][54]
- "We needed an announcement tonight to calm the market, and legislation next week." [TARP][55]
- "That morning, the U.S. government unveiled a package of new programs to boost liquidity and calm the markets." [Various programs][56]
- "This raft of programs, coupled with news reports that we had gone up to the Hill to get new legislation, acted like a tonic to the markets." [Various programs and TARP][57]
- "And we unequivocally knew that the market could not tolerate another failure like that of Lehman."[58]

---

49. If the particular bailout or intervention is not clear from the context of the quote, the relevant transaction is highlighted in brackets.
50. *On the Brink*, 106.
51. *On the Brink*, 116.
52. *On the Brink*, 118.
53. *On the Brink*, 148.
54. *On the Brink*, 246.
55. *On the Brink*, 261.
56. *On the Brink*, 263.
57. *On the Brink*, 264.
58. *On the Brink*, 268.

- "Whatever we did, we felt that by Monday we had to give the market a signal that Morgan Stanley and Goldman Sachs weren't going to fail." [Application as bank holding companies][59]
- "But doing so allowed us to agree on a set of restrictions that the market accepted." [TARP compensation restrictions][60]
- "How did we arrive at the number? I said it was the best estimate we could come up with, and the market would accept no less." [TARP funding][61]
- "But unlike with the WaMu failure, all creditors would also be protected, a hugely important step that signaled to the markets the government's willingness to support our systemically important banks." [Wachovia][62]
- "Congress and the markets expected immediate results, but it was going to take weeks to launch a program to buy toxic assets from banks."[63]
- "The markets needed all the help we could give them." [Coordinated international interventions][64]
- "The markets want to hear that we are going to inject capital, but the politicians and the public don't want to hear it."[65]
- "The markets would not be satisfied by general statements and encouraging words. We needed to show real action—and fast." [Capital purchase program][66]
- "Similarly the markets were expecting me to unveil the details of a program to buy assets."[67]
- "But just as I feared, the markets focused on the facts that there wouldn't be a program to purchase mortgage-related assets. . . ."[68]

---

59. *On the Brink*, 270.
60. *On the Brink*, 281.
61. *On the Brink*, 308.
62. *On the Brink*, 317.
63. *On the Brink*, 330.
64. *On the Brink*, 339.
65. *On the Brink*, 341.
66. *On the Brink*, 351.
67. *On the Brink*, 398.
68. *On the Brink*, 399–400.

- "Capital was the strongest remedy for a weak balance sheet, and the markets needed to see that the government was supporting Citi."[69]
- "Early that evening, I called the president. I explained that we had fashioned a plan we believed the market would accept, enabling us to avoid a chain reaction of failures." [Citigroup bailout][70]

Paulson may say these various interventions were what "the market" wanted, but these actions in preempting failures are absolutely contradictory to a "free market." There are a number of problems with his vision of the market, not the least of which is that "the market" as he defines it perpetually wanted government policy to direct resources its way. Secretary Paulson went along with this desire of the market to be constantly bailed out, no matter the short-term costs or the long-term adverse consequences, although he did at times show some appreciation for the limits under law. It is difficult to believe that individual market players truly held these beliefs regarding heavy intervention, but an exchange in the run-up to consideration of the TARP between Secretary Paulson and Steve Schwarzman, chairman of the Blackstone Group, displays this fear-mongering hysteria combined with a forceful demand for government policy contradictory to a free market:

> **Schwarzman:** Hank, how's your day going?
> **Paulson:** Not well. What do you see out there?
> **Schwarzman:** I have to tell you, the system's going to collapse in the next few days. I doubt you're going to be able to open the banks on Monday. People are shorting financial institutions, they're withdrawing money from brokerage firms because they don't want to be the last people in— like in Lehman—which is going to lead to the collapse of Goldman and Morgan Stanley. Everybody is just pursuing his self interest. You have to do something.
> **Paulson:** We're working on some things. What do you think we should do?

---

69. *On the Brink*, 411.
70. *On the Brink*, 415.

**Schwarzman:** You have to approach what you're doing from the perspective of being a sheriff in a western town where things are out of control and you have to do the equivalent of just walking onto Main Street and shooting your gun up in the air a few times to establish that you're in charge because right now no one is in charge!

**Paulson:** What do you recommend?

**Schwarzman:** Well the first thing you could do is stop short-selling of financial institutions—forget whether it's effective in removing the pressure, although it might be. What will be accomplished is that you will scare the participants in the market, and they will recognize that things are going to change and they can't continue to invest in the exact same way, and that will force people to pause.

**Paulson:** Okay. That's not a bad idea. We've been talking about that. I could do that. What else you got?

**Schwarzman:** I would stop the ability of people to withdraw, you know, transfer their brokerage accounts. Nobody really wants to transfer their account out of Goldman or Morgan. They just feel they have to do it so they're not the last person on a sinking ship.

**Paulson:** I don't have the powers to do that.

**Schwarzman:** You could get rid of the ability for people to write credit default swaps on financial institutions which is putting enormous pressure on financial institutions.

**Paulson:** I don't have the powers to do that either.

**Schwarzman:** Look, you're going to have to announce something very big to rescue the system, some huge amount of money that gets utilized to address the problems of the system.

**Paulson:** Well we're not ready to do that, yet. We've got some ideas.

**Schwarzman:** I don't think that it's relevant if you haven't fully baked everything. You need an announcement tomorrow to stop the collapse and you've got to figure something out that will grab people's attention.[71]

Although Paulson may have seen his actions as a consistent application of what the market wanted, consumers and small business, whose actions drive so

---

71. *Too Big to Fail*, 425–27.

**Figure 9.2.** Matrix of Policy/Decisiveness Regarding Decision-Making

| | |
|---|---|
| Correct policy<br>Indecisive and unclear policy action | Correct policy<br>Decisive and clear policy action |
| Bad policy<br>Indecisive and unclear policy action | Bad policy<br>Decisive and clear policy action |

much of the economy, were absolutely perplexed by the zigs and zags in government policy. Throughout 2008 and early 2009 as the interventions built up, their confidence and optimism plummeted.[72]

Ultimately, the best of all worlds is to be right on policy and also be decisive in the decision-making process. Secretary Paulson was actually in the worst of all worlds regarding destabilization of the markets in that he was both wrong on the substantive policy and also weak on the decisiveness of action and clear articulation of the underlying policy as shown in the lower lefthand corner of the matrix in Figure 9.2.

---

72. Data for January 2008 to February 2009 for consumer confidence went from 87.3 to 25.3 and business confidence went from 91.8 to 82.6.

# 10

# Will the Dodd-Frank Changes Stop the Bailouts?

"I proposed a set of reforms to empower consumers and investors,
to bring the shadowy deals that caused this crisis into the light
of day, and to put a stop to taxpayer bailouts once and for all."
— President Barack Obama in signing the Dodd-Frank legislation[1]

---

**LEGAL SCORECARD**

- Fraud Enforcement and Recovery Act of 2009
- Dodd-Frank Wall Street Reform and Consumer Protection
  Act (2010)

---

## The Obama Administration Plan

**DURING JUNE 2009,** just a few months after taking office, the
Obama Administration took on the task of reforming the financial system.[2]
Like the Depression-era reforms and the changes implemented in the late 1980s
and early 1990s before it, this effort was intended to respond to the perceived
sources of the crisis. President Obama described the reforms as "a sweeping

---

1. The White House, "Remarks By the President at Signing of Dodd-Frank Wall Street
Reform and Consumer Protection Act," July 21, 2010.
2. U.S. Department of the Treasury, "Financial Regulatory Reform, A New Foundation:
Rebuilding Financial Supervision and Regulation," June 17, 2009 [hereinafter, Obama
Reform Document]. C-Span, "Presidential Remarks on Regulatory Reform," run time
20:18, June 17, 2009 [hereinafter, Obama Reform Speech].

overhaul of the financial regulatory system, a transformation on a scale not seen since the reforms that followed the Great Depression."[3] Not unlike Secretary Paulson, President Obama emphasized: "I've always been a strong believer in the power of the free market. It has been, and will remain the engine of America's progress, the source of prosperity that's unrivaled in history."[4] In his remarks, President Obama also criticized the seat-of-the-pants nature of the bailouts during the 2000s: "That's why when this crisis began crucial decisions about what would happen to some of the world's biggest companies, companies employing tens of thousands of people and holding trillions of dollars in assets, took place in emergency meetings in the middle of the night."[5]

In support of the Administration's initiative, Treasury Secretary Geithner and Director of the National Economic Council Lawrence Summers argued on the editorial page of the *Washington Post* that this was an effort that could not wait, but needed to be addressed in a matter of months, not years:

> Some people will say that this is not the time to debate the future of financial regulation, that this debate should wait until the crisis is fully behind us. Such critics misunderstand the nature of the challenges we face. Like all financial crises, the current crisis is a crisis of confidence and trust. Reassuring the American people that our financial system will be better controlled is critical to our economic recovery.[6]

So the formulation of a legislative response began with the goal to quickly approve legislation. However, this push to address the causes of the crisis moved forward in Congress despite the fact that the Congress itself had not received its "official" explanation for the causes of the crisis and the large institution failures, or near failures. An integral part of the Fraud Enforcement and Recovery Act of 2009 was the creation of the FCIC, whose mission was to "examine the causes of the current financial and economic crisis in the United States" and

---

3. Obama Reform Speech at 5:40.
4. Obama Reform Speech at 6:35.
5. Obama Reform Speech at 12:15.
6. Timothy Geithner and Lawrence Summers, "A New Financial Foundation," *Washington Post*, June 15, 2009.

"examine the causes of the collapse of each major financial institution that failed (including institutions that were acquired to prevent their failure) or was likely to have failed if not for the receipt of exceptional Government assistance."[7] The FCIC submitted its report in January 2011.[8]

The Obama Administration plan also completely bypassed the problem of how to permanently address Fannie Mae and Freddie Mac, the institutions that resulted in the greatest direct net cost to the U.S. government during the 2000s crisis. The enterprises had received $148 billion through 2010 and the expected total cost will likely be over $200 billion.[9] Since the bailout of the two GSEs in 2008, they have remained in conservatorship and have made little progress in bringing the long-term budgetary commitment of the government under control. In fact, the actions since the initial bailout decision have actually expanded the commitment. Although the Obama Administration plan did reference Fannie Mae and Freddie Mac, it only committed to having "a wide-ranging initiative to develop recommendations on the future of Fannie Mae and Freddie Mac."[10] These recommendations were submitted in February 2011.[11]

The Obama Administration plan itself only used the word "bailout" one time, couched in the familiar rhetoric of a binary choice between bailouts and an ill-defined "financial collapse":

> . . . provide the government with the tools it needs to manage financial crises. We need to be sure that the government has the tools it needs to manage crises, if and when they arise, so that we are not left with untenable choices between bailouts and financial collapse.[12]

---

7. Public Law 111–21, 123 Stat. 1617 (May 20, 2009). Section 5(c)(1) and 5(c)(2), Fraud Enforcement and Recovery Act of 2009.

8. See http://fcic-static.law.stanford.edu/cdn_media/fcic-reports/fcic_final_report_full.pdf.

9. FHFA, "FHFA Releases Projections Showing Range of Potential Draws for Fannie Mae and Freddie Mac," October 21, 2010.

10. Obama Reform Document, 13.

11. U.S. Department of the Treasury, U.S. Department of Housing and Urban Development, "Reforming America's Housing Finance Market—A Report to Congress," February 2011.

12. Obama Reform Document, 4.

The plan set out a number of proposals to avoid this choice between bailouts and financial collapse:

- A new Financial Services Oversight Council of financial regulators to identify emerging systemic risks and improve interagency cooperation;
- New authority for the Federal Reserve to supervise all firms that could pose a threat to financial stability, even those that do not own banks;
- Stronger capital and other prudential standards for all financial firms, and even higher standards for large, interconnected firms;
- A new regime to resolve nonbank financial institutions whose failure could have serious systemic effects; and
- Revisions to the Federal Reserve's emergency lending authority to improve accountability.[13]

The plan candidly recognized the regulatory breakdowns that had occurred during the 2000s crisis: "To be sure, most of the largest, most interconnected, and most highly leveraged financial firms in the country were subject to some form of supervision and regulation by a federal government agency. But those forms of supervision and regulation proved inadequate and inconsistent."[14] Despite the overwhelming evidence that these supervisors and regulators failed in their role as an advance warning system, the proposed plan relied on these same agencies to flag future problems.

## Dodd-Frank Wall Street Reform and Consumer Protection Act

After months of hearings and markups, in December 2009 the House of Representatives passed the Wall Street Reform and Consumer Protection Act of 2009. Its stated purpose was to "provide for financial regulatory reform, to protect consumers and investors, to enhance Federal understanding of insurance issues, to regulate the over-the-counter derivatives markets, and for other purposes." The Senate passed its companion bill in May 2010, the Restoring American Financial Stability Act of 2010. Its stated purpose was "to promote the

---

13. Obama Reform Document, 3–4.
14. Obama Reform Document, 5.

financial stability of the United States by improving accountability and transparency in the financial system, to end 'too big to fail,' to protect the American taxpayer by ending bailouts, to protect consumers from abusive financial services practices, and for other purposes."

The initial bills were reconciled and the resulting legislation, named after the two leading chairmen of the respective committees in the House and Senate, was signed into law by President Obama on July 21, 2010. In the aftermath of the passage, the bailout-related provisions of the law were trumpeted in releases by the respective committees for accomplishing two major objectives:

- Ends "too big to fail" Bailouts—Ends the possibility that taxpayers will be asked to write a check to bail out financial firms that threaten the economy by creating a safe way to liquidate failed financial firms; by imposing tough new capital and leverage requirements that make it undesirable to get too big; by updating the Fed's authority to allow system-wide support but no longer prop up individual firms; and by establishing rigorous standards and supervision to protect the economy and American consumers, investors, and businesses; and
- Advance Warning System—Creates a Council to identify and address systemic risks posed by large, complex companies, products, and activities before they threaten the stability of the economy.[15]

These objectives are achieved through a number of key provisions in the Dodd-Frank Act that, taken in their entirety, are intended to address the causes of the 2000s financial crisis that led to the bailouts (see Table 10.1).

The overall thrust of the changes as codified in the Dodd-Frank legislation was that: (1) single institution taxpayer bailouts that inure to the benefit of creditors and shareholders are bad policy; (2) insolvent institutions should not be bailed out; and (3) if funding is extended to a financial institution, sufficient collateral should be committed so that no losses are absorbed by the government. Although the effort to put an end to bailouts should be recognized, it also has to be met with a great degree of skepticism, especially in light of the way these provisions have been structured in Dodd-Frank and the history of

---

15. Senate Banking Committee, Brief Summary of the Dodd-Frank Wall Street Reform and Consumer Protection Act, 1 [hereinafter, Dodd-Frank Brief Summary].

**Table 10.1.** Dodd-Frank Bailout-Related Provisions

| Provision | Summary |
|---|---|
| Prohibition on Taxpayer Funding (Sec. 214) | No taxpayer funds allowed to prevent liquidation; all funds expended recovered through asset sales, recoupment of payments made to creditors, or assessments on the industry; taxpayers will bear no losses |
| Creation of a council to identify and address systemic risks (Sec. 111–76) | Financial Stability Oversight Council made up of 10 federal financial regulators and an independent member responsible for identifying and responding to emerging risks throughout the financial system |
| Capital and leverage mandates (Sec. 112, 171) | Authorizes the Council to recommend to the Board of Governors heightened prudential standards for risk-based capital and leverage and impose a 15–1 leverage requirement at a company if necessary to mitigate a grave threat to the financial system |
| Regulation of nonbank financial companies (Sec. 113–15, Sec. 161–76) | Grants the Federal Reserve the power to regulate and subject to prudential standards certain nonbank financial companies if the council believes distress could cause financial instability |
| Divestiture of certain assets or operations (Sec. 121, Sec. 165) | Large complex company to divest some of its holdings if Federal Reserve determines that grave threat to stability exists |
| Orderly liquidation authority (Sec. 201–217) | Grants the power to FDIC to unwind systemically significant financial companies; shareholders and unsecured creditors bear losses and management and culpable directors are removed |
| Revisions to unusual and exigent circumstance lending by Federal Reserve (Sec. 1101–3) | Prohibits emergency lending to an individual entity or insolvent entity, but allows for a program with "broad based eligibility"; collateral must be sufficient to protect taxpayers from losses |
| FDIC Guarantee of solvent insured banks (Sec. 1104–5) | Power to create a widely available program to guarantee obligations of solvent insured depository institutions or solvent depository institution holding companies if there is a "liquidity event determination" |

how the Congress and the various federal banking agencies have responded in the past to financial crises.

### Put a Stop to Taxpayer Bailouts Once and For All

Although the goal of ending taxpayer bailouts once and for all is a noble objective, the likelihood that the Dodd-Frank legislation has accomplished this is quite small. The more likely outcome is that the quotes about putting "a stop to taxpayer bailouts once and for all" will be added to a long line of prospective comments throughout history regarding the salutary effects of new legislation. As is clear from a review of the history, the standard pattern is (1) financial crisis; (2) financial institutions approach failure; (3) panic by regulators and members of Congress; and (4) bailout legislation.[16] In many historical instances, new legislation approved by Congress was the source of the power to undertake the bailouts. This was the case in the 1930s with regard to the RFC; the 1980s with regard to Fannie Mae and the Farm Credit System; and the 2000s with regard to Fannie Mae and Freddie Mac and, of course, TARP. The idea that a present-day Congress can prospectively prevent a future Congress from the standard response of passing an ad hoc bailout in the midst of a crisis is fanciful. Treasury Secretary Geithner gave this honest assessment of how a future Congress might react and the dubious state of a future taxpayer commitment: "The size of the shock that hit our financial system was larger than what caused the Great Depression. In the future we may have to do exceptional things again if we face a shock that large."[17]

Even putting aside the fact that limits on future bailouts are not realistic, Dodd-Frank still does not live up to the rhetoric of its architects. They argue in their press releases that the legislation: "Clearly states taxpayers will not be on the hook to save a failing financial company or to cover the cost of its liquidation." The legislation calls for industry assessments to recapture expenditures. For example, expenditures may be necessary under the FDIC's expanded liquidation authority which grants broad-based authority to provide funding, including making loans, purchasing debt obligations, making guarantees against loss, all

---

16. In some cases, the bailouts were accomplished through some form of regulatory action.
17. SIGTARP Citi Report, 44.

of which might expose the FDIC to potential expenditures.[18] This approach is a tax on well-managed financial institutions to compensate creditors of poorly managed institutions.

### The All-Knowing Council

The Council is charged with "identifying and responding to emerging risks throughout the financial system."[19] It will oversee large financial and nonfinancial institutions that pose systemic risk. The Obama Administration plan of June 2009 suggested such a council, but in that report it glossed over the fact that all along there was a similar umbrella group of agencies responsible for overseeing financial markets: "The Council should replace the President's Working Group on Financial Markets [WGFM] and have additional authorities and responsibilities with respect to systemic risk and coordination of financial regulation." This is particularly relevant in all the discussions regarding confidence during the 2000s crisis as one of the explicit purposes of the WGFM was "maintaining investor confidence."[20]

In fact, the WGFM took the lead on a number of occasions during the course of the crisis as previously noted, and in particular it met and issued a report in March 2008, well before any of the major bailouts, to release an analysis of the market turmoil during late 2007 and early 2008. The analysis was made at the request of President George W. Bush in August 2007 to review the underlying causes and recommend changes to help avoid a repeat of events leading up to the March 2008 issue date. The report confidently noted that its recommendations would "mitigate systemic risk, help restore investor confidence, and facilitate economic growth."[21] As detailed in Chapters 7, 8, and 9 of this book, dramatic increases in systemic risk (as the WGFM defined it), declining investor confidence and sharply reduced growth ensued. Predictably, in the report's

---

18. Dodd-Frank, Section 204(d).
19. Dodd-Frank Brief Summary, 3.
20. Executive Order 12631, Section 2.
21. WGFM, *President's Working Group Issues Policy Statement To Improve Future State of Financial Markets*. WGFM, *Policy Statement on Financial Market Developments*, March 13, 2008 [hereinafter, *Working Group Policy Statement*], http://www.ustreas.gov/press /releases/hp871.htm.

recitation of all of the contributing factors to the market turmoil, it neglected to cite any critique regarding accommodative monetary policy, possibly because the Board of Governors was one of the lead members of the WGFM.[22] Even if one assumes that the working group's recommendations were on point, few of the recommendations were acted upon and the report had no appreciable impact on lessening the worsening crisis.

Based on the structure of the Council as constituted in the Dodd-Frank legislation, it appears that the overall conclusion from the 2000s crisis is that the WGFM would have worked in its efforts to maintain confidence if only the group had been bigger in all respects:

- **More members on the Council**—rather than the mere four members of the WGFM, the newly constituted FSOC has an unwieldy ten members: the four members of the WGFM plus six new members (see comparison in Table 10.2).[23] As in the case of the WGFM, the Council will be headed by the politically driven Treasury Department.

- **More resources**—not only will there be a council, but the Dodd-Frank Act provides for the council to appoint special advisory, technical, or professional committees, to include state regulators; to receive assistance from other federal agencies, including the detailing of government employees; and to have at its disposal an Office of Financial Research.[24] This office, to be headed by a presidential appointee, is described as "a highly sophisticated staff of economists, accountants, lawyers, former supervisors, and other specialists to support the council's work by collecting financial data and conducting economic analysis."

- **More powers**—the vested authorities of the Council primarily focus on its ability to obtain information from a wide variety of sources in order to monitor the financial services marketplace and to identify potential risk to financial stability. The authority to obtain information from any non-bank financial company or bank holding company is expansive.[25] Additionally, the Council has the power to request that the Board of

---

22. *Working Group Policy Statement*, p. 8–10.
23. Dodd-Frank, Sec. 111.
24. Dodd-Frank, Sec. 151.
25. Dodd-Frank, Sec. 112(d)(3).

**Table 10.2.** Comparison Between Members of Oversight Groups

| Members of the Working Group on Financial Markets (1988) | Members of the Financial Stability Oversight Council (2010) |
| --- | --- |
| Secretary of the Treasury (Chair of Group) | Secretary of the Treasury (Chair of Council) |
| Chairman of the Board of Governors of the Federal Reserve | Chairman of the Board of Governors of the Federal Reserve |
| Chairman of the Securities and Exchange Commission | Chairman of the Securities and Exchange Commission |
| Chairman of the Commodities Futures Trading Commission | Chairman of the Commodities Futures Trading Commission |
| | Comptroller of the Currency |
| | Bureau of Consumer Financial Protection |
| | Chairperson of the FDIC |
| | Director of the Federal Housing Finance Agency |
| | Chairman of the National Credit Union Administration Board |
| | Independent Member |

Governors conduct an examination of a nonbank financial company to determine whether it should be supervised by the Board of Governors and ultimately to mandate supervision.[26]

- **More reports**—the Council may require a bank holding company with total assets of $50 billion or more or a non-bank financial company supervised by the Board of Governors to submit reports on its financial condition; on its systems for monitoring and controlling risks; on transactions with subsidiaries that are depository institutions; and the extent to which activities could disrupt financial markets or affect financial stability.[27] The act also allows the Council to make recommendations on

26. Dodd-Frank, Sec. 112(d)(4), 113.
27. Dodd-Frank, Sec. 116(a).

a requirement that nonbank financial companies and large bank holding companies prepare reports on rapid and orderly resolution, so-called funeral plans.[28]

As previously noted, throughout the 2000s crisis Secretary Paulson was quite damning of the workings of the WGFM, detailing that:

- The agencies involved in the working group were often very competitive, which led to difficulties in information sharing. There is already some evidence that such infighting is inherent at the new council;[29]
- Efforts to study various worst-case scenarios (for example, a potential failure of Fannie Mae and Freddie Mac) were cancelled for fear that word would leak out to the press that such scenarios were imminent; and
- Statements of the WGFM rarely achieved their intended objective to calm or otherwise assure markets.

With more players involved in the Council, such infighting, fear of scrutiny, and lack of effectiveness would surely be multiplied.

Examples abound of how the workings of a council, in an environment similar to the 2000s crisis, would fall short of the great expectations of the Dodd-Frank architects. Once a problem area is discovered, even if it is discovered early enough to timely address the problem, there is no assurance that the proper action or actions will be taken. For example, the FDIC did some on-point analysis of the troubling trend in consolidation of megabanks that led researchers in the agency to conclude that the FDIC fund was at great risk if one of these institutions were to fail.[30] It is not clear, however, that much of anything was done through the FDIC or any other agency to act upon this red flag. FDIC research on subprime problems in 2006 and 2007 also met a similar fate. Chairman Bair noted some troubling signs regarding subprime mortgages while she was at the

---

28. Dodd-Frank, Sec. 115(d), 165.
29. Damian Paletta, "Infighting Besets Financial-Oversight Council," *Wall Street Journal*, September 30, 2010.
30. See Kenneth D. Jones and Tim Critchfield, "Consolidation in the U.S. Banking Industry: Is the 'Long, Strange Trip' About to End?" *FDIC Banking Review* 17, no. 4 (2005). Kenneth D. Jones and Chau Nguyen, "Increased Concentration in Banking: Megabanks and Their Implications for Deposit Insurance" (June 2004).

Treasury Department in the early years of President Bush's first term. When she became FDIC chairman in 2006, she directed an effort whereby the FDIC bought a database of subprime loans to study subprime lending more closely, and she was shocked at what was found: "We just couldn't believe what we were seeing. . . . Really steep payment shock loans and subprimes. . . . Very little income documentation, really high prepayment penalties." In March 2007, she initiated the first government action against a subprime lender, Fremont Investment and Loan, a California bank. As in the case of the analysis of megabanks, it is not very clear that anything was done to address the problem early enough to do any good.[31] Another illuminating example is the supervision of AIG. The Office of Thrift Supervision (OTS), an office within the Treasury Department, noted problem areas at the institution throughout 2006, 2007, and 2008. Yet no serious action was taken to address AIG until September 2008. So as to the 2000s crisis, it was not a lack of discussion regarding problems in the financial sector that was to blame, as some good analysis was undertaken in the cited examples at the FDIC and the OTS. The problem is taking the initial analysis that identifies a problem area and getting agreement from the range of council members involved on the necessary follow-through to respond in a way that actually prevents the problem from leading to real or perceived systemic problems. It is not at all clear that the Council with its unwieldy structure and new crop of stakeholders, with all of its resources, powers, and reports, will be able to do much of anything to prevent or limit the damage from the next crisis.

### Capital and Leverage Limitations

One of the authorities of the Council is to make recommendations to the Board of Governors for heightened prudential standards. These include standards for risk-based and mandatory contingent capital and leverage for nonbank financial companies and large, interconnected bank holding companies super-

---

31. Ryan Lizza, "The Contrarian: Sheila Bair and the White House Financial Debate," *New Yorker*, July 6, 2009. Kimberly Blanton, "FDIC Official Urges Curbs on Subprime Loan Firms," *Boston Globe*, March 28, 2007,.http://www.boston.com/business/globe/articles/2007/03/28/fdic_official_urges_curbs_on_subprime_loan_firms/.

vised by the Board of Governors, among other standards.[32] The past twenty-five years have seen untold attempts at achieving the perfect capital and leverage limitations that balance the competing objectives of retaining the flexibility of financial institutions to take on risk, while at the same time maintaining a sufficient capital buffer to protect against potential losses. In the United States, capital limits have been made relatively consistent across banking and savings regulators in the aftermath of the 1980s crisis. The most prominent of these efforts was implementation of the system of prompt corrective action (PCA) under FDICIA. Internationally, an entire series of capital accords under the Basel moniker have also sought the holy grail of the perfect capital standard. Yet Citigroup, Wachovia, Fannie Mae, and Freddie Mac were all subject to what were thought to be stringent capital standards and they still approached failure with relatively short notice of impending capital shortfalls. A system of easily calculated capital limits that if violated result in the closure of financial institutions is preferable to yet another complex regime of capital requirements.

Rather than emitting hope such limits will truly work as planned, the Dodd-Frank efforts at establishing yet more capital and leverage limitations simply highlight how much of a mixed bag the PCA provisions that were implemented in the early 1990s were. The idea behind PCA was to give the regulatory agencies the power to intervene at an early point in time in order to reduce the costs to the FDIC of resolutions. But this has not been the case, likely because capital is a lagging indicator of the problems a troubled institution is facing, meaning that once the indicator raises a red flag, it is likely too late to do much to address the inherent problem indicated by the initial warning.[33]

A quick glimpse of the data for the failures in 2008 and 2009 illustrates this fact as it reveals that those failure costs were actually quite high and little improved over the pre-FDICIA levels. Although it is not a perfect measure of

---

32. Dodd-Frank, Section 112, 115, 171.

33. "Expensive Bank Failures," 4–6. This same point is made in U.S. Department of the Treasury, "Principles for Reforming the U.S. and International Regulatory Capital Framework for Banking Firms," September 3, 2009, 6 ("This highlights how the existing regulatory capital and accounting rules generate capital ratios for banking firms that too often are a lagging indicator of financial distress"), http://www.treas.gov/press/releases/docs/capital-statement_090309.pdf.

the severity of failures as measured by the cost, the ratio of bank resolution costs as a percentage of total assets reveals approximately how big a hole has to be filled in terms of costs after the failure of a bank.[34] During the 1980s and early 1990s, on an annual basis this ratio stayed within a range of 5 to 25 percent with the average over time at about 12 percent.[35] The ratio stayed within the same range for the 2000s crisis, and in some cases such as IndyMac, the most expensive bank resolution in history, it greatly exceeded it. The resolution cost of IndyMac of $10.7 billion on an asset base of $23.5 billion reveals a cost-to-assets ratio of more than 45 percent.[36]

## The New Resolution Options

Under Dodd-Frank the options for resolving institutions reflect the perceptions of each of the resolution options during the 2000s crisis. Thus, it is easiest to understand the new legislation by reviewing how many of the major bailouts and bankruptcies from the crisis would likely have been different if they had occurred under a Dodd-Frank regime. For each of the types of resolutions utilized during the 2000s crisis, the Dodd-Frank legislation reformulates the approach (see Table 10.3).

### *Orderly Liquidation*

The underlying assumption and one of the key lessons reportedly learned from the financial crisis is that the bankruptcy system cannot be relied upon

---

34. See "Expensive Bank Failures," 3, footnote that discusses how banks were likely under regulatory orders to shrink their balance sheets, which would have had the effect of increasing a bank's negative Tier 1 capital ratio when it failed, all else equal. Buchman also notes that these ratios are striking taking into consideration that all of the banks were reporting positive capital levels on the last quarterly call reports that they submitted prior to placement into receivership.

35. Federal Deposit Insurance Corporation, *Managing the Crisis: The FDIC and RTC Experience*, Appendix C—Statistical Data, Chart C.19, Bank Resolution Costs as a Percentage of Total Assets, 810.

36. See "Expensive Bank Failures," Appendix for 2008 and 2009 resolutions through October 2009. This is the calculation at the resolution of the conservatorship in March 2009 after the bank was downsized.

**Table 10.3.** Dodd-Frank Transforms the 2000s Resolution Methods

| 2000s Resolution Method (Institutions) | Dodd-Frank Reformulation |
|---|---|
| File Chapter 11 bankruptcy (Lehman Brothers) | For systemically important institutions, may be addressed under the new orderly liquidation regime (Sec. 201–17) |
| Board of Governors— Unusual and exigent circumstances (Bear Stearns, AIG) | No longer for an individual entity but is allowed for a program or facility with "broad-based eligibility" available to solvent entities; the security must be sufficient. May be addressed under orderly liquidation. (Sec. 1101–3) |
| FDIC temporary liability guarantee program (widely available program primarily benefiting large banks) | Grants permanent authority to create a "widely available program" to guarantee obligations of solvent insured depository institutions or solvent depository institution holding companies if there is a "liquidity event determination" (Sec. 1104–5)[1] |
| FDIC open bank assistance (OBA) (Wachovia, Citigroup, Bank of America) | Exceptions to least cost only available to banks that have been placed in receivership (i.e., closed bank) (Sec. 203) |
| Government sponsored enterprises (Fannie Mae and Freddie Mac) | No changes to structure of Fannie Mae and Freddie Mac or any other GSEs; no change to conservatorship or receivership options; Treasury study of ending the conservatorships required by February 2011 (Sec. 1074) |
| Troubled Asset Relief Program (TARP) (broad-based program primarily benefiting large banks) | Reduces the amount authorized under the TARP to $475 billion, from $700 billion; prohibits Treasury from using repaid TARP funds; and prohibits Treasury from initiating new programs under TARP (Sec. 1302) |

1. Congress must act on an expedited basis.

to handle the liquidation of a systemic financial company. The change to a new process is in line with the descriptor of the new resolution process as orderly, which is apparently meant to contrast with the critical description of disorderly that was applied to the Lehman Brothers bankruptcy. However, as detailed previously, this account of history has little evidence to support it.

The orderly liquidation process has at its core the resolution process the FDIC has historically applied to banks which will now be applied to a broader range of systemic financial companies. This category will include those institutions the Council and the Federal Reserve regulate, as well as those institutions that meet the new "systemic risk determination." This determination is a process that the FDIC or the Board of Governors can initiate on their own or at the request of the Secretary of the Treasury. Once the determination is made, the FDIC will be responsible for overseeing the orderly liquidation process. Much of the language regarding the determination of systemic risk is drawn from the old systemic risk exception in the Federal Deposit Insurance Corporation Act utilized so much during the 2000s crisis regarding serious adverse effects on "financial stability."[37]

The purpose of this orderly liquidation is to mitigate the risks of financial instability while at the same time minimizing moral hazard that might go along with the unwinding of a financial company. This is done by making sure creditors and shareholders bear the losses of the financial company and that the management and all other parties responsible for the deteriorated financial condition of the company bear responsibility through shared losses or loss of their management position.[38] The FDIC is given a broad range of new powers to undertake this orderly liquidation, including general powers, such as transferring the company's assets, forming a bridge financial company, issuing subpoenas, and coordinating with foreign financial regulators to more specific powers related to claims, agreements, and recovery of compensation. An orderly liquidation fund will be used to absorb the costs of the orderly liquidation process through assessments and repayments.[39]

The entire structure of the orderly liquidation process under Dodd-Frank is based upon the conclusion that the FDIC is a much better entity for managing

---

37. Dodd-Frank, Section 203. For brokers or dealers the determination is by the SEC, and the Board of Governors considers whether to make the determination. For insurance companies, the Director of the Federal Insurance Office and the Board of Governors consider whether to make the determination.

38. Dodd-Frank, Section 204.

39. Dodd-Frank, Section 210.

the liquidation of large systemic financial institutions than the courts, which is the narrative that came out of the crisis. This is also the stance of the FDIC as they openly inserted themselves into the discussion by arguing that they would be better positioned than the courts to undertake liquidation of systemic institutions and in so doing undertook an unseemly lobbying campaign for additional powers. Arguments cited by the FDIC included:

- The FDIC's experience with the sale of Washington Mutual, Wachovia, Citigroup, Bank of America, Fannie Mae, and Freddie Mac during the 2000s crisis and Continental Illinois during the 1980s crisis;
- The bankruptcy court's experience with Lehman, which the FDIC describes as involving significant market disruptions, huge fees and expenses, and a drawn-out resolution process;
- The fact that the FDIC's operations are transparent because they are subject to the FOIA;
- The FDIC's resolution process, which allows for a bridge entity that can avoid the continued existence of a "too big to fail" entity; and
- The bankruptcy of Lehman Brothers, which led to a noncompetitive process for the sale of its broker-dealer and investment-management and underwriting businesses.[40]

Notwithstanding the arguments by the FDIC to the contrary, there was very little evidence to support moving the authority from the courts to the FDIC. The key point is that the FDIC has had very limited experience in the liquidation of very large nonbank institutions or bank institutions for that matter, which is the issue at hand. Washington Mutual was the largest financial institution failure in U.S. history at over $300 billion of assets, but it was resolved through sale to JPMorgan on a whole bank basis, meaning essentially all the operations were absorbed by JPMorgan. Other than putting together the purchase and

---

40. A clear exchange detailing the disagreement regarding these issues is stated in an article in the *Wall Street Journal* and the response of the FDIC. See Peter J. Wallison and David Skeel, "The Dodd Bill: Bailouts Forever," *Wall Street Journal*, April 7, 2010, http://online .wsj.com/article/NA_WSJ_PUB:SB10001424052702303493904575167571831270694.html. FDIC, "FDIC Rebuts Inaccurate Op-ed," undated, http://www.fdic.gov/news/letters /rebuttal_04072010.html [hereinafter "FDIC Rebuts"].

assumption agreement the resolution process was not particularly involved.[41] The other larger institutions the FDIC cites, such as Wachovia, Citigroup, and Bank of America, were never liquidated, but were addressed through OBA, which involved propping up the institutions. By no means did these transactions involve winding down their operations as required in the liquidation of Lehman Brothers. Additionally, the Wachovia and Bank of America transactions were not even consummated, as Wachovia was ultimately purchased by Wells Fargo with no FDIC involvement and Bank of America's OBA was never even approved by the Treasury. It is also not clear the extent FDIC was heavily involved in the Fannie Mae and Freddie Mac decision-making. These entities were also not liquidated, but instead were placed in conservatorship, another case of simply propping up the institution and not liquidating it. Finally, the FDIC cites the case of Continental Illinois to support its expanded powers, but as detailed in the relevant chapter of this book, Continental Illinois was resolved a quarter century ago and as a result the FDIC has little management expertise remaining from that experience and it was also not nearly as complex an institution as today's banks or nonbanks.[42]

Alternatively, Lehman Brothers was a much more challenging liquidation than the examples from the 2000s crisis the FDIC has cited. The most significant and time-consuming resolution managed solely by the FDIC during the 2000s crisis was IndyMac, a $32 billion institution when it was taken over by the FDIC that took eight months to dispose of. This compares to the Lehman Brothers bankruptcy, in which a $600 billion institution was handled by the bankruptcy court. As Secretary Paulson has detailed, there was no ready buyer for the entire Lehman operation, as Bank of America and Barclays contemplated such a purchase, but ultimately neither was willing to take on the entire entity. The bankruptcy court was left with breaking up the component parts of

41. FDIC, "JPMorgan Chase Acquires Banking Operations of Washington Mutual," September 25, 2008. Also see Whole Bank Purchase and Assumption Agreement, FDIC and JPMorgan Chase Bank, September 25, 2008, http://www.fdic.gov/about/freedom /Washington_Mutual_P_and_A.pdf.

42. For a discussion of the complexity issue regarding Continental, see William Isaac, "Bank Nationalization Isn't the Answer," *Wall Street Journal*, February 24, 2009, http:// online.wsj.com/article/NA_WSJ_PUB:SB123543631794154467.html.

Lehman Brothers and sold the largest of these parts within a very short period of time of the initial filing, and in so doing retained significant value, all despite the lack of planning for the bankruptcy filing by Lehman Brothers. The court in the Lehman Brothers case and the FDIC in the WaMu case dealt with the same challenge: selling off large financial operations in the midst of a financial crisis with very few players available that were large enough, strong enough, and thus capable of absorbing the institutions in question. It is not clear at all that the FDIC did a better job than the courts, yet the FDIC boldly and publicly criticizes the bankruptcy court for how it sold off the assets in the Lehman bankruptcy in a "noncompetitive process," "arguably at fire sale prices," and the "sale to Barclays is still being litigated." A recent ruling determined the sale was "imperfect," but the judge was not persuaded that the sale should be revisited.[43]

Although the FDIC cites that it is subject to the FOIA as evidence of its transparency and openness and that it is not operating in secret, as has been discussed throughout this book, it regularly invokes exemptions under this act to shield its operations from scrutiny. Finally FDIC cites its authority to create a bridge entity and avoid the creation of a TBTF entity. However, it declined to use this power in the cases of systemic institutions like Wachovia and Citigroup, and it is not clear they even considered these options in their efforts to resolve these two institutions.

### Broad-Based and Widely Available Programs

Another key lesson gleaned from the financial crisis as demonstrated by the Dodd-Frank formulation is that the bailouts of financial institutions should not be on an individual basis, but instead should be undertaken through so-called "broad-based" or "widely available" programs. This approach is evident from the changes to the power of the Federal Reserve under Section 13(3), the power to lend under unusual and exigent circumstances (UEC), which was used in the Bear Stearns and AIG bailouts and considered in the case of Lehman. This power remains, but now requires the prior approval of the secretary of the Treasury,

---

43. FDIC Rebuts. Joseph Checkler and Patrick Fitzgerald, "Judge Sides with Barclays over Lehman," *Wall Street Journal*, February 23, 2011.

and additionally it must be applied to a broad swath of institutions and be approved by Congress on an expedited basis. Additionally, only solvent financial institutions may participate in such a program, and the Federal Reserve must assure that the security for loans is sufficient. If a failure occurred today like Bear Stearns and AIG, they would have to be addressed under such a broadly based program rather than on an individual institution basis.

The same philosophy was also applied to the FDIC's TLGP of 2008, which has been permanently codified as a program to be created by the FDIC that is "widely available" during what is called a "liquidity event," which is

(A) an exceptional and broad reduction in the general ability of financial market participants—
  (i) to sell financial assets without an unusual and significant discount; or
  (ii) to borrow using financial assets as collateral without an unusual and significant increase in margin; or
(B) an unusual and significant reduction in the ability of financial market participants to obtain unsecured credit.[44]

The program, which can now be aptly called the FDIC's Permanent Liquidity Guarantee Program under the Dodd-Frank formulation, allows the FDIC to guarantee obligations of solvent insured depository institutions or solvent depository institution holding companies.[45] This is not unlike the FDIC's TLGP, which was limited to so-called viable institutions.

When the next large institution stumbles like Bear Stearns did, absent special legislation that would address the situation, either the FDIC will approve a widely available program (in the case of an insured institution or holding company) or the Federal Reserve under UEC will approve a broad-based program (in the case of other institutions). But it is quite possible that such a program could be approved that is simply a charade in order to benefit a troubled institution like Bear Stearns. The limitations on these programs are that the institutions must be solvent or not insolvent, as the case may be, but this is not really that

---

44. Dodd-Frank, Section 1104.
45. Dodd-Frank, Section 1105.

binding a restriction.[46] As the history reveals in the case of Continental Illinois, Bear Stearns, and AIG, regulators will tend to see a liquidity problem much more readily than they will see a capital solvency problem. Under the Federal Reserve's UEC authority, there is the further restriction that the security must be sufficient to protect taxpayers from losses, but that was also the case with the Bear Stearns and AIG transactions.

### *Open Bank Assistance*

The provisions for OBA are still on the books. However, the assistance can no longer be provided for systemic institutions unless they are liquidated or the case can be made that OBA is the least costly resolution to pursue. Institutions that were approved by the FDIC for OBA such as Wachovia, Citigroup, and Bank of America could be provided OBA today, but would have to be liquidated, something the FDIC was unwilling to do during the 2000s crisis. In the various minutes and memos it is not clear that liquidation, or more likely a bridge bank followed by liquidation, was even raised as a possibility. So the most likely choice under Dodd-Frank would be to apply the FDIC's widely available program, assuming the determination could credibly be made that the institutions were solvent.

## What the Dodd-Frank Legislation Did to Instill Confidence

The goal of both the Obama Administration proposal and the Dodd-Frank legislation was to instill certainty, confidence, and trust in the financial system that had been badly damaged throughout 2008 and 2009. The release of the legislation was at a time of increasing uncertainty in the financial markets amid concerns about the languishing and slow-growth economy during the summer

---

46. There are differing definitions under the two formulations. *Solvent* is defined as a situation where the value of the assets of an entity exceeds its obligations to creditors under the FDIC program; and *insolvent* is defined as a situation where a borrower is in bankruptcy, resolution under Title II of Dodd-Frank or under any Federal or state insolvency proceeding under the Federal Reserve's 13(3) formulation.

of 2010. The legislation has done little to reduce that uncertainty and in fact, not unlike the interventions during the 2000s crisis, actually may have increased uncertainty. Much of this uncertainty flowed from the lack of specificity in the legislation and the resulting need to promulgate nearly 250 regulations pursuant to the Dodd-Frank legislation, much of it in the realm of bailouts and resolution of troubled financial institutions.[47]

The Obama Administration hoped to tout financial reform, designed to address the financial sector problems left behind by the Bush Administration, as one of the centerpieces of its activist agenda. Additionally, the plan was to address Fannie Mae and Freddie Mac in 2011 under a Democratically-controlled Congress. Rather than a winning issue the Democrats could run on during the 2010 election cycle, the Dodd-Frank legislation instead fueled the developing narrative that Congress simply does not understand the adverse impact of its actions on broader confidence. Dodd-Frank did not help them expand or maintain their majorities in Congress, as along with health care legislation it was in part responsible for losses of historic proportions. But as much as it was a rejection of the Obama Administration's approach, it was also a rejection of the bailout mentality that was ramped up so dramatically during the late months of the George W. Bush Administration. With the House of Representatives now under Republican control, a long-term legislative solution to Fannie Mae and Freddie Mac and the broader housing market now seems quite far off.[48]

---

47. Review and Outlook, "The Uncertainty Principle," *Wall Street Journal*, July 14, 2010, http://online.wsj.com/article/NA_WSJ_PUB:SB10001424052748704288204575363162664835780.html.
48. Nick Timiraos and Victoria McGrane, "Gridlock Could Delay Fannie Reboot," *Wall Street Journal*, November 5, 2010.

# 11

## The Assessment of the History

### There Is Nothing New Under the Sun

IN ONE OF HIS many disputable statements uttered throughout the financial crisis, Secretary Paulson had this take on the historical significance of the crisis: "There is no playbook for responding to turmoil we have never faced."[1] To the contrary, with the analysis of the history of bailouts of the past century in mind, a much more accurate characterization of the recent financial crisis is: "There is nothing new under the sun."[2] The history is replete with eerie instances of déjà vu:

- Two government sponsored enterprises approached failure and were ultimately bailed out; are we talking about the 1980s and Fannie Mae and the Farm Credit System, or the 2000s and Fannie Mae and Freddie Mac?
- A large TBTF commercial bank approached insolvency, causing regulators to raise fears about a rippling effect of failures that proved to be overstated; are we talking about the BOUS during the 1930s, Continental Illinois in the 1980s, or Wachovia and Citigroup in the 2000s?

---

1. Henry M. Paulson, Jr., "Fighting the Financial Crisis, One Challenge at a Time," *New York Times*, November 17, 2008.
2. The author worked at the Oversight Board of the Resolution Trust Corporation (OBRTC) in 1990 and 1991. This Board was made up of a cross section of government representatives to oversee the activities of the RTC. Doug Foster, another staff member at the OBRTC, had a great deal of experience in financial sector regulation, supervision, and intervention at that time. Foster would tell stories about how there was a cycle of repeated history in financial sector regulation, supervision, and interventions. He labeled this phenomenon "There's nothing new under the sun." After researching the history of bailouts in this book, this pattern is very clear.

- A major investment bank approaches failure and arguments surface that the safety net of TBTF bailouts should be extended to cover them; are we talking about Drexel Burnham Lambert in the 1980s or Bear Stearns and Lehman Brothers in the 2000s?
- The economy enters what many see as a period of long-term financial stability, just before a major financial crisis; are we talking about the "New Era" just before the Depression in the 1930s or the "Great Moderation" just before the financial collapse in the 2000s?
- A Republican president undertakes a series of bailouts of unprecedented scope, abandons any veneer of adherence to free-market policy, and is followed in office by a Democratic president who seamlessly continues the efforts to bail out financial institutions with the assistance of some Republican holdovers; are we talking about the Hoover Administration and the transition to the Roosevelt Administration in the 1930s or the George W. Bush Administration and the transition to the Obama Administration in the 2000s?
- Actions are urged to bail out financial institutions in order to maintain "confidence," yet after those bailouts are undertaken, confidence continues to erode and the economic downturn actually accelerates; are we talking about President Hoover who urged passage of the RFC in order to restore confidence in the 1930s or the various regulators who argued that bailouts were essential to restoring confidence in the 2000s?
- The policy response by the government to a so-called systemic banking crisis was to inject capital simultaneously into multiple banks and take back preferred stock; are we talking about the 1930s and the RFC or the 2000s and TARP?
- Scare tactics are deployed to get the Congress's blessing for a financial bailout; are we talking about Continental Illinois' rescue in the 1980s or the TARP in the 2000s?
- A bailout of financial institutions benefits foreign banks, depositors, or creditors; are we talking about Continental Illinois in the 1980s and its predecessor Franklin National Bank in the 1970s, or Fannie Mae, Freddie Mac, Wachovia, Citigroup, and AIG in the 2000s?
- Government intervention results in the long-term nationalization of financial institutions with the government taking an 80 percent owner-

ship stake and replacing management; are we talking about Continental in the 1980s or Fannie Mae, Freddie Mac, and AIG in the 2000s?

- Horror stories are told about how many of the "little people" would lose their jobs, and how many companies would close their doors if a financial institution is not bailed out; are we talking about Continental in the 1980s or Bear Stearns and AIG in the 2000s?

- Bailouts of institutions are justified on the basis of linkages among financial institutions; are we talking about Continental and its array of correspondent banks in the 1930s and 1980s or Bear Stearns and AIG and their web of counterparties in the 2000s?

- Policymakers argue that emergency legislation has to be passed immediately, within a matter of hours or days; are we talking about the RFC that was debated and passed in a single day during the 1930s or the TARP legislation that supposedly needed to pass within a matter of days during the 2000s?

- A government bailout program is proposed during a crisis, and once it is passed into law the initially narrow power envisioned is dramatically broadened and activities far afield from the original proposal proliferate; are we talking about the War Finance Corporation in the 1910s, the Reconstruction Finance Corporation in the 1930s, or the TARP in the 2000s?

- A regulator overseeing a financial institution on the brink of failure publicly announces shortly before its bailout that the institution is not in as bad a shape as rumored; are we talking about Joseph Broderick of the New York State Banking Department regarding Bank of United States in the 1930s, Comptroller C. Todd Conover regarding Continental Illinois in the 1980s, or James Lockhart of the FHFA regarding Fannie and Freddie in the 2000s?

- Supervisors put together an after-the-fact justification for a bailout of a financial institution; are we talking about Continental in the 1980s or Bear Stearns in the 2000s?

- Regulators employ shifting strategies between letting financial institutions fail and bailing them out; are we talking about the slow drift towards being "less solicitous of the interests of the bank's owners and bondholders" during the 1980s crisis or are we talking about the dramatic swings in stated policy between the approach to Bear Stearns, Lehman Brothers, and AIG during the 2000s crisis?

- Congress vows that there will never again be widespread use of bailouts, that they will only be reserved for cases of institutions whose failure will cause the gravest of instability; are we talking about the changes in the 1990s regarding the systemic risk exception in FDICIA or the changes codified in Dodd-Frank during the aftermath of the crisis in the 2000s?

- Pressure is placed on the management of large financial institutions to join a preferred stock program to instill confidence that the program is not just for troubled banks; are we talking about the RFC during the 1930s or the TARP during the 2000s?

- Executives of troubled banks are vilified as overpaid and the Congress scrutinizes pay levels at banks; are we talking about RFC powers during the 1930s, Congressional criticism of Continental during the 1980s, or the criticism that led to the creation of a compensation czar during the 2000s?

- Financial agencies argue that banks were really only illiquid and not insolvent and that they will ultimately be resolved at zero cost; are we talking about Continental during the 1980s or Bear Stearns and AIG during the 2000s?

- To remedy TBTF policies, proposals are offered to tighten capital requirements; are we talking about the Continental hearings in the 1980s and the resulting capital changes in FDICIA in 1991 or financial reform hearings in the 2000s and changes to capital requirements under Dodd-Frank?

- The chosen solution from Washington after a financial panic is to create a panel of wise people in Washington that, so it is alleged, will smooth out the process of booms and busts in the financial cycle that periodically occur in the U.S. economy; are we talking about the creation of the Federal Reserve in 1913, the Working Group on Financial Markets in 1988, or the Financial Stability Oversight Council in 2010?

Although a single generalization cannot be made that addresses all of these phenomena, much of the repeated pattern throughout history reflects the nature of government regulation and intervention. Government regulators and the politicians who grant regulators their powers overestimate their understanding of the financial institutions they oversee. When it becomes very clear that they are working under false assumptions, they respond in panic, implementing a classic "not on my watch" approach. The usual pattern is that they overreact in the midst of a financial crisis because they feel they have to "do something." Most of these actions make matters worse both in the short term as the panic spreads more broadly and the long term as unintended consequences flow from their initial reaction.[3]

## Ever-Expanding, Permanent Bailouts and How We Got Here

Like so many public policy initiatives, the original intention of bailouts was relatively benign: to minimize the negative impact of short-term consequences of turbulent financial periods. The history of bailouts reveals a clear pattern of ignoring the long-term consequences of those actions. The program of bailouts started out during the First World War as a temporary program to focus resources on war efforts. This approach was revived with the RFC during the dire economic circumstances of the Depression as a temporary, two-year measure to stop the scourge of bank failures. As the bailouts transformed after the Depression, they became a permanent authority of the FDIC that was intended to undertake costless bailouts of small institutions that were considered "essential" to their community. But for the existence of these small institutions, it was argued, these communities might not have any banking services at all. However, with each passing financial crisis after that, the number of agencies deploying bailouts multiplied, the safety net became bigger and bigger, and the primary beneficiaries were soon concentrated among the largest of financial institutions, who came to rely on and demand this ready source of government backstopping (see Table 11.1). After each crisis, it was sworn that the next time around the bailouts would just not be allowed again.

---

3. For a model of behavioral economics as applied to the reactions of regulators, see the work of Slavisa Tasic, which is highlighted in Matt Ridley, "Studying the Biases of Bureaucrats," *Wall Street Journal*, October 23, 2010.

**Table 11.1.** Expanding Breadth of Bailouts for Financial Institutions

| *1930s* | *1980s* | *2000s* |
|---|---|---|
| RFC[1] | OBA | OBA |
| | GSEs | GSEs |
| | FOR | UEC |
| | | TARP |
| | | TLGP |
| Economic depression | Deep recession | Deep recession |
| Temporary authority | Permanent authority | Permanent authority |
| Nearly all troubled commercial banks, but of varying sizes | Primarily large commercial bank focus | Expansion to investment banks and insurance companies; expansion to viable institutions |
| $1 billion outlays at time, net cost minimal | Expansion beyond commercial banks to GSEs | Nearly all directed to large institutions |
| | TBTF = 11 multi-national banks | TBTF = 19 financial groups; Fannie Mae and Freddie Mac |
| | Billions in outlays, net cost positive | Trillion in outlays and guarantees, $100s of billions in estimated cost |

RFC = Reconstruction Finance Corporation
OBA = open bank assistance
GSE = government sponsored enterprises
FOR = forbearance

UEC = unusual and exigent circumstances
TARP = Troubled Asset Relief Program
TLGP = Temporary Liquidity Guarantee Program

1. UEC did exist during this period, but it was a tiny share of RFC and of minimal importance.

There is no better example that spans the storied history of bailouts than an institution that was the product of a merger in 1910 between Commercial National Bank and Continental National Bank. In 1929 that bank merged with Illinois Merchants Trust Co., and three years later the bank's name became Continental Illinois National Bank and Trust Co.[4] At about that same time,

---

4. "Continental Illinois National Bank and Trust Company," *Encyclopedia of Chicago*, http://www.encyclopedia.chicagohistory.org/pages/2627.html.

Continental Illinois imprudently lent excessively to utilities in the Chicago area and to out-of-territory borrowers and ultimately was bailed out to the tune of $50 million by the RFC in 1933.[5] As Continental gained a national and international presence in the 1970s and early 1980s, it again lent imprudently, this time to energy companies in far-off states. On the funding side, Continental borrowed from a correspondent banking and international network of financial institutions. Again it was bailed out to the tune of $4 billion and an ultimate net cost of $1.1 billion under the FDIC's OBA powers. Ultimately, what was left of Continental was purchased in 1994 by Bank of America. After Bank of America ventured into investment banking with its purchase of Merrill Lynch in September 2008, it received yet another bailout, this time $45 billion, a combination of funds and commitments from the FDIC OBA, Treasury TARP, and Federal Reserve UEC. One has to wonder what form the firm will take when it is bailed out during the next financial crisis later this century.

## Seat-of-the-Pants Justifications Abound

The implicit assumption in vesting these ever-expanding authorities to intervene with the Federal Reserve, the FDIC, and the Treasury, and in preserving these powers going forward under Dodd-Frank is that the agencies can (1) quickly gain an understanding of the situation causing stress in an individual financial institution or a range of financial institutions; (2) objectively assess the magnitude of the problem and any unintended consequences of interventions; (3) review the options available under law; and (4) put into place a transaction structured to limit the potential damage to the financial system from a so-called systemic failure by taking into account the reactions of all market participants.

Economist Arthur Laffer makes the point that panicked decisions and drunken decisions invariably lead to ugly results.[6] "Seat-of-the-pants" is not a flattering description of the methods of the regulators, but its use is justified to describe the panic-driven actions during the 2000s crisis. It is only natural that

---

5. Irvine H. Sprague, *Bailout* (New York: Basic Books, 1986), 232. As of 1984, Continental, a subsidiary of Continental Illinois Corporation (CIC) since the organization of the holding company in 1969, had been in business for more than 124 years.
6. Arthur B. Laffer and Stephen Moore, *Return to Prosperity: How America Can Regain Its Economic Superpower Status* (New York: Simon and Schuster, 2009), 6.

under deadlines of time pressure judgment will be flawed, mistakes will be made, and taxpayer exposure will be magnified, and that has clearly been the case. With the possible exception of the Lehman Brothers decision, which was made over a number of months, all of the major bailout decisions during the 2000s crisis were made under duress of panic over a very short period of time with very limited information at hand and with the input of a limited number of objective parties involved in the decision-making. Not surprisingly, these seat-of-the-pants responses did not instill confidence, and there was no clear evidence collected that the expected negative fallout would truly have occurred.

During the 2000s crisis, the argument for intervention advanced by the Federal Reserve was, at its core, that although the bailouts appeared to be blatant handouts to the largest banks, the ultimate beneficiary was the average person on "Main Street." Chairman Bernanke tried to dramatize this point during an interview on the news program *60 Minutes*. The interview took place where his family maintained a store during his childhood, which it just so happens stood on Main Street: "I come from Main Street. That's my background. I've never been on Wall Street. And I care about Wall Street for one reason and one reason only, because what happens on Wall Street matters to Main Street."[7]

In that vein, Chairman Bernanke, FRBNY President Geithner, and their colleagues in the Federal Reserve System developed all manner of dubious theories to justify bailouts that were supposedly intended to benefit Main Street. As detailed throughout this book, none holds up under scrutiny, and spreading such poorly supported theories accomplishes little other than undermining the intellectual standing of the Federal Reserve. Four of these nebulous theories apparently developed by the Federal Reserve staff include the following:

- **Disorderly failure**—The argument advanced by Chairman Bernanke and then–FRBNY President Geithner that allowing Bear Stearns or AIG to go through the bankruptcy process would somehow cause all manner of chaos for the financial system and economy more broadly. Under this theory it is justified to inject massive amounts of public funds to cushion the losses of large investors because to do otherwise would lead to disorder for everyone else.

---

7. *60 Minutes*, "Ben Bernanke's Greatest Challenge," June 7, 2009, http://www.cbsnews.com/stories/2009/03/12/60minutes/main4862191_page4.shtml.

- **Unexpected losses**—The argument advanced by the Federal Reserve that allowing institutions to fail would somehow surprise large investors to such an extent that it would undermine confidence in the financial system and the economy more broadly.[8]

- **Outsized losses**—Presumably similar to the concept of unexpected losses, the idea that if losses are beyond those that are considered normal, within one asset category or overall, they need to be covered by the government and that action would reduce broader investor uncertainty.[9]

- **Knock-on effects**—Federal Reserve Vice Chairman Kohn's strained description of the ill-defined cascading effect of what would happen if AIG counterparties were not fully repaid and the necessity to bail out these big investment banks because somehow somewhere down the line of investors there would be knock on effects that would hurt the little-guy investor.[10]

---

8. GAO SRE Report, 17 ("The Federal Reserve reasoned, among other things, that the failures and least-cost resolutions of a number of institutions could impose **unexpected losses** on investors and further undermine confidence in the banking system, which already was under extreme stress"). The concept of unexpected losses is defined as the amount of losses associated with some extreme percentile in the probability distribution. See Office of the Comptroller of the Currency, Board of Governors of the Federal Reserve System, Federal Deposit Insurance System, Office of Thrift Supervision, "Proposed Treatment of Expected and Unexpected Losses Under the New Basel Capital Accord," October 30, 2003.

9. Board of Governors of the Federal Reserve, Monetary Policy Report, February 24, 2009 ("As part of the agreement, the Treasury and Federal Deposit Insurance Corporation (FDIC) are providing capital protection against *outsized losses* on a pool of $306 billion in residential and commercial real estate and other assets"). GAO SRE Report, 26 ("Treasury, FDIC, and the Federal Reserve determined that FDIC assistance under the systemic risk exception, which would complement other U.S. federal assistance and TARP programs, would promote confidence in Citigroup. Specifically, they determined that if the systemic risk exception were invoked, FDIC could provide guarantees that would help protect Citigroup from *outsized losses* on certain assets and thus reduce investor uncertainty regarding the potential for additional losses to weaken Citigroup.").

10. Kohn Testimony is available at C-Span, "Government Intervention and Regulation of AIG," Senate Committee on Banking, Housing, and Urban Affairs, March 5, 2009, and the exchange between Senator Warner and Vice Chairman Kohn is from the 104:40 mark to 115:00, total run time 2:23:18 [hereinafter Kohn Testimony]. There is also reference to the phrase "knock-on to other institutions" in an email, *McKinley v. Board of Governors,* BOG–FOIA 10–251–000612 email from Kim Jensik titled "10:30 call info" to various staff of the Board of Governors, September 15, 2008.

These ruminations are nothing more than ad hoc, seat-of-the-pants creations of the Federal Reserve officials presenting them. At a bare minimum in any serious effort to develop justifications for a bailout, two threshold criteria should be met: 1) The arguments for contagion effects should be quantitatively supported; and 2) Once the quantitative support has been provided, it must be shown that any expenditure of public funds directed toward beneficiaries has its intended impact. In presenting the theories above, the Federal Reserve has failed on both counts.

Yet these justifications have been repeated in the financial press by the three intertwined and self-supporting groups:

- Self-interested cafeteria capitalists that have a vested interest in a system of bailing out large financial institutions and their creditors.[11]
- Current or former regulators that desire the broadest possible range of powers to intervene.[12]
- Politicians who voted for the bailouts and receive financial support from banking and other related interests.

More recently the justification has been put forward that much of the money used for the bailouts has already been or will be paid back, and thus there will be "no loss" and therefore the bailouts were a success.[13] These arguments are not at all convincing. Looking at the full range of bailouts, this analysis completely ignores the case of Fannie Mae and Freddie Mac, which will likely have a public cost in the hundreds of billions of dollars. It also ignores the human costs of the deep economic recession, which were likely higher because of the uncertainty and panic related to the management of bailout policy. It ignores the moral

---

11. For example, see Wilbur Ross on the following: "When Wall Street Nearly Collapsed," CNNMoney, September 14, 2009, http://money.cnn.com/galleries/2009/fortune/0909/gallery.witnesses_meltdown.fortune/20.html. "An Interview with Wilbur Ross," Bloomberg interview by Carol Massar, February 14, 2009, total run time 27:00, http://www.youtube.com/watch?v=aKLarfrXNWA. "Wilbur Ross CNBC.com Exclusive Interview," CNBC interview by Martin Soong, September 14, 2008, total run time 3:41. http://www.cnbc.com/id/15840232?video=856209599.

12. Alan Blinder, "Government to the Economic Rescue," *Wall Street Journal*, June 16, 2010.

13. Chairman Ben S. Bernanke, "Federal Reserve's Exit Strategy," February 10, 2010, http://www.federalreserve.gov/newsevents/testimony/bernanke20100210a.htm.

hazard costs of distorting incentives going forward. It also ignores the economic cost of leaving poorly managed and structured financial institutions in place, rather than applying the cleansing effect of having such institutions exit from the financial system. The fact is that if any troubled financial institution, or even troubled business for that matter, were to receive a proportionately sized loan, equity injection, or guarantee along with the other support that goes along with it, they too would likely be able to pay it all back and get back on their feet. In the case of AIG, the level of commitment to making sure the company did not file bankruptcy was extraordinary. Beyond the direct funding that was provided, all players in the market knew that the Federal Reserve was so thoroughly invested in its efforts regarding AIG that any necessary backstopping that was needed for a decade-long period would be provided. This is evidenced by the multiple restructurings after the initial transaction that was pulled together in September 2008.

The real question is whether the government should draw on its vast resources to give proportionate support to all individual financial institutions or businesses, the classic case of picking winner and losers. The fact that the vast majority of resources in the most recent crisis went to large financial institutions merely highlights the political power wielded by these institutions. The proper approach is to allow any losses to cascade through the system and right those imbalances that led to the crisis in the first place, regardless of the short-term consequences. At bottom these bailouts were just a roll of the dice. There was always the possibility that they would turn out relatively well in the short run, but they also may not have worked out as well as has been the case in many other countries around the world. The recent example of bank bailouts in Ireland that brought the country to near fiscal collapse is the most obvious case.[14]

## Financial Crises Require Governments

Notwithstanding the statements of Chairman Bernanke, President Geithner, and other Federal Reserve officials to the contrary, there is really no clear evidence that the actions taken improved the standing of Main Street, despite

---

14. "Irish Debt Crisis Timeline," *Telegraph*, November 22, 2010, http://www.telegraph.co.uk/finance/financetopics/financialcrisis/8133611/Irish-debt-crisis-timeline.html.

Chairman Bernanke's public relations offensive to make this point and the related argument that a Second Great Depression was avoided by their efforts.[15] Arguing that the United States avoided a depression is the classic case of misdirection. Under the Federal Reserve Act:

> The Board of Governors of the Federal Reserve System and the Federal Open Market Committee shall maintain long run growth of the monetary and credit aggregates commensurate with the economy's long run potential to increase production, so as to promote effectively the goals of maximum employment, stable prices, and moderate long-term interest rates.[16]

Talk of avoiding a depression merely changes the subject. Rather than discuss how the Board of Governors and the Federal Open Market Committee clearly failed in their stated objective in the Federal Reserve Act to promote effectively the goal of maximum employment, Chairman Bernanke and his colleagues manage to lower the bar regarding their legislative objective and effectively rewrite that objective to focus on avoiding a depression. The jury is still out on the achievement of stable prices and moderate long-term interest rates.

Although his knowledge of the history of financial crises is not comparable to that of Chairman Bernanke, Geithner has also focused on the historical context of financial crises and the response of injecting government funds into financial institutions. In his comments during the crisis he comes across as the sage historian imparting his knowledge on what we have supposedly learned from the long history of financial crises:

> There is a basic lesson on financial crises that governments tend to wait too long, underestimate the risks, want to do too little. And it ultimately gets away from them, and they end up spending more money, causing much more damage to the economy. What happened was that the Fed

---

15. Sudeep Reddy, "Bernanke Feared a Second Great Depression," *Wall Street Journal*, July 27, 2009, http://www.pbs.org/newshour/updates/business/july-dec09/bernanke_07–26.html ("I was not going to be the Federal Reserve chairman who presided over the second Great Depression. It wasn't to help the big firms that we intervened. When the elephant falls down, all the grass gets crushed as well.").

16. Federal Reserve Act, Section 2a.

had broader authority than the government did. But this was not going to get solved by liquidity. Financial crises require governments. The tragic mistake was to not get authority earlier, not to ask.[17]

However, the way he has presented the facts to justify bailouts is a complete distortion of the history. The first two sentences do fit into the history. Although he does not cite any supporting historical examples, an example of this phenomenon is the savings and loan crisis during the 1980s. In that case, Congress and the financial agencies delayed action on closing down financial institutions and practiced various forms of forbearance. Institutions were allowed to continue operating, taking on further risk and causing additional losses for the government under deposit insurance exposure. It ultimately made the cost of resolving savings and loans balloon over what it otherwise would have been if the institutions were promptly closed. But Secretary Geithner uses this argument not to justify promptly closing down institutions, as the context would imply, but rather to justify bailing out institutions and making creditors whole. More than any of the major players in the bailouts, he had what has accurately been portrayed as a "proclivity for interventions and rescues."[18]

The remainder of the quote is also telling, especially the direct reference to "[f]inancial crises require governments." Based on the context in this case, Geithner appears to have meant that government action is essential as a response to financial crises, but again he does not make clear at all why government action bailing out financial institutions is the preferable approach over simply closing them down. Based on the history of crises, a meaning differing from Geithner's intention is actually closer to the mark. It is clear that financial crises require governments in the sense that it is government that is responsible for bringing on the crisis. In the 1930s, it was government that was negligent in its management of monetary policy. In the 1980s, it was again mismanagement of monetary policy during an earlier period that led to much of the turbulence. In the 2000s, it was the broad push to homeownership through government policy that led to a bubble in prices facilitated by accommodative monetary policy, and the circumstances were exacerbated by regulatory breakdowns. So based

---

17. Nina Easton, "Inside Obama's Economic Crusade," *Fortune*, February 13, 2009, http://money.cnn.com/2009/02/13/news/economy/easton_economicteam.fortune/index.htm.
18. *In Fed We Trust*, 171.

on the historical evidence, it can be more clearly articulated that it is government that is at the core of the initiation and worsening of financial crises and should only be at the core of the response to the extent of taking swift action to shut down failing financial institutions.

## What Will the Next Crisis Look Like?

Now that the crisis has abated, Congress and the financial agencies talk tough about how future crises should be handled, but they chose not to be so tough when they had a chance during 2008 and early 2009.[19] The Dodd-Frank legislation has not changed the historical trajectory of bailouts. The only certainty about the next crisis is that it will not play out precisely like the previous one, but without a change in trajectory it will likely have many of the same elements as previous crises.

When the next financial crisis brings its usual blend of tightening credit, bank failures, and a significant decline in economic activity, whether it will be brought on by the worsening U.S. fiscal difficulties or some other cause, the general circumstances surrounding it are fairly predictable if the historical pattern is followed:

- Government policy will lead to mal-investment and distortions in the investment decisions of financial institutions;
- Financial institutions that are bigger and more complex than in the 2000s crisis will take on high levels of risk and will fund that risk with volatile sources of funding that are sensitive to financial institution stress;
- The faces will change at the regulatory agencies, but there will be a breakdown at one or more of those financial agencies that will reveal how ill-equipped the agencies are to keep up with financial institution activities;

---

19. A classic case of this is reflected in the remarks of Chairman Sheila C. Bair of the FDIC, who after the bailouts ended stated that "open bank assistance should be prohibited." Yet she chose again and again to lead the FDIC in approving such OBA during 2008 and early 2009. Ronald D. Orol, "Open Bank Assistance Should Be Prohibited, Bair Says," *Market Watch*, September 18, 2009.

- The agencies will step forward and note that they have the situation under control, the problems are manageable, and the likelihood of failures are overstated;
- A singular event will occur that makes clear the seriousness of the circumstances;
- After that event, panic will set in at the regulatory agencies, and the pendulum will swing back in the opposite direction; dark scenarios detailing the great harm that will be done to the financial system and the economy more broadly will be told;
- These scare tactics of regulators will be used to justify heavy-handed intervention by regulators who will possess a "not on my watch" approach to failures;
- When asked to provide details of what adverse consequences would flow from allowing the large institutions to fail, the agencies will recoil and withhold the details, arguing that to reveal such information would result in further damage to an already fragile system; and
- These interventions will heighten the uncertainty in the market and cause a cycle of panic, leading businesses and consumers to respond by pulling back on economic activity, bringing on the problems that the interventions were intended to avoid.

The only way to eclipse this impending scenario is if policymakers at the time are familiar with the history of ever-expanding and panic-driven bailouts and are willing to resist the temptation to take such a very shortsighted approach and ultimately avoid the long-term destructive choice of bailouts. During the next crisis, leaders of the key regulatory agencies and Congress must forgo the reflexive "not on my watch" approach driven by the need to "do something" by using public funds in a pointless attempt to make the short-term circumstances less volatile. The best approach is to simply shutter the failing institution or institutions in question, no matter how large or complex.

# The Freedom of Information Act Lawsuits

"A popular Government without popular information or the means of acquiring it is but a Prologue to a Farce or a Tragedy or perhaps both. Knowledge will forever govern ignorance, and a people who mean to be their own Governors, must arm themselves with the power knowledge gives."      —James Madison[1]

"Systemic Risk"
    —Heading from an FDIC memorandum detailing the systemic risk that would occur absent an intervention to prevent the pending failure of Wachovia Bank. The section ran for 2.5 pages, but every single word of the section was redacted when first released by the FDIC.[2]

## Background

**THE FREEDOM OF INFORMATION ACT** (FOIA)[3] was intended to blunt efforts by the government to conceal documents. FOIA was approved in 1966 out of concerns about a growing federal bureaucracy that was not accountable to the electorate and about the mushrooming growth of

---

1. Letter to W.T. Barry, August 4, 1822, in G.P. Hunt, ed., *IX The Writings of James Madison* edited by Gaillard Hunt (1910), 103.
2. Memorandum to the Board of Directors (Redacted), Wachovia Bank, September 29, 2008. See the full memo, before and after redactions, at the end of the Appendix.
3. Public Law 89–554.

government secrecy. During hearings on the proposed FOIA, Senator Edward Long emphasized that "free people are, of necessity, informed; uninformed people can never be free."[4] Alternatively, no less a critic than Supreme Court Justice Antonin Scalia, in his days before he took a seat on the high court, criticized the reality of FOIA:

> The act and its amendments were promoted as a means of finding out about the operations of government; they have been used largely as a means of obtaining data in the government's hands concerning private institutions. They were promoted as a boon to the press, the public interest group, the little guy; they have been used most frequently by corporate lawyers. They were promoted as a minimal imposition on the operations of government; they have greatly burdened investigative agencies and the courts. . . . In short, it is a far cry from John Q. Public finding out how his government works.[5]

One of the first acts of the Obama Administration in January 2009 was to issue a memorandum and guidelines on FOIA. The memorandum came down clearly on the side of openness, noting that FOIA "should be administered with a clear presumption: In the face of doubt, openness prevails. The Government should not keep information confidential merely because public officials might be embarrassed by disclosure, because errors and failures might be revealed, or because of speculative or abstract fears."[6] However, the follow-through by the Obama Administration has not lived up to this high-minded rhetoric. In fact

---

4. Charles J. Wichmann, III, "Ridding FOIA of Those 'Unanticipated Consequences:' Repaving a Necessary Road to Freedom," *Duke Law Journal* 47, no. 6 (April 1998): 1213, 1217–218.

5. Antonin Scalia, "The Freedom of Information Act Has No Clothes," *Regulation* (March/April 1982): 16.

6. The White House—President Barack Obama, "Memorandum for the Heads of Executive Departments and Agencies—Freedom of Information Act," January 21, 2009, http://www.whitehouse.gov/the_press_office/FreedomofInformationAct/. US Department of Justice—Office of Information Policy, "President Obama's FOIA Memorandum and Attorney General Holder's Guidelines—Creating a New Era of Open Government," January 21, 2009.

**Table App.1.** Most Common FOIA Exemptions Relevant to Bailouts

| Exemption | Justification |
| --- | --- |
| 5 U.S.C. § 552(b)(4) (Exemption 4) | Trade secrets and commercial or financial information obtained from a person and privileged or confidential; |
| 5 U.S.C. § 552(b)(5) (Exemption 5) | Inter-agency or intra-agency memorandums or letters which would not be available by law to a party other than an agency in litigation with the agency; and |
| 5 U.S.C. § 552(b)(8) (Exemption 8) | Contained in or related to examination, operating, or condition reports prepared by, on behalf of, or for the use of an agency responsible for the regulation or supervision of financial institutions. |

in many of the cases discussed throughout this appendix, the Obama Department of Justice has supported agencies such as the Board of Governors of the Federal Reserve (hereinafter, Board) in order to keep documents shielded from public scrutiny whose release would not cause harm.

## The Intersection of FOIA and Bailouts

FOIA requires complete disclosure of requested government agency information unless the information falls into one of nine delineated exemptions. In light of FOIA's goal of promoting full agency disclosure, the exemptions are construed narrowly.[7] The strong presumption in favor of disclosure places the burden on the agency to justify the withholding of any requested documents.[8] With regard to bailouts of financial institutions, the most relevant exemptions and those that have historically been invoked to shield information on bailed-out financial institutions are detailed in Table App.1.

Additionally, a parallel statute, the Government in the Sunshine Act (GISA), may be implicated as part of an FOIA request. This act, which promotes open-

---

7. *United States Dep't of Justice v. Tax Analysts*, 492 U.S. 136, 151 (1989).
8. *United States Dep't of State v. Ray*, 502 U.S. 164, 173 (1991).

**Table App.2.** Additional GISA Exemptions Relevant to Bailouts

| Exemption | Justification |
| --- | --- |
| 5 U.S.C. § 552b(c)(9)(A)(ii) (Exemption 9A(ii)) | In the case of any agency which regulates currencies, securities, commodities, or financial institutions, be likely to significantly endanger the stability of any financial institution; and |
| 5 U.S.C. § 552(b)(9)(B) (Exemption 9B) | In the case of any agency, be likely to significantly frustrate implementation of a proposed agency action. |

ness of government action, is applicable when documents requested under FOIA include minutes for board meetings and related documents that are subject to GISA limitations. A number of these exemptions are identical (exemptions 4, 8) with those codified in FOIA, but there are additional exemptions independent of FOIA as detailed in Table App.2.

The theme of fearmongering by regulatory agencies and the Treasury Department has been duly noted throughout this volume as a key element of the 2000s crisis. This took a number of forms including the arguments set forth that can be summarized as follows: If we don't bail out Bear Stearns (or AIG, Wachovia, or Citigroup, or if you don't pass TARP), then all manner of negative consequences will flow from that decision.

However, this fearmongering was taken one step further to argue that the involved agencies should not even have to disclose the underlying documents key to the decisions made during the crisis. One of the justifications for this was that the release of the information would lead to even more financial instability. The argument was also made that the agencies needed to protect the sanctity of their deliberative process to encourage a full and open internal discussion of the issues going forward. Finally, arguments were made that select financial data should be preserved as confidential. However, documents related to the bailouts, including meeting minutes, memos, emails, and spreadsheets, have been released steadily over the past two years without any noted impact on financial institutions or the agency processes.

Another example of the efforts to avoid disclosure of the events of the 2000s crisis is that communications and strategy sessions within the Board and the FRBNY utilized a loophole in the structure of the GISA in order to avoid public scrutiny. Under the GISA, every portion of every "meeting" of an agency must be open to public observation with narrow exceptions.[9] The term "meeting" means the deliberations of at least the number of individual agency members required to take action on behalf of the agency.[10] For the Board, that number of members translated to four governors, so the solution to avoid scrutiny was to hold meetings with only three of the four governors. In the case of unusual and exigent lending under Section 13(3), the requirement was even greater as five members were required to make a decision.[11] So the most direct means to avoid public scrutiny was to have a meeting of three board members, which avoided triggering the open meeting requirements of the GISA. This was done by having a core group of three of the governors (Bernanke, Kohn, and Warsh) to discuss issues regarding options for addressing troubled financial institutions. Additionally, then–FRBNY President Geithner was also involved in these discussions, as he was not a governor and thus his presence did not trigger the open meeting requirements.[12] The decisions were then ultimately rubber-stamped by the Board at a subsequent meeting.[13]

## *Bloomberg LP v.*
## *Board of Governors of the Federal Reserve System*[14]

> **Relevant FOIA sections:** exemptions 4 and 5

---

9. 5 USC 552b(b).

10. 5 USC 552b(a).

11. 12 USC 343(3).

12. *In Fed We Trust*, 107.

13. For a good summary of the Federal Reserve System, see *McKinley v. Board of Governors*, Paul Orfanedes Attorney for Plaintiff, Plaintiff's Memorandum of Law in Opposition to Defendant Board of Governors' Motion for Summary Judgment and In Support of Plaintiff's Cross-Motion for Summary Judgment, Case 1:09-cv-01263-ESH (D. District of Columbia filed July 8, 2009), http://www.scribd.com/doc/28064418/Opposition-to-Board-of-Governors-SJ-Motion-and-Statement-of-Facts, opinion at http://docs.justia.com/cases/federal/district-courts/district-of-columbia/dcdce/1:2009cv01263/137433/41/.

14. District Court Southern District of New York: 649 F.Supp.2d 262 (2009) [hereinafter, Bloomberg District Court opinion]. United States Court of Appeals 2nd Circuit: 601

The first significant legal challenge to the secrecy demonstrated by the agencies involved in the bailouts, and the case that has gained the most attention, was initiated by Mark Pittman of Bloomberg. Pittman was a Gerald Loeb Award–winning journalist whose work focused on financial issues, and he spent a particularly large amount of his time on the sources of the financial crisis.[15] Pittman recognized the magnitude of the crisis much earlier than most journalists and policymakers, and his contemplation of the seriousness of the crisis and concerns about the government response led him in May 2008 to file a FOIA request with the Board. He later filed a FOIA suit under the name of Bloomberg against the Board in November 2008.

Pittman was focused on the "what" of the bailouts. As part of his investigation of the financial crisis, he sought records from the Board for "all securities posted between April 4, 2008 and May 20, 2008 as collateral to the Primary Dealer Credit Facility, the discount window, the Term Securities Lending Facility, and the Term Auction Facility." More than five months after submitting the request, Bloomberg had not received a response, so the suit was filed. Subsequently, the Board provided a small portion of the requested documents, but withheld more than 200 pages of documents citing exemptions 4 and 5 under FOIA. It also responded that documents held by the FRBNY were not subject to FOIA requests. A colleague of Pittman's, Craig Torres, also submitted a FOIA request for information regarding the bailout of Bear Stearns, and the Board denied the request on the basis of their location at the FRBNY, which is not subject to FOIA, as well as exemptions 4 and 5. When the journalists at Bloomberg were not satisfied with the response from the Board, the requests were combined into a single case in the Federal District Court in New York.[16]

---

*(footnote 14 continued)* F.3d 143 (2010) [2nd Circuit Court opinion]. At the Court of Appeals level, the Clearing House Association, LLC joined the case as an intervenor.

15. The Gerald Loeb Award is given to specialists in business, finance, and the economy.

16. *Bloomberg LP v. Board of Governors of the Federal Reserve System*, Complaint for Declaratory and Injunctive Relief, 5 (November 7, 2008). Amended and Supplemental Complaint for Declaratory and Injunctive Relief, 6, 9 (November 25, 2008), Case No. 08-cv-9595 (LAP).

Tragically Pittman died of a heart-related illness in November 2009 before his case made it through the court system.[17]

Bloomberg was successful at the District Court level as its motion for summary judgment was granted. The court determined that the Board had not conducted an adequate search because it did not search any of the records at the FRBNY that might qualify as records of the Board, and it thus improperly withheld records in response to an FOIA request.[18] The court also determined that requested reports were improperly withheld under FOIA exemptions 4 and 5, and the Board was ordered to produce the reports.

Upon appeal to the 2nd Circuit Court, the Clearing House Association LLC (Clearing House) intervened in the case as a defendant and along with the Board appealed the determination that exemption 4 did not apply. The Clearing House Association is a group of twenty large banks, and its intervention is consistent with the idea of the mutually supporting nature of the actions of the government and the largest banks during the crisis. Bloomberg was also successful in the 2nd Circuit Court as the court affirmed the ruling of the District Court with regard to exemption 4 and noted that there was no basis for the exemption the Board asked the court to read into FOIA.[19]

The next step was for the Board and the Clearing House to decide whether to appeal the 2nd Circuit Court's ruling to the Supreme Court (petition for a writ of certiorari). The Board decided not to petition, but the Clearing House filed a petition. Reportedly, the Board was told by the Obama Administration's Acting Solicitor General Neal Katyal not to appeal.[20] The Supreme Court denied the

---

17. For a summary of Pittman's life, see Bob Ivry, "Mark Pittman, Reporter Who Challenged Fed Secrecy, Dies at 52," Bloomberg.com, November 30, 2009, http://www.bloomberg.com/apps/news?pid=20601109&sid=anOj_XTh.8yo&pos=12.

18. Bloomberg District Court opinion, 24.

19. Bloomberg 2nd Circuit Court opinion, 2, 19. For a video of arguments in the case, see C-Span, "Freedom of Information Cases," January 11, 2010, total run time is 1:49:54.

20. Bob Ivry and Greg Stohr, "Fed Won't Join Bank Supreme Court Appeal on Loan Disclosures," October 26, 2010. Brent Kendall, "Fed Won't Join Banks in Discount-Window Appeal," October 27, 2010. Bob Ivry and Greg Stohr, "Obama's Solicitor General Told Fed Not to Appeal, Banks Say," October 27, 2010.

petition, which left the determination of the lower court standing. Documents were released in March 2011.[21]

### Fox News Network, LLC v. Board of Governors of the Federal Reserve System[22]

> **Relevant FOIA sections:** exemptions 4 and 5

In November 2008, Fox News Network requested similar information as Bloomberg, such as details on borrowers' names, loan amounts, and pledged collateral. Fox News was denied these requests by the Board, and upon filing with the Federal District Court in New York, was not successful, as the Board's motion for summary judgment was granted. The Court determined that the Board performed an adequate search and that exemption 4 could be used to exempt the documents from disclosure. However, Fox was successful at the 2nd Circuit Court in a companion case to Bloomberg's. The court vacated the unfavorable ruling of the District Court with regard to exemption 4 citing the Bloomberg opinion. With regard to whether the Board had adequately searched its records, the 2nd Circuit Court also remanded to the District Court in order to further search records that might be responsive to the initial request.[23] The petition for a writ of certiorari was also denied.[24]

---

21. Craig Torres, "Fed Releases Discount-Window Loan Records Under Court Order," *Bloomberg/Business Week*, March 31, 2011. Bob Ivry and Craig Torres, "Fed's Court Ordered Disclosure Shows Americans' 'Right to Know,'"*Bloomberg/Business Week*, March 22, 2011 [hereinafter, Bloomberg/ Fox disclosure story]. See Greg Stohr and Bob Ivry, "Obama Lawyers Urge Court to Reject Banks on Loans," Bloomberg.com, February 19, 2011, http:// www.bloomberg.com/news/2011–02–18/obama-lawyers-urge-court-to-reject-banks-on -loans.html. Brent Kendall, "Justice Department: High Court Shouldn't Consider Fed Disclosure Case," *Wall Street Journal*, February 18, 2011, http://online.wsj.com/article/SB 10001424052748703959604576152850851617350.html.

22. District Court Southern District of New York: 639 F.Supp.2d 384 (2009). United States Court of Appeals 2nd Circuit: 601 F.3d 158 (2010).

23. For a video of arguments in the case, see C-Span, "Freedom of Information Cases," January 11, 2010, total run time is 1:49:54.

24. Bloomberg/ Fox disclosure story. Bob Ivry and Greg Stohr, "Obama's Solicitor General Told Fed Not to Appeal, Banks Say," Bloomberg.com, October 27, 2010. Brent

**McKinley v. FDIC, Board of Governors of the Federal Reserve System (McKinley I)**[25]

**McKinley v. FDIC (McKinley II)**[26]

**McKinley v. Board of Governors of the Federal Reserve System (McKinley III)**

**McKinley v. Federal Housing Finance Agency (McKinley IV)**[27]

> **Relevant FOIA sections:** exemptions 4, 5, 8
> **Relevant GISA sections:** exemptions 4, 8, 9(A)(ii)

Focusing more on the "why" of the bailouts, the author has filed four cases in federal court, represented by the advocacy group Judicial Watch, in order to find the answer to the question: What negative fallout would there have been if the large, interconnected financial institutions in question were allowed to fail? It has been a long struggle to try to obtain the answer to that question.[28]

- *McKinley I* (July 2009): focus on the FDIC's action in approving open bank assistance for Wachovia and the Board in approving a 13(3) transaction for Bear Stearns. Documents in question included FDIC Board minutes and a related memo on deliberations on Wachovia; and emails,

---

Kendall, "Justice Department: High Court Shouldn't Consider Fed Disclosure Case," *Wall Street Journal*, February 18, 2011.

25. Case 1:09-cv-01263-ESH (D. District of Columbia filed July 8, 2009), opinion at http://docs.justia.com/cases/federal/district-courts/district-of-columbia/dcdce/1:2009cv01263/137433/41/. United States Court of Appeals for the District of Columbia Circuit, No. 10-5353, http://www.cadc.uscourts.gov/internet/opinions.nsf/AAF71C34F40B115C852578A4004DCD17/$file/10-5353-1311337.pdf.

26. Case 1:10-cv-00420-EGS (D. District of Columbia filed March 15, 2010), opinion at http://docs.justia.com/cases/federal/district-courts/district-of-columbia/dcdce/1:2010cv00420/141205/17/.

27. Case 1:10-cv-01165-HHK (D. District of Columbia filed July 12, 2010), opinion at http://docs.justia.com/cases/federal/district-courts/district-of-columbia/dcdce/1:2010cv01165/143012/15/.

28. Review and Outlook, "Who's Too Big To Fail," *Wall Street Journal*, September 13, 2009, http://online.wsj.com/article/SB10001424052970204731804574386932897872954.html.

spreadsheets, and related documents for the Board on deliberations regarding Bear Stearns. After two years of the FDIC fighting the disclosure of the Wachovia documents, a *Wall Street Journal* editorial highlighted the case and the fact that Judge Ellen Segal Huvelle required the FDIC to produce the documents for her review. The editorial demanded that the FCIC, which was in the midst of an investigation of the bailout, release the documents.[29] The FCIC released the documents the next day, and they revealed that the FDIC was pressured to approve the bailout by the Treasury Department; the documents were full of speculative and abstract fears of potential harm; and there was no specific documented evidence of the potential fallout from a Wachovia failure. Judge Huvelle dismissed the FDIC as a party and denied summary judgment on the basis of mootness, given the relevant documents were released. Redactions in the emails, spreadsheets, and related documents that were produced by the Board shielded much of the key information regarding the bailout of Bear Stearns. Judge Huvelle upheld the Board's claimed exemptions under exemptions 5 and 8 and granted the Board's summary judgment motion.[30] This ruling regarding the Board was appealed to the U.S. Court of Appeals for the D.C. Circuit and they upheld the lower court ruling in June 2011.

- *McKinley II* (March 2010): focus on the FDIC's actions in approving open bank assistance for the TLGP, Citigroup, and Bank of America transactions. Documents in question included FDIC Board minutes, a related memo on deliberations, and other requested documents on these approvals. Judge Sullivan's initial opinion criticized the FDIC for not conducting an adequate enough search and for not justifying the withholding of documents. He remanded the matter to the FDIC to address these issues.[31]

---

29. Review and Outlook, "Systemic Risk Stonewall," *Wall Street Journal*, September 1, 2010.

30. Case 1:09-cv-01263-ESH (D. District of Columbia filed July 8, 2009), opinion at http://docs.justia.com/cases/federal/district-courts/district-of-columbia/dcdce/1:2009cv01263/137433/41/.

31. *McKinley v. FDIC*, Case 1:10-cv-00420-EGS (D. District of Columbia filed March 15, 2010), opinion at http://docs.justia.com/cases/federal/district-courts/district-of-columbia/dcdce/1:2010cv00420/141205/17/.

- *McKinley III* (May 2010): focus on the Board's approval of a 13(3) transaction for AIG and consideration of giving the same assistance to Lehman Brothers. The Board in November 2010 produced thousands of pages of heavily redacted emails, spreadsheets, and related documents with no rulings to date.
- *McKinley IV* (July 2010): focus on the intervention by the FHFA in choosing the option of conservatorship over receivership in approving the intervention in the operations of Fannie Mae and Freddie Mac. The FHFA has admitted that it has three documents responsive to this request, but claims various exemptions to shield them from public scrutiny. This case is ongoing in the U.S. District Court for the District of Columbia.[32]

The earliest and most advanced of the line of cases, *McKinley I*, involved an extreme case of redactions. The case is a good example of the thin public policy basis for keeping the shielded documents secret. Out of eleven pages of a key FDIC memorandum in the case, approximately nine were redacted. The entire section on systemic risk, which was all of 2.5 pages, was redacted in its entirety, and the memorandum, before and after redactions, is set forth at the end of this Appendix. In comparing the two versions of the memo it is difficult to see why the FDIC felt the need to fight disclosure. Among other things, the FDIC argued that the information if disclosed would "endanger the stability of financial institutions," but the ultimate release of the documents in September 2010 had no such adverse impact on any financial institutions nor is there evidence that it ever would have had such an adverse impact.

## Other Cases

A number of other FOIA-related cases have also been initiated, and these are at various stages of development, including many that have been dismissed:

---

32. *McKinley v. FHFA*, Case 1:10-cv-01165-HHK (D. District of Columbia filed July 12, 2010), opinion at http://docs.justia.com/cases/federal/district-courts/district-of-columbia /dcdce/1:2010cv01165/143012/15/.

- *The New York Times Company v. Board of Governors* (April 2009)—
  dismissed in November 2009.
- *Judicial Watch v. U.S. Department of the Treasury* (five cases beginning January 2009)—cases on a wide range of issues from the TARP
  program and related meetings, to correspondence between Treasury and
  Congressman Barney Frank, to the bailout of Fannie Mae and Freddie
  Mac, to meetings of the Obama Administration's pay czar with AIG.
- *Judicial Watch v. Federal Housing Finance Agency* (August 2009)—
  access to Fannie Mae and Freddie Mac documents regarding political
  contributions.
- *Judicial Watch v. Board of Governors of the Federal Reserve* (November 2009)—access to visitor logs for meetings with Chairman Bernanke
  and Governor Walsh.[33]
- *Freedom Watch Inc. v. Board of Governors* (February 2009)—
  court granted Board's summary judgment motion in August 2009.
- *Citizens for Responsibility and Ethics in Washington v. Board of Governors* (April 2009)—requested information similar to Bloomberg and
  Fox cases. Dismissed in November 2009 and refiled by the plaintiff that
  same month.[34]
- *Gold Anti-Trust Action Committee v. Board of Governors* (December
  2009)—focus on market interventions in gold swap transactions.[35]

## Why the Lack of Transparency?

By all appearances, the agencies that are resisting disclosure are at the same
time resisting a robust debate regarding the justification for their interventions.

---

33. For all financial crisis–related cases by Judicial Watch, see http://www.judicialwatch
.org/financial-crisis.

34. For current status, see http://www.citizensforethics.org/node/43313.

35. For an update as of February 2011 on this case please see http://gata.org/node/9559.
This lawsuit includes requests on a range of interventions over many years including during the 2000s financial crisis.

An important point is that although they can invoke a range of exemptions, nothing stops them from full disclosure. The agencies' unwillingness to disclose the documents and to publicly articulate the reasons for the interventions seems to indicate the weakness of the underlying arguments for the interventions.

Apparently in reaction to the secrecy of the agencies, the Dodd-Frank legislation contained clear mandates to disclose information withheld by the agencies. The act requires the GAO to conduct an audit by mid-2011 of all the loans and other financial assistance provided by the Federal Reserve and compelled the Federal Reserve to disclose by December 1, 2010, a variety of information regarding financial assistance it has provided.[36]

---

36. Dodd-Frank, Section 1109 (" . . . a one-time audit of all loans and other financial assistance provided during the period beginning on December 1, 2007 and ending on the date of enactment of this Act by the Board of Governors or a Federal reserve bank under the Asset-Backed Commercial Paper Money Market Mutual Fund Liquidity Facility, the Term Asset-Backed Securities Loan Facility, the Primary Dealer Credit Facility, the Commercial Paper Funding Facility, the Term Securities Lending Facility, the Term Auction Facility, Maiden Lane, Maiden Lane II, Maiden Lane III, the agency Mortgage-Backed Securities program, foreign currency liquidity swap lines, and any other program created as a result of section 13(3) of the Federal Reserve Act (as so designated by this title) . . . the Board of Governors shall publish on its website, not later than December 1, 2010, with respect to all loans and other financial assistance provided during the period beginning on December 1, 2007 and ending on the date of enactment of this Act under the Asset-Backed Commercial Paper Money Market Mutual Fund Liquidity Facility, the Term Asset-Backed Securities Loan Facility, the Primary Dealer Credit Facility, the Commercial Paper Funding Facility, the Term Securities Lending Facility, the Term Auction Facility, Maiden Lane, Maiden Lane II, Maiden Lane III, the agency Mortgage-Backed Securities program, foreign currency liquidity swap lines, and any other program created as a result of section 13(3) of the Federal Reserve Act: (1) the identity of each business, individual, entity, or foreign central bank to which the Board of Governors or a Federal reserve bank has provided such assistance; (2) the type of financial assistance provided to that business, individual, entity, or foreign central bank; (3) the value or amount of that financial assistance; (4) the date on which the financial assistance was provided; (5) the specific terms of any repayment expected, including the repayment time period, interest charges, collateral, limitations on executive compensation or dividends, and other material terms; and (6) the specific rationale for each such facility or program.").

MATERIAL REDACTED                    September 29, 2008

MEMORANDUM:    The Board of Directors

THROUGH:       Mitchell L. Glassman, Director *Mitchell L. Glassman*
               Division of Resolutions and Receiverships

               Sandra L. Thompson, Director *Thompson*
               Division of Supervision and Consumer Protection

FROM:          James R. Wigand, Deputy Director *RW*
               Franchise and Asset Marketing Branch
               Division of Resolutions and Receiverships

               Herbert J. Held, Assistant Director *J Held*
               Franchise and Asset Marketing Branch
               Division of Resolutions and Receiverships

SUBJECT:       Wachovia Bank, National Association, Charlotte, North Carolina
               Wachovia Mortgage, FSB, North Las Vegas, Nevada
               Wachovia Bank, FSB, Houston, Texas
               Wachovia Bank of Delaware, National Association, Wilmington, DE
               Wachovia Card Services, National Association, Atlanta, Georgia


               Wachovia Corporation (Bank Holding Company) Information
               (As of June 30, 2008):
               Total Assets:    $781,883,478,000
               Total Deposits (including Foreign): $475,172,374,000
               Uninsured Deposits:  $157,100,000,000
               Foreign Deposits: $53,170,000,000
               Tier 1 Leverage/Total Risk Based (Lead Bank): 6.27%/11.58%


Recommendation

65

Executive Summary

Wachovia Bank, NA (Bank) is a nationally chartered bank founded in 1879 that is wholly owned by Wachovia Corporation, a financial holding company regulated by the Federal Reserve. The Bank is the fourth largest bank in the country and the predominant legal entity within Wachovia Corporation, representing 83 percent of consolidated holding company assets. The insured legal entities of Wachovia Corporation consist of three national banks and two Federal savings banks. Other significant holding company subsidiaries include Wachovia Capital Markets, LLC, and Wachovia Securities, LLC. The Bank operates approximately 3,400 banking centers in 21 states, primarily along the eastern and gulf coasts and in California, and engages in foreign activities.

65, 8

2

b 5,8

er

MATERIAL REDACTED

Based on the analysis of Citigroup's proposal, staff recommends accepting the Citigroup, Inc. bid to resolve the five insured depository institutions and to resolve the systemic risk posed by a possible failure of Wachovia Corporation and its affiliate banks and thrifts.

Supervisory History and Condition

3

b4
b5

b8

`t

*Supervisory History*

The insured legal entities of Wachovia Corporation are shown in the table below.

**Wachovia Bank, NA**

5

MATERIAL REDACTED

b5, 8

MATERIAL REDACTED

The Bank's former chief executive officer, Ken Thompson, was removed on June 2, 2008, and Robert Steel was selected as his replacement on July 9, 2008. The Bank's chief financial officer and chief risk officer were also subsequently replaced.

**Wachovia Mortgage FSB and Wachovia Bank FSB**

b5, 8

**Wachovia Bank of Delaware NA and Wachovia Card Services**

Wachovia Bank of Delaware NA represents a more traditional institution with no pay-option ARM exposure. Likewise, Wachovia Card Services is a recently formed credit card lending operation.

<u>Marketing</u>

7

On September 28, 2008, FDIC staff began discussions with Citigroup and Wells Fargo, both of which submitted bids to the FDIC on the same day. Both bids sought open bank assistance from the FDIC.

b5, 8

The Citigroup bid requests that the FDIC provide loss sharing on a $312 billion pool of assets. Losses would be shared as follows: (i) the first $30.0 billion of losses in the pool, Citigroup assumes 100 percent, and (ii) Citigroup assumes $4 billion a year of losses for three years. Additionally, FDIC will receive face value of $12 billion in preferred stock and warrants.

However, based upon the terms of the Citigroup proposal, these losses would be absorbed by Citigroup and result in no loss to the Deposit Insurance Fund.

Systemic Risk

65

9

b5

b5

*Conclusion*

b5,6

**Other Information**

If you have any questions concerning this case, please call Herbert Held at extension

or Sharon Yore at extension

12

This recommendation is prepared by:

_Sharon Yore_
Sharon Yore
Franchise and Asset Marketing
DRR - Washington

This recommendation is supported by:

_____
George French
Deputy Director, DSC

_John V Thomas for_
Sara A. Kelsey
General Counsel

13

## Fully Disclosed Version of FDIC Board Memo
## (Two Years after the Meeting)

September 29, 2008

MEMORANDUM: The Board of Directors

THROUGH: Mitchell L. Glassman, Director *Mitchell L. Glassman*
Division of Resolutions and Receiverships

Sandra L. Thompson, Director
Division of Supervision and Consumer Protection

FROM: James R. Wigand, Deputy Director
Franchise and Asset Marketing Branch
Division of Resolutions and Receiverships

Herbert J. Held, Assistant Director
Franchise and Asset Marketing Branch
Division of Resolutions and Receiverships

SUBJECT: Wachovia Bank, National Association, Charlotte, North Carolina
Wachovia Mortgage, FSB, North Las Vegas, Nevada
Wachovia Bank, FSB, Houston, Texas
Wachovia Bank of Delaware, National Association, Wilmington, DE
Wachovia Card Services, National Association, Atlanta, Georgia

Wachovia Corporation (Bank Holding Company) Information
(As of June 30, 2008):
Total Assets:     $781,883,478,000
Total Deposits (including Foreign): $475,172,374,000
Uninsured Deposits:   $157,100,000,000
Foreign Deposits: $53,170,000,000
Tier 1 Leverage/Total Risk Based (Lead Bank): 6.27%/11.58%

UFIR Rating (Lead Bank): 3-3-3-4-5-2/3 (9/28/08 Interim Downgrade)

Recommendation

Staff recommends that the Board find that the failure of Wachovia Corporation and its

affiliate banks and thrifts would have serious adverse effects on economic conditions and financial

stability. Its failure would seriously and negatively affect already disrupted credit markets, including short-term interbank lending, counterparty relationships in Qualified Financial Contract markets, and bank senior and subordinated debt markets, and would further disrupt the related markets in derivative products and other markets. Staff recommends that the Board accept the bid of Citigroup, Inc., as the least costly available method of dealing with this systemic risk, and that the Board authorize staff to take all steps needed to implement this decision. Based on preliminary information, staff estimates no loss to the Deposit Insurance Fund.

Executive Summary

Wachovia Bank, NA (Bank) is a nationally chartered bank founded in 1879 that is wholly owned by Wachovia Corporation, a financial holding company regulated by the Federal Reserve. The Bank is the fourth largest bank in the country and the predominant legal entity within Wachovia Corporation, representing 83 percent of consolidated holding company assets. The insured legal entities of Wachovia Corporation consist of three national banks and two Federal savings banks. Other significant holding company subsidiaries include Wachovia Capital Markets, LLC, and Wachovia Securities, LLC. The Bank operates approximately 3,400 banking centers in 21 states, primarily along the eastern and gulf coasts and in California, and engages in foreign activities. The risk profile of the Bank is declining rapidly because of deteriorating liquidity and poor quality assets. Liquidity has reached crisis proportions, such that the Bank is unable to meet its obligations. Most recently, on Friday, September 26, 2008, the Bank was unable to roll $1.1 billion of its asset backed commercial paper. More short term obligations are due this week that the Bank will likely be unable to pay and there are an estimated $157.1 billion in uninsured deposits.

The company's rapidly deteriorating financial condition is due largely to its portfolio of pay-option ARM products, commercial real estate portfolio, and weakened liquidity position. On Friday September 26, 2008, market acceptance of Wachovia liabilities ceased as the company's stock plunged, credit default swap spreads widened in excess of 1,400 points (to over 2,000 points), some parties declined to advance the Bank overnight funds, and counterparties advised that they would require greater collateralization on any transactions with the Bank.

Citigroup, Inc., and Wells Fargo performed due diligence in an attempt to acquire the Banks in a private transaction; however, neither were able to reach definitive agreements. The FDIC entered into negotiations with Citigroup and Wells Fargo on September 28, 2008. Both Banks submitted open bank assistance bids to the FDIC on September 28, 2008; however, only the Citigroup proposal resulted in serious negotiations.

Based on the analysis of Citigroup's proposal, staff recommends accepting the Citigroup, Inc. bid to resolve the five insured depository institutions and to resolve the systemic risk posed by a possible failure of Wachovia Corporation and its affiliate banks and thrifts.

<u>Supervisory History and Condition</u>

*Condition*

Unless the Bank immediately attracts a merger partner, the FDIC and other regulators project that the Bank will likely be unable to pay obligations or meet expected deposit outflows.

3

The FDIC and the OCC anticipate a number of funding outflows during the week beginning September 29, 2008. Near-term funding outflows include:

- Maturing asset-backed commercial paper, which is not expected to be placed with external parties and, therefore, will need to be funded by the Bank;

- Maturing repurchase agreements, which are not expected to be placed with external parties and, therefore, will need to be funded by the Bank;

- Maturing Variable Rate Demand Notes supported by liquidity facilities/letters of credit issued by the Bank which are not expected to be placed and will be put to the Bank;

- The loss of overnight sweep deposit representing large commercial deposits;

- The loss of a substantial portion of money swept from retail brokerage accounts maintained with affiliated entities; and

- An assumed 1.5 percent daily deposit run-off, which is based on recent experience by other large insured institutions experiencing extreme stress.

| Wachovia Bank, N.A. Liquidity Analysis | 9/26/08 |
|---|---|
| ($BN) | |
| Overnight FFS | 8.0 |
| Federal Reserve | 2.6 |
| T-Bills & Term CP | 10.0 |
| Less: Overnight FFP | -3.5 |
| **Cash Equivalents** | **17.1** |
| Discount Window (Post Haircut) | 52.0 |
| Unpledged Securities (Pre-Haircut) | 29.0 |
| FHLB | 5.0 |
| **Available Sources** | **86.0** |
| **Total Cash Equivalents & Sources** | **103.1** |

| FDIC Stress Scenario ($BN) | 10/7/08 |
|---|---|
| **Total Cash Equivalents & Sources** | **103.1** |
| **Less: Actual Maturity & Stress** | |
| 1. 1.5% Daily Deposit Outflow | -42.0 |
| 2. Corporate Sweeps 100% outflow | -12.0 |
| 3. Retail Brokerage Outflow | -30.0 |
| 4. VRDN Maturity & Stress | -15.8 |
| 5. Maturing Debt | -9.7 |
| 6. ABCP (VFCC) Maturity | -3.3 |
| 7. Maturing Repo Agreements | -2.7 |
| | -12.4 |

4

Potentially available funding sources considered in the above analysis include $17 billion in liquid assets, $52 billion of "after-haircut" borrowing capacity based on collateral already posted with the Federal Reserve, $29 billion in unencumbered securities, and $5 billion of available funding from the Federal Home Loan Bank. Additional eligible collateral for pledging totals $117 billion and is comprised of $97 billion in commercial loans and $20 billion in consumer loans that are not pay option ARMs.

Uninsured deposits are reported at $157.1 billion as of June 30, 2008, with $76 billion comprised of corporate, non-time deposits that are considered highly sensitive. This could result in deposit outflows greater than the 1.5 percent daily withdrawals included in the FDIC stress scenario depicted above.

*Supervisory History*

The insured legal entities of Wachovia Corporation are shown in the table below.

| Entities (6/30/08) | Assets | Deposits | CAMELS | Exam Date |
|---|---|---|---|---|
| Wachovia Bank, N.A. | 670,639 | 450,929 | 2-3-3-3-2-2/3 [a] | 6/30/08 |
| Wachovia Mortgage, FSB | 76,795 | 18,009 | 3-3-2-4-2-1/3 | 4/30/08 Offsite |
| Wachovia Bank, FSB | 27,992 | 2,809 | 3-3-2-4-2-1/3 | 4/30/08 Offsite |
| Wachovia Card Services, N.A. | 2,224 | 0 | 2-2-2-2-2-2/2 | 6/30/08 |
| Wachovia Bank of Delaware, N.A. | 4,814 | 4,175 | 2-2-2-2-2-2/2 | 6/30/08 |

(a) 9/28/08 - OCC downgraded Capital to a 3, Earnings to a 4, and Liquidity to a 5

**Wachovia Bank, NA**

The Bank is subject to a continuous examination program by the Office of the Comptroller of the Currency (OCC). The June 30, 2008, OCC examination of the Bank resulted in a composite rating downgrade to a "3." The following table displays the Bank's historical examination and financial data:

5

| Wachovia Bank, N.A. | 6/30/08 OCC | 6/30/07 OCC | 6/30/06 OCC | 6/30/05 OCC |
|---|---|---|---|---|
| UFIR | 2-3-3-3-2-2/3 (a) | 2-2-2-2-1-2/2 | 2-2-2-2-1-2/2 | 2-2-2-2-1-2/2 |
| Classifications/T1+ALLL | 33% | 9% | 10% | 13% |
| Enforcement Action | MOU | None | None | None |
| Financial Data | 6/30/2008 | 12/31/2007 | 12/31/2006 | 12/31/2005 |
| Total Assets | $670,639,000 | $653,269,000 | $518,123,000 | $472,143,000 |
| Total Loans | $413,994,000 | $413,349,000 | $302,764,000 | $262,173,000 |
| Total Deposits | $450,929,000 | $458,186,000 | $353,234,000 | $33,780,000 |
| Tier 1 Leverage Ratio | 6.27% | 6.71% | 6.66% | 6.26% |
| Total Risk Based Capital Ratio | 11.58% | 11.45% | 10.90% | 10.70% |
| Option ARM's/Tier 1+ALLL | 138% | 146% | 0% | 0% |
| Brokered Deposits to Total Deposits | 10.98% | 8.97% | 10.20% | 11.48% |

(a) 9/28/08 - OCC downgraded Capital to a 3, Earnings to a 4, and Liquidity to a 5

The Bank operates under a Memorandum of Understanding issued in August 2008 that addresses weaknesses cited in the most recent OCC report of examination.

On October 12, 2007, the Bank acquired from Wachovia Mortgage FSB and Wachovia Bank FSB (formerly World Savings Bank FSB and World Savings Bank Texas FSB, respectively) all of those institutions' retail deposits totaling $76 billion. The Bank also acquired almost $90 billion dollars in assets, including approximately $65 billion in pay-option ARM mortgage loans. The pay-option ARM portfolio is concentrated in the California and Florida markets, which represent approximately 60 percent and 10 percent of the total portfolio, respectively. Since the loans were transferred, significant declines in home prices, combined with the effects of previously lax collateral-based underwriting by the World Savings Bank entities, led to serious deterioration in the pay-option ARM portfolio; rising nonperforming loan levels and the need for considerable provisions to the allowance for loan and lease losses resulted in quarterly losses. During the week of September 22, 2008, the Bank increased its cumulative loss estimates for the pay option ARM portfolio from 12 percent to 20 percent. The pay-option portfolio represents approximately 138 percent of capital and reserves.

6

The Bank's former chief executive officer, Ken Thompson, was removed on June 2, 2008, and Robert Steel was selected as his replacement on July 9, 2008. The Bank's chief financial officer and chief risk officer were also subsequently replaced. These actions to replace senior management failed to dispel market concerns regarding the Bank's condition.

**Wachovia Mortgage FSB and Wachovia Bank FSB**

The two thrifts retain almost $70 billion in residential mortgage exposure, which consists almost entirely of pay option ARMs sharing the same risk characteristics as the pay-option ARM portfolio in the Bank. During the first and second quarters of 2008, both thrifts required substantial capital contributions from Wachovia Corporation in order to maintain capital ratios at satisfactory levels.

**Wachovia Bank of Delaware NA and Wachovia Card Services**

Wachovia Bank of Delaware NA represents a more traditional institution with no pay-option ARM exposure. Likewise, Wachovia Card Services is a recently formed credit card lending operation.

Marketing

An electronic data room was established by the Banks for potential buyers to perform due diligence. No proposals were accepted.

7

On September 28, 2008, FDIC staff began discussions with Citigroup and Wells Fargo, both of which submitted bids to the FDIC on the same day. Both bids sought open bank assistance from the FDIC. The Wells Fargo bid requires that the FDIC cover potential losses on a pool up to $127.3 billion in assets (includes $80.7 billion funded). Wells Fargo assumes the first $2 billion in losses on the pool of assets, following which the FDIC will share in the losses at the rate of 80 percent. Wells Fargo proposed that total FDIC loss exposure be capped at $20 billion. Staff estimated this proposal would cost the FDIC between $5.6 ~~million~~ billion to $7.2 billion.

The Citigroup bid requests that the FDIC provide loss sharing on a $312 billion pool of assets. Losses would be shared as follows: (i) the first $30.0 billion of losses in the pool, Citigroup assumes 100 percent, and (ii) Citigroup assumes $4 billion a year of losses for three years. Additionally, FDIC will receive face value of $12 billion in preferred stock and warrants.

Wachovia Corporation submitted an open bank assistance proposal. Approximately $200 billion of the Bank's loans would receive FDIC credit protection, of which the Bank would provide $25 billion of first loss protection. In return, Wachovia would issue to FDIC, $10 billion of preferred stock and warrants on common shares.

Considering current market conditions, staff estimates the Citigroup transaction could result in aggregate losses ranging from approximately $35 to $52 billion. However, based upon the terms of the Citigroup proposal, these losses would be absorbed by Citigroup and result in no loss to the Deposit Insurance Fund.

All proposals submitted required some form of regulatory capital relief from their primary federal regulators.

## Systemic Risk

Given the forecasted size of the losses at Wachovia Bank NA, it appears likely that any transaction effected by the FDIC under a least-cost framework would require the FDIC to impose significant losses on the Bank's subordinated debt-holders and, possibly, senior note holders. In addition, absent invocation of the systemic risk exception available under the FDI Act, the FDIC is prohibited from using deposit insurance funds to benefit senior or secured debt-holders of a company.

However, staff believes that a least-cost resolution of Wachovia Bank NA would have significant adverse effects on economic conditions and the financial markets. Term funding markets have been under considerable stress for more than a year, and these pressures have increased greatly following the failure of Lehman Brothers, the difficulties at AIG, and the closing of Washington Mutual. LIBOR rates have increased more than 100 basis points since early September; commercial paper rates have also risen dramatically, and the volume of financial paper outstanding has declined sharply. In both of these markets, the maturity of new issues has shortened a great deal as investors have become much less willing to lend beyond overnight. Concerns about actual and potential losses on financial institutions' obligations have caused outflows from prime money market mutual funds totaling nearly $400 billion over the past two weeks. Since these funds are normally substantial purchasers of commercial paper and short-term bank obligations, these outflows have added to the pressures in those markets. More generally, investors appear to have become more concerned about the outlook of a number of U.S. banking organizations, putting downward pressure on their stock prices and upward pressure on their collateralized debt security spreads.

In this environment, a least-cost resolution of Wachovia Bank NA with no assistance to creditors and the potential for meaningful losses imposed on the Bank's debt would be expected to have significant systemic consequences. A default by Wachovia Corporation and a partial payout to debtors of Wachovia Bank NA would intensify liquidity pressures on other U.S. banks, which are extremely vulnerable to a loss of confidence by wholesale suppliers of funds. Investors would likely be concerned about direct exposures of other financial firms to Wachovia Corporation or Wachovia Bank NA. Furthermore, the failure of Wachovia Corporation would lead investors to doubt the financial strength of other institutions that might be seen as similarly situated. Wachovia's sudden failure could also lead investors to reassess the risk in U.S. commercial banks more broadly, particularly given the current fragility of financial markets generally and the term funding markets for financial institutions.

In addition, if a least-cost resolution did not support foreign depositors (who are considered non-deposit, general creditors under the FDI Act); the resolution could imperil this significant source of funding for other U.S. financial institutions. More generally, given Wachovia's international presence, global liquidity pressures could increase and confidence in the dollar could decline. Further, losses on Wachovia Corporation and Wachovia Bank NA paper could lead more money market mutual funds to "break the buck," accelerating runs on those and other money funds. The resulting liquidations of fund assets, along with the further

10

loss of confidence in financial institutions, might well lead short-term funding markets to virtually cease. Moreover, the individuals and businesses whose deposits have been swept into non-deposit investments or foreign deposits (e.g., at a Cayman branch) would find all or part of their funds unavailable and likely face losses. In the current environment, such an event could shake the public's confidence in bank deposits. All of these effects would likely cause investors to sharply raise their assessment of the risks of investing in similar (albeit smaller) regional banks, making it much less likely that those institutions would be able to raise capital and other funding.

Staff believes the consequences of a least-cost resolution could extend to the broader economy. The financial turmoil that could result from a least-cost resolution of Wachovia Bank NA and the likely consequent failure of Wachovia Corporation would further undermine business and household confidence. In addition, with the liquidity of banking organizations further reduced and their funding costs increased, banking organizations would become even less willing to lend to businesses and households. These effects would contribute to weaker economic performance, further damage financial markets, and have other material negative effects.

*Conclusion*

Staff believes that the imposition of a least-cost resolution on Wachovia would almost surely have major systemic effects. Both financial stability and overall economic conditions would likely be adversely affected for the reasons discussed above. A resolution that protects all

11

depository institution and holding company creditors would best mitigate the adverse effects of the failure on the financial markets and the broader economy.

In creating the systemic risk exception, Congress clearly envisioned that circumstances could arise in which the exception should be used. In view of the current intense financial strains, as well as the likely consequences to the general economy and financial system of a least-cost resolution of the fourth-largest commercial bank in the United States, staff believes that circumstances such as Congress envisioned are clearly present and that invocation of the systemic risk exception is justified. Staff further believes that the Citigroup proposal represents the least cost alternative available for dealing with this systemic risk.

Other Information

If you have any questions concerning this case, please call Herbert Held at extension 8-7329, or Sharon Yore at extension 8-7336.

12

This recommendation is prepared by:


_Sharon Yore_
Sharon Yore
Franchise and Asset Marketing
DRR - Washington


This recommendation is supported by:


_____
George French
Deputy Director, DSC


_John V. Thomas for_
Sara A. Kelsey
General Counsel


13

# Selected Bibliography

Adrian, Tobias, Christopher Burke, and James J. McAndrews. "The Federal Reserve's Primary Dealer Credit Facility." In *Federal Reserve Bank of New York—Current Issues in Economics and Finance* 15, no. 4 (2009): 1–11.

*Agricultural Credit Act of 1987: House of Representatives.* 100th Congress, 1st Session, August 28, 1987.

*Amendments to Federal Deposit Insurance Act: Subcommittee of the Committee on Banking and Currency*, 2nd Session, January 11, 23, and 30, 1950.

Ayotte, Kenneth A., and David A. Skeel. "Bankruptcy or Bailouts." *Journal of Corporation Law* 35 (2010): 469, 490.

Baker, James. "How Washington Can Prevent Zombie Banks." *Financial Times*, March 1, 2009.

"Banking: Out of Hock." *Time*, November 27, 1939.

Bekesha, Michael, and Paul Orfanedes. "Plaintiff's Memorandum in Opposition to Defendant Board of Governors' Motion for Summary Judgment and in Support of Plaintiff's Cross-Motion for Summary Judgment." In *McKinley v. Board of Governors* (2010). http://www.scribd.com/doc/28064418/Opposition-to-Board-of-Governors-SJ-Motion-and-Statement-of-Facts.

Bennett, Rosalind. "Failure Resolution and Asset Liquidation: Results of an International Survey of Deposit Insurers." *FDIC Banking Review* 14, no. 1 (2001): 12.

Benston, George and George G. Kaufman. "FDICIA after Five Years: A Review and Evaluation." In *Federal Reserve Bank of Chicago Working Paper 97–1* (1997): 1–42.

Bernanke, Ben S. *Economic Outlook Testimony: Before the Joint Economic Committee of the U.S. Congress*, September 24, 2008.

Blinder, Alan. "Government to the Economic Rescue." *Wall Street Journal*, June 16, 2010.

Blinder, Alan, and Mark Zandi. "How We Ended the Great Recession." Published electronically July 27, 2010. http://www.economy.com/mark-zandi/documents/End-of-Great-Recession.pdf.

Bradley, Christine M. "A Historical Perspective on Deposit Insurance Coverage." *FDIC Banking Review* 13, no. 2 (2000): 16.

Brady, Nicholas F., Eugene A. Ludwig, and Paul A. Volcker. "Resurrect the Resolution Trust Corporation." *Wall Street Journal*, September 17, 2008.

Brinkmann, Emile J., Paul M. Horvitz, and Ying-Lin Huang. "Forbearance: An Empirical Analysis." *Journal of Financial Services Research* 10, no. 1 (1996): 27–41. DOI: 10.1007/BF00120144.

Brockmeijer, Jan. "Report from the Task Force on the Winding Down of Large and Complex Financial Institutions." In *Basel Committee on Banking Supervision*, 2001.

Buchman, John. "Expensive Bank Failures and Their Implications for Regulatory Reform." In *ABA Banking Law Committee, Fall Meeting* (2009), 1–41.

Calomiris, Charles W., and Joseph R. Mason. "Contagion and Bank Failures During the Great Depression: The June 1932 Chicago Banking Panic." *The American Economic Review* 87, no. 5 (December 1997): 863–83.

Calomiris, Charles W., and Joseph R. Mason. "How to Restructure Failed Banking Systems: Lessons from the U.S. in the 1930s and Japan in the 1990s." In *National Bureau of Economic Research* (2003).

Carlson, Mark. "A Brief History of the 1987 Stock Market Crash with a Discussion of the Federal Reserve Response." In *Finance and Economics Discussion Series-Division of Research and Statistics and Monetary Affairs* 2007–13, (2006): 1–25.

Cihak, Martin, and Erlend Nier. "The Need for Special Resolution Regimes for Financial Institutions—the Case of the European Union." In *IMF Working Paper, WP/09/200* (2009).

Clift, Eleanor. "The 'Former Member' Club." In *Newsweek* (2010). Published electronically December 17. http://www.newsweek.com/2010/12/17/congress-reflects-on-the-year-what-went-wrong.html.

CNBC. "Reuters, Paulson Raised RTC-Type Solution." CNBC, 2008.

*Comprehensive Deposit Insurance Reform and Taxpayer Protection Act of 1991*: *Before the Senate Committee on Banking, Housing, and Urban Affairs*, 102nd Congress, 1st Session.

Corston, John. "Statement of John Corston, Acting Deputy Director." 11: Complex Financial Institutions Branch, FDIC, 2010.

Critchfield, Tim, and Kenneth D. Jones. "Consolidation in the U.S. Banking Industry: Is the 'Long, Strange Trip' About to End?" *FDIC Banking Review* 17, no. 4 (2005): 31–61.

Crittenden, Michael R., and Patrick Yoest. "Resolution Trust Plan Is Floated." *Wall Street Journal*, September 18, 2008.

Dash, Eric, and Julie Creswell. "The Reckoning: Citigroup Saw No Red Flags Even as It Made Bolder Bets." *New York Times*, November 22, 2008.

DeYoung, Robert, and Jack Reidhill. "A Theory of Bank Resolution: Political Economics and Technological Change." (Powerpoint presentation) January 31, 2008.

*Economic Implications of the "Too Big to Fail" Policy: Hearing Before the Subcommittee on Economic Stabilization of the Committee on Banking, Finance, and Urban Affairs*, 102nd Congress, 1st Session, May 9, 1991.

Eland, Ivan. *Recarving Rushmore: Ranking the Presidents on Peace, Prosperity, and Liberty*. Oakland, California: The Independent Institute, 2009.

FDIC. "FDIC Rebuts Inaccurate Op-Ed." In *FDIC Online* (2010). Published electronically April 8, 2010. http://www.fdic.gov/news/letters/rebuttal _04072010.html.

Freeman, James. "Bear Stearns: The Fed's Original 'Systemic Risk' Sin." *Wall Street Journal*, March 16, 2009.

———. "Fighting Geithnerism." *Wall Street Journal*, March 28, 2009.

Friedman, Milton, and Anna Jacobson Schwartz. *A Monetary History of the United States, 1867–1960*. Princeton, New Jersey: Princeton University Press, 1971.

Gibson, Dunn, and Crutcher. "Overview of the FDIC as Conservator or Receiver." In *Gibson, Dunn, and Crutcher Report* (2008). http://blogs.law. harvard.edu/corpgov/files/2008/10/092608-overview-fdicasconvervator -receiver.pdf.

Glass, Carter. "Congressional Record 77, S 3728." 1933.

Glassman, Mitchell. "FDIC Guarantee of Bank Debt." In *Memorandum to the Board of Directors of the FDIC*, 2008.

Gould, George D. *The Conclusions and Recommendations of the President's "Working Group on Financial Markets": Before the Committee on Banking, Housing, and Urban Affairs*, 100th Congress, 2nd Session, May 24, 1988 (Report by George D. Gould, Under Secretary for Finance, Department of Treasury).

Greenspan, Alan. *Private-Sector Refinancing of the Large Hedge Fund, Long-Term Capital Management: Testimony Before the House Committee on Banking and Financial Services,"* 105th Congress, 2nd Session, 1998.

*Hearings before the Committee on Banking, Housing, and Urban Affairs*, 98th Congress, July 25 and 31, 1984.

*Hearing before the Senate Committee on Banking, Housing, and Urban Affairs, Deposit Insurance Reform and Financial Modernization*, 101st Congress, 2nd Session, April 3, 1990.

Helwege, Jean. "Financial Firm Bankruptcy and Systemic Risk." *Regulation Magazine*, (2009): 27.

_____. "Financial Firm Bankruptcy and Systemic Risk." *Journal of International Financial Markets, Institutions & Money* 20 (2010): 6.

_____. "A New Systemic Risk Regulator and Too Big to Fail." 3: Center for the Study of Financial Regulation, 2010.

Helwege, Jean, Nicole M. Boyson, and Jan Jindra. "Crises, Liquidity Shocks, and Fire Sales at Financial Institutions." Published electronically July 2, 2010. http://papers.ssrn.com/sol3/papers.cfm?abstract_id=1633042.

Helwege, Jean, Samuel Maurer, Asani Sarker, and Yuan Wang. "Credit Default Swap Auctions." In *Federal Reserve Bank of New York Staff Reports*, 2009.

Hitt, Gregory. "Congress Pledges Action." *Wall Street Journal*, September 20, 2008.

Hoover, Herbert. "Annual Message to the Congress on the State of the Union." 1931.

Humphrey, Thomas M. "Lender of Last Resort: What It Is, Whence It Came, and Why the Fed Isn't It." *Cato Journal* 30, no. 2 (2010): 333.

*Inquiry into Continental Illinois Corporation and Continental Illinois National Bank: Before the Subcommittee on Financial Institutions Supervision, Regu-*

*lation, and Insurance of the Committee on Banking, Finance and Urban Affairs*, 98th Congress, 2nd Session, September 18–19, October 4, 1984.

Jickling, Mark. "Averting Financial Crisis." Congressional Research Service Report for Congress, 2008.

Jones, Kenneth D., and Chau Nguyen. "Increased Concentration in Banking: Megabanks and Their Implications for Deposit Insurance." Published electronically July 20, 2004. http://papers.ssrn.com/sol3/papers.cfm?abstract_id=566041.

Jones, Kenneth D., and Robert C. Oshinsky. "The Effect of Industry Consolidation and Deposit Insurance Reform on the Resiliency of the U.S. Bank Insurance Fund." Published electronically July 7, 2007. http://papers.ssrn.com/sol3/papers.cfm?abstract_id=997844.

Kane, Edward. "Incentives for Banking Megamergers: What Motives Might Regulators Infer from Event-Study Evidence." *Journal of Money, Credit, and Banking* 32, no. 3 (2000): 6–9.

Labaton, Stephen. "Treasury to Set Executives' Pay at 7 Ailing Firms." *New York Times*, June 10, 2009.

Laeven, Luc, and Fabian Valencia. "Systemic Banking Crises: A New Database." In *IMF Working Paper, WP/08/224*, 2008.

———. "Resolution of Banking Crises: The Good, the Bad, and the Ugly." In *IMF Working Paper, WP/10/146*, 2010.

Laffer, Arthur B., and Stephen Moore. *Return to Prosperity: How America Can Regain Its Economic Superpower Status*. New York: Simon and Schuster, 2009.

*Legislative Proposals to Ensure the Safety and Soundness of Government-Sponsored Enterprises: Senate Hearing*, May 10, 1991.

Leuchtenburg, William E. "The New Deal and the Analogue of War." In *Change and Continuity in Twentieth-Century America*, edited by John Braeman et al., 81–143. Columbus, Ohio: Ohio State University Press, 1964.

Lewis, Michael. *The Big Short: Inside the Doomsday Machine*. New York: W.W. Norton & Company, Inc., 2010.

*McKinley v. Board of Governors*, Case 1:09-cv-1263, (2011).

*McKinley v. FDIC*, Case 1:10-cv-00420, (2010).

*McKinley v. FHFA*, Case 1:10-cv-01165-HHK, (2010).

Norris, Floyd. "The Regulatory Failure Behind the Bear Stearns Debacle." *New York Times*, April 4, 2008.

Olson, James S. *Saving Capitalism: The Reconstruction Finance Corporation and the New Deal 1933–1940*. Princeton, New Jersey: Princeton University Press, 1988.

*Oversight Hearings into the Effectiveness of Federal Bank Regulation: Subcommittee of the Committee on Government Operations*, 94th Congress, 2nd Session, February 10, May 25–6, and June 1, 1976.

Paulson, Henry M., Jr. "Fighting the Financial Crises, One Challenge at a Time." *New York Times*, November 17, 2008.

———. *On the Brink: Inside the Race to Stop the Collapse of the Global Financial System*. New York: Business Plus, 2010.

Pelofsky, Jeremy. "Paulson Raised RTC-Style Concept with Congress: Source." *Reuters*, September 18, 2008.

Reconstruction Finance Corporation Liquidation Act, Small Business Act of 1953. Public Law 83–163.

Reddy, Sudeep. "A Necessary Step or Slippery Slope?" *Wall Street Journal*, March 15, 2009.

———. "Bernanke Feared a Second Great Depression." *Wall Street Journal*, July 27, 2009.

*Reforming America's Housing Finance Market: A Report to Congress*. U.S. Department of the Treasury, U.S. Department of Housing and Urban Development, 2011.

Reidhill, Jack, Lee Davison, and Elizabeth Williams. "The History of Bridge Banks in the United States." FDIC, 2005.

Reinhart, Carmen and Kenneth Rogoff, "This Time is Different: Eight Centuries of Financial Folly," see video of Carmen Reinhart at "May 3: 800 Years of Financial Crises," May 5, 2010, at http://video.ft.com/v/82349517001/May-3–800-years-of-financial-crises.

*Review of the Findings of the President's Working Group on Financial Markets and the Use of Stock Index Futures and Other Recent Market Developments: Before the Committee on Agriculture*, 100th Congress, 2nd Session, June 14 and July 13, 1988.

Seidman, L. William, and David C. Cooke. "What We Learned from Resolution Trust." *Wall Street Journal*, September 25, 2008.

Shumway, Robert. "Continental Illinois National Bank and Trust Company of Chicago-Section 13 (C)(2) Assistance, Memo to the Board of Directors of the Federal Deposit Insurance Corporation." 1984.

SIGTARP. "Quarterly Report to Congress." 2010.

Skeel, David A. *The New Financial Deal: Understanding the Dodd-Frank Act and Its (Unintended) Consequences*. Hoboken, New Jersey: Wiley, 2011.

Smith, James E. *Letter from the Federal Reserve as Quoted in Franklin Oversight Hearings*. Detailed Affidavit of James E. Smith, OCC, U.S. District Court of the Eastern District of New York, 1974.

Sorkin, Andrew Ross. *Too Big to Fail*. New York: Viking, 2009.

Sparshott, Jeffrey, and Kevin Kingsbury. "AIG Rescue Will Prove Profitable, Treasury Says." *Wall Street Journal*, November 2, 2010.

"Statement by the U.S. Treasury Department on AIG Exit Plan." Treasury Department Office of Financial Stability, 2010.

Stewart, Jon. "Clusterf#@K to the Poor House—Wall Street Burns." *Daily Show with Jon Stewart*: Comedy Central, 2010.

Title XIII, Public Law 102–550, United States Code Congressional and Administrative News, 102nd Congress, 2nd Session, 1991.

Todd, Walker F. "History of and Rationales for the Reconstruction Finance Corporation." *Federal Reserve Bank of Cleveland Economic Review* 28, no. 4 (1992): 24.

———. "FDICIA's Emergency Liquidity Provisions." *Federal Reserve Bank of Cleveland Economic Review* 29, no. 3 (1993).

"Troubled Asset Relief Program: Two Year Perspective." 4: U.S. Treasury Department, Office of Financial Stability, 2010.

United States Code Congressional and Administrative News. 100th Congress, 1st Session, 1987.

United States Code Congressional and Administrative News. 102nd Congress, 1st Session, 1991.

United States Statutes at Large, 73rd Congress, 1933–1934.

United States Statutes at Large, 81st Congress 1950–1951.

Valukas, Anton. "Report of Anton Valukas, Bankruptcy Examiner."
In *Lehman Brothers Holdings Inc., Case No. 08-13555* (2010): 617–18.
http://lehmanreport.jenner.com/VOLUME%201.pdf.

Wallison, Peter J., and David A. Skeel. "The Dodd Bill: Bailouts Forever," *Wall Street Journal* (2010). Published electronically April 7, 2010. http://online.wsj.com/article/NA_WSJ_PU
:SB10001424052702303493904575167571831270694.html.

*War Finance Corporation Act: House of Representatives Report No. 369*. 65th
Congress, 2nd Session, 1918.

Wessel, David. *In Fed We Trust*. New York: Crown Business, 2009.

"When Wall Street Nearly Collapsed—Wilbur Ross: Lehman's Death a
Tragic Mistake." *Fortune*, September 14, 2009.

White, Ben, and Vikas Bajaj. "Woes at Citigroup Began with Failed Bid for
Wachovia." *New York Times*, November 21, 2008.

"Wilbur Ross Expects 1000 Bank Failures." *YouTube* (video), 2008.

"Will Sell Stock to RFC; First National Bank of Chicago Limits It to
$15,000,000." *New York Times*, November 11, 1933.

Young, Owen D. "Owen D. Young, Deputy Chairman of the Board of
Directors of the New York Federal Reserve Bank, in Comments be-
fore the Directors, July 7, 1932." In *Monetary History*, edited by Milton
Friedman and Anna Jacobson Schwartz. 330–31. Princeton, New Jersey:
Princeton University Press, 1971.

Zubrow, Barry. "Written Testimony of Barry Zubrow, Chief Risk Officer,
JPMorgan before FCIC." 7–8, 2010.

# Index

**A**

ABN Amro, 196*t*
accountability, 108, 280–81
advance warning systems, 6, 24, 280, 281
affordable housing, 118, 219
Agency Mortgage Backed Securities Program,
125, 327n36
Agricultural Credit Act of 1987, 97
AIG Financial Products Division, 181–191
Alaska Mutual Bank, 95n66
Alix, Mike, 14. *See also* Bear Stearns
Alt-A mortgages, 219, 219n284
Alvarez, Scott, 14, 142–43, 206, 237
Alvarez and Marsal, 173
American Bankers Association, 65n10, 97n69,
105, 250
American International Group (AIG)
  bailout of, 31–32, 205–11, 206–8*t*, 209nn249–
    50, 210n254, 230, 262, 291*t*
  bankruptcy option, 200–201, 205
  beneficiaries of bailout, 216–17
  benefits of bailout to creditors, 32, 216
  capital injection estimates, 200–201
  circumstances leading to stress, 181–88,
    181n167, 182nn175–76, 183nn177–78,
    184n179, 185n180, 186n182, 187n183,
    188n185
  collateral in bailout of, 177*t*, 181–82, 188–89,
    193, 197, 200–201, 210, 212
  collateral requirement, 210
  commercial paper holdings, 193, 198
  Congress role, 258–59
  counterparty payments, 215–16, 216n278
  credit default swap sales by, 181, 186, 196, 197,
    198n225
  credit default swaps, 181, 185, 186, 196–97
  credit rating downgrade, 181–82, 194
  derivatives contracts held by, 186, 191–97
  discount window borrowing, 188, 189n191,
    201–2
  final deal, 212–13, 212n263
  government secrecy involving, 208–9,
    209n249, 211
  hedge funds, 182, 182n175, 193
  impact of, 173, 174–79*t*, 193, 193n210,
    197nn220–23, 198n225, 213–18, 214n271
  information quality, 181, 189–93, 189nn190–
    91, 193n210, 195, 195n218, 197–98, 198n225,
    199–200, 209n250, 215
  insolvency, 201, 205, 211
  institutional exposure to, 193–95, 195n218,
    196*t*
  justifications for intervention, 195–98,
    197nn220–23, 198n225, 203–5, 210–11, 213,
    216–18
  "knock-on" effects, 216–17, 307, 307n10
  legal authority, 212, 258–59
  liquidity issues, 181, 186, 188–94, 199–204,
    210–11, 271, 297
  loan request by, 193–94, 201, 207*t*, 209
  lobbying of government on behalf of, 203–5
  loss estimates, 214–15
  maintenance of secrecy in, 325
  options review, 199–211, 199n228, 201nn232–
    34, 202nn236–39, 206–8*t*, 209nn249–50,
    210n254
  OTS scrutiny of, 183–86, 183n178, 184n179,
    185n180, 188
  PDCF role, 189–90, 189nn190–91
  regulatory breakdowns in oversight of, 122,
    186–87, 187n183, 288
  regulatory system exploitation by, 182–83,
    182nn175–76
  resolution costs, 214–15

shareholders, 212
solvency, 181–82, 199–200, 202n237, 209
systemic risk assessment, 188–99, 188n185,
    189nn190–91, 191n200, 193n210, 195n218,
    196t, 197nn220–23, 198n225
uncertainty issue, 200, 213–15
Anderson, Roger A., 93n57
Annunzio, Frank, 82
Anti-Deficiency Act, 20
Aozora Bank of Tokyo, 169–71
Asset-Backed Commercial Paper Money
    Market Fund Liquidity Facility, 219t
asset bubbles, 33, 35, 74
"Averting Financial Crisis" (Jickling), 34n26

**B**
Bacon, Louis, 163
Bagehot, Walter, 27–30, 27n13, 28n14
Bailey, Deborah P., 12, 16n30, 17–18, 132nn33–34,
    133n36
bailouts, 30–33, 32n21, 33n22. *See also* financial
    institution bailouts
Bair, Sheila
    Citigroup role, 253
    on limits of bank failures, 123–24
    on OBA prohibition, 312n19
    subprime market analysis by, 287–88
    Wachovia role, 236–39, 236n12, 243–44,
        244nn33–35
Banco Santander, 196t
BancTexas Group Inc., 94, 95n66
bank failures
    Bair on limits of, 123–24
    costs of historically, 289–90, 290n34
    historically, 35–38, 36t, 37f, 37n28
    1980s recessions, 72–75, 72nn4–5, 74n6, 74t
    recession 2007, 123–24, 124t
    resolution costs, 289–90
    *See also specific institutions*
Bank Insurance Fund (BIF), 235
Bank of America
    AIG exposure, 196t
    bailout of, 37, 291t, 294, 305
    cost of subsidy, 256
    domination of industry by, 122
    Lehman Brothers role, 158, 159, 165, 174t
    maintenance of secrecy in, 324
    purchase of Continental Illinois by, 90, 305
    purchase of Merrill Lynch by, 305
    regulatory breakdowns in oversight of, 123,
        256
Bank of New England, 94–95, 104, 104n3

Bank of New York Mellon, 165
Bank of United States, 43–45, 45nn16–20
Banking Act of 1933, 57
banking crisis. *See* financial crises
Barclay's
    AIG exposure, 196t
    Lehman Brothers role, 148n77, 158, 165,
        173, 295
Basel Committee on Banking Supervision, 155
Bates Numbers, 10n4
Baxter, Thomas Jr., 205
Bear Stearns
    bankruptcy filing by, 14, 291t
    capital loss to creditors, 24, 25, 133, 138,
        141–42, 141nn56–58, 142, 142n59, 152t
    cash balance drop, 14, 14n23
    collapse as imbalance, 33–34
    collateral in bailout of, 12, 133, 137, 152t
    contagion risk level, 30–31
    credit default swaps, 16, 18, 132, 132n33, 135
    derivatives contracts held by, 13, 131, 150
    factors leading to stress of, 129–31
    firm level exposure to, 14, 16, 132nn33–34
    government intervention in, 17–21, 20n47,
        136–38, 137n45, 262
    government review of, 9–12, 131–36, 132nn33–
        34, 133nn1–2, 133t, 134n36, 135n39
    hedge funds, 23–24
    impact of, 143–44, 168–69
    information quality, 12–13, 13n21, 132–35,
        132nn33–34, 133t
    insolvency of, 24–25, 27, 129–30, 142
    JPMorgan Chase buyout of, 15–21, 20n47,
        136–38, 137n45
    justification of intervention, 29, 33, 131–36,
        132nn33–34, 133nn1–2, 133t, 134n36,
        135n39, 138–42, 141nn56–58, 142n59
    large financial institutions (LFIs) reactions
        to, 11, 12, 131–32, 132nn33–34, 133n36
    legal authority, 212
    Lehman Brothers *vs.*, 151–52, 152t, 155–56
    liquidity issues, 9–15, 19, 23–24, 130–34, 140,
        144–45, 152t, 297
    maintenance of secrecy in, 324
    as moral hazard incentive, 142–43, 153, 169
    overview, 23–24, 24nn3–4, 37, 208
    regulatory breakdowns in oversight of, 123,
        130–31
    repos, 12, 134, 135, 135n39
    run on, 12, 14, 25–27, 26n9
    SEC role, 9–17, 12n14, 27, 134n36, 138–39, 220
    shareholders in, 137, 142

solvency of, 142n59
systemic risk assessment, 16, 16n30, 132–34,
    132nn33–34, 133n36, 133t, 154, 168–69, 170f
taxpayer losses, 141n57
uncertainty issue, 14
Belgium, 247n41
Bennett, Robert, 2n2, 4–5
Berkshire Hathaway, 145
Bernanke, Ben
    AIG bailout role, 182–83, 182nn175–76, 186,
        194, 199, 202, 205–8, 209n249, 214
    Bear/JP Morgan buyout role, 16–17, 19–20
    Citigroup role, 253
    financial crisis policies, 125–26, 126n21
    GSE bailout role, 221–23, 226
    justification of interventions by, 140–41,
        306–10, 307nn8–10
    Lehman Brothers role, 146, 149–53, 158–60,
        158n120, 160n128, 162n6
    maintenance of secrecy by, 319
    seeking of legislative authorities by, 258, 262
    on subprime housing market, 120–21
    TARP sales pitch, 263–64
Black Monday 1987, 99
Blackrock, 223
Bloomberg LP, 30n18
BNP Paribas, 170–71, 196t
Board of Governors of the Federal Reserve
    System
    AIG role, 190, 193–94, 199–205, 201n234,
        209n249, 210–11
    bailout program detail availability, 218,
        218n282, 219t
    Bear/JP Morgan merger role, 15–21, 20n47,
        132–36
    GSE role, 221
    justification of interventions by, 138–39, 156
    Lehman Brothers role, 146–51, 147n73, 156,
        160–62, 161–63t, 174–78t
    proposed mergers policy, 147n77, 148–49
    quality of Bear Stearns information, 12–13,
        13n21
    review of Bear Stearns by, 9–12
    support of FOIA secrecy by, 316–19
    on "too big to fail" policy reform, 109–15,
        110n15, 112n20, 112nn19–20, 115nn24–25,
        259
*Board of Governors of the Federal Reserve*
    *System, Bloomberg LP v.*, 30n18, 319–22,
    319nn13–14
*Board of Governors of the Federal Reserve System,*
    *Citizens for Responsibility and Ethics in*
    *Washington v.*, 326

*Board of Governors of the Federal Reserve System,*
    *Fox News Network, LLC v.*, 322
*Board of Governors of the Federal Reserve System,*
    *Freedom Watch Inc. v.*, 326
*Board of Governors of the Federal Reserve System,*
    *Gold Anti-Trust Action Committee v.*, 326
*Board of Governors of the Federal Reserve System,*
    *Judicial Watch v.*, 326
*Board of Governors of the Federal Reserve System,*
    *McKinley v.*, 20n47, 323–25
*Board of Governors of the Federal Reserve System,*
    *New York Times Company v.*, 326
Boesky, Hayley, 192–93
Bolten, Josh, 243
Borah, William, 53
Break the Glass Bank Recapitalization Plan
    (BTG), 257–63, 261nn15–17
"breaking of the buck," 168, 179
Breeden, Richard C., 100, 100n80
Bretton Woods System, 73
bridge banks, 94, 233, 233n2, 253n66, 295
Broderick, Joseph, 44, 45, 301
Buchman, John, 290n34
Buffett, Warren, 149, 200
Bunning, Jim, 209
Burch, Natalie, 162n6
Bureau of Consumer Financial Protection, 286t
Bush, George H. W., 107
Bush, George W.
    AIG role, 188n185
    bailout analysis report, 284–85
    Bear/JP Morgan buyout role, 18, 23
    Lehman Brothers role, 174–78t
    message to Congress on crisis, 257
    TARP sales pitch, 263–64

**C**

cafeteria capitalism, 4, 163, 203, 308
Calomiris, Charles W., 48n30, 52n41
Calyon (Credit Agricole), 154, 154n106, 155t, 196t
Campbell, John, 213
Capital Assistance and Deposit Insurance
    Flexibility Act, 77n15
capital forbearance program, 98n73
Capital Purchase Program (CPP), 266–68, 268t
Carnell, Richard, 114
Carper, Richard, 71
Cassano, Joseph, 185n180
central banks
    crisis lending role, 27–30, 27n13
    establishment of, 40
    *See also* Federal Reserve System

Change in Bank Control Act, 244
Charlton, Richard, 206t
Chase Manhattan Bank, 105
China Investment Corporation, 148, 148n78
Citigroup
  AIG as topic of discussion by, 181n167
  AIG exposure, 196t
  circumstances leading to stress, 251
  creditors as beneficiaries of, 252
  domination of industry by, 122
  failure of, 37, 261n16, 289, 291t, 294
  GAO role, 255–56
  government guarantee of assets, 254–55,
    306n9
  impact of, 255–56
  information quality, 255–56
  insolvency of, 244n35
  justification for intervention, 251–53, 253n61,
    253n66
  liquidity issues, 251–53
  maintenance of secrecy in, 324
  nationalization of, 254–55
  preferred stock purchase, 254–55
  purchase of Wachovia by, 238–39, 244,
    244nn33–35, 245, 245n38, 251
  regulatory breakdowns in oversight of, 123
  systemic risk assessment, 251–53, 253n61,
    253n66
  uncertainty issue, 251
*Citizens for Responsibility and Ethics in
  Washington v. Board of Governors,* 326
Clarke, Robert, 109–10, 110n15
Clearing House Association LLC, 319n14, 321
Clouse, James, 203
Cohn, Gary, 195. *See also* Goldman Sachs
Cole, Roger, 132n33, 134n36, 167n45
collateral
  AIG requirement, 210
  borrowing capacity relationship, 27–32
  CDS *vs.* repo market, 135, 161
  Dodd-Frank legislation, 281–83, 282t
  lender of last resort facility, 125–26
  loan *vs.* bailout characterization, 33, 126
  PDCF, 140, 156n111, 166–67, 166n144, 193,
    320
  RFC requirements, 54–55, 55n49
  TLGP requirements, 296
  *See also specific financial institutions*
commercial paper
  as competitive pressure, 73
  drop in levels of, 168
  Federal Reserve Act on, 41–42

Federal support programs, 125, 174–77t, 219t,
  327n36
  Lehman Brothers holdings, 142
  *See also specific financial institutions*
Commercial Paper Funding Facility, 125, 177t,
  219t, 327n36
Commodity Credit Corpoation, 62
Commodity Futures Trading Commission
  (CFTC), 187
Competitive Equality Banking Act of 1987, 94
concentrations of credit, 85n39
Congress
  access to liquidity authority, 115n25
  AIG role, 258–59
  Alt-A mortgages, 219
  bailouts as finest moment of, 4–5
  Bear Stearns role, 143
  BTG plan role, 262–63
  Continental Illinois role, 81–83, 91–92
  Dodd-Frank legislation (*See* Dodd-Frank
    legislation)
  Fannie Mae role, 95–96
  financial crisis definitions, 34n26
  Great Depression role, 52–54, 55n50, 61
  GSE role, 95–96, 115–17, 116n26, 225–26
  information quality within, 278
  OBA role, 64, 76–77, 95–96
  oversight role generally, 175–77t
  RFC role, 52–54, 61
  systemic risk exception role, 112, 112n20,
    253
  TARP sales pitch to, 263–64, 265n35, 269–
    70, 269n45
  too big to fail policy reform, 105–6
Congressional Budget Office (CBO), 89,
  255n72
Congressional Oversight Panel (COP), 5, 6n9,
  97–198, 211, 269t, 1189n191
Conover, C. Todd, 81, 83, 83n34, 87–92, 92n55
conservatorship described, 227, 233, 233n2
contagion
  defined, 26–27
  Great Depression role, 48
  as justification, 133t, 135
  *See also* systemic risk; *specific financial
    institutions*
Continental Illinois Bank and Trust Company
  bailout of, 71, 168, 233, 262, 294
  bondholder protection, 103n1
  capital ratio requirement, 92
  Congress role, 81–83, 91–92
  cost analysis, 83–86, 84nn35–36, 85n38,

86n41, 89–90, 89n48
creditors as beneficiaries of bailouts, 79, 81,
92, 95
executive compensation packages, 93, 93n57
factors precipitating bailout of, 78–81,
78nn17–18, 79nn21–23, 304–5
foreign bank bailouts, 92, 92n55
impact of, 168
information quality, 84n35, 87, 87n43,
89–90, 89n48
insolvency of, 58, 89
justification for intervention, 81–88, 83n34,
84nn35–36, 85nn38–39, 86nn41–42,
87n43, 88n45, 131–32, 136
legislative response, 94, 95n66
liquidity issues, 88–89, 297
moral hazard, market discipline issues,
92–93, 122
policy issues, 88–93, 89nn46–49, 90n50,
91n51, 92n55593n57
preferred stock sale by, 57, 58
reprivatization of, 90, 90n50
shareholders, 89n47
solvency of, 88–89, 92
"too big to fail" issue, 88, 88n45, 90–91, 91n51
uncertainty issue, 91, 131–32
corporatism, 5
Costigan, Edward, 56
Cox, Christopher, 12n14, 138, 160
credit contraction (crunch)
described, 34–35
historically 1920-21, 42, 44t; 1930s, 43–46,
44t; 1980s, 72; 2000s, 34, 124n15, 168n151
credit default swaps
AIG, 181, 185, 186, 196–97
AIG sales of, 181, 186, 196, 197, 198n225
Bear Stearns, 16, 18, 132, 132n33, 135
Lehman Brothers, 152, 154
repos as collateral *vs.*, 135, 161
value in market fragility, 18, 132, 135, 186,
186n182, 274
Credit Suisse, 140n52, 165, 196t
creditors
Bank of New England, 94–95, 104, 104n3
Bear Stearns, 24, 25, 133, 138, 141–42,
141nn56–58, 142, 142n59, 152t
as beneficiaries generally, 46, 64, 68, 235, 237,
272, 292, 300, 308, 311
benefits of AIG bailout to, 32, 216
benefits of Lehman bailout to, 156, 168–71,
179
as cause of bank runs, 24–27

Citigroup as beneficiaries, 252
Continental Illinois as beneficiaries, 79, 81,
92, 95
Dodd-Frank protections, 281–84, 282t,
297n46
First City Holding Company, 103n1
Long Term Capital Management, 128–29,
129n26
risk shifting, 138
TLGP as beneficiaries, 249
tightening of lending standards, 124, 267,
268t
Wachovia, 238–39, 245–46
Cummings, Walter J., 58
Curl, Gregory, 158
Curry, Thomas, 249
Custodial Trust Corporation, 134n37

**D**
D'Amato, Alfonse, 117
Danske, 196t
Davis, Michele, 159
Default Management Group (DMG), 151,
151n100
Defense Plant Corporation, 62
Defense Supplies Corporation, 62
Delta Airlines, 135
Department of Housing and Urban Develop-
ment, 96
deposit insurance
effects on bank runs, 26, 26n9
flexibility, 77, 77n15
*See also* Federal Deposit Insurance
Corporation (FDIC)
deposit to currency ratios, 46–48, 46f, 58
Depository Institutions Deregulation
and Monetary Control Act of 1980
(DIDMCA), 73
derivatives
AIG contracts, 186, 191–97
Bear Stearns contracts, 13, 131, 150
Dodd-Frank regulation of, 280
Lehman Brothers contracts, 150–51, 150n95,
155t
potential risk in, 155
Deutsche Bank, 154, 154n106, 155t, 196t
Dimon, Jamie, 4, 15, 17
Disaster Loan Corporation, 62
discount window borrowing
AIG, 188, 189n191, 201–2
described, 30n18, 112
Fannie/Freddie, 221

FOIA requests regarding, 320
Franklin, 67n17, 69nn21–22
JPMorgan Chase, 18
Lehman Brothers, 146
oversight of, 108
disorderly bankruptcy theory, 168–70, 170f
disorderly failure justification, 133t, 140–41, 168,
    210, 306
Dobbeck, Dianne, 13n21, 19
Dodd, Christopher, 115, 263
Dodd-Frank legislation
    bailout program detail availability, 218,
      218n282, 219t
    bailout provisions, 32n21, 280–83, 282t
    capital, leverage mandates, 282t, 288–90
    on collateral, 281–83, 282t
    commercial paper, 327n36
    creditor protections in, 281–84, 282t,
      297n46
    derivatives regulation, 280
    disclosure requirements in, 327
    Fannie/Freddie options report, 228
    FDIC expanded liquidation authority, 282t,
      283–84, 290–95, 291t, 292n37
    Financial Stability Oversight Council
      (FSOC), 282t, 284–88, 286t, 290n34
    impact of, 297–98
    on insolvency, 281, 282t, 296–97, 297n46
    limitations of, 278–79
    moral hazard mitigation by, 292
    Office of Financial Research, 285
    Open Bank Assistance reform, 282t, 291t,
      297
    on regulatory breakdowns, 280
    sales pitch, 277–80
    self-interest in passage of, 5
    shareholders in, 281, 282t
    on solvency, 291t, 296–97, 297n46
    taxpayer funding provision, 282t, 283–84
    unusual and exigent circumstances (UEC)
      powers reform, 282t, 291t, 295–97,
      297n46
domino theory, 30, 75, 76, 86–87, 87n43, 197,
    233
Drake, Peter, 11n9
Dresdner, 196t
Drexel Burnham Lambert, 100–101, 100n80,
    106, 127
Dudley, William, 157–58
Dugger, Robert, 85n38, 87n43
Duke, Elizabeth, 205

**E**

economic stimulus package, 121
Eland, Ivan, 49n32
elastic currency concept, 41–42
Electronic Home and Farm Authority, 62
Ely, Bert, 220n285
Emergency Banking Act, 55n51
Emergency Banking Relief Act of 1933, 55–56
Emergency Economic Stabilization Act of 2008
    (EESA), 235, 235n37, 265, 266n37
Emergency Relief and Construction Act of
    1932, 54n47, 59, 59n63
essentiality test, 76, 80, 88n45
executive compensation, 93, 93n57, 326n36
exit strategy, 24
Export-Import Bank, 62

**F**

failure. *See* bank failures
Fannie Mae
    bailout of, 31, 96–97, 97n69, 116, 159, 218,
      229, 262, 294
    capitalization requirement of, 220, 289
    circumstances leading to stress, 218–24,
      219n284, 220nn285–87, 221n290,
      222n296, 224n302
    Congress role, 95–96
    discount window borrowing, 221
    impact of bailout, 230–31, 279
    implied government guarantee of, 219–21,
      220nn285–86
    justification for intervention, 228
    maintenance of secrecy in, 325
    placement into conservatorship, 227–29,
      228nn317–18, 229n320
    preferred stock purchase, 229, 229n322
    regulatory breakdowns in oversight of,
      223–24, 224n302
    review of options, 227–28, 228nn317–18
    systemic risk assessment, 224–26, 226n311
Farm Credit System (FCS), 97, 116, 116n26,
    262
Farm Credit System Financial Assistance
    Corporation, 97
*FDIC, McKinley v.*, 323–25
FDIC Fund, 57, 124, 287
fear mongering
    AIG, 181, 198, 217
    Citigroup, 253n66, 256
    contagion, 128, 135, 299
    FOIA document requests, 240–42
    in frozen economy, 257, 272–73

GSE bailouts, 116n26, 223, 226
insolvency, 27
LCTM bailout, 128
in maintenance of secrecy, 316–18
in policy making, 272–73, 287
in TARP sales pitch, 263–64, 267
"too big to fail" policy, 109
Federal Deposit Insurance Corporation (FDIC)
Bank Insurance Fund (BIF), 235
bondholder protection by, 103n1, 107n10
bridge bank creation by, 94, 233, 233n2, 253n66, 295
change of bailout policy by, 103–5, 103n1
Citigroup role (*See* Citigroup)
Continental Illinois role, 80–81, 85–89, 86nn41–42, 89n48
Dodd-Frank provisions affecting, 282t, 283–84, 290–95, 291t, 292n37
establishment of, 57–58, 125n18
Franklin National Bank role, 68, 69n21
impact of, 58–59
insolvency of, 74–75, 124
interbank liability limitations, 112n19
maintenance of secrecy by, 323–25
Open Bank Assistance (*See* Open Bank Assistance)
prompt corrective action system implementation, 112, 113, 122, 289
refusal of document disclosure by, 238–39, 239n23, 248
standing bailout powers for, 61
Temporary Liquidity Guarantee Program role (*See* Temporary Liquidity Guarantee Program)
"too big to fail" policy reform, 105–15, 106n8, 107n10, 109n13, 110nn15–16, 112nn19–20, 115nn24–25
Wachovia role (*See* Wachovia)
Washington Mutual failure role, 236–37, 236n12
Federal Deposit Insurance Corporation Act of 1950, 64n8
Federal Deposit Insurance Corporation Improvement Act (FDICIA) of 1991, 92, 111–15, 112nn19–20, 115nn24–25, 137–38, 234, 250, 289
federal financial agency roles generally, 183, 183n177
Federal Home Loan Banks, 48
Federal Housing Finance Agency (FHFA), 222–29. *See also* Office of Federal House Enterprise Oversight (OFHEO)

*Federal Housing Finance Agency, Judicial Watch v.*, 326
*Federal Housing Finance Agency, McKinley v.*, 323–25
Federal Reserve Act
expansion of lending authority, 59, 59n63, 137–38
growth objective maintenance, 310
lender of last resort authority, 27–28, 30n18, 76, 142, 221
passage of, 39–41
reserve allocation by, 41–42
Section 10B, 30n18
special power codification, 48
unusual and exigent circumstances powers (*See* unusual and exigent circumstances powers)
Federal Reserve Bank of New York (FRBNY)
AIG role, 188–211, 188n185, 189nn190–91, 195n218, 197nn220–23, 198n225, 201n234, 209nn249–50
Bear/JP Morgan buyout role, 15–21, 20n47, 131, 136–38, 137n45
BOUS role historically, 44–45, 45nn16–17
Citigroup role (*See* Citigroup)
Freedom of Information Act authority, 128n24
Lehman Brothers role, 146–51, 147n73, 155–67, 161–63t, 174–78t
quality of Bear Stearns information, 12–13, 13n21
review of Bear Stearns by, 9–12, 16
Federal Reserve Bank of Richmond, 238, 242
Federal Reserve System
AIG loss estimates, 214–15
AIG role, 186–87
Continental Illinois role, 80–81
expansion of lending authority, 59, 59n63
extension of funding policy, 125–26
FDIC conflicts with, 65n10
Franklin National Bank role, 67–69, 67n17, 69n22
Great Depression role, 47–48, 48n30
as liquidity provider, 19, 28, 40, 59n63, 80, 112n19, 115, 177t, 178t, 265, 282t
1980s recession role, 72–73, 72n4
regulatory breakdowns in oversight by, 122–23
regulatory gap role of, 129, 129n26
role of historically, 40–42, 130–31, 319, 319n13
Senior Loan Officer Opinion Survey, 72n4, 124, 267

as systemic risk regulator, 127–29, 128n24,
128t, 129n26
on "too big to fail" policy reform, 109–10,
110n15
Federal Savings and Loan Corporation
(FSLIC), 77n16
financial crises
defined, 33–35, 33n24, 34nn26–27, 35t, 36t, 37f
future predictions on, 312–13, 312n19
government as requirement in, 309–12,
310n15
institution failures historically, 35–38, 36t,
37f, 37n28
Financial Crisis Inquiry Commission (FCIC),
135n39, 153, 239, 278–79, 324
financial institution bailouts
bailout defined, 30–33, 32n21, 33n22
critical analysis, self-interest in, 4–5, 137, 263
déjà vu patterns in, 299–303, 299n2
failure defined, 23–25, 24nn3–4
literature review, 3–4, 3nn4–6, 4n7
Main Street as beneficiary justification,
306–8, 307nn8–10
panic basis of decisions, 305–6
permanent and expanding, 303–5, 304t
perspectives on, 1–3, 1n1, 2n2, 299–303,
299n2
proposed mergers policy, 147n77, 148–49
quantitative support requirement, 308
run defined, 25–27, 25nn6–7, 26n7
seat of the pants justifications for, 305–9,
307nn8–10
self-interest in, 308–9
Financial Institutions Reform, Recovery, and
Enforcement Act of 1989, 261n15
financial safety net, 24–25, 224
Financial Services Authority (FSA), 158, 162
financial stability
bank failure impacts on, 43n12, 118, 169
Federal Reserve System oversight of, 99,
112n20, 187, 234, 280
as justification, 221, 292, 300
preservation of, 21, 221
Restoring American Financial Stability Act
of 2010, 280–81 (*See also* Dodd-Frank
legislation)
financial stability as, 221, 292, 300
Financial Stability Oversight Council (FSOC),
282t, 284–88, 286t, 290n34
First City Bancorporation of Texas, 94, 95n66,
104
First City Holding Company, 103n1

First National Bank of Chicago, 57
First Pennsylvania Bank, 75, 79, 122
First Republic Bank, 104
fiscal policy, 143–44
forbearance
described, 97–99, 98nn72–73, 114
expansion of, 304t
foreign bank bailouts, 92, 92n55, 223
Foster, Doug, 299n2
*Fox News Network, LLC v. Board of Governors of
the Federal Reserve System*, 7n9, 322
fractional-reserve banking, 25, 25n7
fragility of markets, 21, 133, 136, 151–52, 152t, 198,
223, 262–63, 313
Frank, Barney, 147
Franklin National Bank of New York, 66–69,
67n17, 69nn21–22, 79, 89, 122
Fraud Enforcement and Recovery Act of 2009,
278
Freddie Mac
bailout of, 31, 96–97, 97n69, 159, 218, 229,
262, 294
capitalization requirement of, 220, 289
circumstances leading to stress, 218–24,
219n284, 220nn285–87, 221n290,
222n296, 224n302
discount window borrowing, 221
impact of bailout, 230–31, 279
implied government guarantee of, 219–21,
220nn285–86
justification for intervention, 228
maintenance of secrecy in, 325
placement into conservatorship, 227–29,
228nn317–18, 229n320
preferred stock purchase, 229, 229n322
regulatory breakdowns in oversight of,
223–24, 224n302
review of options, 227–28, 228nn317–18
systemic risk assessment, 224–26,
226n311
free market, 52, 270–71, 273, 278, 300
Freedom of Information Act
background, 315–17
document withholding under, 238–39,
239n23, 325
exemptions, 317–19, 317t, 318t
FDIC as subject to, 295
information redaction under, 11n9, 13n16,
325
lawsuits, 7n9, 315–26
requests generally, 7n9, 128n24

*Freedom Watch Inc. v. Board of Governors,* 326
Fremont Investment and Loan, 288
Friedman, Milton, 63n4
Fuld, Dick, 145, 159, 160, 214. *See also* Lehman
  Brothers
full faith and credit, 76, 117
*Full Faith and Credit: The Great S&L Debacle
  and Other Washington Sagas* (Seidman),
  103n1

**G**

GAO. *See* Government Accountability Office
  (GAO)
Garn, Jake, 116n26
Garner, John Nance, 53
Garn–St Germain Depository Institutions Act
  of 1982, 73, 76–77
Geithner, Timothy
  AIG role, 188–90, 188n185, 189nn190–91, 196,
    202–3, 205–8, 207–8t, 213, 214
  Bear/JP Morgan merger role, 14, 16–17,
    19–20, 131, 136–37
  on beneficiaries of AIG bailout, 216–17
  Dodd-Frank sales pitch, 278
  justification of interventions by, 138–39, 283,
    306–8, 307nn8–10, 310–12
  justification Paulson, Bernanke by, 263
  Lehman Brothers role, 147n73, 148–49,
    151n100, 157n115, 161–63t, 165–66
  maintenance of secrecy by, 319
  Wachovia role, 243
  Washington Mutual failure role, 236–37,
    236n12
General Electric, 145
Gerald Loeb Award, 320, 320n15
Germany, 247n41
Glauber, Robert, 107–8, 116n27, 117n28
*Gold Anti-Trust Action Committee v. Board of
  Governors,* 326
Golden West Financial Corporation, 238
Goldman Sachs
  AIG exposure, 195, 196t
  hedge funds withdrawals from, 168
  lobbyists in legislative reform, 115, 115n25
Gonzalez, Henry, 107
Government Accountability Office (GAO)
  Citigroup role, 255–56
  Long Term Capital Management role, 129
  roles of generally, 5, 6n9, 112, 112n20, 327
  TLGP role, 248, 250
  on too big to fail issue, 109–10, 234
  Wachovia role, 245–46

Government in the Sunshine Act (GISA),
  317–19, 318t
government-sponsored enterprises (GSEs)
  Alt-A mortgages, 219, 219n284
  authority to purchase securities, 221–23,
    222n296, 229
  bailout of, 31, 96–97, 97n69, 116, 159, 218,
    229, 304t
  circumstances leading to stress, 218–24,
    219n284, 220nn285–87, 221n290,
    222n296, 224n302
  Congress role, 95–96, 115–17, 116n26,
    225–26
  described, 96–97
  discount window borrowing, 221
  foreign investor reactions, 223
  impact of bailout, 230–31
  information quality, 223–24, 224n302
  insolvency, 96–97, 115–17, 220, 223, 225
  insolvency risks, scrutiny of, 115–18,
    116nn26–27, 117n28
  justification for intervention, 228
  maintenance of secrecy in, 325
  placement into conservatorship, 227–29,
    228nn317–18, 229n320
  preferred stock purchase, 229, 229n322
  regulatory breakdowns in oversight of,
    223–24, 224n302
  review of options, 227–28, 228nn317–18
  solvency of, 227
  systemic risk assessment, 224–26, 226n311
  uncertainty issue, 227–30
  *See also* Fannie Mae; Freddie Mac
Gramm-Leach-Bliley Act of 1999, 130, 184
Grayson, Alan, 256
Great Depression
  bank liquidity issues, 47, 47n25
  bank suspensions, 42–43, 43n12, 44t
  banking system meltdown, 43–46, 43n13,
    44t, 45nn16–20, 46f, 58
  bond decline, 47, 47n24
  Congress role, 52–54, 55n50, 61
  contagion as cause of, 27
  deposit to currency ratios, 46–48, 46f, 58
  factors precipitating generally, 39–41, 40n3,
    46–48, 47nn24–25
  Federal Reserve Act (*See* Federal Reserve
    Act)
  financial history preceding, 41–44
  legal scorecard, 39
  Reconstruction Finance Corporation (*See*
    Reconstruction Finance Corporation)

stock of money decline, 46–47, 135
Great Moderation, 120, 300
Greenspan, Alan, 25n5, 128, 128n24

**H**
haircuts, 10, 156, 239
Hanc, George, 72n5
Harvey, John, 167
hedge funds
    AIG, 182, 182n175, 193
    Bear Stearns, 23–24
    impact of withdrawals by, 168, 204
    on Lehman Brothers, 146, 163
    LTCM (*See* Long Term Capital
        Management)
Helping Families Save Their Homes Act of
    2009, 235, 235n9
Hiratsuka, Jon, 162n6
Homan, Paul, 75
homeownership, 5, 122, 123*t*, 223, 311
Hoover, Herbert, 48–53, 49n32, 50n35
House Committee on Banking, Finance, and
    Urban Affairs, 81–88, 83n34, 84nn35–36,
    85nn38–39, 86nn41–42, 87n43, 88n45
House Concurrent Resolution 290, 76–77
Housing and Community Development Act of
    1992, 117–18
Housing and Economic Recovery Act of 2008
    (HERA), 221–23, 222n296, 227
Hoyt, Robert, 20, 147
HSBC, 196*t*
Hu Jintao, 148
Hubbard, Carroll, 89n46
Huvelle, Ellen Segal, 324

**I**
*In Fed We Trust* (Wessel), 4n7
income maintenance agreements, 98n73
IndyMac FSB, 122, 123, 235–37, 290
inflation, 39, 72–73, 76, 97, 98n73
information quality
    AIG, 181, 189–93, 189nn190–91, 193n210,
        195, 195n218, 197–98, 198n225, 199–200,
        209n250, 215
    Bear Stearns, 12–13, 13n21, 132–35, 132nn33–
        34, 133*t*
    Citigroup, 255–56
    in Congress, 278
    Continental Illinois, 84n35, 87, 87n43,
        89–90, 89n48
    GSE capitalization, 223–24, 224n302
    justification of interventions, 309–12, 310n15

resolution cost data, 69n21, 89–90
TARP, 262, 268–69
Temporary Liquidity Guarantee Program,
    247–49, 248nn45–46, 249nn48–49
Wachovia, 239–44, 239n23, 241–42*t*, 324
ING, 196*t*
Inhofe, James, 263
insolvency
    AIG, 201, 205, 211
    assessment of, 40
    Bank of United States, 44
    Bear Stearns, 24–25, 27, 129–30, 142
    Continental Illinois, 58, 89
    correction of, 58, 73, 106n8
    as credit issue, 24, 40
    defined, 297n46
    as déjà vu, 299
    in discount window lending misuse, 69n22
    Dodd-Frank legislation on, 281, 282*t*,
        296–97, 297n46
    of FDIC, 74–75, 124
    forbearance in regard to, 73, 98, 114
    Franklin, 67–68
    GSEs, 96–97, 115–17, 220, 223, 225
    Lehman Brothers, 129–30, 158–59, 165
    in prompt corrective action, 113
    in systemic risk, 110–11
    in too big to fail reform, 106n8
    Wachovia/Citigroup, 244n35
International Monetary Fund (IMF), 246–47
Isaac, William, 77–79, 77n15, 79nn21–22,
    82, 84n35, 85n38, 86n42, 87–93, 89n48, 94,
    95, 98n73, 233, 294n42

**J**
Jester, Dan, 265n35
Jickling, Mark, 34n26
Jones, Jesse, 52n40, 57, 57n58, 58
JPMorgan Chase
    AIG exposure, 196*t*
    counterparty positions analysis, 154,
        154n106, 155*t*
    discount window borrowing, 18
    Lehman Brothers role, 156, 163*t*, 164–65
    Morgan Stanley merger, 149
    shareholders in, 137, 142
    Washington Mutual sale to, 293–95
Judicial Watch, 7n9, 322
*Judicial Watch v. Board of Governors of the
    Federal Reserve*, 326
*Judicial Watch v. Federal Housing Finance
    Agency*, 326

*Judicial Watch v. U.S. Department of the Treasury,* 326
justifications
  contagion as, 133*t,* 135
  disorderly failure, 133*t,* 140–41, 168, 210, 306
  fear-mongering (*See* fear mongering)
  financial stability as, 221, 292, 300
  free market, 19, 52, 270–71, 273, 278, 300
  knock-on effects, 216–17, 307, 307n10
  outsized losses, 307, 307n9
  unexpected losses, 248–49, 307, 307n8

**K**

Kashkari, Neel, 218, 237, 257, 259, 261, 261n17, 263
Katyal, Neal, 321
Kaufman, George, 110–11
Kazakhstan, 247n41
knock-on effects, 216–17, 307, 307n10
Kohn, Donald
  AIG role, 186–87, 187n183, 194, 200–202, 201n234, 216, 216n278
  Bear Stearns role, 15–17, 19–20
  Lehman Brothers role, 146
  maintenance of secrecy by, 319
Korea Development Bank, 150
Kroszner, Randall, 15–16, 18, 132, 132n33
Kucinich, Dennis, 261n16

**L**

La Follette, Robert M. Jr., 56
LaTorre, Alejandro, 208*t*
Labrecque, Thomas, 105–6, 106n8
Laffer, Arthur, 305
Latvia, 247n41
LaWare, John, 109–10, 110n15
Leach, James, 86, 90–92
least cost resolution, 112, 241–42*t,* 245, 249n48, 307n8
Lehman Brothers
  AIG exposure, 196*t*
  automatic stay rule, 173
  bank holding company option, 157–58, 157n115, 165–66
  bankruptcy filing, 151, 153–54, 159–63, 161–63*t,* 165–67, 165n137, 202, 205, 230, 291*t*
  Bear Stearns *vs.,* 151–52, 152*t,* 155–56
  benefits of bailout to creditors, 156, 168–71, 179
  collateral in bailout of, 154–55, 158–59, 158n120, 166–67, 166n144, 170–71, 203

commercial paper holdings, 142
counterparty positions analysis, 154, 154n106, 155*t*
credit default swaps, 152, 154
Default Management Group (DMG), 151, 151n100
derivatives contracts held by, 150–51, 150n95, 155*t*
discount window borrowing, 146
disorderly bankruptcy theory, 168–70, 170*f*
factors leading to stress of, 129–31, 145–50, 147n73, 148n77, 149n90
failure of, 37
Federal Reserve authority, 159, 160, 165–66
funding gap, 146, 158–59, 158n120, 210
government operation of, 156–57
government scrutiny of, 146–47, 155–56
hedge funds on, 146, 163
impact of, 167–80, 168n150, 170*f,* 170n159, 172*f,* 174–79*t,* 198n225, 203–4, 293
insolvency of, 129–30, 158–59, 165
justification of intervention, 151–53, 152*t,* 156, 214
LIBOR— OIS Spread, 171–72, 172*f*
liquidation of, 293–95
liquidity issues, 146–50, 152*t,* 156–58, 157n115, 161–64, 163*t*
maintenance of secrecy in, 325
merger pressure on, 147–49
as moral hazard beneficiary, 142, 153, 159n123, 169, 179
options analysis, 155–67, 156nn111–12, 157n115, 158n116, 158nn119–20, 160n128, 161–63*t,* 165n137, 166n144
PDCF role, 146, 156, 156n111, 166, 174*t*
playbook development, 151, 151n100
policy analysis focus, 144–45, 145n65
political issues in bailout of, 159–63, 159n123, 160n128, 161–63*t*
price of insurance for, 154
regulatory breakdowns in oversight of, 123
repurchase agreements, 151, 154–55, 165
sale of business units by, 173
SEC role, 146–47, 160, 174–78*t*
shareholders in, 168, 169
solvency of, 156
systemic risk assessment, 150–55, 150n95, 151n100, 152*t,* 154nn106–7, 155*t*
tri-party borrowings issues, 156, 156n112, 164–66

uncertainty issue, 180, 203
lender of last resort authority, 27–28, 30n18,
    76, 142, 221
"Lender of Last Resort Policies," 56n55
lending standards tightening, 124, 267, 268t
Lewis, Ken, 147, 159
Liang, Nellie, 161
Liberty Bonds, 49
Liberty Loans, 49
Liesman, Steve, 207t
liquidity
    AIG, 181, 186, 188–94, 199–204, 210–11, 271,
        297
    Bear Stearns, 9–15, 19, 23–24, 130–34, 140,
        144–45, 152t, 297
    Black Monday, 99
    Citigroup, 251–53
    Continental Illinois, 88–89, 297
    credit standards tightening and, 268t
    EESA, 265
    events, 296
    Federal Reserve System as provider of, 19,
        28, 40, 59n63, 80, 112n19, 115, 177t, 178t,
        265, 282t
    foreign currency liquidity swap lines,
        327n36
    Great Depression, 47, 47n25
    Lehman Brothers, 146–50, 152t, 156–58,
        157n115, 161–64, 163t
    as solution to crises, 310–11
    TLGP (*See* Temporary Liquidity Guarantee
        Program (TLGP))
    Wachovia, 241t
Lockhart, James, 220n287, 221
London Interbank Offered Rate (LIBOR), 168,
    171–72, 241t
Long, Edward, 316
Long Term Capital Management, 115n25,
    127–29, 128n24, 128t, 129n26, 165,
    165n137

**M**
Madigan, Brian, 29–30, 30n18, 193–94, 199,
    209n250
Madison, James, 315
Maiden Lane LLC, 137, 137n45, 157
Main Street, 2, 138, 143, 217, 274, 306, 309
maintenance of secrecy, 126–27, 126n1, 319,
    323–27
market discipline, 26, 92–93, 95, 100n80, 106–7,
    106n8, 114, 224
    Continental Illinois, 92–93, 122

Marsal, Bryan, 150n95, 173
Maryland Casualty Company, 58
Mason, Joseph R., 48n30, 52nn40–41
McAdoo, William, 49n33
McAndrews, Jamie, 19–20
McCabe, Thomas B., 61, 64, 64n9
McConnell, Meg, 135n39, 150n95, 154n106,
    193n210
*McKinley v. Board of Governors*, 20n47, 323–25
*McKinley v. FDIC*, 323–25
*McKinley v. Federal Housing Finance Agency*,
    323–25
McKinney, Stewart, 88
MCorp, 104
Mehle, Roger W. Jr., 77n16
Memorandum of Understanding (MoU),
    244
Menendez, Robert, 262
Merrill Lynch, 196t, 305
Metals Reserve Company, 62
Miller, Harvey, 153
Miscellaneous Revenue Act of 1982, 96, 97n69
Mitsubishi UFJ, 148
Mizuho International, 154, 154n106, 155t, 170
Molinaro, Sam, 137
monetary policy, 5, 43n12, 47–48, 120, 122,
    139–44, 189n190, 285, 311
Money Market Investor Funding Facility, 125
Moore, Dennis, 226
moral hazard
    Bear Stearns as, 142–43, 153, 169
    Continental Illinois, 92–93, 122
    Dodd-Frank mitigation of, 292
    Lehman as beneficiary, 153, 159n123, 169, 179
    recession 2007, 122
    Wachovia, 246–47
Morgan Stanley
    AIG exposure, 196t
    counterparty positions analysis, 154,
        154n106, 155t
    GSE bailout role, 223
    hedge funds withdrawals from, 168
Mosser, Patricia, 159, 208t
multinational banks, 88, 92
Murkowski, Lisa, 2n2

**N**
Nason, David, 265n35
National Bureau of Economic Research
    (NBER), 34, 34n27, 36, 37, 42n8, 72n2,
    72n3, 105n7, 120n3, 121n10
National City Bank of New York, 57

National City Corporation of Ohio, 261n16
National Credit Union Administration, 286t
nationalization, 80, 90–91, 90n50, 180, 221,
    254–55, 300–301
Nelson, William, 201, 209n249
net-worth certificate program, 98n73
New Era, 42, 300
New York Clearing House, 40n3
*New York Times,* 6
*New York Times Company v. Board of Governors,*
    326
Norton, Jeremiah, 265n35
Nye, Gerald, 56

**O**

Obama, Barack, 31, 277–78, 281
Obama Administration Plan. *See* Dodd-Frank
    legislation
Office of Federal House Enterprise Oversight
    (OFHEO), 118, 122, 218, 220n287, 222–26.
    *See also* Federal Housing Finance Agency
    (FHFA)
Office of Financial Research, 285
Office of the Comptroller of the Currency
    (OCC)
    Bear Stearns role, 10
    Continental Bank role, 78, 79
    Franklin bank role, 67, 67n17
    regulatory breakdowns in oversight by, 123
    on "too big to fail" policy reform, 109–10,
        110n15
    Wachovia role, 238
Office of Thrift Supervision (OTS)
    as AIG supervisor, 183–86, 183n178, 184n179,
        185n180, 188
    IndyMac ratings, 235–36
    regulatory breakdowns in oversight by, 122,
        235–36, 288
Olson, James, 50n35
*On the Brink: Inside the Race to Stop the Collapse
    of the Global Financial System* (Paulson),
    3n4
Open Bank Assistance
    Congress role, 64, 76–77, 95–96
    Continental Illinois bailout by, 94–95,
        95n66, 233
    deposit insurance flexibility changes to,
        75–77, 77nn13–16
    Dodd-Frank revision of, 291t, 292t, 297,
        312n19
    Federal Deposit Insurance Corporation
        Improvement Act (FDICIA) of 1991,

111–15, 112nn19–20, 115nn24–25, 137–38,
    234, 250, 289
    overview, 63–66, 64nn7–9, 65n12, 66n13, 305
    post-1980s use of, 104, 233–34, 262, 304t
    systemic risk exception, 105–12, 106n8,
        107n10, 109n13, 110nn15–16, 112nn19–20,
        233–34
    TLGP (*See* Temporary Liquidity Guarantee
        Program)
    Washington Mutual failure, 236–37, 236n12,
        237n14
    *See also specific institutions*
option-adjustable rate mortgages (ARMs), 238
orderly liquidation, 282, 290–95
OTS. *See* Office of Thrift Supervision (OTS)
outsized losses justification, 307, 307n9
Overend, Gurney, and Co., 28–30
oversight
    Congressional Oversight Panel (COP), 5,
        6n9, 97–198, 211, 269t, 1189n191
    described, 183, 183n177
    of financial stability, 99, 112n20, 187, 234, 280
    Office of Federal House Enterprise Over-
        sight (OFHEO), 118, 122, 218, 220n287,
        222–26 (*See also* Federal Housing Finance
        Agency (FHFA))
    regulatory breakdowns in, 123, 130–31,
        223–24, 224n302
    TARP, 6n9, 125
Oversight Board of the Resolution Trust
    Corporation (OBRTC), 299n2

**P**

Pandit, Vikram, 181n167
Panic of 1907, 40, 40n3
Parkinson, Patrick, 147n73, 151n100, 156, 157n115,
    160, 191n200
Paterson, David, 182
Patman, Wright, 88n45, 91–93
Patrikis, Ernest T., 183n177
Paul, Ron, 76–77
Paulson, Henry M. Jr.
    AIG bailout role, 187–88, 205, 208t, 211,
        217–18
    on bailouts in general, 31, 299
    Bear/JP Morgan buyout role, 17–18, 17n35,
        136–37
    *On the Brink: Inside the Race to Stop the Col-
        lapse of the Global Financial System,* 3n4
    Citigroup role, 251, 253
    GSE bailout role, 220–23, 220n287, 222n296,
        226–30

justification of Bear Stearns by, 33
justification of TARP, 269n45, 270–75, 275f
Lehman Brothers role, 145–48, 148n77, 151,
153, 159–61, 161–63t, 166, 214
seeking of legislative authorities by, 259–60,
262
on subprime housing market, 121
TARP role, 263–64, 269–75, 269nn44–45,
275f
on WGFM, 287
PDCF. *See* primary dealer credit facility (PDCF)
Penn Square Bank of Oklahoma, 78
Perli, Roberto, 13n16, 132n34
Permanent Liquidity Guarantee Program, 296.
*See also* Temporary Liquidity Guarantee
Program (TLGP)
Peters, Brian, 9–10, 207–8t
Pickle, Jake, 116n26
Pittman, Mark, 320
Pointer, Tanshel, 208t
Polakoff, Scott, 183n178, 184, 186–87, 187n183.
*See also* American International Group
(AIG)
policy making
financial system failure risk evidence, 6
history of, 5–6
interventions, results of, 6, 246, 247n41
proposed mergers, 147n77, 148–49
quality of information in (*See* information
quality)
regulatory breakdowns in, 6, 122–23, 223–24,
224n302, 235–36
scrutiny, limitations on, 6–7, 6n9
self-interest in, 4–5, 137, 263, 308–9
*See also specific institutions*
preferred stock purchases
Citigroup, 254–55
Continental Illinois, 57, 58
Fannie/Freddie, 229, 229n322
Fannie Mae, 229, 229n322
Freddie Mac, 229, 229n322
GSEs, 229, 229n322
RFC program, 55–58, 56n55, 57nn57–58
primary dealer credit facility (PDCF)
AIG role, 189–90, 189nn190–91
on collateral, 140, 156n111, 166–67, 166n144,
193, 320
creation of, 139–40, 140n52
GSE role, 221
Lehman Brothers role, 146, 156, 156n111, 166,
174t
prompt corrective action (PCA) system, 112,

113, 122, 289
Prudence Company of New York, 58
Public Law 97–320, 77n13
Public-Private Investment Program (PPIP), 256
purchase-and-assumption transaction, 33, 63, 94

**R**

Reagan, Ronald, 77, 270
receivership, 227
recessions generally
cycle post-1930, 35, 36t
1980s, 72–75, 72nn4–5, 74n6, 74t, 104–5
2007 (*See* 2000s recession)
Reconstruction Finance Corporation
authority of, 53
bailout methods of, 52–53, 52n40, 262, 266,
304t
capitalization issues, 53–56, 55n50
collateral securities required by, 54–55, 55n49
Congress role, 52–54, 61
development of, 48–51, 49nn32–33, 50nn35–
36, 51n38, 262
impact of, 53–54, 55n56, 58–59, 58n61
institution management by, 58
loan recipient name disclosure, 54, 54n47,
126n21
poor structure arguments, 53–55
post-Depression roles, 62–63, 63n4
preferred stock purchase program, 55–58,
56n55, 57nn57–58
salary regulation by, 58
Reconstruction Finance Corporation
Liquidation Act of 1953, 62–63
regulation described, 183, 183n177
regulatory breakdowns, 6, 122–23, 220, 223–24,
224n302, 235–36
Reich, John, 186, 253
Reinhart, Carmen, 33n24
Reinhart, Vincent, 259
Reno National Bank, 55
repurchase agreements (repos)
Bear Stearns, 12, 134, 135, 135n39
as collateral *vs.* CDS, 135, 161
Drexel, 100n80
Franklin, 66
Lehman (tri-party), 151, 154–55, 165
Wachovia, 238
Reserve Primary Fund, 25n7, 168, 179
resolution costs
AIG, 214–15
bank failures, 289–90
IndyMac, 290

quality of data, 69n21, 89–90
Resolution Trust Corporation (RTC), 260–61
Restoring American Financial Stability Act
    of 2010, 280–81. *See also* Dodd-Frank
    legislation
Riegle, Donald Jr., 93, 116–17
Roosevelt, Franklin D., 49n32, 55–57, 55n51,
    57n58
Ross, Katie J., 162n6
Ross, Wilbur, 167
Royal Bank of Scotland, 165
Rubber Reserve Company, 62
runs, defined, 25–27, 25nn6–7, 26n7
Russo, Martin, 116n27
Russo, Tom, 146. *See also* Lehman Brothers
Rutledge, William, 208*t*
Ryan, Tony, 17

**S**
Sasser, James, 106
*Saving Capitalism: The Reconstruction Finance
    Corporation and the New Deal 1933–1940*
    (Olson), 50n35
Scalia, Antonin, 316
Schultz, Fred, 75
Schwartz, Alan, 11, 15. *See also* Bear Stearns
Schwartz, Anna, 69, 69n22
Schwarzman, Steve, 273–74
secrecy, maintenance of, 126–27, 126n1, 319,
    323–27
Securities and Exchange Commission (SEC)
    Bear Stearns role, 9–17, 12n14, 27, 134n36,
        138–39, 220
    Dodd-Frank reform of, 292n37
    Drexel role, 100, 100n80, 106–7
    Lehman Brothers role, 146–47, 160, 174–78*t*
    oversight by generally, 286*t*, 292n37
    regulatory breakdowns by, 123, 220, 226
    regulatory role of, 129–31, 129n26
    representation on WGFM, 99, 187, 226, 286*t*
    too big to fail policy, 100, 100n80, 106–7
securities markets turmoil, 1980s, 99–101,
    100n80
Seidman, L. William, 103, 104, 109, 109n13
self-interest, 4–5, 137, 263, 308–9
Senior Loan Officer Opinion Survey, 72n4,
    124, 267
Shafran, Steve, 151n100, 158n116
shareholders
    AIG, 212
    as beneficiaries of bailouts, 32, 64, 91n51, 95,
        116n27, 142, 212

Continental Illinois, 89n47
    in Dodd-Frank legislation, 281, 282*t*
    JP Morgan/Bear Stearns merger, 137, 142
    Lehman Brothers, 168, 169
    loss of assets by, 31, 168, 237, 292
    Wachovia, 238–39
    WaMu, 237
Sheerin, James, 14
Sheets, Nathan, 204
Shinsei Bank, 170–71
Shipstead, Henrick, 56
Shlaes, Amity, 257
Sirri, Erik, 17
Small Business Administration (SBA), 62–63
Smith, Michelle, 207*t*, 209n250, 210
Societe Generale, 196*t*
solvency
    AIG, 181–82, 199–200, 202n237, 209
    Bank of United States, 44
    Bear Stearns, 142n59
    Continental, 88–89, 92
    as credit requirement, 27, 28n14, 51–52
    Dodd-Frank legislation on, 291*t*, 296–97,
        297n46
    as FDIC membership requirement, 57–58,
        282*t*
    Franklin, 67n17
    GSEs, 227
    importance of funding to, 24n4, 25n6, 27,
        28n14
    as indicator, 23
    Lehman, 156
    uncertainty in assessments of, 29, 40
Sorkin, Andrew Ross, 4n7, 214n271
Special Inspector General for the Troubled Asset
    Relief Program (SIGTARP), 5, 6n9, 256
Sprague, Irvine, 75, 305n5
St. Germain, Fernand J., 81–83, 83n34, 84n35,
    86–88, 87n43, 93
Stanton, Thomas, 220n285
State Street, 165
Steel, Robert, 17, 220n286, 238
Stefansson, Coryann, 12–13, 18, 132nn33–34, 167
stigma, 30n18, 54, 57, 126, 146, 267
stock of money, 46–47, 135
Strauss-Kahn, Dominique, 247
subprime mortgage market
    Bair analysis, 287–88
    Clinton/Bush Administration
        encouragement of, 219
    federal official appraisal of, 120–21
    major player exposure to, 129–30

option-adjustable rate mortgages (ARMs),
238
uncertainty issue, 227–30
*See also specific institutions*
Summers, Lawrence, 278
supervision described, 183, 183n177
"Survey Evidence of Tighter Credit Conditions:
What Does it Mean?", 72n4
Swagel, Phillip, 257
Swanson, Claude, 39–41
Sweden, 247n41
systemic risk
assessment of (*See under specific financial
institutions*)
consolidation phenomenon, 234–35, 235t
described, 30–31, 128n24
determination, Dodd-Frank revision of, 292
Dodd-Frank provisions on, 282t
exception, 105–12, 106n8, 107n10, 109n13,
110nn15–16, 112nn19–20, 233–34
Federal Reserve System as regulator of,
127–29, 128n24, 128t, 129n26
systemically important financial institution,
140–41, 246

**T**
TARP. *See* Troubled Asset Relief Program
(TARP)
taxpayers
Bear Stearns losses, 141n57
in Drexel bailout, 100n80
as financially responsible party, 1n1, 7, 95,
116–17
as having no say in bailouts, 91n51
protection of, 105–6, 210, 258, 281–83, 282t,
297
TARP sales pitch, 265
Taylor, John, 171–72
tea parties, 2n2
Temporary Liquidity Guarantee Program
(TLGP)
circumstances leading to stress, 247
collateral requirements, 296
creditors as beneficiaries of, 249
Dodd-Frank reform of, 296
expansion of, 304t
final deal, 249–50, 250n53
GAO role, 248, 250
impact of, 250
information quality, 247–49, 248nn45–46,
249nn48–49
justification for intervention, 247–49,

248nn45–46, 249nn48–49
maintenance of secrecy in, 324
systemic risk assessment, 247–49, 248nn45–
46, 249nn48–49
Term Asset-Backed Securities Loan Facility
(TALF), 219t
Term Securities Lending Facility Options
Program, 125
Tester, Jon, 262
Texas, 73–74, 74n6
Thain, John, 165n137
Thornton, Henry, 27–28, 27n13
*Too Big to Fail* (Sorkin), 4n7
"too big to fail" policy
Continental Illinois, 88, 88n45, 90–91, 91n51
Dodd-Frank ending of, 281, 293
FDIC reform of, 105–15, 106n8, 107n10,
109n13, 110nn15–16, 112nn19–20,
115nn24–25
GAO on, 109–10, 234
insolvency in reform of, 106n8
reform, Board of Governors on, 109–15,
110n15, 112n20, 112nn19–20, 115nn24–25,
259
risks of mergers to, 149
SEC role in, 100, 100n80, 106–7
uncertainty in, 91
Torres, Craig, 320
Trading with the Enemy Act of 1917, 55–56
transparency, 54, 108, 149, 226, 280–81, 295,
326–27
Troubled Asset Relief Program (TARP)
AIG bailout by, 212, 212n262, 215
beneficiaries of, 267–69, 269f, 269nn44–45,
270–73
Bennett on, 4–5, 5n8
circumstances leading to stress, 257–59
Dodd-Frank revision of, 291t
Emergency Economic Stabilization Act of
2008 (EESA), 265, 266n37
estimated cost of, 262
expansion of, 304t
as healthy bank program, 261n16
impact of, 265–75, 265n35, 266n37, 268t,
269f, 269nn44–45, 275f
implementation, oversight of, 6n9, 125
information quality, 262, 268–69
participation as requirement, 266–67
rush to pass, 262
sales pitch, 263–64, 265n35, 269–70, 269n45
shifting strategies of, 265–66, 265n35,
266n37, 269nn44–45, 304t

systemic risk assessment, 259–63, 261nn15–17
uncertainty issue, 265
Tucker, Paul, 28n14
2000s recession
 bailout policy, 125
 bank failures during, 123–24, 124t
 extension of funding policy, 125–26
 factors precipitating, 121–23, 122n12, 123f
 FDIC Fund insolvency, 124
 homeownership increase, 121–22, 122n12, 123f
 monetary policy issues, 122
 moral hazard incentives, 122
 overview, 121–22
 regulatory breakdowns, 122–23
 secrecy policy, 126–27, 126n21
 tightening of lending standards, 124, 267, 268t

**U**

UBS, 196t
Ukraine, 247n41
uncertainty
 AIG, 200, 213–15
 Bear Stearns, 14
 Citigroup, 251
 Continental Illinois, 91, 131–32
 in financial markets, 91, 144, 169, 172, 172t, 214, 257, 297–98, 307
 government leaders as cause of, 264, 308–9
 GSEs, 227–30
 Lehman Brothers, 180, 203
 as lending issue, 34
 in solvency assessments, 29, 40
 in subprime mortgage market, 227–30
 in systemic risk exception, 234
 TARP, 265
 as "too big to fail" issue, 91
unexpected losses, 248–49, 307, 307n8
United Bank of Alaska, 95n66
United States Commercial Company, 62
unsound institutions, 28, 30, 45, 69n22, 126, 201, 218, 221. *See also specific institutions*
unusual and exigent circumstances powers
 Bear Stearns, 21
 Dodd-Frank reform of, 282t, 291t, 295–97, 297n46
 Dodd-Frank reformulation of, 291t
 expansion of, 137–38, 291t, 304t
 as false narrative, 127
 maintenance of secrecy, 319
 overview, 59, 114–15, 115nn24–25

*U.S. Department of the Treasury, Judicial Watch v.*, 326
U.S. Treasury Department
 AIG role, 197–98, 205, 215
 authority of to authorize bailouts, 18, 20
 authority to purchase securities, 221–23, 222n296, 229
 Bear/JP Morgan buyout role, 15–20
 Break the Glass Bank Recapitalization Plan (BTG), 257–63, 261nn15–17
 BTG authorities given to, 258
 Citigroup role (*See* Citigroup)
 Fannie/Freddie preferred stock purchase, 229, 229n322
 GSE bailout role, 220–23, 220n287, 222n296, 226–30
 Lehman Brothers role, 174–78t
 lending stimulation by, 265, 267
 TLGP role, 249n49
 Wachovia guarantee by, 242–43
 Working Group on Financial Markets (WGFM) (*See* Working Group on Financial Markets (WGFM))

**V**

Vento, Bruce F., 86, 90n50, 92n55
viable institutions, 250, 261–62, 266, 296. *See also specific institutions*
Volcker, Paul, 80, 89, 93, 187n183, 260n12

**W**

Wachovia
 circumstances leading to stress, 237–38
 Citigroup purchase of, 238–39, 244, 244nn33–35, 245, 245n38, 251
 commercial paper holdings, 238, 241t
 creditors, 238–39, 245–46
 documentation, 324, 327–54
 domination of industry by, 122
 failure of, approaching, 37, 289, 291t, 294
 GAO role, 245–46
 impact of, approaching, 245–47, 245n38, 247n41
 information quality, 239–44, 239n23, 241–42t, 324
 insolvency of, 244n35
 justification for intervention, 239–44, 239n23, 241–42t
 liquidity issues, 241t
 as moral hazard issue, 246–47
 regulatory breakdowns in oversight of, 123, 238

repurchase agreements (repos), 238
review of options, 242–44, 242n26,
    244nn33–35
shareholders, 238–39
systemic risk assessment, 238–42, 239n23,
    241–42*t*
Wells Fargo purchase by, 245n38, 294
Wachtell, Lipton, Rosen, and Katz, 227
*Wall Street Journal,* 7n9
Wall Street Reform and Consumer Protec-
    tion Act of 2009. *See* Dodd-Frank
    legislation
Wallison, Peter, 142–43, 158n120, 220n285
War Finance Corporation, 48–51, 49nn32–33
Warner, Mark, 216, 216n278
warning systems, 6, 24, 280, 281
Warren, Elizabeth, 213
Warsh, Kevin
    AIG bailout role, 199–200, 202, 205, 207*t*
    Bear Stearns role, 17–20
    Lehman Brothers role, 158n120, 166–67
    maintenance of secrecy by, 319
Washington Mutual
    failure of, 236–37, 236n12, 237n14
    liquidation of, 293–95
    OBA assistance for, 236–37, 236n12, 237n14,
        239

regulatory breakdowns in oversight of, 122
    shareholders in, 237
Weil, Gotshal and Manges, 153
Wells Fargo Bank
    Lehman Brothers role, 176*t*
    purchase of Wachovia by, 245n38, 294
Wessel, David, 4n7, 143, 145n65, 214n271
widely available programs, 282*t*, 291*t*, 295–97
Wilkinson, Jim, 159–60
Willumstad, Robert, 4, 31–32, 188–90, 193,
    195, 199, 201, 206. *See also* American
    International Group (AIG)
Wilson, Woodrow, 40–41, 49n32
Woodruff, Judy, 123
Working Group on Financial Markets (WGFM)
    AIG role, 187–88
    creation of, 99–100
    Fannie/Freddie role, 226
    FSOC *vs.,* 284–85, 286*t*
    inability of, 123, 187–88, 226
    Paulson's criticism of, 287
    representation on, 99, 187, 226, 286*t*
World War I, 49–50, 55
World War II, 62
Wylie, Chalmers, 88, 89n48

**Y**
Yingling, Edward, 250

# About the Author

VERN MCKINLEY, Research Fellow at the Independent Institute, holds degrees in finance and economics from the University of Illinois and a J.D. from the National Law Center at George Washington University. He has worked for the International Monetary Fund, Asian Development Bank, World Bank, KfW Bankengruppe (Germany), U.S. Treasury, USAID, Deloitte / BearingPoint, PricewaterhouseCoopers, and Morrison & Foerster.

During the past twelve years he has been a legal advisor and regulatory policy expert for central banks and financial agencies in the United States, China, Nigeria, Indonesia, Ukraine, Latvia, Eastern Caribbean Currency Union, Libya, the Philippines, Kazakhstan, Palestine, Montenegro, Kosovo, Morocco, Serbia, Tajikistan, Kyrgyzstan, Kenya, Sudan, Afghanistan, and Armenia. During the recent global financial crisis he has worked in six countries in various stages of crisis, either in the early stages of identifying developing problems or as responsive reform measures were under development.

Prior to his time as an advisor, McKinley worked in legal, supervision, research, deposit insurance, and liquidation-related positions for the Board of Governors of the Federal Reserve, Federal Deposit Insurance Corporation (FDIC), Resolution Trust Corporation (RTC), and Office of Thrift Supervision. He worked at the FDIC in the 1980s during the banking crisis in Texas and at the RTC in the 1990s as it resolved hundreds of insolvent savings and loans.

McKinley has been credited with correctly predicting, in a policy analysis in 1997, that the structure of Fannie Mae and Freddie Mac would one day lead to the meltdown of the two institutions. He has contributed a chapter to *Central Bank Modernisation* and has had articles in *Forbes*, the *Washington Times*, *Regulation Magazine*, *Sacramento Bee*, and *USA Today Magazine*.

# Independent Studies in Political Economy

THE ACADEMY IN CRISIS | *Ed. by John W. Sommer*

AGAINST LEVIATHAN | *Robert Higgs*

ALIENATION AND THE SOVIET ECONOMY | *Paul Craig Roberts*

AMERICAN HEALTH CARE | *Ed. by Roger D. Feldman*

ANARCHY AND THE LAW | *Ed. by Edward P. Stringham*

ANTITRUST AND MONOPOLY | *D. T. Armentano*

ARMS, POLITICS, AND THE ECONOMY | *Ed. by Robert Higgs*

BEYOND POLITICS | *Randy T. Simmons*

CAN TEACHERS OWN THEIR OWN SCHOOLS? | *Richard K. Vedder*

THE CAPITALIST REVOLUTION IN LATIN AMERICA | *Paul Craig Roberts & Karen Araujo*

THE CHALLENGE OF LIBERTY | *Ed. by Robert Higgs & Carl P. Close*

CHANGING THE GUARD | *Ed. by Alexander Tabarrok*

THE CHE GUEVARA MYTH AND THE FUTURE OF LIBERTY | *Alvaro Vargas Llosa*

THE CIVILIAN AND THE MILITARY | *Arthur A. Ekirch, Jr.*

CUTTING GREEN TAPE | *Ed. by Richard L. Stroup & Roger E. Meiners*

THE DECLINE OF AMERICAN LIBERALISM | *Arthur A. Ekirch, Jr.*

DEPRESSION, WAR, AND COLD WAR | *Robert Higgs*

THE DIVERSITY MYTH | *David O. Sacks & Peter A. Thiel*

DRUG WAR CRIMES | *Jeffrey A. Miron*

ELECTRIC CHOICES | *Ed. by Andrew N. Kleit*

THE EMPIRE HAS NO CLOTHES | *Ivan Eland*

ENTREPRENEURIAL ECONOMICS | *Ed. by Alexander Tabarrok*

THE ENTERPRISE OF LAW | *Bruce L. Benson*

FAULTY TOWERS | *Ryan C. Amacher & Roger E. Meiners*

FINANCING FAILURE | *Vern McKinley*

FIRE & SMOKE | *Michael I. Krauss*

THE FOUNDERS' SECOND AMENDMENT | *Stephen P. Halbrook*

FREEDOM, FEMINISM, AND THE STATE | *Ed. by Wendy McElroy*

GOOD MONEY | *George Selgin*

HAZARDOUS TO OUR HEALTH? | *Ed. by Robert Higgs*

HOT TALK, COLD SCIENCE | *S. Fred Singer*

HOUSING AMERICA | *Ed. by Randall G. Holcombe & Benjamin Powell*

JUDGE AND JURY | *Eric Helland & Alexander Tabarrok*

LESSONS FROM THE POOR | *Ed. by Alvaro Vargas Llosa*

LIBERTY FOR LATIN AMERICA | *Alvaro Vargas Llosa*

LIBERTY FOR WOMEN | *Ed. by Wendy McElroy*

MAKING POOR NATIONS RICH | *Ed. by Benjamin Powell*

MARKET FAILURE OR SUCCESS | *Ed. by Tyler Cowen & Eric Crampton*

MONEY AND THE NATION STATE | *Ed. by Kevin Dowd & Richard H. Timberlake, Jr.*

NEITHER LIBERTY NOR SAFETY | *Robert Higgs*

THE NEW HOLY WARS | *Robert H. Nelson*

NO WAR FOR OIL | *Ivan Eland*

OPPOSING THE CRUSADER STATE | *Ed. by Robert Higgs & Carl P. Close*

OUT OF WORK | *Richard K. Vedder & Lowell E. Gallaway*

PARTITIONING FOR PEACE | *Ivan Eland*

PLOWSHARES AND PORK BARRELS | *E. C. Pasour, Jr. & Randal R. Rucker*

A POVERTY OF REASON | *Wilfred Beckerman*

PRIVATE RIGHTS & PUBLIC ILLUSIONS | *Tibor R. Machan*

PROPERTY RIGHTS | *Ed. by Bruce L. Benson*

THE PURSUIT OF JUSTICE | *Ed. by Edward J. López*

RACE & LIBERTY IN AMERICA | *Ed. by Jonathan Bean*

RECARVING RUSHMORE | *Ivan Eland*

RECLAIMING THE AMERICAN REVOLUTION | *William J. Watkins, Jr.*

REGULATION AND THE REAGAN ERA | *Ed. by Roger E. Meiners & Bruce Yandle*

RESTORING FREE SPEECH AND LIBERTY ON CAMPUS | *Donald A. Downs*

RESURGENCE OF THE WARFARE STATE | *Robert Higgs*

RE-THINKING GREEN | *Ed. by Robert Higgs & Carl P. Close*

SCHOOL CHOICES | *John Merrifield*

SECURING CIVIL RIGHTS | *Stephen P. Halbrook*

STRANGE BREW | *Douglas Glen Whitman*

STREET SMART | *Ed. by Gabriel Roth*

TAXING CHOICE | *Ed. by William F. Shughart, II*

TAXING ENERGY | *Robert Deacon, Stephen DeCanio, H. E. Frech, III, & M. Bruce Johnson*

THAT EVERY MAN BE ARMED | *Stephen P. Halbrook*

TO SERVE AND PROTECT | *Bruce L. Benson*

TWILIGHT WAR | *Mike Moore*

VIETNAM RISING | *William Ratliff*

THE VOLUNTARY CITY | *Ed. by David T. Beito, Peter Gordon, & Alexander Tabarrok*

WINNERS, LOSERS & MICROSOFT | *Stan J. Liebowitz & Stephen E. Margolis*

WRITING OFF IDEAS | *Randall G. Holcombe*